The
Modern
World

A HISTORY READER

ANDREA FINKELSTEIN
and the History Department

BRONX COMMUNITY COLLEGE
CITY UNIVERSITY OF NEW YORK

PEARSON

Custom
Publishing

Printed in the United States of America

10 9 8 7 6 5 4 3 2 1

ISBN 0-536-63864-0

2007300145

ED/MJ

Please visit our web site at *www.pearsoncustom.com*

PEARSON CUSTOM PUBLISHING
501 Boylston Street, Suite 900, Boston, MA 02116
A Pearson Education Company

Table of Contents

Topic I—The Age of Revolution: Ideas and Politics, 1650-1800

1. The English Bill of Rights (1689) 3
2. The Second Treatise of Government (1690), John Locke 5
3. On Commerce and Toleration (1734 & 1764), Voltaire 9
4. Letter on Smallpox Inoculation (1718), Lady Mary Wortley Montagu 11
5. The Spirit of the Laws (1748), Charles de Secondat, Baron de Montesquieu 13
6. The Social Contract (1762), Jean-Jacques Rousseau 16
7. Common Sense (1776), Thomas Paine 19
8. The United States Declaration of Independence (1776) 22
9. The American Bill of Rights (1791) 26
10. The French Declaration of the Rights of Man and Citizen (1789) 28
11. The Declaration of the Rights of Woman and Citizen (1791), Olympe de Gouges 31
12. The Interesting Narrative of the Life of Olaudah Equiano, or Gustavus Vasa, The African, Written by Himself (1789), Olaudah Equiano 34
13. Address to the National Congress of Venezuela (1819), Simón Bolívar 37

Topic II—Industrial Transformation and the Birth of Modern Societies

14. Lectures on the Industrial Revolution (1879–1883), Arnold Toynbee 43
15. Sadler Report on Child Labor (1832) 47
16. Mine Commissioners' Reports (1842) 50

Topic III—Social and Economic Thought in Early Industrial Society

17. The Wealth of Nations (1776), Adam Smith 55
18. Essay on the Principle of Population (1798), Thomas Robert Malthus 59
19. A New View of Society (1813), Robert Owen 62
20. The Communist Manifesto (1848), Karl Marx and Friedrich Engels 65

21. Evolutionary Socialism (1899), Eduard Bernstein ... 72
22. Wealth and its Uses (1902), Andrew Carnegie ... 75
23. Rerum Novarum (1891), Pope Leo XIII ... 79

Topic IV—Nationalism Across the Globe

24. Duties to Your Country (1858), Giuseppe Mazzini ... 85
25. The Ems Dispatch (1870), Otto von Bismarck ... 88
26. The Welfare State (1884), Otto von Bismarck ... 91
27. Incidents in the Life of a Slave Girl (1861),
    Harriet Ann Jacobs ... 93
28. The Dred Scott Decision (1857) ... 96
29. First Inaugural Address (1861), Abraham Lincoln ... 98
30. Abraham Lincoln's Reply to Horace Greeley
    (August 22, 1862), Abraham Lincoln ... 102
31. The Equality of All Men (1865), Frederick Douglass ... 103
32. The Reconstruction Amendments (1865–1870) ... 106
33. Plessy v. Ferguson (1896) ... 108
34. The Edict of Closure (1635) ... 110
35. A Dutch Anatomy Lesson in Japan (1771),
    Sugita Gempaku ... 111
36. Japan Industrializes, Shibuzawa Eiichi ... 113
37. Mitsubishi Letter to Employees (1876), Iwasaki Yatarō ... 115
38. Article 27, The Mexican Constitution (1917) ... 117

Topic V—The New Imperialism

39. The Economic History of India under British Rule (1901),
    Romesh C. Dutt ... 121
40. Emperor Ch'ien Lung to George III (1793) ... 124
41. The Treaty of Tientsin (1858) ... 127
42. Letter to Sir George Grey (1858) from Moshweshwe I ... 128
43. A School Examination in German Togo (1909) ... 131
44. "The White Man's Burden" (1899),
    Rudyard Kipling ... 133
45. "The Brown Man's Burden" (1899),
    Henry du Pré Labouchère ... 135
46. Imperialism (1902), John A. Hobson ... 137
47. Confession of Faith, Cecil Rhodes ... 141
48. Annual Message to Congress (1823), James Monroe ... 143
49. Annual Message to Congress (1904),
    Theodore Roosevelt ... 145

50. Letter to the Editor, New York Evening Post,
    March 25, 1889, José Marti   147

Topic VI—The Evolution of Liberalism in Nineteenth Century Society

51. On Liberty (1859), John Stuart Mill   153
52. Declaration of Sentiments (1848), Elizabeth Cady Stanton   157
53. Wages and the Franchise (1870), Susan Brownell Anthony   160
54. Speeches on Women's Rights (1851 & 1867),
    Sojourner Truth   163
55. "Why We Are Militant" (1913), Emmeline Pankhurst   165
56. Nineteenth-Century Chinese Marriage Contracts   168
57. "An Address to Two Hundred Million Fellow
    Countrywomen," Ch'iu Chin   170
58. Natural Selection (1859 & 1872), Charles Darwin   172
59. On the Inequality of the Races (1853–1855), Joseph Arthur,
    Comte de Gobineau   178
60. On the Concentration of Wealth, William Graham Sumner   180
61. The "Will to Power" and the Self-Evolution of the Superior
    Man, Friedrich Nietzsche   182

Topic VII—World War I and its Consequences

62. The Greatness of War (1897), Heinrich von Treitschke   189
63. Austria's Ultimatum to Serbia (July 23, 1914)   191
64. The "Willy-Nicky" Telegrams (29 July–1 August, 1914)   194
65. Count Johann von Bernstorff to the U. S. Secretary of State:
    Unrestricted Submarine Warfare (1917)   198
66. "Dulce et Decorum est" (1917), Wilfred Owen   202
67. The Fourteen Points (1918), Woodrow Wilson   204
68. The War Guilt Clause: Article 231,
    Treaty of Versailles (1919)   208
69. The Economic Consequences of the Peace (1919),
    John Maynard Keynes   209
70. The Balfour Declaration (1917), Arthur James Balfour   212
71. The Mandate System: Article 22, League of Nations
    Charter (1919)   213
72. The Jewish State (1896), Theodor Herzl   215
73. Resolutions of the General Syrian Congress (1919)   218
74. Tenets of the New Party (1907), Bal Gangadhar Tilak   220
75. Hind Swaraj (Indian Home Rule, 1921),
    Mohandas Karamchand Gandhi   222

76. San Min Chu I (Three Principles of the People, 1924–1925),
    Sun Yat-sen   225
77. The Pan-African Congress of 1919   229

Topic VIII—Mass Politics, Mass Societies, and the Expansion of State Power

78. Leninism, Vladimir Ilyich Lenin   233
79. Stalin against the Kulaks (1933), Josef Stalin   237
80. The Nature of Fascism (1935), Benito Mussolini   239
81. Speech in Munich (1923), Adolf Hitler   243
82. The Nuremberg Laws (1935)   245
83. A Red Record (1895), Ida Bell Wells-Barnett   248

Topic IX—World War II

84. The Appeasement Debate (1938), Neville Chamberlain &
    Winston Churchill   253
85. Treaty of Non-Aggression Between Germany and the
    Union of Soviet Socialist Republics (1939)   257
86. The Four Freedoms (1941), Franklin Delano Roosevelt   259
87. Speech to SS Leaders (1943), Heinrich Himmler   262
88. The Death Camp at Treblinka, Jean-François Steiner   264
89. Burma under the Japanese, 1942–1945, U Nu   268
90. Government Information Manual for the Motion
    Picture Industry (1942)   270
91. Korematsu v. United States (1944)   274
92. A Strategic Dilemma (1944), A. Leon Kubowitzki &
    John J. McCloy   276
93. The Yalta Protocols (1945)   278

Topic X—The Cold War, 1945–1991

94. The Iron Curtain (1946), Winston Churchill   285
95. The "Long Telegram" (1946), George Frost Kennan   288
96. "Equal Opportunity" (1946),
    Vyacheslav Mikhailovich Molotov   292
97. Address to Congress (1947), Harry S. Truman   294
98. NSC 68 (1950), Paul H. Nitze   298
99. 100 Things You Should Know About Communism
    and Education (1950), H.U.A.C.   301
100. A Marxist Condemns Stalin (1956), Nikita Khrushchev   305
101. The Military-Industrial Complex (1961),
     Dwight David Eisenhower   308
102. Speech at the United Nations (1988), Mikhail Gorbachev   311

Topic XI—The End of Empire in Asia and the Middle East

103. Toward Freedom (1941), Jawaharlal Nehru   317
104. The Call for Pakistan (1940), Muhammad Ali Jinnah   321
105. Bandung Declaration (1955)   324
106. The 28th Anniversary of the Chinese Communist Party (1949), Mao Zedong   327
107. China Under Deng Xiaoping   330
108. The Vietnamese Declaration of Independence (1945)   333
109. Camp David Agreement (1978)   336

Topic XII—Liberation and Dependency in Africa and Latin America

110. The Freedom Charter of the African National Congress (1955)   341
111. South African Women's Charter (1954)   345
112. "The Widows of the Reserves" (1960), Phyllis Ntantala   349
113. "Our March to Freedom is Irreversible" (1990), Nelson Rolihlahla Mandela   353
114. Four Years of Independence (1962), Ahmed Sékou Touré   355
115. Perón Expounds His Doctrine (1948), Juan Domingo Perón   359
116. History Will Absolve Me (1953), Fidel Castro   361
117. "The Death of Victor Jara" (1973)   364
118. Chiapas: The Southeast in Two Winds, A Storm and a Prophecy (1992), Subcomandante Marcos   366

Topic XIII—The Contemporary World

119. Civilization and Its Discontents (1930), Sigmund Freud   373
120. The Universal Declaration of Human Rights (1948)   376
121. Brown v. Board of Education (1954)   381
122. "I Have a Dream" (1963), Martin Luther King, Jr.   384
123. "The Great Society" (1964), Lyndon Baines Johnson   387
124. The Feminine Mystique (1963), Betty Friedan   390
125. Roe v. Wade (1973)   394
126. A Lakota at Boarding School, Luther Standing Bear   397
127. The Quranic School, Assia Djebar   401
128. The Hidden Face of Eve, Nawal El Saadawi   407
129. 'Message' to UNCED (1992), Fidel Castro   409

Copyright Acknowledgments

Topic I

The Age of Revolution: Ideas and Politics,

1650–1800

1

The English Bill of Rights (1689)

In 1688, after nearly a century of struggle between Parliament and the Crown over control of England's government and religion, a "Glorious Revolution" gave Parliament the power of the purse as well as ultimate control over the succession to the throne. Catholic James II was forced into exile in France, the throne was given to his Protestant daughter Mary and her husband William, and the "Rights of Englishmen" were enshrined in an Act of Parliament that remains the model for declarations of human rights the world over.

. . . . Whereas the late King James the Second, by the assistance of divers evil counselors, judges and ministers employed by him, did endeavor to subvert and extirpate the Protestant religion and the laws and liberties of this kingdom;

By assuming and exercising a power of dispensing with and suspending of laws and the execution of laws without consent of Parliament; . . .

By levying money for and to the use of the Crown by pretense of prerogative for other time and in other manner than the same was granted by Parliament;

By raising and keeping a standing army within this kingdom in time of peace without consent of Parliament, and quartering soldiers contrary to law;

By causing several good subjects being Protestants to be disarmed at the same time when papists were both armed and employed contrary to law;

By violating the freedom of election of members to serve in Parliament; . . .

And whereas of late years partial corrupt and unqualified persons have been returned and served on juries in trials, and particularly divers jurors in trials for high treason which were not freeholders;

And excessive bail hath been required of persons committed in criminal cases to elude the benefit of the laws made for the liberty of the subjects;

And excessive fines have been imposed;

And illegal and cruel punishments inflicted; . . . .

All which are utterly and directly contrary to the known laws and statutes and freedom of this realm;

And whereas the said late King James the Second having abdicated the government and the throne being thereby vacant . . .

3

[The Lords Spiritual and Temporal and Commons (Parliament)] asserting their ancient rights and liberties declare:

That the pretended power of suspending the laws or the execution of laws by regal authority without consent of Parliament is illegal; . . .

That levying money for or to the use of the Crown by pretense of prerogative, without grant of Parliament, for longer time, or in other manner than the same is or shall be granted, is illegal;

That it is the right of the subjects to petition the king, and all commitments and prosecutions for such petitioning are illegal;

That the raising or keeping a standing army within the kingdom in time of peace, unless it be with consent of Parliament, is against law;

That the subjects which are Protestants may have arms for their defense suitable to their conditions and as allowed by law;

That election of members of Parliament ought to be free;

That the freedom of speech and debates or proceedings in Parliament ought not to be impeached or questioned in any court or place out of Parliament;

That excessive bail ought not to be required, nor excessive fines imposed, nor cruel and unusual punishments inflicted;

That jurors ought to be duly impaneled and returned, and jurors which pass upon men in trials for high treason ought to be freeholders;

And that for redress of all grievances, and for the amending, strengthening and preserving of the laws, Parliaments ought to be held frequently.

And they do claim, demand and insist upon all and singular the premises as their undoubted rights and liberties. . . .

[And] the said Lords Spiritual and Temporal and Commons assembled at Westminster do resolve that William and Mary, prince and princess of Orange, are and be declared king and queen of England, France and Ireland and the dominions thereunto belonging, to hold the crown and royal dignity of the said kingdoms and dominions to them . . . , and after their deceases the said crown and royal dignity of the same kingdoms and dominions to be to the heirs of the body of the said princess, and for default of such issue to the Princess Anne of Denmark and the heirs of her body, and for default of such issue to the heirs of the body of the said prince of Orange. . . .

And whereas it hath been found by experience that it is inconsistent with the safety and welfare of this Protestant kingdom to be governed by a popish prince, or by any king or queen marrying a papist, the said Lords Spiritual and Temporal and Commons do further pray that it may be enacted, that all and every person and persons that is, are or shall be reconciled to or shall hold communion with the see or Church of Rome, or shall profess the popish religion, or shall marry a papist, shall be excluded and be for ever incapable to inherit, possess or enjoy the crown and government of this realm. . . . [the restriction of the monarchy to Protestants was enacted in the Act of Settlement, 1701]

2

The Second Treatise
of Government (1690)

JOHN LOCKE

*A physician and philosophy professor from a gentry family with com-
mercial roots, John Locke (1632–1704) left Oxford University for politics as private secretary to the leader of a Parliamentary faction
struggling with the Crown for control of England's government.
Locke's* Two Treatises of Government *defended Parliament's rights.
Forced into exile in 1683 when his side appeared to have lost the struggle, Locke was unable to publish the* Two Treatises *until Parliament's
final victory in 1689. The* First Treatise *attacked the Biblically-based
argument that kings were appointed by God to serve as "absolute" mon-
archs. Instead, the* Second Treatise *argued that government was created by the people in a "Social Contract" designed to protect humanity's
"natural rights." His ideas laid the foundation for modern republican
government.*

[I§3] *Political Power* then I take to be *a Right* of making Laws with Penalties of Death, and consequently all less Penalties, for the Regulating and Preserving of Property, and of employing the force of the Community, in the
Execution of such Laws, and in the defense of the Common-wealth from
Foreign Injury, and all this only for the Public Good.

[II§4] To understand Political Power right, and derive it from the Original, we must consider what State all Men are naturally in, and that is, a *State
of perfect Freedom* to order their Actions, and dispose of their Possessions, and
Persons as they think fit, within the bounds of the Law of Nature, without
asking leave, or depending upon the Will of any other Man.

A *State* also of *Equality,* wherein all the Power and Jurisdiction is reciprocal, no one having more than another: there being nothing more evident,
than that Creatures of the same species and rank promiscuously born to all
the same advantages of Nature, and the use of the same faculties, should also
be equal one amongst another without Subordination or Subjection. . . .

[II§6] But though this be a *State of Liberty*, yet it is *not a State of Licence*. . . . The *State of Nature* has a Law of nature to govern it, which obliges every one: And Reason, which is that Law, teaches all Mankind, who will but consult it, that being all equal and independent, no one ought to harm another in his Life, Health, Liberty, or Possessions. For Men being all the Workmanship of one Omnipotent, and infinitely wise Maker; All the Servants of one Sovereign Master, sent into the World by his order and about his business, they are his Property, whose Workmanship they are, made to last during his, not one another's Pleasure. . . .

[IV§22] The *Natural Liberty* of Man is to be free from any Superior Power on Earth, and not to be under the Will or Legislative Authority of Man, but to have only the Law of nature for his Rule. The *Liberty of Man, in Society*, is to be under no other Legislative Power but that established, by consent, in the Common-wealth, nor under the Dominion of any Will, or Restraint of any Law, but what the Legislative shall enact, according to the Trust put in it. . . .

[IV§23] This *Freedom* from Absolute, Arbitrary Power, is so necessary to, and closely joined with a man's preservation, that he cannot part with it, but by what forfeits his Preservation and life together. For a Man, not having the Power of his own Life, *cannot*, by Compact, or his own Consent, *enslave himself* to any one, nor put himself under the Absolute, Arbitrary Power of another, to take away his Life, when he pleases. No body can give more Power than he has himself; and he that cannot take away his own Life, cannot give another power over it. . . .

[VIII§95] Men being, as has been said, by nature, all free, equal and independent, no one can be put out of this Estate, and subjected to the Political Power of another, without his own *Consent*. The only way whereby any one divests himself of his Natural Liberty, and *puts on the bonds of Civil Society* is by agreeing with other Men to join and unite into a Community, for their comfortable, safe, and peaceable living one amongst another, in a secure Enjoyment of their Properties, and a greater Security against any that are not of it. . . .

[VIII§97] And thus every Man, by consenting with others to make one Body Politic under one Government, puts himself under an Obligation to every one of that Society, to submit to the determination of the *majority*, and to be concluded by it; or else this *original Compact*, whereby he with others incorporates into *one Society*, would signify nothing, and be no Compact, if he be left free, and under no other ties, than he was in before in the State of Nature. . . .

[IX§123] If Man in the State of Nature be so free, as has been said; If he be absolute Lord of his own Person and Possessions, equal to the greatest, and subject to no Body, why will he part with his freedom? Why will he give up this Empire, and subject himself to the Dominion and Control of any other power? To which 'tis obvious to Answer, that though in the state of Nature he hath such a right, yet the Enjoyment of it is very uncertain, and constantly exposed to the Invasion of others. For all being Kings as much as he is, every Man his equal, and the greater part no strict Observers of equity and Justice, the enjoyment of the property he had in this state is very unsafe, very unsecure. This makes him willing to quit this Condition, which however free, is full of fears and continual dangers: And 'tis not without reason, that he seeks out, and is willing to join in Society with others who are already united, or have a mind to unite for the mutual *Preservation* of their Lives, Liberties and Estates, which I call by the general Name, *Property*. . . .

❀

[IX§124] The great and *chief end* therefore, of Mens uniting into Commonwealths, and putting themselves under Government, *is the Preservation of their Property*. . . .

[IX§131] But though Men when they enter into Society, give up the equality, Liberty, and Executive Power they had in the State of Nature, into the hands of the Society, to be so far disposed of by the Legislative, as the good of the Society shall require; yet it be being only with an intention in every one the better to preserve himself his Liberty and Property; (For no rational Creature can be supposed to change his condition with an intention to be worse) the power of the Society, or *Legislative* constituted by them, *can never be supposed to extend farther than the common good;* but is obliged to secure every ones Property by providing against those . . . defects . . . that made the State of Nature so unsafe and uneasy. . . .

[XII§144] But because the Laws, that are at once, and in a short time made, have a constant and lasting force, and need a *perpetual Execution,* or an attendance thereunto: Therefore 'tis necessary there should be a *Power always in being,* which should see to the *Execution* of the Laws that are made, and remain in force. . . .

[VIII§107] . . . in the beginning of things, the Father's Government of the Childhood of those who sprung from him, having accustomed them to the *Rule of one Man.* . . . [men naturally turned to] that Form of Government, which from their Infancy they had all been accustomed to. . . . [and because they were unaware of] the Inconveniences of Absolute Power, which Monarchy, in Succession, was apt to lay claim to, and bring upon them, it was not at all strange, that they should not much trouble themselves to think of Methods of restraining any Exorbitance of those, to whom they had given the Authority over them, and of balancing the Power of Government, by placing several parts of it [*i.e.,* the legislature and executive] in different hands. . . .

[XIII§149] Though in a Constituted Commonwealth . . . there can be but *one Supreme Power,* which is *the Legislative,* to which all the rest are and must be subordinate, yet the Legislative being only a Fiduciary power to act for certain ends, there remains still *in the People a Supreme Power* to remove or *alter the Legislative,* when they find the *Legislative* act contrary to the trust reposed in them. . . .

[XIX§223] To this perhaps it will be said, that the People being ignorant, and always discontented, to lay the Foundation of Government in the unsteady Opinion, and uncertain Humor of the People, is to expose it to certain ruin; And *no Government will be able long to subsist,* if the People may set up a new Legislative whenever they take offence at the old one. To this, I Answer: Quite the contrary. People are not so easily got out of their old Forms, as some are apt to suggest. They are hardly to be prevailed with to amend the acknowledged Faults, in the Frame they have been accustomed to. . . .

[XIX§229] The end of Government is the good of Mankind, and which is *best for Mankind,* that the People should always be exposed to the boundless will of Tyranny, or that the rulers should be sometimes liable to be opposed, when they grow exorbitant in the use of their Power, and employ it for the destruction, and not the preservation of the Properties of their People?

On Commerce and Toleration
(1763 & 1764)

VOLTAIRE

François-Marie Arouet (1694–1778), better known by his pen name "Voltaire," was the century's most successful writer, but his satirical pen earned him two terms of imprisonment in the Bastille. In exile in England to avoid another stay in jail, he developed a deep appreciation for the English constitution, respect for science, and a relatively tolerant view of religious differences. When he returned to France he helped translate Newton's work into French to spread the new learning. The selection "On Commerce" is taken from Philosophical Letters on England *(1734), and "Tolerance" is taken from his* Philosophical Dictionary *(1764). Like his fellow philosophes, Voltaire was not an armchair theorist, but an agitator for intellectual and social change. Despite his fame, he found it prudent to retire to an estate near the Swiss border where it would be easier to escape the clutches of an increasingly conservative French monarchy.*

On Commerce

Commerce, which has enriched the citizens of England, has helped to make them free, and this freedom has extended their commerce in return, and that has made this nation great. Little by little, commerce created the navy that has made the English masters of the seas. They have, at present, nearly two hundred warships. Posterity may be surprised to learn that a tiny island with only a little lead, tin, fuller's earth, and coarse wool grew strong enough from trade to send (in 1723), three fleets to three different corners of the world at the same time: one fleet to Gibraltar, conquered and held by its forces, a second to Porto-Bello to keep the King of Spain from enjoying the treasures of the West Indies, and a third into the Baltic Sea to stop a war between the Northern Powers.

When the armies of Louis XIV (the king of France) were about to take the Italian city of Turin, Prince Eugène . . . had no money to march to its relief, so he had applied for a loan from some English merchants. In half an hour they lent him fifty million. With that money, he saved Turin, defeated the French, and wrote this little thank-you note to the merchants: 'Sirs, I have received your money, and I flatter myself I have employed it to your satisfaction.'

All this makes an English merchant justifiably proud and leads him to compare himself, not unreasonably, to a Roman citizen. Nor do the younger sons of English Lords despise commercial matters. . . . [while French nobles] look down on businessmen, and French businessmen hear so much criticism of their profession they are foolish enough to blush. However, I'm not certain who is more useful to a country, a nobleman who knows when the King gets up or goes to bed, and gives himself grand airs while playing the part of a slave in some Minister's hallway, or a business man who makes his country rich . . . and contributes to the well-being of the world.

Tolerance

What is tolerance? It is our due as human beings. We are all foolish; we all make mistakes. Let us pardon each other's follies. This is the first law of nature. . . .

We all agree that every private person who persecutes a man, his brother, because he disagrees with him is a monster. This admits of no difficulty. But the government, the magistrates, the princes!—how do they react to people whose faith is different from their own? If they are powerful foreigners, princes always form alliances with them. The Most Christian Francis I [King of France] allies with Muslims against the Most Catholic Charles V [Holy Roman Emperor of Germany]. Francis I gives money to the Lutherans in Germany, to support their rebellion against the Emperor, but, as usual, he will first have French Lutherans burned at the stake. Policy dictates he pay them in Germany and burn them in France. But what happens?

Persecutions make converts. France will soon be filled with new Protestants. At first they will let themselves be hanged; afterwards they will hang their opponents in turn. . . . If your country is divided between two religions, they massacre each other; if you have thirty sects, they live in peace. Look at the Grand Turk: he governs Guegers, Banians, Greek Catholics, Nestorians, and Roman Catholics. The first to stir up trouble is impaled; and all is peaceful. . . .

The name of any religious sect is no more than a name of some error; but there are no sects of geometricians, algebraists, or arithmeticians because all the propositions of geometry, algebra, and arithmetic are true. In all the other sciences, anyone can be mistaken.

4

Letter on Smallpox Inoculation (1718)

LADY MARY WORTLEY MONTAGU

Lady Mary Wortley Montagu (1689–1762) was an Earl's daughter who rebelled against an arranged marriage to elope with a British diplomat. In the letter below she tells a friend about the smallpox inoculations she saw while traveling with her husband in the Ottoman Empire. Her interest in smallpox was personal. Her brother had been one of the thousands to die in the periodic epidemics, and she herself was among the tens of thousands more left scarred by the disease. When she returned home she kept the resolution she made in this letter to convince her own people to submit to inoculation, but this was difficult to do: the treatment involved the risk of scarring resulting from the mild infection the inoculation produced. Even a safer vaccine, made from cowpox (a much milder disease), developed by Edward Jenner (1749–1825) in 1796, had to battle for acceptance. The British government did not make it mandatory until 1883, and that law was not really enforced for two more decades.

Apropos of distempers, I am going to tell you a thing that will make you wish yourself here. The smallpox, so fatal, and so general amongst us, is here entirely harmless, by the invention of ingrafting, which is the term they give it. There is a set of old women, who make it their business to perform the operation, every autumn, in the month of September, when the great heat is abated. People send to one another to know if any of their family has a mind to have the smallpox; they make parties for this purpose, and when they are met (commonly fifteen or sixteen together) the old woman comes with a nutshell full of the matter the best sort of small pox, and asks what vein you please to have opened. She immediately rips open that [vein] you offer to her, with a large needle (which gives you no more pain than a common scratch), and puts into the vein as much matter as can lie upon the head of her needle, and after that, binds up the little wound with a hollow bit of shell, and in this manner opens four of five veins. The Grecians have commonly the superstition of opening one in the middle of the forehead, one in each arm, and one in the breast, to mark the sign of the cross; but this has a very ill effect, all these wounds leaving little scars, and is not done by those that are not superstitious, who choose to have them in the legs, or that part of the arm that is concealed. The children or young patients play together all the rest of the day, and are in perfect health to the eighth.

Then the fever begins to seize them, and they keep to their beds two days, very seldom three. They have very rarely above twenty or thirty in their faces, which never mark, and in eight days time they are as well as before their illness. Where they are wounded, there remain running sores during the distemper, which I don't doubt is a great relief to it. Every year thousands undergo this operation, and the French ambassador says pleasantly that they take the smallpox here by way of diversion, as they take the waters in other countries. There is no example of anyone that has died from it, and you may believe I am well satisfied of the safety of this experiment, since I intend to try it on my dear little son [which she did the following year]. I am patriot enough to take pains to bring this useful invention into fashion in England, and I should not fail to write to some of our doctors very particularly about it, if I knew anyone of them that I thought had virtue enough to destroy such a considerable branch of their revenue, for the good of mankind. But that distemper is too beneficial to them, not to expose to all their resentment the hardy wight that should undertake to put an end to it. Perhaps if I live to return, I may, however have the courage to war with them. Upon this occasion, ad mire the heroism in the heart of

Your friend, etc. etc.

5

The Spirit of the Laws (1748)

CHARLES DE SECONDAT, BARON DE MONTESQUIEU

The son of a French magistrate, Charles de Secondat, Baron de la Brède et de Montesquieu (1689–1755), was president (chief judge) of the Parlement (chief court) in Bordeaux. Like Voltaire, Montesquieu looked first to England when he wanted to understand how governments could foster responsible liberty. In the end, however, he decided no one government could meet the needs of all men at all times. His master work, The Spirit of the Laws, *explores the need to fit laws to the unique "general spirits" created in populations by such things as climate, history, religion, and the size of the territory. But, as any student of the American constitution will recognize, its most immediately influential sections concerned the need to separate and divide the functions of governments to secure individual freedoms from tyrannical regimes.*

Many things govern men: climate, religion, laws, constitutional maxims, the example of the past, mores, and manners. From these, arises a general spirit. . . . And it is up to the legislator to follow the spirit of the nation (in so far as it is not contrary to the principles of government) if he wishes his laws to be obeyed. [3.19.4 & 3.19.5]

Although all States have the same general function, which is to maintain themselves, each State also has an aim unique to itself. Rome's aim was expansion, Sparta's war, Israel's religion, Marseilles' trade, China's public tranquility. . . . [But] there is one nation in the world [Great Britain] whose constitution aims for political liberty. We are going to examine the principles by which Britain secures this liberty. If the principles are sound, liberty will appear in these pages as if in a mirror. . . . [2.11.5]

The British Constitution: Separation of Powers

There are three different kinds of powers in every government: legislative . . . executive . . . and judicial. . . .

Political liberty in citizens is a tranquility of spirit that comes from their belief in their own safety. In order for them to have such safety, the government must be so arranged that no one citizen is afraid of any other.

When legislative and executive power are united in any individual or single ruling body, there is no liberty, because citizens fear that those who made tyrannical laws will carry them out tyrannically.

There is also no liberty if judicial power is not separated from the legislative and the executive. If judicial power were joined to the legislative, the judge would be the lawmaker and his power over the lives and liberty of the citizens would be arbitrary. If judicial power were joined to the executive, judges would have the power of oppressors.

All would be lost if the same man or the same group of nobles, aristocrats, or commoners held all three powers: law making, law enforcing, and judging crimes and disagreements between citizens. . . . As executives, the magistrates would retain all their legislative power: they could plunder the state through their combined will. And, since they would also have judicial power, they could destroy any citizen through their individual decisions. . . .

Judicial power should not rest in a permanent court but be exercised by individuals drawn from the body of the people . . . in a tribunal that lasts only as long as necessity requires. . . . [But] judgments should be so set that they are never anything but a precise copy of the law. If they were just one judge's individual opinion, no one in society would ever know what was actually required of them.

Furthermore, judges must be of the same status as the accused, his peers, so he won't imagine he has fallen into the hands of people inclined to do him violence . . . .

Every citizen, except those whose humble status makes them dependent on the will of others, should have a voice in choosing his district's representative. . . . But, in every country, there are always some people distinguished by birth, wealth, or honors. If they are counted together with the commoners and have no more say than others, the common liberty would be their enslavement, and they would have no desire to defend it, because most of the decisions would be against them. Therefore, they should have a part in legislation in proportion to their social advantages, in a second legislative body with the right to check the actions of the common people, as the common people have the right to check theirs.

Executive power should be vested in a monarch, because the part of government needing immediate action is better administered by one man than by several, whereas lawmaking is often better ordered by many men than by one. . . .

If the executive does not have the right to check the actions of the legislature, the legislature will be despotic, for giving itself all the power it can imagine, it will easily be able to destroy the other two powers.

But the legislature must not have the reciprocal faculty of checking the executive. For, as execution is limited to things of the moment by its very nature, it is useless to try to limit it further. . . .

But if, in a free state, the legislature should not have the right to check the executive, it must have the right and the ability to examine the way in which its laws have been carried out . . . [and be able to hold ministers] accountable for their administrations. . . . [2.11.6]

The French Constitution: Division of Powers

Intermediate powers are also essential to monarchical constitutions, and the most natural intermediate and subordinate power is that of the nobility. Nobility is the essence of monarchy, whose fundamental maxim is: *no monarch, no nobility: no nobility, no monarch;* instead, you have a despot. . . .

Abolish the prerogatives of the lords, clergy, nobility, and towns in a monarchy, and you will soon have a democracy or a tyranny. . . . Just as the sea, that might so easily cover the whole planet, is halted by the grass and gravel on the shore, so the seemingly unstoppable pride and power of kings is checked by the slightest obstacles, by petition and prayer. . . . [1.2.4]

The Social Contract (1762)

JEAN-JACQUES ROUSSEAU

Questions regarding civic virtue and freedom were at the heart of the Enlightenment. A music teacher who immigrated to France to escape the suffocating puritanism of Geneva, Jean-Jacques Rousseau (1712–1778) challenged the optimism of the philosophes who thought progress was the cure all for society's ills. Rousseau believed that civilization, property and even the arts corrupted humanity's natural nobility, but knew that the freedom of humanity's original state of Nature could not be regained. Instead, he sought to create a state that could teach people to be virtuous, could "force" people to be free. His writings found their first influence in the radicals like Robespierre who took control of the French Revolution in 1792, but historians and political scientists have been arguing ever since whether Rousseau was promoting democracy or a dictatorship of the majority.

'To find a form of association that defends and protects the person and property of every member with the whole strength of the community, and through which each member, uniting with all, nevertheless obeys only himself, and remains as free as before.' Such is the fundamental problem of which the Social Contract provides the solution. . . .

The clauses of this contract are everywhere the same:

'Each of us puts in common his person and his whole strength under the supreme direction of the general will; and we accept every member of the body politic as an indivisible part of the whole' [I.6].

We see from this formula that the act of association contains a reciprocal engagement between the public and the individual. . . .

As soon as people are thus united in one body, we cannot injure one of the members without attacking the whole, still less injure the body without the members feeling the effects. Thus duty and interest equally oblige the two contracting parties [the individual and the community] to assist each other. . . .

In truth, everyone may, as individuals, have particular wishes contrary or dissimilar to the general will we have as citizens; our private interests may prompt us quite differently from the common interest; [but] whoever refuses to obey the general will shall be made to do so by the whole body: this means nothing other than that the community will force him to be free [I.7].

Although a citizen gives up many advantages that he had in the natural state, he gets back advantages equally great: his faculties are exercised and developed; his ideas are expanded; his feelings are ennobled; his whole soul is so elevated that, if the abuses of this new condition did not often degrade him below the state he has quit, he ought to bless without ceasing the happy moment that released him from it for ever, and transformed him from a stupid and ignorant animal into an intelligent being and a man.

Let us reduce this whole balance to terms easy to compare: what man loses by the social contract is his natural liberty and an unlimited right to all that tempts him and that he can attain; what he gains is civil liberty and property in all that he possesses. . . .

What's more, we could add to this, that moral liberty of the civil state that alone makes a man truly master of himself; for the impetus of appetite alone is slavery, while obedience to a self-prescribed law is liberty [I.8].

The first and most important consequence of the principles established above is that the general will alone can direct the forces of the State according to the object of its institution, which is the common good; for if the opposition of private interests has made the establishment of societies necessary, it is the agreement between these same interests that makes it possible. . . .

In order for a will to be general, it is not always necessary for it to be unanimous, but all views must be counted; any legal exclusions preclude a true generality [II.1].

Just as nature gives every man an absolute power over all his limbs, the Social Contract gives the body politic an absolute power over all its members. . . .

The agreements that tie us to the social body are only obligatory because they are mutual; and their nature is such that in fulfilling them we cannot work for others without also working for ourselves [II.4].

The people, submissive to the laws should be their authors. . . .

But while the people always want what is good, they do not always recognize it. The general will is always right, but the judgment that guides it is not always enlightened. People must be made to see things as they are, sometimes even as they ought to be. They must be shown the good path they seek, and guarded from the seduction of private interests. . . . They must be taught to recognize what they really need. Then public enlightenment will create a union of the understanding and will in the social body [II.6].

There is only one law that, by its nature, demands unanimous consent: the Social Contract. Civil association is the most voluntary act in the world: every man being born free and master of himself, no one can, under any pretext whatsoever, subjugate him without his consent. To decide that the son of a slave is born a slave is to decide that he is not born a man.

If, then, at the creation of the Social Contract, some people find themselves opposed to it, their opposition does not invalidate the Contract; it only prevents their inclusion: they become foreigners amongst the citizenry. Once the State is established, consent lies in residence; to live within in its territory is to submit to its sovereignty.

Except for this original Contract, the vote of the majority always binds the rest. This is a consequence of the Contract itself. But some will ask how a man can be free while forced to conform to wills not his own. How can opponents be free while subject to laws to which they have not consented ? . . .

I reply that the question is wrongly put. Citizens consent equally to all the laws, to those passed against their will, to those that punish their violation. The constant will of all the members of the State is the general will; this is what makes them citizens and free. When we consider a law in the communal assembly, we are not really asked if we approve or reject it, but whether or not it conforms to the general will, which is our own. . . . . . When an opinion contrary to my own prevails, it simply shows me that I was mistaken in my understanding of the general will [IV.2].

Common Sense (1776)

THOMAS PAINE

Thomas Paine (1737–1809) was the son of a Quaker corset maker. He lost his job in the British Excise Office for insisting public servants were entitled to regular wages. At the urging of Benjamin Franklin, Paine emigrated to America in 1774. There, he became a magazine editor and helped draft Pennsylvania's first Constitution. In 1776, Paine's revolutionary propaganda piece, Common Sense, *became a runaway "bestseller" by making the case that independence was the only logical path for Great Britain's American colonies. He continued to make waves defending the early phases of the French Revolution and fighting for political reform in Britain. But Paine died a disappointed man as he watched Napoleon subdue Europe, Britain restrict the right to demonstrate, and the United States fail to live up to his egalitarian hopes.*

The sun never shone on a cause of greater worth [than American independence]. 'Tis not the affair of a city, a county, a province, or a kingdom; but of a continent—of at least one eighth part of the habitable globe. . . .

I have heard it asserted by some, that as America has flourished under her former connection with Great Britain, the same connection is necessary towards her future happiness, and will always have the same effect. Nothing can be more fallacious than this kind of argument. We may as well assert that because a child has thrived upon milk, that it is never to have meat, or that the first twenty years of our lives is to become a precedent for the next twenty. But even this is admitting more than is true; for I answer roundly, that America would have flourished as much, and probably much more, had no European power taken any notice of her. The commerce by which she hath enriched herself are the necessaries of life, and will always have a market while eating is the custom of Europe.

But she has protected us, say some. That she hath engrossed us is true, and defended the continent at our expense as well as her own, is admitted; and she would have defended Turkey from the same motive, *viz.* for the sake of trade and dominion.

Alas! we have been long led away by ancient prejudices and made large sacrifices to superstition. We have boasted the protection of Great Britain, without considering, that her motive was *interest* not *attachment;* and that she did not protect us from *our enemies* on *our account;* but from her *enemies* on *her own account,* from those who had no quarrel with us on any *other account,* and who will always be our enemies on the *same account.* . . .

But Britain is the parent country, say some. Then the more shame upon her conduct. Even brutes do not devour their young, nor savages make war upon their families; wherefore, the assertion, if true, turns to her reproach; but it happens not to be true, or only partly so, and the phrase *parent* or *mother country* hath been jesuitically adopted by the king and his parasites, with a low papistical design of gaining an unfair bias on the credulous weakness of our minds. Europe, and not England, is the parent country of America. This new world hath been the asylum for the persecuted lovers of civil and religious liberty from *every part* of Europe. Hither have they fled, not from the tender embraces of the mother, but from the cruelty of the monster; and it is so far true of England, that the same tyranny which drove the first emigrants from home, pursues their descendants still.

In this extensive quarter of the globe, we forget the narrow limits of three hundred and sixty miles (the extent of England) and carry our friendship on a larger scale; we claim brotherhood with every European Christian, and triumph in the generosity of the sentiment. . . . All Europeans meeting in America, or any other quarter of the globe, are *countrymen;* for England, Holland, Germany, or Sweden, when compared with the whole, stand in the same places on the larger scale, which the divisions of street, town, and county do on the smaller ones; distinctions too limited for continental minds. Not one third of the inhabitants, even of this province, [Pennsylvania], are of English descent. Wherefore, I reprobate the phrase of parent or mother country applied to England only, as being false, selfish, narrow and ungenerous. . . .

Much hath been said of the united strength of Britain and the colonies, that in conjunction they might bid defiance to the world. But this is mere presumption; the fate of war is uncertain, neither do the expressions mean any thing; for this continent would never suffer itself to be drained of inhabitants, to support the British arms in either Asia, Africa or Europe.

Besides, what have we to do with setting the world at defiance? Our plan is commerce, and that, well attended to, will secure us the peace and friendship of all Europe; because it is the interest of all Europe to have America a free port. Her trade will always be a protection, and her barrenness of gold and silver secure her from invaders.

I challenge the warmest advocate for reconciliation to show a single advantage that this continent can reap by being connected with Great Britain. I repeat the challenge; not a single advantage is derived. Our corn will fetch its price in any market in Europe, and our imported goods must be paid for, buy them where we will.

But the injuries and disadvantages which we sustain by that connection, are without number; and our duty to mankind at large, as well as to ourselves, instruct us to renounce the alliance: because, any submission to, or dependence on, Great Britain, tends directly to involve this continent in European wars and quarrels, and set us at variance with nations who would otherwise seek our friendship, and against whom we have neither anger nor complaint. As Europe is our market for trade, we ought to form no partial connection with any part of it. It is the true interest of America to steer clear of European contentions, which she never can do, while, by her dependence on Britain, she is made the make-weight in the scale of British politics.

As to government matters, 'tis not in the power of Britain to do this continent justice: the business of it will soon be too weighty and intricate to be managed with any tolerable degree of convenience, by a power so distant from us, and so very ignorant of us; for if they cannot conquer us, they cannot govern us. To be always running three or four thousand miles with a tale or a petition, waiting four or five months for an answer, which, when obtained, requires five or six more to explain it in, will in a few years be looked upon as folly and childishness. There was a time when it was proper, and there is a proper time for it to cease.

Small islands not capable of protecting themselves are the proper objects for government to take under their care; but there is something absurd, in supposing a Continent to be perpetually governed by an island. In no instance hath nature made the satellite larger than its primary planet; and as England and America, with respect to each other, reverse the common order of nature, it is evident that they belong to different systems. England to Europe: America to itself. . . .

America is only a secondary object in the system of British politics. England consults the good of this country no further than it answers her own purpose. Wherefore, her own interest leads her to suppress the growth of ours in every case which doth not promote her advantage, or in the least interferes with it. . . .

A government of our own is our natural right. . . .

The United States Declaration of Independence (1776)

When thirteen of Britain's North American colonies rebelled in 1775, they drew inspiration from John Locke's defense of the people's right to overthrow governments that attacked their natural rights to "life, liberty and property." Thomas Jefferson (1743–1826), a Virginia slave owner, served on the Continental Congress committee that prepared the Declaration justifying the colonies' decision to proclaim their independence from Great Britain. After a hot debate over which offenses against the rights of the colonists should be included (and the refusal of the Southern Colonies to support any condemnation of slavery), an edited version of Jefferson's draft Declaration was accepted by the Continental Congress. Published on July 4, 1776, the American Declaration of Independence continues to influence republican revolutions of the present day.

When in the Course of human events, it becomes necessary for one people to dissolve the political bands which have connected them with another, and to assume among the Powers of the earth, the separate and equal station to which the Laws of Nature and of Nature's God entitle them, a decent respect to the opinions of mankind requires that they should declare the causes which impel them to the separation.

We hold these truths to be self-evident, that all men are created equal, that they are endowed by their Creator with certain unalienable Rights, that among these are Life, Liberty and the pursuit of Happiness. That to secure these rights, Governments are instituted among Men, deriving their just powers from the consent of the governed, That whenever any Form of Government becomes destructive of these ends, it is the Right of the People to alter or to abolish it, and to institute new Government, laying its foundation on such principles and organizing its powers in such form, as to them shall seem most likely to effect their Safety and Happiness. Prudence, indeed, will dictate that Governments long established should not be changed for light and transient causes; and accordingly all experience hath shown, that mankind are more disposed to suffer, while evils are sufferable, than to right themselves by abolishing the forms to which they are accustomed. But when a long train of abuses and usurpations, pursuing invariably the same Object evinces a design to reduce them under absolute Despotism, it is their right, it is their duty, to throw off such Government, and to provide new Guards for their future security.—Such has been the patient sufferance of these Colonies; and such is now the necessity which constrains them to alter their former Systems of Government. The history of the present King of Great Britain is a history of repeated injuries and usurpations, all having in direct object the establishment of an absolute Tyranny over these States. To prove this, let Facts be submitted to a candid world.

He has refused his Assent to Laws, the most wholesome and necessary for the public good.

He has forbidden his Governors to pass Laws of immediate and pressing importance, unless suspended in their operation till his Assent should be obtained; and when so suspended, he has utterly neglected to attend to them.

He has refused to pass other Laws for the accommodation of large districts of people, unless those people would relinquish the right of Representation in the Legislature, a right inestimable to them and formidable to tyrants only.

He has called together legislative bodies at places unusual, uncomfortable, and distant from the depository of their Public Records, for the sole purpose of fatiguing them into compliance with his measures.

He has dissolved Representative Houses repeatedly, for opposing with manly firmness his invasions on the rights of the people.

He has refused for a long time, after such dissolutions, to cause others to be elected; whereby the Legislative Powers, incapable of Annihilation, have returned to the People at large for their exercise; the State remaining in the mean time exposed to all the dangers of invasion from without, and convulsions within.

He has endeavored to prevent the population of these States; for that purpose obstructing the Laws of Naturalization of Foreigners; refusing to pass others to encourage their migration hither, and raising the conditions of new Appropriations of Lands.

He has obstructed the Administration of Justice, by refusing his Assent to Laws for establishing Judiciary Powers.

He has made Judges dependent on his Will alone, for the tenure of their offices, and the amount and payment of their salaries.

He has erected a multitude of New Offices, and sent hither swarms of Officers to harass our People, and eat out their substance.

He has kept among us, in times of peace, Standing Armies without the Consent of our legislature.

He has affected to render the Military independent of and superior to the Civil Power.

He has combined with others to subject us to a jurisdiction foreign to our constitution, and unacknowledged by our laws; giving his Assent to their acts of pretended legislation:

For quartering large bodies of armed troops among us:

For protecting them, by a mock Trial, from Punishment for any Murders which they should commit on the Inhabitants of these States:

For cutting off our Trade with all parts of the world:

For imposing taxes on us without our Consent:

For depriving us in many cases, of the benefits of Trial by Jury:

For transporting us beyond Seas to be tried for pretended offences:

For abolishing the free System of English Laws in a neighboring Province, establishing therein an Arbitrary government, and enlarging its Boundaries so as to render it at once an example and fit instrument for introducing the same absolute rule into these Colonies:

For taking away our Charters, abolishing our most valuable Laws, and altering fundamentally the Forms of our Governments:

For suspending our own legislature, and declaring themselves invested with Power to legislate for us in all cases whatsoever.

He has abdicated Government here, by declaring us out of his Protection and waging War against us.

He has plundered our seas, ravaged our Coasts, burnt our towns, and destroyed the lives of our people.

He is at this time transporting large armies of foreign mercenaries to complete the works of death, desolation and tyranny, already begun with circumstances of Cruelty & perfidy scarcely paralleled in the most barbarous ages, and totally unworthy the Head of a civilized nation.

He has constrained our fellow Citizens taken Captive on the high Seas to bear Arms against their Country, to become the executioners of their friends and Brethren, or to fall themselves by their Hands.

He has excited domestic insurrections amongst us, and has endeavored to bring on the inhabitants of our frontiers, the merciless Indian Savages, whose known rule of warfare, is an undistinguished destruction of all ages, sexes and conditions.

In every stage of these Oppressions We have Petitioned for Redress in the most humble terms: Our repeated Petitions have been answered only by repeated injury. A Prince, whose character is thus marked by every act which may define a Tyrant, is unfit to be the ruler of a free People.

Nor have We been wanting in attention to our British brethren. We have warned them from time to time of attempts by their legislature to extend an unwarrantable jurisdiction over us. We have reminded them of the circumstances of our emigration and settlement here. We have appealed to their native justice and magnanimity, and we have conjured them by the ties of our common kindred to disavow these usurpations, which, would inevitably interrupt our connections and correspondence. They too have been deaf to the voice of justice and of consanguinity. We must, therefore, acquiesce in the necessity, which denounces our Separation, and hold them, as we hold the rest of mankind, Enemies in War, in Peace Friends.

We, therefore, the Representatives of the United States of America, in General Congress, Assembled, appealing to the Supreme Judge of the world for the rectitude of our intentions, do, in the Name, and by Authority of the good People of these Colonies, solemnly publish and declare, That these United Colonies are, and of Right ought to be Free and Independent States; that they are Absolved from all Allegiance to the British Crown, and that all political connection between them and the State of Great Britain, is and ought to be totally dissolved and that as Free and Independent States, they have full Power to levy War, conclude Peace, contract Alliances, establish Commerce, and to do all other Acts and Things which Independent States may of right do. And for the support of this Declaration, with a firm reliance on the Protection of Divine Providence, we mutually pledge to each other our Lives, our Fortunes and our sacred Honor.

The American Bill of Rights (1791)

The success of the American Revolution would not be secure until it had a national government strong enough to function but not powerful enough to oppress its citizens. The American Constitution *(1787), now the world's oldest written charter of government, was the mechanism whereby thirteen sovereign states established that government. The* Constitution *divided power between the federal government and the individual states and, at the national level, separated power between three co-equal branches of government (executive, legislative, judicial), while affirming that ultimate power remained with "the people." Responding to popular demand that individual liberties be specifically protected from federal interference, ten amendments were ratified in 1791, creating a "Bill of Rights" for the new Constitution. The model for the American "Bill of Rights" was the "Bill of Rights" passed by the English Parliament in 1689 after the success of their "Glorious Revolution."*

Amendment I. Congress shall make no law respecting an establishment of religion, or prohibiting the free exercise thereof; or abridging the freedom of speech, or of the press; or the right of the people peaceably to assemble, and to petition the Government for a redress of grievances.

Amendment II. A well regulated Militia, being necessary to the security of a free State, the right of the people to keep and bear Arms shall not be infringed.

Amendment III. No Soldier shall, in time of peace, be quartered in any house, without the consent of the Owner, nor in time of war, but in a manner to be prescribed by law.

Amendment IV. The right of the people to be secure in their persons, houses, papers, and effects, against unreasonable searches and seizures, shall not be violated, and no Warrants shall issue, but upon probable cause, supported by Oath or affirmation, and particularly describing the place to be searched, and the persons or things to be seized.

Amendment V. No person shall be held to answer for a capital or otherwise infamous crime, unless on a presentment or indictment of a Grand jury, except in cases arising in the land or naval forces, or in the Militia, when in actual service in time of War or public danger; nor shall any person be subject for the same offence to be twice put in jeopardy of life or limb; nor shall be compelled in any criminal case to be a witness against himself, nor be deprived of life, liberty, or property, without due process of law; nor shall private property be taken for public use, without just compensation.

Amendment VI. In all criminal prosecutions, the accused shall enjoy the right to a speedy and public trial, by an impartial jury of the State and district wherein the crime shall have been committed, which district shall have been previously ascertained by law, and to be informed of the nature and cause of the accusation; to be confronted with the witnesses against him; to have compulsory process for obtaining witnesses in his favor, and to have the Assistance of Counsel for his defense.

Amendment VII. In suits at common law, where the value in controversy shall exceed twenty dollars, the right of trial by jury shall be preserved, and no fact tried by a jury, shall be otherwise reexamined in any Court of the United States, than according to the rules of the common law.

Amendment VIII. Excessive bail shall not be required, nor excessive fines imposed, nor cruel and unusual punishments inflicted.

Amendment IX. The enumeration in the Constitution, of certain rights, shall not be construed to deny or disparage others retained by the people.

Amendment X. The powers not delegated to the United States by the Constitution, nor prohibited by it to the States, are reserved to the States respectively, or to the people.

10

The French Declaration of the Rights of Man and Citizen (1789)

In 1789 the people of France took up the Enlightenment call for "natural rights" and demanded a real share of power in the absolutist monarchy of France. King Louis XVI watched in horror as a National Assembly was organized in May, mobs destroyed the Bastille on July 14, and the feudal rights of the Church and the Nobility were abolished on August 4. On August 26 the representatives of the National Assembly adopted a Declaration of the Rights of Man and Citizen *that owed much to English and American models. This new* Declaration *was meant to be the first step in turning France into a constitutional monarchy, but the impasse between Louis and the revolutionary leadership brought on a series of increasing radical revolutions that ended in the dictatorship of Napoleon Bonaparte (1769–1821) in 1799.*

The representatives of the people of France, formed into a National Assembly, considering that ignorance, neglect, or contempt of human rights, are the sole causes of public misfortunes and corruptions of Government, have resolved to set forth in a solemn declaration, these natural, imprescriptible, and inalienable rights: that this declaration being constantly present to the minds of the members of the body social, they may be for ever kept attentive to their rights and their duties; that the acts of the legislative and executive powers of government, being capable of being every moment compared with the end of political institutions, may be more respected; and also, that the future claims of the citizens being directed by simple and incontestable principles, may always tend to the maintenance of the Constitution, and the general happiness.

For these reasons, the National Assembly doth recognize and declare, in the presence of the Supreme Being, and with the hope of his blessing and favor, the following *sacred* rights of men and of citizens:

I. Men are born, and always continue, free and equal in respect of their rights. Civil distinctions, therefore, can be founded only on public utility.

II. The end of all Political associations, is the preservation of the natural and imprescriptible rights of man; and these rights are liberty, property, security, and resistance of oppression.

III. The nation is essentially the source of all sovereignty; nor can any individual, or any body of men, be entitled to any authority which is not expressly derived from it.

IV. Political liberty consists in the power of doing whatever does not injure another. The exercise of the natural rights of every man, has no other limits than those which are necessary to secure to every *other* man the free exercise of the same rights; and these limits are determinable only by the law.

V. The law ought to prohibit only actions hurtful to society. What is not prohibited by the law, should not be hindered; nor should any one be compelled to that which the law does not require.

VI. The law is an expression of the will of the community. All citizens have a right to concur, either personally, or by their representatives, in its formation. It should be the same to all, whether it protects or punishes; and all being equal in its sight, are equally eligible to all honours, places, and employments, according to their different abilities, without any other distinction than that created by their virtues and talents.

VII. No man should accused, arrested, or held it confinement, except in cases determined by the law, and according to the forms which it has prescribed. All who promote, solicit, execute, or cause to be executed, arbitrary orders, ought to be punished, and every citizen called upon, or apprehended by virtue of the law, ought immediately to obey, and renders himself culpable by resistance.

VIII. The law ought to impose no other penalties but such as are absolutely and evidently necessary; and no one ought to be punished, but in virtue of a law promulgated before the offence, and legally applied.

IX. Every man being presumed innocent till he has been convicted, whenever his detention becomes indispensable, all rigor to him, more than is necessary to secure his person, ought to be provided against by the law.

X. No man ought to be molested on account of his opinions, not even on account of his *religious* opinions, provided his avowal of them does not disturb the public order established by the law.

XI. The unrestrained communication of thoughts and opinions being one of the most precious rights of man, every citizen may speak, write, and publish freely, provided he is responsible for the abuse of this liberty, in cases determined by the law.

XII. A public force being necessary to give security to the rights of men and of citizens, that force is instituted for the benefit of the community and not for the particular benefit of the persons to whom it is intrusted.

XIII. A common contribution being necessary for the support of the public force, and for defraying the other expenses of government, it ought to be divided equally among the members of the community, according to their abilities.

XIV. Every citizen has a right, either by himself or his representative, to a free voice in determining the necessity of public contributions, the appropriation of them, and their amount, mode of assessment, and duration.

XV. Every community has a right to demand of all its agents an account of their conduct.

XVI. Every community in which a separation of powers and a security of rights is not provided for, wants a constitution.

XVII. The right to property being inviolable and sacred, no one ought to be deprived of it, except in cases of evident public necessity, legally ascertained, and on condition of a previous just indemnity.

11

The Declaration of the Rights of Woman and Citizen (1791)

OLYMPE DE GOUGES

Olympe de Gouges (1748–1793) was a butcher's daughter turned actress and playwright who believed women had as much of a "natural" right as men to share in the government being created in France in 1789. When the Declaration of the Rights of Man *was silent on the subject of women, she challenged the revolutionary leadership to live up to its promises of equality with a* Declaration of the Rights of Woman *(1791). She called for new marriage laws, equal property rights, and educational opportunities in addition to votes for women. Two years later Robespierre sent her to the guillotine for her feminism, her defense of the constitutional monarchy, and her criticism of the "Reign of Terror" launched that year by the dictatorial Committee of Public Safety.*

The mothers, daughters, sisters, female representatives of the nation, ask to constitute a National Assembly. Considering that ignorance, neglect or contempt of the rights of woman are the sole causes of public miseries, and governmental corruption, they have resolved to set forth in a solemn declaration, the natural, inalienable, and sacred rights of woman, so that this declaration, being ever present to all members of the social body, may unceasingly remind them of their rights and their duties; in order that the acts of women's power, as well as those of men, may be judged constantly against the aim of all political institutions, and thereby be more respected for it, in order that the complaints of women citizens, based henceforth on simple and indisputable principles, may ever tend toward maintaining the Constitution, good morals, and the welfare of all.

In consequence, the sex superior in beauty and the courage so requisite in maternal suffering, recognizes and declares, in the presence and under the auspices of the Supreme Being, the following rights of woman and of the female citizen:

I. Woman is born free and remains equal to man in rights. Social distinctions must be based only on common utility.

II. The aim of every political association is the preservation of the natural and imprescriptible rights of man and woman. These rights are liberty, prosperity, security, and, above all, resistance to oppression.

III. The source of all sovereignty resides essentially in the nation, which is nothing but the union of man and woman; no body, no individual, can exercise authority that does not emanate expressly from it.

IV. Liberty and justice consist in giving back to others all that belongs to them; thus the only limits on the exercise of woman's natural rights are the perpetual tyranny by which man opposes her; these limits must be reformed according to the laws of nature and of reason.

V. The laws of nature and reason prohibit all actions harmful to society; all that is not forbidden by these wise and divine laws should not be prevented, and no one should be forced to do what they do not prescribe.

VI. Law must be the expression of the general will: all citizens, men and women alike must take part in its formation, personally or through their representatives. It must be the same for all: all citizens, men and women alike, being equal before it, must be equally eligible for all high offices, dignities, and public employments, according to their abilities, and without distinctions other than that of their virtues and talents.

VII. No woman can be exempted: she will be accused, apprehended and detained in cases determined by law; women, like men, will obey this rigorous rule.

VIII. The law must establish only those penalties that are strictly and clearly necessary, and no women may be punished except by virtue of a law established and promulgated prior to the offense and legally applied to women.

IX. When a woman is declared guilty, the full severity of the law should be exercised.

X. No one ought to be disturbed for one's fundamental opinions. As a woman has the right to mount the scaffold, she must also have the right to address the nation, provided her interventions do not disturb the public order as established by law.

XI. The free communication of ideas and opinions is one of the most precious rights of woman, since this freedom ensures the recognition of children by their fathers. Every woman citizen can therefore say freely "I am the mother of your child," without being forced to conceal the truth because of a barbaric prejudice, as long as she is answerable for abuse of this liberty as determined by law.

XII. The guarantee of the rights of woman and of the woman citizen, as a public benefit, entails public enforcement; it must be enforced for the advantage of all and not the personal benefit of those to whom it is entrusted.

XIII. For the upkeep of public forces and for administration expenses, the contributions of woman and man are equal; a woman shares in all the labors required by law, in the painful tasks; she must therefore have an equal share in the distribution of offices, employments, trusts, dignities and work.

XIV. Women and men citizens have the right to ascertain, by themselves or through their representatives, the necessity of public taxes. Women citizens will not only assume an equal part in providing the wealth but also in the public administration and in determining the quota, the assessment, the collection, and the duration of the taxes.

XV. The mass of women, joined together to contribute their taxes with those of men, have the right to demand an accounting of their administration from all public officials.

XVI. Any society in which the guarantee of rights is not assured, nor the separation of powers determined, has no constitution. Any constitution is null and void if the majority of the individuals comprising the nation has not participated in its drafting.

XVII. Ownership of property is for both sexes, mutually or separately; it is for each a sacred and inviolable right. No one can be deprived of it as a true inheritance from nature, unless a public necessity, legally established, obviously demands it, and then on condition of a just and prior compensation.

Afterword:

Women, wake up! The alarm bell of reason resounds throughout the universe; recognize your rights. The powerful empire of nature is no longer beset by prejudices, fanaticism, superstition, and lies. The torch of truth has dispelled the clouds of folly and usurpation. The enslaved man has multiplied his force but requires yours to break his chains. Emancipated himself, he has become unjust to his companion. O Women! Women, when will you stop being blind? What advantages have you received from the Revolution?

The Interesting Narrative of the Life of Olaudah Equiano, or Gustavus Vasa, the African, Written by Himself (1789)

OLAUDAH EQUIANO

The success of the American and French Revolutions inspired the European ruling class in the Central and South American colonies to fight for their own independence. This battle was complicated by the simultaneous struggle of the African, Indian, and mixed populations of those colonies for freedom from their "white" colonial masters. The autobiography of Olaudah Equiano (1745–1797), the youngest son of an Ibo chieftain kidnaped into slavery, offers a unique glance into this multilayered Latin American society as well as the differences between slavery in the Americas and in Ibo society. After serving an English master in several military campaigns, and secretly learning to read and write, Equiano sailed on a merchant ship and saved enough money to purchase his freedom (1766). Taking the name Gustavus Vasa, he participated in explorations in the Arctic, sailed the Mediterranean, and worked as a plantation overseer before finally settling in Britain. There he campaigned for an end to the slave trade.

Equiano's Account of Slavery in Africa

Our land is uncommonly rich and fruitful, and produces all kinds of vegetables in great abundance. We have plenty of Indian corn, and vast quantities of cotton and tobacco. Our pine apples grow without culture; they are about the size of the largest sugar-loaf, and finely flavored. We have also spices of different kinds, particularly pepper; and a variety of delicious fruits which I have never seen in Europe; together with gums of various kinds, and honey in abundance. All our industry is exerted to improve those blessings of nature. Agriculture is our chief employment; and every one, even children and women, are engaged in it. Thus we are all habituated to labor from our earliest years. Every one contributes something to the common stock; and as we are unacquainted with idleness, we have no beggars. . . .

Our tillage is exercised in a large plain or common, some hours walk from our dwellings, and all the neighbors resort thither in a body. They use no beasts of husbandry; and their only instruments are hoes, axes, shovels, and beaks, or pointed iron to dig with. Sometimes we are visited by locusts, which come in large clouds, so as to darken the air, and destroy our harvest. This however happens rarely, but when it does, a famine is produced by it. I remember an instance or two wherein this happened. This common is often the theater of war; and therefore when our people go out to till their land, they not only go in a body, but generally take their arms with them, for fear of a surprise. . . . From what I can recollect of these battles, they appear to have been irruptions of one little state or district on the other, to obtain prisoners or booty. Perhaps they were incited to this by those traders who brought the European goods I mentioned [iron farm implements and weapons] amongst us. Such mode of obtaining slaves in Africa is common; and I believe more are procured this way [the purchase of war captives], and by kidnapping, than any other. . . . We have firearms, bows and arrows, broad two-edged swords and javelins; we have shields also, which cover a man from head to foot. All are taught the use of the weapons. Even our women are warriors, and march boldly out to fight along with the men. . . . I was once a witness to a battle in our common. We had been all at work in it one day as usual when our people were suddenly attacked. I climbed a tree at some distance, from which I beheld the fight. There were many women as well as men on both sides; among others my mother was there and armed with a broad sword. After fighting for a considerable time with great fury, and many had been killed, our people obtained the victory. . . . those prisoners which were not sold or redeemed [ransomed by their families] we kept as slaves: but how different was their condition from that of the slaves in the West-Indies! With us they do no more work that other members of the community, even their master. Their food, clothing, and lodging were nearly the same as theirs; except that they were not permitted to eat with those who were freeborn and there was scarce any other difference between them, than a superior degree of importance which the head of a family possesses in our state, and that authority which, as such, he exercises over every part of his household. Some of these slaves have even slaves under them, as their own property, and for their own use. . . .

Equiano's Account of Slavery in the Caribbean

While I was thus employed by my master, I was often a witness to cruelties of every kind, which were exercised on my unhappy fellow slaves. I used frequently to have different cargoes of new Negroes in my care for sale; and it was almost a constant practice with our clerks, and other whites, to commit violent depredations on the chastity of the female slaves; and these I was, though with reluctance, obliged to submit to at all times, being unable to help them. . . . And yet in Montserrat I have seen a Negro man staked to the ground, and cut most shockingly [castrated], and then his ears cut off bit by bit, because he had been connected with a white woman who was a common prostitute. . . .

One Mr. Drummond told me that he had sold 41,000 Negroes, and that he once cut off a Negro man's leg for running away.—I asked him, if that man had died in the operation? How he, as a Christian, could answer for the horrid act before God? And he told me, answering was a thing of another world; but what he thought and did were policy. I told him that the Christian doctrine taught us to do unto others as we would that others should do unto us. He then said that his scheme had the desired effect—it cured that man and some others of running away. . . .

It was very common in several of the islands, particularly in St. Kitt's, for the slaves to be branded with the initial letters of their master's name, and a load of heavy iron hooks hung about their necks. Indeed, on the most trifling occasions they were loaded with chains, and often other instruments of torture were added. The iron muzzle, thumb-screws, &c. are so well-known, as not to need a description, and were sometimes applied for the slightest faults. I have seen a Negro beaten till some of his bones were broken, for only letting a pot boil over. It is not uncommon, after a flogging, to make slaves go on their knees, and thank their owners, and pray, or rather say, God bless them. I have often asked many of the men slaves (who used to go several miles to their wives, and late in the night, after having been wearied with a hard day's labor) why they went so far for wives, and why they did not take them of their own master's Negro women, and particularly those who lived together as household slaves? Their answers have ever been—"Because when the master or mistress choose to punish the women, they make the husbands flog their own wives, and that they could not bear to do."

Address to the National Congress of Venezuela (1819)

SIMÓN BOLÍVAR

As a member of Venezuela's colonial aristocracy, Simón Bolívar (1783–1830) was educated in Spain where he learned the ideals of the Enlightenment. Dubbed the "Liberator" for freeing Colombia, Venezuela, Bolivia, Ecuador, and Peru from Spanish rule, Bolívar struggled unsuccessfully to unite them into a union strong enough to resist the economic encroachment of an expanding United States. This speech by Bolívar to the National Congress of Venezuela explores another problem facing the new Latin American republics: could the "liberal" political system of the United States be adapted to colonies that did not have a tradition of local self-rule? Or did Montesquieu's theory of the uniqueness of cultures, laid out in his L'Esprit des lois *[Spirit of the Laws], doom Latin American states to authoritarian rule?*

We are not Europeans; we are not Indians; we are but a mixed species of aborigines and Spaniards. Americans by birth and Europeans by law, we find ourselves engaged in a dual conflict: we are disputing with the natives for titles of ownership, and at the same time we are struggling to maintain ourselves in the country that gave us birth against the opposition of the invaders. Thus our position is most extraordinary and complicated. But there is more. As our role has always been strictly passive and our political existence nil, we find that our quest for liberty is now even more difficult of accomplishment. . . .

Subject to the threefold yoke of ignorance, tyranny, and vice, the American people have been unable to acquire knowledge, power, or [civic] virtue. The lessons we received and the models we studied, as pupils of such pernicious teachers, were most destructive. We have been ruled more by deceit than by force, and we have been degraded more by vice than by superstition. Slavery is the daughter of Darkness: an ignorant people is a blind instrument of its own destruction. Ambition and intrigue abuse the credulity and experience of men lacking all political, economic, and civic knowledge; they adopt pure illusion as reality; they take license for liberty, treachery for patriotism, and vengeance for justice. . . .

If a people, perverted by their training, succeed in achieving their liberty, they will soon lose it, for it would be of no avail to endeavor to explain to them that happiness consists in the practice of virtue; that the rule of law is more powerful than the rule of tyrants, because, as the laws are more inflexible, everyone should submit to their beneficent austerity; that proper morals, and not force, are the bases of law; and that to practice justice is to practice liberty. Therefore, Legislators, your work is so much the more arduous, inasmuch as you have to reeducate men who have been corrupted by erroneous illusions and false incentives. Liberty, says Rousseau, is a succulent morsel, but one difficult to digest. Our weak fellow-citizens will have to strengthen their spirit greatly before they can digest the wholesome nutriment of freedom. . . .

The more I admire the excellence of the federal Constitution of Venezuela, the more I am convinced of the impossibility of its application to our state. And, to my way of thinking, it is a marvel that its prototype in North America endures so successfully and has not been overthrown at the first sign of adversity or danger. Although the people of North America are a singular model of political virtue and moral rectitude; although that nation was cradled in liberty, reared on freedom, and maintained by liberty alone; and—I must reveal everything—although those people, so lacking in many respects, are unique in the history of mankind, it is a marvel, I repeat, that so weak and complicated a government as the federal system has managed to govern them in the difficult and trying circumstances of their past. But, regardless of the effectiveness of this form of government with respect to North America, I must say that it has never for a moment entered my mind to compare the position and character of two states as dissimilar as the English-American and the Spanish-American. Would it not be most difficult to apply to Spain the English system of political, civil, and religious liberty? Hence, it would be even more difficult to adapt to Venezuela the laws of North America. Does not *L'Esprit des lois* state that laws should be suited to the people for whom they are made; that it would be a major coincidence if those of one nation could be adapted to another; that laws must take into account the physical conditions of the country, climate, character of the land, location, size, and mode of living of the people; that they should be in keeping with the degree of liberty that the Constitution can sanction respecting the religion of the inhabitants, their inclinations, resources, number, commerce, habits, and customs? This is the code we must consult, not the code of Washington! . . .

Therefore, let the entire system of government be strengthened, and let the balance of power be drawn up in such a manner that it will be permanent and incapable of decay because of its own tenuity. Precisely because no form of government is so weak as the democratic, its framework must be firmer, and its institutions must be studied to determine their degree of stability. Unless this is done, we must plan on the establishment of an experimental rather than a permanent system of government; and we will have to reckon with an ungovernable, tumultuous, and anarchic society, not with a social order where happiness, peace, and justice prevail. . . .

. . .We must not aspire to the impossible, lest, in trying to rise above the realm of liberty, we again descend into the realm of tyranny. Absolute liberty invariably lapses into absolute power, and the mean between these two extremes is supreme social liberty. Abstract theories create the pernicious idea of unlimited freedom. Let us see to it that the strength of the public is kept within the limits prescribed by reason and interest.

Topic II

Industrial Transformation and the Birth of Modern Societies

Lectures on the Industrial Revolution (1879–1883)

ARNOLD TOYNBEE

From the middle of the eighteenth century to the middle of the nine-teenth, Great Britain underwent a series of changes in the way it pro-duced goods—from human to machine power, from domestic to factory production—that, even today, continue to transform people's lives. These changes, called the "Industrial Revolution," turned Great Britain into "the Workshop of the World." While the Industrial Revolution helped Britain create an Empire that spanned the globe, it also created unprecedented social turmoil within Britain itself. In a series of lectures given between 1879 and 1883, the historian Arnold Toynbee (1852–1883) made the first systematic attempt to assess a transforma-tion that created "wealth without producing well-being."

Coming to the facts of the Industrial Revolution, the first thing that strikes us is the far greater rapidity which marks the growth of population. Before 1751 the largest decennial increase, so far as we can calculate from our imperfect materials, was 3 per cent. For each of the next three decennial periods the increase was 6 per cent.; then between 1781 and 1791 it was 9 per cent.; between 1791 and 1801, 11 per cent.; between 1801 and 1811, 14 per cent.; between 1811 and 1821, 18 per cent. This is the highest figure ever reached in England, for since 1815 a vast emigration has been always tending to moderate it; between 1815 and 1880 over eight millions (including Irish) have left our shores. But for this our normal rate of increase would be 16 or 18 instead of 12 per cent. in every decade.

Next we notice the relative and positive decline in the agricultural population. In 1811 it constituted 35 per cent. of the whole population of Great Britain; in 1821, 33 per cent.; in 1831, 28 per cent. . . . [percent of population employed in agriculture: 1841 = 13%, 1851 = 10%, 1861 = 8.7%, 1871 = 6.4%]

An agrarian revolution plays as large part in the great industrial change of the end of the eighteenth century as does the revolution in manufacturing

43

industries, to which attention is more usually directed. Our next inquiry must therefore be: What were the agricultural changes which led to this noticeable decrease in the rural population? The three most effective causes were: the destruction of the common-field system of cultivation; the enclosure, on a large scale, of common and waste lands; and the consolidation of small farms into large. We have already seen that while between 1710 and 1760 some 300,000 acres were enclosed, between 1760 and 1843 nearly 7,000,000 underwent the same process. Closely connected with the enclosure system was the substitution of large for small farms. . . . The consolidation of farms reduced the number of farmers, while the enclosures drove the laborers off the land, as it became impossible for them to exist without their rights of pasturage for sheep and geese on common lands.

Severely, however, as these changes bore upon the rural population, they wrought, without doubt, distinct improvement from an agricultural point of view. They meant the substitution of scientific for unscientific culture.

Passing to manufactures, we find here the all-prominent fact to be the substitution of the factory for the domestic system, the consequence of the mechanical discoveries of the time. Four great inventions altered the character of the cotton manufacture: the spinning-jenny, patented by Hargreaves in 1770; the water-frame, invented by Arkwright the year before; Crompton's mule introduced in 1779, and the self-acting mule, first invented by Kelly in 1792, but not brought into use till Roberts improved it in 1825. None of these by themselves would have revolutionized the industry. But in 1769—the year in which Napoleon and Wellington were born—James Watt took out his patent for the steam-engine. Sixteen years later it was applied to the cotton manufacture. In 1785 Boulton and Watt made an engine for a cotton-mill at Papplewick in Notts, and in the same year Arkwright's patent expired. These two facts taken together mark the introduction of the factory system. . . . At first, in fact, machinery raised the wages of spinners and weavers owing to the great prosperity it brought to the trade. In fifteen years the cotton trade trebled itself, from 1788 to 1803 has been called "its golden age"; for, before the power-loom but after the introduction of the mule and other mechanical improvements by which for the first time yarn sufficiently fine for muslin and a variety of other fabrics was spun, the demands became such that "old barns, cart-houses, outbuildings of all descriptions were repaired, windows broke through the old blank walls, and all fitted up for loom-shops; new weavers' cottages with loom-shops arose in every direction, every family bringing home weekly from 40 to 120 shillings per week." At a later date, the condition of the workman was very different. Meanwhile, the iron industry had been equally revolutionized by the invention of smelting by pit-coal brought into use between 1740 and 1750, and by the application in 1788 of the steam-engine to blast furnaces. In the eight years which followed this latter date, the amount of iron manufactured nearly doubled itself.

A further growth of the factory system took place independent of machinery, and owed its origin to the expansion of trade, an expansion which was itself due to the great advance made at this time in the means of communication. The canal system was being rapidly developed throughout the country. In 1777 the Grand Trunk canal, 96 miles in length, connecting the Trent and Mersey, was finished; Hull and Liverpool were connected by one canal while another connected them both with Bristol; and in 1792, the Grand Junction canal, 90 miles in length, made a waterway from London through Oxford to the chief midland towns. Some years afterwards, the roads were greatly improved under Telford and Macadam; between 1818 and 1829 more than a thousand additional miles of turnpike road were constructed; and the next year, 1830, saw the opening of the first railroad. These improved means of communication caused an extraordinary increase in commerce, and to secure a sufficient supply of goods it became the interest of the merchants to collect weavers around them in great numbers, to get looms together in a workshop, and to give out the warp themselves to the workpeople. To these latter this system meant a change from independence to dependence; at the beginning of the century the report of a committee asserts that the essential difference between the domestic and the factory system is, that in the latter the work is done "by persons who have no property in the goods they manufacture." Another direct consequence of this expansion of trade was the regular recurrence of periods of overproduction and of depression, a phenomenon quite unknown under the old system, and due to this new form of production on a large scale for a distant market.

These altered conditions in the production of wealth necessarily involved an equal revolution in its distribution. In agriculture the prominent fact is an enormous rise in rents. Up to 1795, though they had risen in some places, in others they had been stationary since the Revolution. But between 1790 and 1833, according to Porter, they at least doubled. . . . Whatever may have been its causes, however, it represented a great social revolution, a change in the balance of political power and in the relative position of classes. The farmers shared in the prosperity of the landlords; for many of them held their farms under beneficial leases, and made large profits by them. In consequence, their character completely changed; they ceased to work and live with their laborers, and became a distinct class. . . . Meanwhile, the effect of all these agrarian changes upon the condition of the laborer was an exactly opposite and most disastrous one. He felt all the burden of high prices, while his wages were steadily falling, and he had lost his common-rights. It is from this period, *viz.*, the beginning of the present century, that the alienation between farmer and laborer may be dated.

Exactly analogous phenomena appeared in the manufacturing world. The new class of great capitalist employers made enormous fortunes, they took little or no part personally in the work of their factories, their hundreds of workmen were individually unknown to them; and as a consequence, the old relations between masters and men disappeared, and a "cash nexus" was substituted for the human tie. The workmen on their side resorted to combination, and Trades-Unions began a fight which looked as if it were between mortal enemies rather than joint producers. The misery which came upon large sections of the working people at this epoch was often, though not always, due to a fall in wages, for, as I said above, in some industries they rose. But they suffered likewise from the conditions of labor under the factory system, from the rise of prices, especially from the high price of bread before the repeal of the corn-laws, and from those sudden fluctuations of trade, which, ever since production has been on a large scale, have exposed them to recurrent periods of bitter distress. The effects of the Industrial Revolution prove that free competition may produce wealth without producing well-being.

Sadler Report on Child Labor (1832)

Although children had always worked beside their parents on the farm, capitalism's use of child labor in the mines, factories, and textile mills of Great Britain led to increasing opposition to children in the workplace. Michael Thomas Sadler (1780–1835) chaired the Parliamentary Commission charged with investigating child labor in the factories as Parliament considered reform legislation. The following is one of the thousands of interviews Sadler's Commission conducted. As a result of the investigation, Parliament passed the Factory Act of 1833; it set the minimum working age in factories at nine and mandated a half-day maximum for children under the age of fourteen.

What is your occupation?—A blanket manufacturer.

Have you ever been employed in a factory?—Yes.

At what age did you first go to work in one?—Eight.

How long did you continue in that occupation?—Four years.

Will you state the hours of labor at the period when you first went to the factory, in ordinary times?—From 6 in the morning to 8 at night.

Fourteen hours?—Yes.

With what intervals for refreshment and rest?—An hour at noon.

Then you had no resting time allowed in which to take your breakfast, or what is in Yorkshire called your "drinking"?—No.

When trade was brisk what were your hours?—From 5 in the morning to 9 in the evening.

Sixteen hours?—Yes.

With what intervals at dinner?—An hour.

How far did you live from the mill?—About two miles.

Was there any time allowed for you to get your breakfast in the mill?—No.

Did you take it before you left home?—Generally.

During those long hours of labor could you be punctual, how did you awake?—I seldom did awake spontaneously. I was most generally awoke or lifted out of bed, sometimes asleep, by my parents.

Were you always in time?—No.

What was the consequence if you had been too late?—I was most commonly beaten.

Severely?—Very severely, I thought.

In whose factory was this?—Messrs. Hague & Cook's of Dewsbury.

Will you state the effect that those long hours had upon the state of your health and feelings?—I was, when working those long hours, commonly very much fatigued at night, when I left my work, so much so that I sometimes should have slept as I walked if I had not stumbled and started awake again, and so sick often that I could not eat, and what I did eat I vomited. . . .

In what situation were you in that mill?—I was a piecener.

Will you state to the Committee whether piecening is a very laborious employment for children, or not?—It is a very laborious employment. Pieceners are continually running to and fro, and on their feet the whole day.

The duty of the piecener is to take the cardings from one part of the machinery, and to place them on another?—Yes.

So that the labor is not only continual, but it is unabated to the last?—It is unabated to the last. . . .

State the condition of the children towards the latter part of the day, who have thus to keep up with the machinery?—It is as much as they can do when they are not very much fatigued to keep up with their work, and towards the close of the day, when they come to be more fatigued, they cannot keep up with it very well, and the consequence is that they are beaten to spur them on.

Were you beaten under those circumstances?—Yes.

Frequently?—Very frequently.

And principally at the latter end of the day?—Yes.

And is it your belief that if you had not been so beaten, you should not have got through the work?—I should not if I had not been kept up to it by some means.

Does beating then principally occur at the latter end of the day, when the children are exceedingly fatigued?—It does at the latter end of the day, and in the morning sometimes, when they are very drowsy, and have not got rid of the fatigue of the day before.

What were you beaten with principally?—A strap.

Any thing else?—Yes, a stick sometimes; and there is a kind of roller which runs on the top of the machine called a billy, perhaps two or three yards in length. . . .

Were you beaten with that instrument?—Yes.

Have you yourself been beaten, and have you seen other children struck severely with that roller?—I have been struck very severely with it myself, so much so as to knock me down, and I have seen other children have their heads broken with it.

You think that it is a general practice to beat the children with the roller?—It is.

You do not think then that you were worse treated than other children in the mill?—No, I was not, perhaps not so bad as some were. . . .

Can you speak as to the effect of this labor in the mills and factories on the morals of the children, as far as you have observed?—As far as I have observed with regard to morals in the mills, there is every thing about them that is disgusting to every one conscious of correct morality.

Do you find that the children, the females especially, are very early demoralized in them?—They are.

Is their language indecent?—Very indecent; and both sexes take great familiarities with each other in the mills, without at all being ashamed of their conduct. . . .

Have not a considerable number of the females employed in mills illegitimate children very early in life?—I believe there are; I have known some of them have illegitimate children when they were between 16 and 17 years of age.

Mine Commissioners' Reports (1842)

The Factory Act of 1833 did not affect the use of child labor in the coal mines. While men wielded the pick-axes that freed the coal from the walls of the mine pits, women and children were used to retrieve ("hurry") the chunks of coal from the narrow tunnels. Women and children as young as seven were tied by a belt at the waist to a chain used to pull the "corves" (wagons) of coal along the tunnel rails. The evidence gathered by the Parliamentary Commission that produced the report excerpted below led to the passage of the Mines Act (1842) forbidding women and children under the age of ten from working below ground in the mines.

Ann Hague, Examined February 18th:—

I am turned of 13 years old. I hurry the same as the last girl, in Webster's Pit. I draw the corve with a chain and belt. There is a little girl, my sister, who pushes behind. We go at six in the morning and come away at two in the afternoon. We have our breakfast before we go, and take our dinner with us and get it when we can at the pit: when we've a minute to spare. We often stop as much as half an hour. We don't feel tired a deal at night; but we do a little sometimes. We have 24 corves to go in and out with every day. . . . I can read, but I cannot write. . . I go to the Sunday school, all but when I'm poorly. Having to pull so hard in the pit makes me poorly sometimes. They teach me to read in the Testament at the Sunday school. Jesus Christ was the Son of God, but I don't know what he came on earth for.

❀

Elizabeth Day, aged 17. Examined March 13th; working at Messrs. Hopwood's pit at Barusley:—

I have been nearly nine years in the pit. . . . I have to hurry up hill with the loaded corves, quite as much up as down. . . . We always hurry in trousers as you saw to-day when you were in the pit. Generally I work naked down to the waist like the rest, I had my shift on to-day when I saw you, because I had to wait, and was cold: but generally the girls hurry naked down to the waist. It is very hard work for us all. It is harder work than we ought to do a deal. I have been lamed in my ankle, and strained in my back; it caused a great lump to rise in my ankle-bone once. The men behave well to us, and never insult or ill-use us, I am sure of that. We go to work between five and six, but we begin to hurry when we get down. We stop an hour to dinner at 12; we generally have bread and a bit of fat for dinner, and some of them a sup of beer; that's all; we have a whole hour for dinner, and we get out from four to five in the evening; so that it will be 11 hours before we get out. We drink the water that runs through the pit. I am not paid wages myself. The man who employs me pays my father; but I don't know how much it is. I have never been at school. I had to begin working when I ought to have been at school. I don't go to Sunday-school. The truth is, we are confined bad enough on week-days, and want to walk about on Sundays; but I go to chapel on Sunday night. I can't read at all. Jesus Christ was Adam's son, and they nailed him on to a tree; but I don't rightly understand these things.

Topic III

Social and Economic Thought in Early Industrial Society

The Wealth of Nations (1776)

ADAM SMITH

Industrial Capitalism—the economic system created by the change from human-powered to machine-powered production—was still in its infancy and under tight government control when Adam Smith (1723–1790), a Professor of Moral Philosophy at Glasgow University, wrote An Inquiry into the Nature and the Causes of the Wealth of Nations *(1776). He used the analogy of the industrial "division of labor" to explain why the new economic system would work best when government interfered with it the least. However, the "self-interest" he believed set the marketplace's natural laws in motion was not mindless greed but the rational self-interest esteemed by Enlightenment philosophers. His book became the cornerstone of modern economic theory and of laissez-faire capitalism.*

The greatest improvement in the productive powers of labor, and the greater skill, dexterity, and judgment with which it is any where directed, or applied, seem to have been the effects of the division of labor.

The effects of the division of labor, in the general business of society, will be more easily understood, by considering in what manner it operates in some particular manufactures. . . .

To take an example, therefore, from a very trifling manufacture; but one in which the division of labor has been very often taken notice of, the trade of the pin-maker; a workman not educated to this business (which the division of labor has rendered a distinct trade), nor acquainted with the use of the machinery employed in it (to the invention of which the same division of labor has probably given occasion), could scarce, perhaps, with his utmost industry, make one pin in a day, and certainly could not make twenty. But in the way in which this business is now carried on, not only the whole work is a peculiar trade, but it is divided into a number of branches, of which the greater part are likewise peculiar trades. One man draws out the wire, another straightens it, a third cuts it, a fourth points it, a fifth grinds it at the top for receiving the head: to make the head requires two or three distinct operations; to put it on, is a peculiar business; to whiten the pins is another;

it is even a trade by itself to put them into the paper; and the important business of making a pin is, in this manner, divided into about eighteen distinct operations, which, in some factories, are all performed by distinct hands, though in others the same man will sometimes perform two or three of them. I have seen a small factory of this kind where ten men only were employed, and where some of them consequently performed two or three distinct operations. But though they were very poor, and therefore but indifferently accommodated with the necessary machinery, they could, when they exerted themselves, make among them about twelve pounds of pins in a day. There are in a pound upwards of four thousand pins of a middling size. Those ten persons, therefore, could make among them upwards of forty-eight thousand pins in a day. Each person, therefore, making a tenth part of forty-eight thousand pins, might be considered as making four thousand eight hundred pins in a day. But if they had all wrought separately and independently, and without any of them having been educated to this peculiar business, they certainly could not each of them have made twenty, perhaps not one pin in a day. . . .

The real price of everything, what everything really costs to the man who wants to acquire it, is the toil and trouble of acquiring it. What every thing is really worth to the man who has acquired it, and who wants to dispose of it or exchange it for something else, is the toil and trouble which it can save to himself, and which it can impose upon other people. What is bought with money or with goods is purchased by labor, as much as what we require by the toil of our own body. That money or those goods indeed save us this toil. They contain the value of a certain quantity of labor, which we exchange for what is supposed at the time to contain the value of an equal quantity. Labor was the first price, the original purchase money that was paid for all things. It was not by gold or by silver, but by labor, that all the wealth of the world was originally purchased; and its value, to those who possess it, and who want to exchange it for some new productions, is precisely equal to the quantity of labor which it can enable then to purchase or command.

Wealth, as Mr. Hobbes says, is power. But the person who either acquires, or succeeds to a great fortune, does not necessarily acquire or succeed to any political power, either civil or military. His fortune may perhaps, afford him the means of acquiring both, but the mere possession of that fortune does not necessarily convey to him either. The power which that possession immediately and directly conveys to him, is the power of purchasing; a certain command over all the labor, or over all the produce of labor which is then in the market. His fortune is greater or less precisely in proportion to the extent of this power; or to the quantity of other men's labor, or, what is the same thing, of the produce of other men's labor which it enables him to purchase or command. . . .

Every individual, therefore, endeavors as much as he can both to employ his capital in the support of domestic industry, and so to direct that industry that its produce may be of the greatest value, every individual necessarily labors to render the annual revenue of the society as great as he can. He generally, indeed, neither intends to promote the public interest, nor knows how much he is promoting it. By preferring the support of domestic to that of foreign industry, he intends only his own security; and by directing that industry in such a manner as its produce may be of the greatest value, he intends only his own gain, and he is in this, as in many other cases, led by an invisible hand to promote an end which was no part of his intention. Nor is it always the worse for the society that it was no part of it. By pursuing his own interest he frequently promotes that of the society more effectually than when he really intends to promote it. I have never known much good done by those who affected to trade for the public good. It is an affectation, indeed, not very common among merchants, and very few words need be employed in dissuading them from it.

What is the species of domestic industry which his capital can employ, and of which the produce is likely to be of the greatest value, every individual, it is evident, can, in this local situation, judge much better than any statesman or lawgiver can do for him. The statesman, who should attempt to direct private people in what manner they ought to employ their capitals, would not only load himself with a most unnecessary attention, but assume an authority which could safely be trusted, not only to no single person, but to no council or senate whatever, and which would nowhere be so dangerous as in the hands of a man who had folly and presumption enough to fancy himself fit to exercise it.

To give the monopoly of the home market to the produce of domestic industry, in any particular art or manufacture, is in some measure to direct private people in what manner they ought to employ their capitals, and must, in almost all cases, be either a useless or a hurtful regulation. If the produce of domestic [industry] can be brought there as cheap as that of foreign industry, the regulation is evidently useless. If it cannot, it must generally be hurtful. It is the maxim of every prudent master of a family, never to attempt to make at home what it will cost him more to make than to buy. The tailor does not attempt to make his own shoes, but buys them of the shoemaker. The shoemaker does not attempt to make his own clothes, but employs a tailor. The farmer attempts to make neither the one nor the other, but employs those different artificers. All of them find it for their interest to employ their whole industry in a way in which they have some advantage over their neighbors, and to purchase with a part of its produce, or what is the same thing, with the price of a part of it, whatever else they have occasion for.

What is prudence in the conduct of every private family, can scarce be folly in that of a great kingdom. If a foreign country can supply us with a commodity cheaper than we ourselves can make it, better buy it of them with some part of the produce of our own industry, employed in a way in which we have some advantage. The general industry of the country, being always in proportion to the capital which employs it, will not thereby be diminished, no more than that of the above-mentioned artificers; but only left to find out the way in which it can be employed with the greatest advantage. It is certainly not employed to the greatest advantage when it is thus directed towards an object which it can buy cheaper than it can make. The value of its annual produce is certainly more or less diminished, when it, is thus turned way from producing commodities evidently of more value than the commodity which it is directed to produce. According to the supposition, that commodity could be purchased from foreign countries cheaper than it can be made at home. It could, therefore, have been purchased with a part only of the commodities, or, what is the same thing, with a part only of the price of the commodities, which the industry employed by an equal capital would have produced at home, had it been left to follow its natural course. . . .

But in the system of laws which has been established for the management of our American and West Indian colonies, the interest of the home-consumer has been sacrificed to that of the producer with a more extravagant profusion than in all our other commercial regulations. A great empire has been established for the sole purpose of raising up a nation of customers, who should be obliged to buy from the shops of our different producers all the goods with which these could supply them. For the sake of that little enhancement of price which this monopoly might afford our producers, the home-consumers have been burdened with the whole expense of maintaining and defending that empire. For this purpose, and for this purpose only, in the two last wars more than two hundred millions have been spent, and a new debt of more than a hundred and seventy millions has been contracted over and above all that had been expended for the same purpose in former wars. The interest of this debt alone is not only greater than the whole extraordinary profit which, it ever could be pretended, was made by the monopoly of the colony trade, but than the whole value of that trade, or than the value of the goods, which at an average have been annually exported to the colonies.

It cannot be very difficult to determine who have been the contrivers of this whole mercantile system; not the consumers, we may believe, whose interest has been entirely neglected, but the producers, whose interest has been so carefully attended to; and among this latter class our merchants and manufacturers have been by far the principal architects. In the mercantile regulations, which have been taken notice of in this chapter, the interest of our manufacturers has been most peculiarly attended to; and the interest, not so much of the consumers as that of some other sets of producers, has been sacrificed to it.

Essay on the Principle
of Population (1798)

THOMAS ROBERT MALTHUS

Many Enlightenment philosophers believed applying Newtonian science to the problems of society would create a paradise on Earth. Thomas Robert Malthus (1766–1834), a British clergyman and the first man to hold a university appointment in economics, disagreed. His Essay on the Principle of Population *(1798) used the latest population figures from Britain and the Americas to demonstrate that government programs (such as Britain's Poor Laws, an early form of welfare) only aggravated the social problems (unemployment, family abandonment, illegitimate births) they tried to cure. Influential in Britain's switch from a "welfare" to a "workfare" relief system, the conclusions reached by Malthus also had a considerable impact on Charles Darwin's theory of evolution.*

I have read some of the speculations on the perfectibility of man and society with great pleasure. I have been warmed and delighted with the enchanting picture which they hold forth. I ardently wish for such happy improvements. But I see great, and, to my understanding, unconquerable difficulties in the way to them. . . .

I think I may fairly make two postulata.

First, That food is necessary to the existence of man.

Secondly, That the passion between the sexes is necessary and will remain nearly in its present state.

These two laws, ever since we have had any knowledge of mankind, appear to have been fixed laws of our nature, and, as we have not hitherto seen any alteration in them, we have no right to conclude that they will ever cease to be what they now are . . . .

Assuming then my postulata as granted, I say, that the power of population is indefinitely greater than the power in the earth to produce subsistence for man.

Population, when unchecked, increases in a geometrical ratio. Subsistence increases only in an arithmetical ratio. A slight acquaintance with numbers will shew the immensity of the first power in comparison of the second.

By that law of our nature which makes food necessary to the life of man, the effects of these two unequal powers must be kept equal.

This natural inequality of the two powers of population and of production in the earth, and that great law of our nature which must constantly keep their efforts equal, form the great difficulty that to me appears insurmountable in the way to the perfectibility of society. . . .

In the United States of America, where the means of subsistence have been more ample, the manners of the people more pure, and consequently the checks to early marriages fewer, than in any of the modern states of Europe, the population has been found to double itself in twenty-five years. This ratio of increase, though short of the utmost power of population, yet as the result of actual experience, we will take as our rule, and say, that population, when unchecked, goes on doubling itself every twenty-five years or increases in a geometrical ratio. . . .

If I allow that by the best possible policy, by breaking up more land and by great encouragements to agriculture, the produce of this Island [Britain] may be doubled in the first twenty-five years, I think it will be allowing as much as any person can well demand.

In the next twenty-five years, it is impossible to suppose that the produce could be quadrupled. It would be contrary to all our knowledge of the qualities of land. The very utmost that we can conceive, is, that the increase in the second twenty-five years might equal the present produce. Let us then take this for our rule, though certainly far beyond the truth, and allow that, by great exertion, the whole produce of the Island might be increased every twenty-five years, by a quantity of subsistence equal to what it at present produces. . . .

Yet this ratio of increase is evidently arithmetical. . . .

Taking the population of the world at any number, a thousand millions, for instance, the human species would increase in the ratio of—1, 2, 4, 8, 16, 32, 64, 128, 256, 512, etc. and subsistence as—1, 2, 3, 4, 5, 6, 7, 8, 9, 10, etc. In two centuries and a quarter, the population would be to the means of subsistence as 512 to 10. . . .

To remedy the frequent distresses of the common people, the poor laws of England have been instituted; but it is to be feared, that though they have alleviated a little the intensity of individual misfortune, they have spread the general evil over a much larger surface. . . . [Their] obvious tendency is to increase population without increasing the food for its support. A poor man may marry with little or no prospect of being able to support a family to independence. They [the Poor Laws] may be said therefore in some measure to create the poor which they maintain. . . .

The laboring poor, to use a vulgar expression, seem always to live from hand to mouth. Their present wants employ their whole attention, and they seldom think of the future. Even when they have an opportunity of saving they seldom exercise it, but all that is beyond their present necessities goes, generally speaking, to the ale-house. . . .

It is a general complaint among master manufacturers that high wages ruin all their workmen, but it is difficult to conceive that these men would not save a part of their high wages for the future support of their families, instead of spending it in drunkenness and dissipation, if they did not rely on [Poor Relief for assistance]. . . .

To remove the wants of the lower classes of society is indeed an arduous task. The truth is that the pressure of distress on this part of a community is an evil so deeply seated that no human ingenuity can reach it. Were I to propose a palliative, and palliatives are all that the nature of the case will admit, it should be, in the first place, the total abolition of all the present [Poor Laws] . . . .

[In their place,] for cases of extreme distress, county workhouses might be established, supported by rates upon the whole kingdom, and free for persons of all counties, and indeed of all nations. The fare should be hard, and those that were able obliged to work. It would be desirable that they should not be considered as comfortable asylums in all difficulties, but merely as places where severe distress might find some alleviation. . . .

Famine seems to be the last, the most dreadful resource of nature. The power of population is so superior to the power in the earth to produce subsistence for man, that premature death must in some shape or other visit the human race. The vices of mankind are active and able ministers of depopulation. They are the precursors in the great army of destruction; and often finish the dreadful work themselves. But should they fail in this war of extermination, sickly seasons, epidemics, pestilence, and plague advance in terrific array, and sweep off their thousands and then thousands. Should success be still incomplete, gigantic inevitable famine stalks in the rear, and with one mighty blow levels the population with the food of the world. . . .

The lower classes of people in Europe may at some future period be much better instructed than they are at present; they may be taught to employ the little spare time they have in many better ways than at the ale-house; they may live under better and more equal laws than they have ever hitherto done, perhaps, in any country; and I even conceive it possible, though not probable, that they may have more leisure; but it is not in the nature of things that they can be awarded such a quantity of money or subsistence as will allow them all to marry early, in the full confidence that they shall be able to provide with ease for a numerous family.

A New View of Society (1813)

ROBERT OWEN

*Robert Owen (1771–1858) rose from worker to supervisor in the fac-
tories of Manchester, England, married the boss's daughter, and took
over management of a complex of textile mills in New Lanark, Scotland. There he put into action the series of reforms described in his* New
View of Society *(1813). Working from the Enlightenment doctrine
derived from John Locke's tabula rasa argument (in Locke's* Essay on
Human Understanding*) that people were products of their environment, Owen argued that "villages of cooperation" run by workers could
replace harsh factory life and create superior citizens. He spent his life
and his fortune supporting a wide range of radical reforms, among them
a short-lived (1825–1828) cooperative community in New Harmony,
Indiana.*

 "Any general character, from the best to the worst, from the most igno-
rant to the most enlightened, may be given to any community, even to the
world at large, by the application of proper means; which means are to great
extent at the command and under the control of those who have influence in
the affairs of men." . . .

Children can be trained to acquire "any language, sentiments, belief, or any
bodily habits and manners, not contrary to human nature."

For that this has been done, the history of every nation of which we have
records, abundantly confirms; and that this is, and may be again done, the
facts would exhibit around us and throughout all the countries in the world,
prove to demonstration.

Possessing, then, the knowledge of a power so important, which, when
understood, is capable of being wielded with the certainty of a law of nature,
and which would gradually remove the evils which now chiefly afflict
mankind, shall we permit it to remain dormant and useless, and suffer the
plagues of society perpetually to exist and increase? . . .

Some of the best intentioned among the various classes in society may still
say, "All this is *very delightful and beautiful in theory,* but *visionaries* alone
expect to see it *realized.*" To this remark only one reply *can* or *ought* to be

made; that *these principles have been carried most successfully into practice* [at his mills in New Lanark, Scotland] . . . .

[There, the] system of receiving apprentices from public charities was abolished; permanent settlers with large families were encouraged, and comfortable houses were built for their accommodation.

The practice of employing children in the mills, of six, seven and eight years of age, was discontinued, and their parents advised to allow them to acquire health and education until they were ten years old. (It may be remarked, that even this age is too early to keep them at constant employment in factories, from six in the morning to seven in the evening. Far better would it be for the children, their parents, and for society, that the first should not commence employment until they attain the age of twelve, when their education might be finished, and their bodies would be more competent to undergo the fatigue and exertions required of them. When parents can be trained to afford this additional time to their children without inconvenience, they will, of course, adopt the practice now recommended.)

The children were taught reading, writing, and arithmetic, during five years, that is, from five to ten, in the village school, without expense to their parents. All the modern improvements in education have been adopted, or are in the process of adoption. (To avoid the inconveniences which must ever arise from the introduction of a particular creed into a school, the children are taught the elements of Christian religion which are common to all denominations.). . .

Their houses were rendered more comfortable, their streets were improved, the best provisions were purchased, and sold to them at low rates, yet covering the original expense, and under such regulations as taught them how to proportion their expenditure to their income. Fuel and clothes were obtained for them in the same manner; and no advantage was attempted to be taken of them, or means used to deceive them. . . .

Those employed became industrious, temperate, healthy, faithful to their employers, and kind to each other; while the proprietors were deriving services from their attachment, almost without inspection, far beyond those which could be obtained by any other means than those of mutual confidence and kindness. . . .

The end of government is to make the governed and the governors happy.

That government, then, is the best, which in practice produces the greatest happiness to the greatest number; including those who govern, and those who obey. . . .

If there be one duty therefore more imperative than another, on the government of every country, it is, that it should adopt, without delay, the proper means to form those sentiments and habits in the people, which shall give the most permanent and substantial advantages to the individuals and to the community. . . .

The next measure for the general improvement of the British population should be to revise the laws relative to the poor. . . . Benevolence says, that the destitute must not starve; and to this declaration political wisdom readily assents. Yet can that system be right, which compels the industrious, temperate, and comparatively virtuous, to support the ignorant, the idle, and comparatively vicious? Such, however, is the effect of the present British Poor Laws. . . . These laws should be progressively undermined by a system of an opposite nature, and ultimately rendered altogether nugatory. . . .

For this purpose an Act should be passed for the instruction of all the poor and laboring classes in the three kingdoms. . . . For the establishment of seminaries [teacher-training schools] in which those individuals who shall be destined to form the minds and bodies of the future subjects of these realms should be well initiated in the arts and matter of instruction. . . .[and] For supplying the requisite expenditure for the building and support of those seminaries. . . .

Malthus is, however, correct, when he says that the population of the world is ever adapting itself to the quantity of food raised for its support; but he has not told us how much more food an intelligent and industrious people will create from the same soil, than will be produced by one ignorant and ill governed. It is, however, as one to infinity.

For man knows not the limit to his power of creating food. How much has this power been latterly increased in these islands! . . . Shall we then continue to allow misery to predominate, and the labor of man to be most absurdly applied or wasted, when it might be easily directed to remove that misery? . . .

The Communist Manifesto (1848)

KARL MARX AND FRIEDRICH ENGELS

As the Industrial Revolution spread across western Europe, so did the social upheaval it created. Deriding the programs of Robert Owen and other early reformers as "Utopian" dreams, Karl Marx (1818–1883) and his lifelong collaborator Friedrich Engels (1820–1895) developed an alternate theory they called "Scientific Socialism." They claimed the "scientific laws" of history proved that workers would continue to be exploited by their bourgeois employers until Capitalism itself produced the proletarian revolution that would destroy it. They expected that revolution to begin in their native Germany any day. Encouraged by a wave of revolutions in Europe in 1848, Marx and Engels introduced their theories to the world in The Communist Manifesto *(1848), a call to arms to workers everywhere.*

A specter is haunting Europe—the specter of Communism. All the powers of Old Europe have entered into a holy alliance to exorcize this specter; Pope and Czar, Metternich and Guizot, French Radicals and German police-spies.

Where is the party in opposition that has not been decried as communistic by its opponents in power? Where the opposition that has not hurled back the branding reproach of Communism, against the more advanced opposition parties, as well as against its reactionary adversaries?

Two things result from this fact.

I. Communism is already acknowledged by all European powers to be in itself a power.

II. It is high time that Communists should openly, in the face of the whole world, publish their views, their aims, their tendencies, and meet this nursery tale of the specter of Communism with a Manifesto of the party itself.

To this end Communists of various nationalities have assembled in London, and sketched the following Manifesto to be published in the English, French, German, Italian, Flemish and Danish languages.

Bourgeois and Proletarians

The history of all hitherto existing society is the history of class struggles.

Freeman and slave, patrician and plebeian, lord and serf, guild-master and journeyman, in a word, oppressor and oppressed, stood in constant opposition to one another, carried on an uninterrupted, now hidden, now open fight, that each time ended, either in a revolutionary reconstitution of society at large, or in the common ruin of the contending classes.

In the earlier epochs of history we find almost everywhere a complicated arrangement of society into various orders, a manifold gradation of social rank. In ancient Rome we have patricians, knights, plebeians, slaves; in the middle ages, feudal lords, vassals, guild-masters, journeymen, apprentices, serfs; in almost all of these classes, again, subordinate gradations.

The modern bourgeois society that has sprouted from the ruins of feudal society, has not done away with class antagonisms. It has but established new classes, new conditions of oppression, new forms of struggle in place of the old ones.

Our epoch, the epoch of the bourgeoisie, possesses, however, this distinctive feature; it has simplified the class antagonisms. Society as a whole is more and more splitting up into two great hostile camps, into two great classes directly facing each other: Bourgeoisie and Proletariat.

From the serfs of the middle ages sprang the chartered burghers of the earliest towns. From these burgesses the first elements of the bourgeoisie were developed. . . .

We see, therefore, how the modern bourgeoisie is itself the product of a long course of development, of a series of revolutions in the modes of production and of exchange.

Each step in the development of the bourgeoisie was accompanied by a corresponding political advance of that class. An oppressed class under the sway of the feudal nobility, an armed and self-governing association in the mediaeval commune, here independent urban republic (as in Italy and Germany), there taxable "third estate" of the monarchy (as in France), afterwards, in the period of manufacture proper, serving either the semi-feudal or the absolute monarchy as a counterpoise against the nobility, and, in fact, cornerstone of the great monarchies in general. The bourgeoisie has at last, since the establishment of Modern Industry and of the world's market, conquered for itself, in the modern representative State, exclusive political sway. The executive of the modern State is but a committee for managing the common affairs of the whole bourgeoisie.

The bourgeoisie, historically, has played a most revolutionary part.

The bourgeoisie, wherever it has got the upper hand, has put an end to all feudal, patriarchal, idyllic relations. It has pitilessly torn asunder the motley feudal ties that bound man to his "natural superiors," and has left remaining no other nexus between man and man than naked self-interest, than callous "cash payment." It has drowned the most heavenly ecstasies of religious fervor, of chivalrous enthusiasm, of Philistine sentimentalism, in the icy water of egotistical calculation. It has resolved personal worth into exchange value, and in place of the numberless indefeasible chartered freedoms, has set up that single, unconscionable freedom—Free Trade. In one word, for exploitation, veiled by religious and political illusions, it has substituted naked, shameless, direct, brutal exploitation.

The bourgeoisie has stripped of its halo every occupation hitherto honored and looked up to with reverent awe. It has converted the physician, the lawyer, the priest, the poet, the man of science, into its paid wage-laborers.

The bourgeoisie has torn away from the family its sentimental veil, and has reduced the family relation to a mere money relation. . . .

The bourgeoisie has through its exploitation of the world's market given a cosmopolitan character to production and consumption in every country. . . .

The bourgeoisie, by the rapid improvement of all instruments of production, by the immensely facilitated means of communication, draws all, even the most barbarian, nations into civilization. The cheap prices of its commodities are the heavy artillery with which it batters down all Chinese walls, with which it forces the barbarians' intensely obstinate hatred of foreigners to capitulate. It compels all nations, on pain of extinction, to adopt the bourgeois mode of production; it compels them to introduce what it calls civilization into their midst, *i.e.,* to become bourgeois themselves. In one word, it creates a world after its own image. . . .

The bourgeoisie keeps more and more doing away with the scattered state of the population, of the means of production, and of property. It has agglomerated population, centralized means of production, and has concentrated property in a few hands. The necessary consequence of this was political centralization. Independent, or but loosely connected provinces, with separate interests, laws, governments, and systems of taxation, became lumped together into one nation, with one government, one code of laws, one national class interest, one frontier, and one customs tariff.

The bourgeoisie, during its rule of scarce one hundred years, has created more massive and more colossal productive forces than have all preceding generations together. Subjection of Nature's form to man, machinery, application of chemistry to industry and agriculture, steam navigation, railways, electric telegraphs, clearing of whole continents for cultivation, canalization of rivers . . . what earlier century had even a presentment that such productive forces slumbered in the lap of social labor? . . .

A similar movement is going on before our own eyes. Modern bourgeois society with its relations of production, of exchange, and of property, a society that has conjured up such gigantic means of production and of exchange, is like the sorcerer, who is no longer able to control the powers of the nether world whom he has called up by his spells. For many a decade past the history of industry and commerce is but the history of the revolt of modern productive forces against modern conditions of production, against the property relations that are the conditions for the existence of the bourgeoisie and of its rule. It is enough to mention the commercial crises that by their periodical return put on its trial, each time more threateningly, the existence of the bourgeois society. In these crises a great part not only of the existing products, but also of the previously created productive forces, is periodically destroyed. In these crises there breaks out an epidemic that, in all earlier epochs, would have seemed an absurdity—the epidemic of overproduction. Society suddenly finds itself put back into a state of momentary barbarism; it appears as if a famine, a universal war of devastation, had cut off the supply of every means of subsistence; industry and commerce seem to be destroyed; and why? Because there is too much civilization, too much means of subsistence, too much industry, too much commerce. The productive forces at the disposal of society no longer tend to further the development of the conditions of bourgeois property; on the contrary, they have become too powerful for these conditions, by which they are fettered, and as soon as they overcome these fetters, they bring disorder into the whole of bourgeois society, endanger the existence of bourgeois property. The conditions of bourgeois society are too narrow to comprise the wealth created by them. And how does the bourgeoisie get over these crises? On the one hand by enforced destruction of a mass of productive forces; on the other, by the conquest of new markets, and by the more thorough exploitation of the old ones. That is to say, by paving the way for more extensive and more destructive crises, and by diminishing the means whereby crises are prevented.

The weapons with which the bourgeoisie felled feudalism to the ground are now turned against the bourgeoisie itself.

But not only has the bourgeoisie forged the weapons that bring death to itself; it has also called into existence the men who are to wield those weapons—the modern working class—the proletarians.

In proportion as the bourgeoisie, *i.e.,* capital, is developed, in the same proportion is the proletariat, the modern working class, developed; a class of laborers, who live only so long as they find work, and who find work only so long as their labor increases capital. These laborers, who must sell themselves piecemeal, are a commodity, like every other article of commerce, and are consequently exposed to all the vicissitudes of competition, to all the fluctuations of the market.

Owing to the extensive use of machinery and to division of labor, the work of the proletarians has lost all individual character, and, consequently, all charm for the workman. He becomes an appendage of the machine, and it is only the most simple, most monotonous, and most easily acquired knack, that is required of him. Hence, the cost of production of a workman is restricted almost entirely to the means of subsistence that he requires for his maintenance, and for the propagation of his race. But the price of a commodity, and therefore also of labor, is equal to its cost of production. In proportion, therefore, as the repulsiveness of the work increases, the wage decreases. . . .

. . . Masses of laborers, crowded into factories, are organized like soldiers. As privates of the industrial army they are placed under the command of a perfect hierarchy of officers and sergeants. Not only are they the slaves of the bourgeois class, and of the bourgeois State, they are daily and hourly enslaved by the machine. . . .

The lower strata of the Middle class—the small tradespeople, shopkeepers, and retired tradesmen generally, the handicraftsmen and peasant—all these sink gradually into the proletariat, partly because their diminutive capital does not suffice for the scale on which modern industry is carried on, and is swamped in the competition with the large capitalists, partly because their specialized skill is rendered worthless by new methods of production. Thus the proletariat is recruited from all classes of the population. . . .

But with the development of industry the proletariat not only increases in number; it becomes concentrated in greater masses, its strength grows and it feels that strength more. The various interests and conditions of life within the ranks of the proletariat are more and more equalized, in proportion as machinery obliterates all distinctions of labor, and nearly everywhere reduces wages to the same low level. The growing competition among the bourgeois, and the resulting commercial crises, make the wages of the workers even more fluctuating. The unceasing improvement of machinery, ever more rapidly developing, makes their livelihood more and more precarious; the collisions between individual workmen and individual bourgeois take more and more the character of collisions between two classes. Thereupon the workers begin to form combinations (Trades' Unions) against the bourgeois; they club together in order to keep up the rate of wages; they found permanent associations in order to make provision beforehand for these occasional revolts. Here and there the contest breaks out into riots.

Now and then the workers are victorious, but only for a time. The real fruit of their battles lies not in the immediate result but in the ever-improved means of communication that are created by modern industry, and that place the workers of different localities in contact with one another. It was just this contact that was needed to centralize the numerous local struggles, all of the same character, into one national struggle between classes. But every class struggle is a political struggle. And that union, to attain which the burghers of the Middle Ages, with their miserable highways, required centuries, the modern proletarians, thanks to railways, achieve in a few years.

This organization of the proletarians into a class, and consequently into a political party, is continually being upset again by the competition between the workers themselves. But it ever rises up again; stronger, firmer, mightier. . . .

All the preceding classes that got the upper hand sought to fortify their already acquired status by subjecting society at large to their conditions of appropriation. The proletarians cannot become masters of the productive forces of society, except by abolishing their own previous mode of appropriation, and thereby also every other previous mode of appropriation. They have nothing of their own to secure and to fortify; their mission is to destroy all previous securities for, and insurances of, individual property.

All previous historical movements were movements of minorities, or in the interest of minorities. The proletarian movement is the self-conscious, independent movement of the immense majority, in the immense majority. The proletariat, the lowest stratum of our present society, cannot stir, cannot raise itself up, without the whole super-incumbent strata of official society being sprung into the air.

Though not in substance, yet in form, the struggle of the proletariat with the bourgeoisie is at first a national struggle. The proletariat of each country must, of course, first of all settle matters with its own bourgeoisie.

In depicting the most general phases of the development of the proletariat, we traced the more or less veiled civil war, raging within existing society, up to the point where that war breaks out into open revolution, and where the violent overthrow of the bourgeoisie lays the foundation for the sway of the proletariat.

The essential condition for the existence, and for the sway of the bourgeois class, is the formation and augmentation of capital; the condition for capital is wage-labor. Wage-labor rests exclusively on competition between the laborers. The advance of industry, whose involuntary promoter is the bourgeoisie, replaces the isolation of the laborers, due to competition, by their revolutionary combination, due to association. The development of modern industry, therefore, cuts from under its feet the very foundation on which the bourgeoisie produces and appropriates products. What the bourgeoisie therefore produces, above all, are its own grave-diggers. Its fall and the victory of the proletariat are equally inevitable. . . .

Position of the Communists in Relation to the Various Existing Opposition Parties

. . .The Communists fight for the attainment of the immediate aims, for the enforcement of the momentary interests of the working class; but in the movement of the present they also represent and take care of the future of that movement. In France the Communists ally themselves with the Social-Democrats, against the conservative and radical bourgeoisie, reserving, however, the right to take up a critical position in regard to phrases and illusions traditionally handed down from the great Revolution.

In Switzerland they support the Radicals, without losing sight of the fact that this party consists of antagonistic elements, partly of Democratic Socialists, in the French sense, partly of radical bourgeois.

In Poland they support the party that insists on an agrarian revolution, as the prime condition for national emancipation, that party which fomented the insurrection of Cracow in 1846.

In Germany they fight with the bourgeoisie whenever it acts in a revolutionary way against the absolute monarchy, the feudal squirearchy, and the petty bourgeoisie.

But they never cease, for a single instant, to instill into the working class the clearest possible recognition of the hostile antagonism between bourgeoisie and proletariat, in order that the German workers may straightway use, as so many weapons against the bourgeoisie the social and political conditions that the bourgeoisie must necessarily introduce along with its supremacy, and in order that, after the fall of the reactionary classes in Germany, the fight against the bourgeoisie itself may immediately begin.

The Communists turn their attention chiefly to Germany, because that country is on the eve of a bourgeois revolution that is bound to be carried out under more advanced conditions of European civilization, and with a much more developed proletariat, than that of England was in the seventeenth, and of France in the eighteenth century, and because the bourgeois revolution in Germany will be but the prelude to an immediately following proletarian revolution.

In short, the Communists everywhere support every revolutionary movement against the existing social and political order of things.

In all these movements they bring to the front, as the leading question in each, the property question, no matter what its degree of development at the time.

Finally, they labor everywhere for the union and agreement of the democratic parties of all countries.

The Communists disdain to conceal their views and aims. They openly declare that their ends can be attained only by the forcible overthrow of all existing social conditions. Let the ruling classes tremble at a Communistic revolution. The proletarians have nothing to lose but their chains. They have a world to win.

Working men of all countries, unite!

Evolutionary Socialism (1899)

EDUARD BERNSTEIN

As the nineteenth century drew to a close, the final clash between own-
ers and workers predicted by The Communist Manifesto failed to mate-
rialize. Socialist parties were left struggling to explain the how the real
gains in voting power, wages, and living conditions made by workers
since 1848 could be reconciled with Marx's theories. In Germany,
Eduard Bernstein (1850–1932) argued that workers, by organizing
themselves into political parties, could gradually alter the socioeconomic
system without resorting to revolution. Marx's followers derided Bern-
stein's view as "revisionism," but Bernstein's Evolutionary Socialism
(1899) became a cornerstone of the democratic-socialist movement in
western Europe.

I set myself against the notion that we have to expect shortly a collapse of
the bourgeois economy, and that social democracy should be induced by the
prospect of such an imminent, great, social catastrophe to adapt its tactics to
that assumption. That I maintain most emphatically.

The adherents of this theory of a catastrophe base it especially on the conclusions of the *Communist Manifesto*. This is a mistake in every respect.

The theory which the *Communist Manifesto* sets forth of the evolution of
modern society was correct as far as it characterized the general tendencies
of that evolution. But it was mistaken in several special deductions, above all
in the estimate of the time the evolution would take. The last has been unre-
servedly acknowledged by Friedrich Engels, the joint author with Marx of
the *Manifesto*, in his preface to the *Class War in France*. But it is evident that
if social evolution takes a much greater period of time than was assumed, it
must also take upon itself forms and lead to forms that were not foreseen and
could not be foreseen then.

Social conditions have not developed to such an acute opposition of things
and classes as is depicted in the *Manifesto*. It is not only useless, it is the
greatest folly to attempt to conceal this from ourselves. The number of members of the possessing classes is to-day not smaller but larger. The enormous
increase of social wealth is not accompanied by a decreasing number of large

capitalists but by an increasing number of capitalists of all degrees. The middle classes change their character but they do not disappear from the social scale.

The concentration in productive industry is not being accomplished even to-day in all its departments with equal thoroughness and at an equal rate. In a great many branches of production it certainly justifies the forecasts of the socialist critic of society; but in other branches it lags even to-day behind them. The process of concentration in agriculture proceeds still more slowly. . . .

In all advanced countries we see the privileges of the capitalist bourgeoisie yielding step by step to democratic organizations. Under the influence of this, and driven by the movement of the working classes which is daily becoming stronger, a social reaction has set in against the exploiting tendencies of capital, a counteraction which, although it still proceeds timidly and feebly, yet does exist, and is always drawing more departments of economic life under its influence. Factory legislation, the democratization of local government, and the extension of its area of work, the freeing of trade unions and systems of cooperative trade from legal restrictions, the consideration of standard conditions of labor in the work undertaken by public authorities—all these characterize this phase of the evolution.

But the more the political organizations of the modern nations are democratized the more the needs and opportunities of great political catastrophes are diminished. He who holds firmly to the catastrophic theory of evolution must, with all his power, withstand and hinder the evolution described above, which, indeed, the logical defenders of that theory formerly did. But is the conquest of political power by the proletariat simply to be by a political catastrophe? Is it to be the appropriation and utilization of the power of the State by the proletariat exclusively against the whole non-proletarian world?

He who replies in the affirmative must be reminded of two things. In 1872 Marx and Engels announced in the preface to the new edition of the *Communist Manifesto* that the Paris Commune had exhibited a proof that "the working classes cannot simply take possession of the ready-made State machine and set it in motion for their own aims." . . . [And in *War of the Classes* (1895), Friedrich Engels said that] the next task of the party should be "to work for an uninterrupted increase of its vote" or to carry on a slow *propaganda of parliamentary activity*. . . . [If] one subscribes to his conclusions, one cannot reasonably take any offense if it is declared that for a long time yet the task of social democracy is, instead of speculating on a great economic crash, "to organize the working classes politically and develop them as a democracy and to fight for all reforms in the State which are adapted to raise the working classes and transform the state in the direction of democracy." That is what I have said in my impugned article and what I still maintain. . . . No one has questioned the necessity for the working classes to gain the control of government. The point at issue is between the theory of social cataclysm and the question whether with the given social development in

Germany and the present advanced state of its working classes in the towns and the country, a sudden catastrophe would be desirable in the interest of social democracy. I have denied it and deny it again, because in my judgment a greater security for lasting success lies in a steady advance than in . . . a catastrophic crash.

And as I am firmly convinced that important periods in the development of nations cannot be leapt over I lay the greatest value on the next tasks of social democracy, on the struggle for the political rights of the working man, on the political activity of working men in town and country for the interests of their class, as well as on the work of the industrial organization of the workers. . . .

The conquest of political power by the working classes, the expropriation of capitalists, are not ends in themselves but only means for the accomplishment of certain aims and endeavors. As such they are demands in the program of social democracy and are not attacked by me. Nothing can be said beforehand as to the circumstances of their accomplishments; we can only fight for their realization. But the conquest of political power necessitates the possession of political *rights;* and the most important problem of tactics which German social democracy has at the present time to solve, appears to me to be to devise the best ways for the extension of the political and economic rights of the German working classes.

Wealth and its Uses (1902)

ANDREW CARNEGIE

After the Civil War ended in 1865, the United States of America industrialized so rapidly that it led the world in productive capacity by 1900. As in Europe, the transformation was tumultuous and painful, creating "Captains of Industry" who traveled by private railroad car and militant workers who torched the railroad yards to win fairer wages. Andrew Carnegie (1835–1915) was a Scottish immigrant to the United States who became the world's foremost steel-maker by pioneering the "vertically integrated" corporation and taking as hard a line against his workers as they took against him. But he also emphasized the responsibilities that came with moneymaking in Wealth and its Uses (1902). Practicing what he preached, Carnegie virtually invented modern philanthropy, giving away almost 90% of his wealth. Among other projects, he endowed more than 1700 public libraries in the United States and Britain.

The principal complaint against our industrial conditions of to-day is that they cause great wealth to flow into the hands of the few. Well, of the very few, indeed, is this true. It was formerly so, as I have explained, immediately after the new inventions had changed the conditions of the world. To-day it is not true. Wealth is being more and more distributed among the many. The amount of combined profits of labor and capital which goes to labour was never so great as to-day, the amount going to capital never so small. While the earnings of capital have fallen more than one-half, in many cases have been entirely obliterated, statistics prove that the earnings of labor were never so high as they were previous to the recent unprecedented depression in business, while the cost of living,—the necessaries of life,—have fallen in some cases nearly one-half. . . .

You may be sure, gentlemen, that the question of the distribution of wealth is settling itself rapidly under present conditions, and settling itself in the right direction. The few rich are getting poorer, and the toiling masses are getting richer. Nevertheless, a few exceptional men may yet make fortunes, but these will be more moderate than in the past. This may not be quite as fortunate for the masses of the people as is now believed, because great accumulations of wealth in the hands of one enterprising man who still toils on are sometimes most productive of all the forms of wealth. Take the richest man the world ever saw, who died in New York some years ago. What was found in his case? That, with the exception of a small percentage used for daily expenses, his entire fortune and all its surplus earnings were invested in enterprises which developed the railway system of our country, which gives to the people the cheapest transportation known.

Whether the millionaire wishes it or not, he cannot evade the law which under present conditions compels him to use his millions for the good of the people. All that he gets during the few years of his life is that he may live in a finer house, surround himself with finer furniture, and works of art which may be added: he could even have a grander library, more of the gods around him; but, as far as I have known millionaires, the library is the least used part of what he would probably consider "furniture" in all his mansion. He can eat richer food and drink richer wines, which only hurt him. But truly the modern millionaire is generally a man of very simple tastes and even miserly habits. He spends little upon himself, and is the toiling bee laying up the honey in the industrial hive, which all the inmates of that hive, the community in general, will certainly enjoy.

The bees of a hive do not destroy the honeymaking bees, but the drones. It will be a great mistake for the community to shoot the millionaires, for they are the bees that make the most honey, and contribute most to the hive even after they have gorged themselves full. Here is a remarkable fact, that the masses of people in any country are prosperous and comfortable just in proportion as there are millionaires. Take Russia, with its population little better than serfs, and living at the point of starvation upon the meanest possible fare, such fare as none of our people could or would eat, and you do not find one millionaire in Russia, always excepting the Emperor and a few nobles who own the land, owing to their political system. . . . In the old home of our race, in Britain, which is the richest country in all Europe—the richest country in the world save one, our own—there are more millionaires than in the whole of the rest of Europe, and its people are better off than in any other. . . .

The inventions of to-day lead to concentrating industrial and commercial affairs into huge concerns. You cannot work the Bessemer process successfully without employing thousands of men upon one spot. You could not make the armor for ships without first expending seven millions of dollars, as the Bethlehem Company has spent. You cannot make a yard of cotton goods in competition with the world without having an immense factory and thousands of men and women aiding in the process. The great electric establishment here in your town succeeds because it has spent millions, and is prepared to do its work upon a great scale. Under such conditions it is impossible but that wealth will flow into the hands of a few men in prosperous times beyond their needs. . . .

But assuming that surplus wealth flows into the hands of a few men, what is their duty? How is the struggle for dollars to be lifted from the sordid atmosphere surrounding business and made a noble career? Now, wealth has hitherto been distributed in three ways: The first and chief one is by willing it at death to the family. Now, beyond bequeathing to those dependent upon one the revenue needful for modest and independent living, is such a use of wealth either right or wise? I ask you to think over the result, as a rule, of millions given over to young men and women, the sons and daughters of the millionaire. You will find that, as a rule, it is not good for the daughters, and this is seen in the character and conduct of the men who marry them. As for the sons, you have their condition as described in the extract which I read you from *The Sun*. Nothing is truer than this, that as a rule the "almighty dollar" bequeathed to sons or daughters by millions proves an almighty curse. . . .

There is a second use of wealth, less common than the first, which is not so injurious to the community, but which should bring no credit to the testator. Money is left by millionaires to public institutions when they must relax their grasp upon it. There is no grace, and can be no blessing, in giving what cannot be withheld. It is no gift, because it is not cheerfully given, but only granted at the stern summons of death. The miscarriage of these bequests, the litigation connected with them, and the manner in which they are frittered away seem to prove that the Fates do not regard them with a kindly eye. We are never without a lesson that the only mode of producing lasting good by giving large sums of money is for the millionaire to give as close attention to its distribution during his life as he did to its acquisition. We have to-day the noted case of five or six millions of dollars left by a great lawyer to found a public library in New York, an institution needed so greatly that the failure of this bequest is a misfortune. It is years since he died; the will is pronounced invalid through a flaw, although there is no doubt of the intention of the donor. It is sad commentary upon the folly of men holding the millions which they cannot use until they are unable to put them to the end they desire. Peter Cooper, Pratt of Baltimore, and Pratt of Brooklyn, and others are the type of men who should be taken by you as your model; they distributed their surplus during life.

The third use, and the only noble use of surplus wealth, is this: That it be regarded as a sacred trust, to be administered by its possessor, into whose hands it flows, for the highest good of the people. Man does not live by bread alone, and five or ten cents a day more revenue scattered over thousands would produce little or no good. Accumulated into a great fund and expended as Mr. Cooper expended it for the Cooper Institute, it establishes something that will last for generations. It will educate the brain, the spiritual part of man. It furnishes a ladder upon which the aspiring poor may climb; and there is no use whatever, gentlemen, trying to help people who do not help themselves. You cannot push any one up a ladder unless he be willing to climb a little himself. When you stop boosting, he falls, to his injury. Therefore, I have often said, and I now repeat, that the day is coming, and already we see its dawn, in which the man who dies possessed of millions of available wealth which was free and in his hands ready to be distributed will die disgraced. Of course I do not mean that the man in business may not be stricken down with his capital in the business, which cannot be withdrawn, for capital is the tool with which he works his wonders and produces more wealth. I refer to the man who dies possessed of millions of securities which are held simply for the interest they produce, that he may add to his hoard of miserable dollars. By administering surplus wealth during life great wealth may become a blessing to the community, and the occupation of the business man accumulating wealth may be elevated so as to rank with any profession. In this way he may take rank even with the physician, one of the highest of our professions, because he too, in a sense, will be a physician, looking after and trying not to cure, but to prevent, the ills of humanity.

Rerum Novarum (1891)

POPE LEO XIII

In 1891 Pope Leo XIII (r. 1878–1903) issued Rerum Novarum (Of New Things). *In it, he offered the Catholic Church's solution to the social upheaval accompanying the Industrial Revolution. Opposed to both Marxism and liberalism, Leo XIII sought a Christian way to ease tensions between capital and labor. Rejecting "the notion that class is naturally hostile to class," he endorsed Catholic labor unions, state aid to the poor, and inter-class cooperation. His encyclical called for social justice engineered from above at a time when the working class was trying to force change from below. The debate over the right way to reform society continues—inside the Catholic Church as well as outside it—today.*

That the spirit of revolutionary change, which has long been disturbing the nations of the world, should have passed beyond the sphere of politics and made its influence felt in the cognate sphere of practical economics is not surprising. The elements of the conflict now raging are unmistakable in the vast expansion of industrial pursuits and the marvelous discoveries of science; in the changed relations between masters and workmen; in the enormous fortunes of some few individuals, and the utter poverty of the masses; in the increased self-reliance and closer mutual combination of the working classes; as also, finally, in the prevailing moral degeneracy. The momentous gravity of the state of things now obtaining fills every mind with painful apprehension . . . .

The great mistake made in regard to the matter now under consideration is to take up with the notion that class is naturally hostile to class, and that the wealthy and the workingmen are intended by nature to live in mutual conflict. So irrational and so false is this view, that the direct contrary is the truth. Just as the symmetry of the human frame is the resultant of the disposition of the bodily members, so in a State is it ordained by nature that these two classes should dwell in harmony and agreement, and should, as it were, groove into one another, so as to maintain the balance of the body politic. Each needs the other: Capital cannot do without Labor, nor Labor without Capital. Mutual agreement results in pleasantness of life and the beauty of good order; while perpetual conflict necessarily produces confusion and savage barbarity. Now, in preventing such strife as this, and in uprooting it, the efficacy of Christian institutions is marvelous and manifold. First of all, there is no intermediary more powerful than Religion (whereof the Church is the interpreter and guardian) in drawing the rich, and the poor bread-winners, together, by reminding each class of its duties to the other, and especially of the obligations of justice. Thus Religion teaches the laboring man and the artisan to carry out honestly and fairly all equitable agreements freely entered into; never to injure the property, nor to outrage the person, of an employer; never to resort to violence in defending their own cause, nor to engage in riot or disorder; and to have nothing to do with men of evil principles, who work upon the people with artful promises, and excite foolish hopes which usually end in useless regrets, followed by insolvency. Religion teaches the wealthy owner and the employer that their work-people are not to be accounted their bondsmen; that in every man they must respect his dignity and worth as a man and as a Christian; that labor is not a thing to be ashamed of, if we lend ear to right reason and to Christian philosophy, but is an honorable calling, enabling a man to sustain his life in a way upright and creditable; and that it is shameful and inhuman to treat men like chattels to make money by, or to look upon them merely as so much muscle or physical power. Again, therefore, the Church teaches that, as Religion and things spiritual and mental are among the workingman's main concerns, the employer is bound to see that the worker has time for his religious duties; that he be not exposed to corrupting influences and dangerous occasions; and that he be not led away to neglect his home and family, or to squander his earnings. . . .

Rights must be religiously respected wherever they exist; and it is the duty of the public authority to prevent and to punish injury, and to protect every one in the possession of his own. Still, when there is a question of defending the rights of individuals, the poor and helpless have a claim to especial consideration. The richer class have many ways of shielding themselves, and stand less in need of help from the State; whereas those who are badly off have no resources of their own to fall back upon, and must chiefly depend upon the assistance of the State. And it is for this reason that wage-earners, who are undoubtedly among the weak and necessitous, should be specially cared for and protected by the Government.

Here, however, it is expedient to bring under special notice certain matters of moment. It should ever be borne in mind that the chief thing to be realized is the safeguarding of private property by legal enactment and public policy. Most of all it is essential, amid such a fever of excitement, to keep the multitude within the line of duty; for if all may justly strive to better their condition, neither justice nor the common good allows any individual to seize upon that which belongs to another, or, under the futile and shallow pretext of equality, to lay violent hands on other people's possessions. Most true it is that by far the larger part of the workers prefer to better themselves by honest labor rather than by doing any wrong to others. But there are not a few who are imbued with evil principles and eager for revolutionary change, whose main purpose is to stir up tumult and bring about measures of violence. The authority of the State should intervene to put restraint upon such firebrands, to save the working classes from their seditious arts, and protect lawful owners from spoliation. . . .

If we turn now to things external and corporeal, the first concern of all is to save the poor workers from the cruelty of greedy speculators, who use human beings as mere instruments of moneymaking. It is neither just nor human so to grind men down with excessive labor as to stupefy their minds and wear out their bodies. Man's powers, like his general nature, are limited, and beyond these limits he cannot go. His strength is developed and increased by use and exercise, but only on condition of due intermission and proper rest. Daily labor, therefore, should be so regulated as not to be protracted over longer hours than strength admits. How many and how long the intervals of rest should be must depend on the nature of the work, on circumstances of time and place, and on the health and strength of the workmen. Those who work in mines and quarries, and extract coal, stone, and metals from the bowels of the earth, should have shorter hours in proportion as their labor is more severe and trying to health. Then, again, the season of the year should be taken into account; for not infrequently a kind of labor is easy at one time which at another is intolerable or exceedingly difficult. Finally, work which is quite suitable for a strong man cannot reasonably be required from a woman or a child. And, in regard to children, great care should be taken not to place them in workshops and factories until their bodies and minds are sufficiently developed. For just as very rough weather destroys the buds of spring, so does too early an experience of life's hard toil blight the young promise of a child's faculties, and render any true education impossible. Women, again, are not suited for certain occupations; a woman is by nature fitted for home work, and it is that which is best adapted at once to preserve her modesty and to promote the good bringing up of children and the well-being of the family. As a general principle it may be laid down that a workman ought to have leisure and rest proportionate to the wear and tear of his strength; for waste of strength must be repaired by cessation from hard work. . . .

In the last place—employers and workmen may of themselves effect much in the matter we are treating, by means of such associations and organizations as afford opportune aid to those who are in distress, and which draw the two classes more closely together. Among these may be enumerated societies for mutual help; various benevolent foundations established by private persons to provide for the workman, and for his widow or his orphans, in case of sudden calamity, in sickness, and in the event of death; and what are called "patronages," or institutions for the care of boys and girls, for young people, as well as homes for the aged.

The most important of all are workingmen's unions; for these virtually include all the rest. History attests what excellent results were brought about by the artificers' guilds of olden times. They were the means of affording not only many advantages to the workmen, but in no small degree of promoting the advancement of art. . . . Such unions should be suited to the requirements of this our age—an age of wider education, of different habits, and of far more numerous requirements in daily life.

Topic IV

Nationalism Across the Globe

Duties to Your Country (1858)

GIUSEPPE MAZZINI

A doctor's son, Giuseppe Mazzini (1805–1872) fled the Italian King-dom of Piedmont-Sardinia after the failure of his earliest attempts at revolution. Condemned to death in absentia by the authorities, Mazzini continued to preach the cause of Italian independence and unification from exile. "Duties to Your Country" (1858) is one of a series of essays promoting Mazzini's liberal nationalism. This form of nationalism pays as much attention to the rights of individuals within the nation as to the political independence of the nation as a whole. Mazzini was devastated when a finally united Italy (1861) became a constitutional monarchy instead of a republic. Refusing to live under a king, Mazzini spent the rest of his life in self-imposed exile.

Like a wise overseer of labour, who distributes the different parts of the work according to the capacity of the workmen, he [God] divided Human-ity into distinct groups upon the face of our globe, and thus planted the seeds of nations. Bad governments have disfigured the design of God, which you may see clearly marked out, as far, at least, as regards Europe, by the courses of the great rivers, by the lines of the lofty mountains, and by other geo-graphical conditions; they have disfigured it by conquest, by greed, by jeal-ousy of the just sovereignty of others; disfigured it by so much that, to-day there is perhaps no nation except England and France whose confines corre-spond to this design. They [the bad governments] did not, and they do not, recognise any country except their own families or dynasty, the egoism of caste. But the divine design will infallibly be fulfilled. Natural divisions, the innate spontaneous tendencies of the peoples will replace the arbitrary divi-sions sanctioned by bad governments. The map of Europe will be re-made. The Countries of the People will rise, defined by voice of the free, upon the ruins of the Countries of Kings and privileged castes. Between these Coun-tries there will be harmony and brotherhood. And then the common work of Humanity for the general amelioration, for the gradual discovery and appli-cation of the real law of life, carried on in association and distributed accord-ing to local capacities, will be accomplished by peaceful and progressive development; then each of you, strong in the affections and in the aid of many millions of men speaking the same language, endowed with the same tendencies, and educated by the same historic tradition, may hope by your personal effort to be able to benefit the whole of Humanity. . . .

O my brothers! love your Country. Our country is our home, the home which God has given us, placing therein a numerous family which we love and are loved by, and with which we have a far more intimate and quicker communion of feeling and thought than with others; a family which by its concentration upon a given spot, and by the homogenous nature of its elements, is destined for a special kind of activity. Our Country is our field of labor; the products of our activity must go forth from it for the benefit of the whole earth; but the instruments of labour which we can use best and most effectively exist in it, and we may not reject them without being unfaithful to God's purpose and diminishing our own strength. In laboring according to true principles for our Country we are laboring for Humanity; our Country is the fulcrum of the lever which we have to wield for the common good. If we give up this fulcrum we run the risk of becoming useless to our Country and to Humanity. Before *associating* ourselves with the Nations which compose Humanity we must exist as a Nation. There can be no association except among equals; and you have no recognised collective existence.

Humanity is a great army moving to the conquest of unknown lands, against powerful and wary enemies. The Peoples are the different corps and divisions of that army. Each has a post entrusted to it; each a special operation to perform; and the common victory depends on the exactness with which the different operations are carried out. Do not disturb the order of the battle. Do not abandon the banner which God has given to you. Wherever you may be, into the midst of whatever people circumstances may have driven you, fight for the liberty of that people if the moment calls for it; but fight as Italians, so that the blood which you shed may win honour and love, not for you only, but for your Country. . . . Do not say *I*; say *we*. Be every one of you an incarnation of your Country, and feel himself and make himself responsible for his fellow-countrymen; let each one of you learn to act in such a way that in him men shall respect and love his Country.

Your Country is one and indivisible. As the members of a family cannot rejoice at the common table if one of their number is far away, snatched from the affection of his brothers, so you should have no joy or repose as long as a portion of the territory upon which your language is spoken is separated from the Nation.

Your country is the token of the mission which God has given you to fulfil in Humanity. The faculties, the strength of *all* its sons should be united for the accomplishment of this mission. . . .

A Country is a fellowship of free and equal men bound together in a brotherly concord of labour towards a single end. You must make it and maintain it such. A Country is not an aggregation, it is an *association*. There is no true Country without a uniform right. There is no true Country where the uniformity of that right is violated by the existence of castes, privilege, and inequality—where the powers and faculties of a large number of individuals are suppressed or dormant—where there is no common principle accepted, recognised, and developed by all. In such a state of things there can be no Nation, no People, but only a multitude, a fortuitous agglomeration of men whom circumstances have brought together and different circumstances will separate. In the name of your love for your Country you must combat without truce the existence of every privilege, every inequality, upon the soil which has given you birth. One privilege only is lawful—the privilege of Genius when Genius reveals itself in brotherhood with Virtue; but it is a privilege conceded by God and not by men, and when you acknowledge it and follow its inspirations, you acknowledge it freely by the exercise of your own reason and your own choice. Whatever privilege claims your submission in virtue of force or heredity, or any right which is not a common right, is a usurpation and a tyranny, and you ought to combat it and annihilate it. Your Country should be your Temple. God at the summit, a People of equals at the base. Do not accept any other formula, any other moral law, if you do not want to dishonour your Country and yourselves. Let the secondary laws for the gradual regulation of your existence by the progressive application of this supreme law.

And in order that they should be so, it is necessary that *all* should contribute to the making of them. The laws made by one fraction of the citizens only can never by the nature of things and men, do otherwise than reflect the thoughts and aspirations and desires of that fraction; they represent, not the whole country, but a third, a fourth part, a class, a zone of the country. The law must express the general aspiration, promote the good of all, respond to a beat of the nation's heart. The whole nation therefore should be, directly or indirectly, the legislator. By yielding this mission to a few men, you put the egoism of one class in the place of the Country, which is the union of *all* the classes.

A Country is not a mere territory; the particular territory is only its foundation. The Country is the idea which rises upon that foundation; it is the sentiment of love, the sense of fellowship which binds together all the sons of that territory. So long as a single one of your brothers is not represented by his own vote in the development of the national life—so long as a single one vegetates uneducated among the educated—so long as a single one able and willing to work languishes in poverty for want of work—you have not got a Country such as ought to be, the Country of all and for all. *Votes, education, work* are the three main pillars of the nation; do not rest until your hands have solidly erected them. . . .

And because you will be ready to die for Humanity, the life of your Country will be immortal.

The Ems Dispatch (1870)

OTTO VON BISMARCK

Nineteenth-century nationalism was dominated by Realpolitik, a dedication to the strength of the state above all else. Realpolitik was often identified with the career of Otto von Bismarck (1815–1898) who provoked, fought, and won three wars in six years to create a unified Germany dominated by his native Prussia. As Bismarck himself explains in this excerpt from his Memoirs, his manipulation of a dispatch (official telegram) from his own king (Wilhelm I of Prussia) brought on the last of those unifying wars. The telegram reported one step in the basically friendly negotiations between France and Prussia over the future of the Spanish monarchy, but as altered by Bismarck and published in the state-controlled press, it provoked the desired French attack. When the Franco-Prussian War (1870–71) was over, Prussia and its allies united to become Germany, drastically altering the balance of power in Europe. Bismarck's account is followed by the "before" and "after" versions of the Ems Dispatch.

I invited Generals Moltke and Roon to have dinner with me on July 13th, and spoke to them concerning my views and intentions. During the dinner conversation it was reported to me that a code telegram had been received from Ems, and it was then in process of decoding. I then read it to my guests, who were so crushed that they refused to eat or drink.

All considerations, conscious or unconscious, strengthened my opinion that war could be avoided only at the cost of the honor of Prussia and of the national confidence in her.

Under this conviction I made use of the royal authority communicated to me through Abeken to publish the contents of the telegram. In the presence of my guests I reduced the telegram by deleting words, but without adding or altering a single word. . . .

The difference in the effect of the shortened text of the Ems telegram as compared with that of the original was not the result of stronger words, but of the form, which made the announcement appear decisive.

After I had read the condensed version to my two guests, Moltke said:

"Now it has a quite different ring. In its original form it sounded like a parley. Now it is like a flourish in answer to a challenge!"

I went on to explain:

"If, in execution of His Majesty's order, I immediately communicate this text, which contains no changes in or additions to the telegram, not only to the newspapers, but also by wire to all our embassies, it will be known in Paris before midnight. Not only on account of its contents, but also because of the manner of its distribution, it will have the effect of a red flag on the Gallic bull.

"We must fight if we do not want to act the part of the defeated without a battle. However, success depends essentially upon the impression which the beginning of the war makes upon us and others. It is most important that we should be the ones attacked. Gallic insolence and sensitivity will bring this about if we announce before all Europe, as far as we can without the speaking tube of the Reichstag, that we are courageously meeting the public threats of France."

This explanation drew from both generals a metamorphosis into a more joyous mood, whose liveliness surprised me. They had suddenly recovered their desire to eat and drink and began to speak in a more cheerful tone.

Roon said: "Our God of old still lives, and will not let us die in disgrace."

Moltke relinquished his passive equanimity so much that, glancing up joyously to the ceiling and abandoning his usual punctiliousness of speech, he pounded his chest with his hand and exclaimed:

"If I may but live to lead our armies in such a war, then right afterwards let the devil come and haul away the old carcass."

The Original Dispatch:

"M. Benedetti [the French Ambassador] intercepted me on the Promenade in order to demand of me most insistently that I should authorize him to telegraph immediately to Paris that I shall oblige myself for all future time never again to give my approval to the candidacy of the Hohenzollerns should it be renewed. I refused to agree to this, that last time somewhat severely, informing him that one dare not and cannot assume such obligations forever. Naturally, I informed him that I had received no news as yet, and since he had been informed earlier than I by way of Paris and Madrid, he could easily understand why my government was once again out of the matter."

"*[Appended memo from Wilhelm's Secretary:]* Since then His Majesty has received a dispatch from the Prince [the German candidate for the Spanish throne]. As His Majesty has informed Count Benedetti that he was expecting news from the Prince, His Majesty himself, in view of the above-mentioned demand and inconsonance with the advice of Count Eulenberg and myself, decided not receive the French Ambassador again but to inform him through an adjutant that His Majesty had now received from the Prince confirmation of the news which Benedetti had already received from Paris, and that he had nothing further to say to the Ambassador. His Majesty leaves it to the judgment of Your Excellency whether or not to communicate at once the new demand by Benedetti and its rejection to our ambassadors and to the press."

The Dispatch as Edited by Bismarck:

After the reports of the renunciation by the Hereditary Prince of Hohenzollern had been officially transmitted by the Royal Government of Spain to the Imperial Government of France, the French Ambassador presented to His Majesty the King at Ems the demand to authorize him to telegraph to Paris that His Majesty the King would obligate himself for all future time never again to give his approval to the candidacy of the Hohenzollerns should it be renewed.

His Majesty the King thereupon refused to receive the French Ambassador again and informed him through an adjutant that His Majesty had nothing further to say to the Ambassador.

The Welfare State (1884)

OTTO VON BISMARCK

Bismarck's diplomatic achievements as Chancellor of Germany were easier to achieve than the internal unity of the newly created German Reich (state/empire). Bismarck was eventually forced to abandon a campaign against the Catholic Church that dominated the southern German states. He was also faced with the threat of a growing Marxist-Socialist movement. To ensure worker support for his government, Bismarck created the first "welfare state," providing workers with sickness, accident, and old age insurance. This undermined the appeal of the Socialist Party while enlisting the masses in support of Bismarck's policies. In this speech to the Reichstag (legislature), Bismarck justified his reforms as Christian rather than socialist. Was this another example of Realpolitik?

We have bestirred ourselves to improve the laborers' position in three directions. One, at a time when opportunity for work is slight and wages have become low, we have taken the necessary steps to protect work in our native land against competition; in other words, we have introduced protective tariffs to protect domestic labor. As a result of these measures, a real improvement of wages and a diminution of unemployment has taken place. Since then, work has reappeared more and more, and you trouble yourself in vain in seeking other grounds for that. On the contrary, I believe this event must have a considerable effect in the quietening down of socialist efforts. . . .

A second plan, which is in the government's mind, is the improvement of tax conditions, in that a fit division of them is sought, by which particularly oppressive [sales taxes] on account of small amounts are, if not eliminated, then, at least, decreased, which perhaps will lead to a further decrease. [Sales taxes] have earlier destroyed and broken down many small individuals in the working class and the few *groschen* [pennies] which they brought in taxes at the stipulated time also often were the reason why a family, which did not stand right on the lowest rung of affluence, was thrown back into want. . . .

The third branch of reforms, which we strive for, lies in direct provision for the workers. The question of labor time and wage increases is extraordinarily difficult to solve through state intervention, through legislation at all; for in any settlement that one makes, one runs the danger of interfering very considerably and unnecessarily in the personal freedom of getting value for one's services. . . . Then the worker suffers from that as well as the entrepreneur. That therefore is the governing borderline, and every legislative intervention must stop before that. . . . The workers' real sore point is the insecurity of his existence. He is not always sure he will always have work. He is not sure he will always be healthy, and he foresees some day he will be old and incapable of work. But also if he falls into poverty as a result of long illness, he is completely helpless with his own powers, and society hitherto does not recognize a real obligation to him beyond ordinary poor relief, even when he has worked ever so faithfully and diligently before. But ordinary poor relief leaves much to be desired, especially in the great cities where it is extraordinarily much worse than in the country. . . . We read in Berlin newspapers of suicide because of difficulty in making both ends meet, of people who died from direct hunger and have hanged themselves because they have nothing to eat, of people who announce in the paper they were tossed out homeless and have no income. . . .

For the worker it is always a fact that falling into poverty and onto poor relief in a great city is synonymous with misery, and this insecurity makes him hostile and mistrustful of society. That is humanly not unnatural, and as long as the state does not meet him halfway, just as long will this trust in the state's honesty be taken from him by accusations against the government, which he will find where he wills; always running back again to the socialist quacks . . . and, without great reflection, letting himself be promised things, which will not be fulfilled. On this account, I believe that accident insurance, with which we show the way, especially as soon as it covers agriculture completely, the construction industry above all, and all trades, will still work amelioratingly on the anxieties and ill-feeling of the working class. . . .

We derive our right to let the exceptional law continue from duty and from the fulfillment of the duty of Christian legislation. On the Progressive side, you call it "socialist legislation"; I prefer the term "Christian." At the time of the Apostles, socialism went very much further still. If perhaps you will read the Bible once, you will find out various things about it in the Acts of the Apostles. I don't go as far in our own times. But I get the courage for repressive measures only from my good intention of working to the end that, so far as a Christian-minded state society may do it, the real grievances, the real hardships of fate, about which the workers have to complain, will be alleviated and will be redressed.

Incidents in the Life of a Slave Girl (1861)

HARRIET ANN JACOBS

Harriet Ann Jacobs (1813–1897) was born to a family of mulatto slaves in North Carolina. After the death of her first owners she was left by will to the family of a physician who subjected her to the sexual abuse recounted in this excerpt from her autobiography. Eventually escaping to the north, she lived for many years as a nursemaid in New York City. Joining the abolitionist movement, she began publishing her memoirs as a series of articles in the New York Tribune, but public complaints about the graphic nature of the story convinced the newspaper to stop publishing the story before it was finished. It first appeared as a book in 1861 as part of the abolitionist movement's campaign to raise awareness in the northern states of the true nature of slavery. After working as a nurse during the Civil War, Jacobs spent the last years of life living in the nation's capital as the legally free woman she had, by Constitutional Amendment, now become.

During the first years of my service in Dr. Flint's family, I was accustomed to share some indulgences with the children of my mistress. Though this seemed to me no more than right, I was grateful for it, and tried to merit the kindness by the faithful discharge of my duties. But I now entered on my fifteenth year—a sad epoch in the life of a slave girl. My master began to whisper foul words in my ear. Young as I was, I could not remain ignorant of their import. I tried to treat them with indifference or contempt. The master's age, my extreme youth, and the fear that his conduct would be reported to my grandmother, made him bear this treatment for many months. He was a crafty man, and resorted to many means to accomplish his purposes. Sometimes he had stormy, terrific ways, that made his victims tremble; sometimes he assumed a gentleness that he thought must surely subdue. Of the two, I preferred his stormy moods, although they left me trembling. He tried his utmost to corrupt the pure principles my grandmother had instilled. He peopled my young mind with unclean images, such as only a vile monster could think of. I turned from him with disgust and hatred. But he was my master. I was compelled to live under the same roof with him—where I saw a man forty years my senior daily violating the most sacred commandments of nature. He told me I was his property; that I must be subject to his will in all things. My soul revolted against the mean tyranny. But where could I turn for protection? No matter whether the slave girl be as black as ebony or as fair as her mistress. In either case, there is no shadow of law to protect her from insult, from violence, or even from death; all these are inflicted by fiends who bear the shape of men. The mistress, who ought to protect the helpless victim, has no other feelings towards her but those of jealousy and rage. The degradation, the wrongs, the vices, that grow out of slavery, are more than I can describe. They are greater than you would willingly believe. Surely, if you credited one half the truths that are told you concerning the helpless millions suffering in this cruel bondage, you at the north would not help to tighten the yoke. You surely would refuse to do for the master, on your own soil, the mean and cruel work which trained bloodhounds and the lowest class of whites do for him at the south.

Every where the years bring to all enough of sin and sorrow; but in slavery the very dawn of life is darkened by these shadows. Even the little child, who is accustomed to wait on her mistress and her children, will learn, before she is twelve years old, why it is that her mistress hates such and such a one among the slaves. Perhaps the child's own mother is among those hated ones. She listens to violent outbreaks of jealous passion, and cannot help understanding what is the cause. She will become prematurely knowing in evil things. Soon she will learn to tremble when she hears her master's footfall. She will be compelled to realize that she is no longer a child. If God has bestowed beauty upon her, it will prove her greatest curse. That which commands admiration in the white woman only hastens the degradation of the female slave. I know that some are too much brutalized by slavery to feel the humiliation of their position; but many slaves feel it most acutely, and shrink from the memory of it. I cannot tell how much I suffered in the presence of these wrongs, nor how I am still pained by the retrospect. My master met me at every turn, reminding me that I belonged to him, and swearing by heaven and earth that he would compel me to submit to him. If I went out for a breath of fresh air, after a day of unwearied toil, his footsteps dogged me. If I knelt by my mother's grave, his dark shadow fell on me even there. The light heart which nature had given me became heavy with sad forebodings. The other slaves in my master's house noticed the change. Many of them pitied me; but none dared to ask the cause. They had no need to inquire. They knew too well the guilty practices under that roof, and they were aware that to speak of them was an offence that never went unpunished.

I longed for some one to confide in. I would have given the world to have laid my head on my grandmother's faithful bosom, and told her all my troubles. But Dr. Flint swore he would kill me, if I was not as silent as the grave. Then, although my grandmother was all in all to me, I feared her as well as loved her. I had been accustomed to look up to her with a respect bordering upon awe. I was very young, and felt shamefaced about telling her such impure things, especially as I knew her to be very strict on such subjects. Moreover, she was a woman of a high spirit. She was usually very quiet in her demeanor; but if her indignation was once roused, it was not very easily quelled. I had been told that she once chased a white gentleman with a loaded pistol, because he insulted one of her daughters. I dreaded the consequences of a violent outbreak; and both pride and fear kept me silent. But though I did not confide in my grandmother, and even evaded her vigilant watchfulness and inquiry, her presence in the neighborhood was some protection to me. Though she had been a slave, Dr. Flint was afraid of her. He dreaded her scorching rebukes. Moreover, she was known and patronized by many people; and he did not wish to have his villainy made public. It was lucky for me that I did not live on a distant plantation, but in a town not so large that the inhabitants were ignorant of each other's affairs. Bad as are the laws and customs in a slaveholding community, the doctor, as a professional man, deemed it prudent to keep up some outward show of decency. . . .

The Dred Scott Decision (1857)

The place of individuals of African descent (whether slave or free), the largest minority in the new American nation, was hotly debated throughout the nineteenth century. In this 1857 Supreme Court decision, Chief Justice Roger Brooke Taney (1777-1864) excluded "Negroes" from any hope of citizenship. Scott, the slave of an Army surgeon, claimed freedom because he had accompanied his master into Illinois (a free state) and a territory where slavery was prohibited (Louisiana north of 36 degrees, 30 minutes). Complicated maneuvering guaranteed that Scott would be freed no matter the outcome of the case, but Taney's decision inflamed anti-slavery advocates and helped hasten the onset of the Civil War (1861–1865).

. . . The question is simply this: Can a Negro, whose ancestors were imported into this country, and sold as slaves, become a member of the political community formed and brought into existence by the Constitution of the United States, and as such become entitled to all the rights, and privileges, and immunities guarantied by that instrument to the citizen? One of which rights is the privilege of suing in a court of the United States in the cases specified in the Constitution.

We think . . . [the people of the Negro race] . . . are not included, and were not intended to be included, under the words "citizens" in the Constitution, and can therefore claim none of the rights and privileges which that instrument provides for and secures to citizens of the United States. On the contrary, they were at that time considered as a subordinate and inferior class of beings, who had been subjugated by the dominant race, and, whether emancipated or not, yet remained subject to their authority, and had no rights or privileges but such as those who held the power and the Government might choose to grant them. . . .

No one, we presume, supposes that any change in public opinion or feeling, in relation to this unfortunate race, in the civilized nations of Europe or in this country, should induce the court to give to the words of the Constitution a more liberal construction in their favor than they were intended to bear when the instrument was framed and adopted. Such an argument would be altogether inadmissible in any tribunal called on to interpret it. If any of its provisions are deemed unjust, there is a mode prescribed in the instrument itself by which it may be amended; but while it remains unaltered, it must be construed now as it was understood at the time of its adoption. It is not only the same in words, but the same in meaning, and delegates the same powers to the Government, and reserves and secures the same rights and privileges to the citizen; and as long as it continues to exist in its present form, it speaks not only in the same words, but with the same meaning and intent with which it spoke when it came from the hands of its framers, and was voted on and adopted by the people of the United States. Any other rule of construction would abrogate the judicial character of this court, and make it the mere reflex of the popular opinion of the day. . . .

The act of Congress, upon which the plaintiff relies, declares that slavery and involuntary servitude, except as a punishment for crime, shall be forever prohibited in all that part of the territory ceded by France, under the name of Louisiana, which lies north of thirty-six degrees thirty minutes north latitude, and not included within the limits of Missouri. And the . . . inquiry is whether Congress was authorized to pass this law under any of the powers granted to it by the Constitution; for if the authority is not given by that instrument, it is the duty of this court to declare it void and inoperative, and incapable of conferring freedom upon any one who is held as a slave under the laws of any one of the States. . . .

. . . An Act of Congress which deprives a citizen of the United States of his liberty or property, merely because he came himself or brought his property into a particular Territory of the United States, and who had committed no offense against the laws, could hardly be dignified with the name of due process of law. . . .

Upon these considerations, it is the opinion of the court that the act of Congress which prohibited a citizen from holding and owning property of this kind in the territory of the United States north of the line therein mentioned, is not warranted by the Constitution, and is therefore void; and that neither Dred Scott himself, nor any of his family, were made free by being carried into this territory; even if they had been carried there by the owner, with the intention of becoming a permanent resident. . . .

First Inaugural Address (1861)

ABRAHAM LINCOLN

The 1860 election of Abraham Lincoln (1809–1865), who opposed the expansion of slavery in the western territories, as President of the United States led eleven southern states to secede from the Union. They declared themselves an independent republic, the Confederate States of America. In his First Inaugural Address (1861), Lincoln rejected their action, putting forward legal, geographic, historical, and emotional reasons for the indivisibility of the United States, and making the case that, despite their differences, Americans were truly one nation.

A disruption of the Federal Union, heretofore only menaced, is now formidably attempted.

I hold that, in contemplation of universal law and of the Constitution, the Union of these States is perpetual. Perpetuity is implied, if not expressed, in the fundamental law of all national governments. It is safe to assert that no government proper ever had a provision in its organic law for its own termination. Continue to execute all the express provisions of our national Constitution, and the Union will endure forever—it being impossible to destroy it except by some action not provided for in the instrument itself.

Again, if the United States be not a government proper, but an association of States in the nature of contract merely, can it as a contract be peaceably unmade by less than all the parties who made it? One party to a contract may violate it—break it, so to speak; but does it not require all to lawfully rescind it?

Descending from these general principles, we find the proposition that in legal contemplation the Union is perpetual confirmed by the history of the Union itself. The Union is much older than the Constitution. It was formed, in fact, by the Articles of Association in 1774. It was matured and continued by the Declaration of Independence in 1776. It was further matured, and the faith of all the then thirteen States expressly plighted and engaged that it should be perpetual, by the Articles of Confederation in 1778. And, finally, in 1787 one of the declared objects for ordaining and establishing the Constitution was "to form a more perfect Union."

But if the destruction of the Union by one or by a part only of the States be lawfully possible, the Union is less perfect than before the Constitution, having lost the vital element of perpetuity.

It follows from these views that no State upon its own mere motion can lawfully get out of the Union; that resolves and ordinances to that effect are legally void; and that acts of violence, within any State or States, against the authority of the United States, are insurrectionary or revolutionary, according to circumstances.

I therefore consider that, in view of the Constitution and the laws, the Union is unbroken; and to the extent of my ability I shall take care, as the Constitution itself expressly enjoins upon me, that the laws of the Union be faithfully executed in all the States. Doing this I deem to be only a simple duty on my part; and I shall perform it so far as practicable, unless my rightful masters, the American people, shall withhold the requisite means, or in some authoritative manner direct the contrary. I trust this will not be regarded as a menace, but only as the declared purpose of the Union that it will constitutionally defend and maintain itself.

Before entering upon so grave a matter as the destruction of our national fabric, with all its benefits, its memories, and its hopes, would it not be wise to ascertain precisely why we do it? Will you hazard so desperate a step while there is any possibility that any portion of the ills you fly from have no real existence? Will you, while the certain ills you fly to are greater than all the real ones you fly from—will you risk the commission of so fearful a mistake?

All profess to be content in the Union if all constitutional rights can be maintained. Is it true, then, that any right, plainly written in the Constitution, has been denied? I think not. Happily the human mind is so constituted that no party can reach to the audacity of doing this. Think, if you can, of a single instance in which a plainly written provision of the Constitution has ever been denied. If by the mere force of numbers a majority should deprive a minority of any clearly written constitutional right, it might, in a moral point of view, justify revolution—certainly would if such a right were a vital one. But such is not our case. All the vital rights of minorities and of individuals are so plainly assured to them by affirmations and negations, guaranties and prohibitions, in the Constitution, that controversies never arise concerning them. But no organic law can ever be framed with a provision specifically applicable to every question which may occur in practical administration. No foresight can anticipate, nor any document of reasonable length contain, express provisions for all possible questions. Shall fugitives from labor be surrendered by national or by State authority? The Constitution does not expressly say. *May* Congress prohibit slavery in the Territories? The Constitution does not expressly say. *Must* Congress protect slavery in the Territories? The Constitution does not expressly say.

From questions of this class spring all our constitutional controversies, and we divide upon them into majorities and minorities. If the minority will not acquiesce, the majority must, or the Government must cease. There is no other alternative; for continuing the Government is acquiescence on one side or the other.

If a minority in such case will secede rather than acquiesce, they make a precedent which in turn will divide and ruin them; for a minority of their own will secede from them whenever a majority refuses to be controlled by such minority. For instance, why may not any portion of a new confederacy a year or two hence arbitrarily secede again, precisely as portions of the present Union now claim to secede from it? All who cherish disunion sentiments are now being educated to the exact temper of doing this.

One section of our country believes slavery is right, and ought to be extended, while the other believes it is wrong, and ought not to be extended. This is the only substantial dispute. The fugitive slave clause of the Constitution and the law for the suppression of the foreign slave trade are each as well enforced, perhaps, as any law can ever be in a community where the moral sense of the people imperfectly supports the law itself. The great body of the people abide by the dry legal obligation in both cases, and a few break over in each. This, I think, cannot be perfectly cured; and it would be worse in both cases after the separation of the sections than before. The foreign slave trade, now imperfectly suppressed, would be ultimately revived, without restriction, in one section, while fugitive slaves, now only partially surrendered, would not be surrendered at all by the other.

Physically speaking, we cannot separate. We cannot remove our respective sections from each other, nor build an impassable wall between them. A husband and wife may be divorced and go out of the presence and beyond the reach of each other; but the different parts of our country cannot do this. They cannot but remain face to face, and intercourse, either amicable or hostile, must continue between them. Is it possible, then, to make that intercourse more advantageous or more satisfactory after separation than before? Can aliens make treaties easier than friends can make laws? Can treaties be more faithfully enforced between aliens than laws can among friends? Suppose you go to war, you cannot fight always; and when, after much loss on both sides, and no gain on either, you cease fighting, the identical old questions as to terms of intercourse are again upon you.

This country, with its institutions, belongs to the people who inhabit it. Whenever they shall grow weary of the existing government, they can exercise their constitutional right of amending it, or their revolutionary right to dismember or overthrow it. I cannot be ignorant of the fact that many worthy and patriotic citizens are desirous of having the national Constitution amended. . . .

Why should there not be a patient confidence in the ultimate justice of the people? Is there any better or equal hope in the world? In our present differences is either party without faith of being in the right? If the Almighty Ruler of nations, with his eternal truth and justice, be on your side of the North, or on yours of the South, that truth and that justice will surely prevail by the judgment of this great tribunal of the American people.

By the frame of the government under which we live, this same people have wisely given their public servants but little power for mischief; and have, with equal wisdom, provided for the return of that little to their own hands at very short intervals. While the people retain their virtue and vigilance, no administration, by any extreme of wickedness or folly, can very seriously injure the government in the short space of four years.

My countrymen, one and all, think calmly and well upon this whole subject. Nothing valuable can be lost by taking time. If there be an object to hurry any of you in hot haste to a step which you would never take deliberately, that object will be frustrated by taking time; but no good object can be frustrated by it. Such of you as are now dissatisfied still have the old Constitution unimpaired, and, on the sensitive point, the laws of your own framing under it; while the new administration will have no immediate power, if it would, to change either. If it were admitted that you who are dissatisfied hold the right side in the dispute, there still is no single good reason for precipitate action. Intelligence, patriotism, Christianity, and a firm reliance on Him who has never yet forsaken this favored land, are still competent to adjust in the best way all our present difficulty.

In your hands, my dissatisfied fellow-countrymen, and not in mine, is the momentous issue of civil war. The government will not assail you. You can have no conflict without being yourselves the aggressors. You have no oath registered in heaven to destroy the government, while I shall have the most solemn one to "preserve, protect, and defend" it.

I am loath to close. We are not enemies, but friends. We must not be enemies. Though passion may have strained, it must not break, our bonds of affection. The mystic chords of memory, stretching from every battlefield and patriot grave to every living heart and hearthstone all over this broad land, will yet swell the chorus of the Union when again touched, as surely they will be, by the better angels of our nature.

Abraham Lincoln's Reply to Horace Greeley (August 22, 1862)

ABRAHAM LINCOLN

Lincoln was reluctant to turn the Civil War into a divisive referendum on slavery. He argued the war was being fought to preserve the Union despite pressure from abolitionists pressing for an "Emancipation Proclamation" and from advocates of a negotiated peace recognizing the Confederacy. In this response to criticism from newspaper publisher Horace Greeley (1811–1872), Lincoln lays special emphasis on the oath of office every president takes to defend the Constitution.

Hon. Horace Greeley:

. . . As to the policy I "seem to be pursuing," as you say, I have not meant to leave any one in doubt.

I would save the Union. I would save it the shortest way under the Constitution. The sooner the National authority can be restored, the nearer the Union will be "the Union as it was." If there be those who would not save the Union unless they could at the same time *save* Slavery, I do not agree with them. If there be those who would not save the Union unless they could at the same time *destroy* Slavery, I do not agree with them. My paramount object in this struggle *is* to save the Union, and is *not* either to save or destroy Slavery. If I could save the Union without freeing *any* slave, I would do it; and if I could do it by freeing *all* the slaves, I would do it; and if I could do it by freeing some and leaving others alone, I would also do that. What I do about Slavery and the colored race, I do because I believe it helps to save this Union; and what I forbear, I forbear because I do *not* believe it would help to save the Union. I shall do *less* whenever I shall believe what I am doing hurts the cause, and I shall do *more* whenever I shall believe doing more will help the cause. I shall try to correct errors when shown to be errors; and I shall adopt new views so fast as they shall appear to be true views. I have here stated my purpose according to my view of *official* duty, and I intend no modification of my oft-expressed *personal* wish that all men, everywhere, could be free.

Yours,

A. Lincoln

The Equality of All Men (1865)

FREDERICK DOUGLASS

The North's victory in the Civil War did not, by itself, settle the question of the place of people of African descent in the United States. Born into slavery, Frederick Douglass (1817–1895) fled north and joined the abolitionist movement. During the Civil War, he campaigned for Negro enlistment, and his sons served in the Massachusetts 54th, a Negro regiment. As the war came to an end, Douglass fought for constitutional amendments guaranteeing Negro citizenship and a universal franchise. Basing his arguments on the special importance of citizenship in democratic governments, he called upon the nation to live up to its rhetoric of equality in this 1865 speech to the Massachusetts Anti-Slavery Society.

I have had but one idea for the last three years to present to the American people, and the phraseology in which I clothe it is the old abolition phraseology. I am for the "immediate, unconditional, and universal" enfranchisement of the black man, in every State in the Union. [Loud applause.] Without this, his liberty is a mockery; without this, you might as well almost retain the old name of slavery for his condition; for in fact, if he is not the slave of the individual master, he is the slave of society, and holds his liberty as a privilege, not as a right. He is at the mercy of the mob, and has no means of protecting himself.

It may be objected, however, that this pressing of the Negro's right to suffrage is premature. Let us have slavery abolished, it may be said, let us have labor organized, and then, in the natural course of events, the right of suffrage will be extended to the Negro. I do not agree with this. The constitution of the human mind is such, that if it once disregards the conviction forced upon it by a revelation of truth, it requires the exercise of a higher power to produce the same conviction afterwards. The American people are now in tears. The Shenandoah has run blood—the best blood of the North. All around Richmond, the blood of New England and of the North has been shed—of your sons, your brothers and your fathers. We all feel, in the existence of this Rebellion, that judgments terrible, wide-spread, far-reaching, overwhelming, are abroad in the land; and we feel, in view of these judgments, just now, a disposition to learn righteousness. This is the hour. Our streets are in mourning, tears are falling at every fireside, and under the chastisement of this Rebellion we have almost come up to the point of conceding this great, this all-important right of suffrage. I fear that if we fail to do it now, if abolitionists fail to press it now, we may not see, for centuries to come, the same disposition that exists at this moment. [Applause.] Hence, I say, now is the time to press this right.

It may be asked, "Why do you want it? Some men have got along very well without it. Women have not this right." Shall we justify one wrong by another? This is a sufficient answer. Shall we at this moment justify the deprivation of the Negro of the right to vote, because some one else is deprived of that privilege? I hold that women, as well as men, have the right to vote [applause], and my heart and my voice go with the movement to extend suffrage to woman; but that question rests upon another basis than on which our right rests. We may be asked, I say, why we want it. I will tell you why we want it. We want it because it is our *right*, first of all. No class of men can, without insulting their own nature, be content with any deprivation of their rights. We want it again, as a means for educating our race. Men are so constituted that they derive their conviction of their own possibilities largely from the estimate formed of them by others. If nothing is expected of a people, that people will find it difficult to contradict that expectation. By depriving us of suffrage, you affirm our incapacity to form an intelligent judgment respecting public men and public measures; you declare before the world that we are unfit to exercise the elective franchise, and by this means lead us to undervalue ourselves, to put a low estimate upon ourselves, and to feel that we have no possibilities like other men. Again, I want the elective franchise, for one, as a colored man, because ours is a peculiar government, based upon a peculiar idea, and that idea is universal suffrage. If I were in a monarchial government, or an autocratic or aristocratic government, where the few bore rule and the many were subject, there would be no special stigma resting upon me, because I did not exercise the elective franchise. It would do me no great violence. Mingling with the mass I should partake of the strength of the mass; I should be supported by the mass, and I should have the same incentives to endeavor with the mass of my fellow-men; it would be no particular burden, no particular deprivation; but here where universal suffrage is the rule, where that is the fundamental idea of the government, to rule us out is to make us an exception, to brand us with the stigma of inferiority, and to invite to our heads the missiles of those about us; therefore, I want the franchise for the black man.

I know that we are inferior to you in some things—virtually inferior. We walk about among you like dwarfs among giants. Our heads are scarcely seen above the great sea of humanity. The Germans are superior to us; the Irish are superior to us; the Yankees are superior to us [Laughter]; they can do what we cannot, that is, what we have not hitherto been allowed to do. But while I make this admission, I utterly deny, that we are originally, or naturally, or practically, or in any way, or in any important sense, inferior to anybody of this globe. [Loud applause.] This charge of inferiority is an old dodge. It has been made available for oppression on many occasions. It is only about six centuries since the blue-eyed and fair-haired Anglo-Saxons were considered inferior by the haughty Normans, who once trampled upon them. If you read the history of the Norman Conquest, you will find that this proud Anglo-Saxon was once looked upon as of coarser clan than his Norman master, and might be found in the highways and byways of old England laboring with a brass collar on his neck, and the name of his master marked upon it. You were down then! [Laughter and applause.] You are up now. I am glad you are up, and I want you to be glad to help us up also. [Applause.]

The story of our inferiority is an old dodge, as I have said; for wherever man oppress their fellows, wherever they enslave them, they will endeavor to find the needed apology for such enslavement and oppression in the character of the people oppressed and enslaved. . . . So, too, the Negro, when he is to be robbed of any right which is justly his, is an "inferior man." It is said that we are ignorant; I admit it. But if we know enough to be hung, we know enough to vote. If the Negro knows enough to pay taxes to support the government, he knows enough to vote; taxation and representation should go together. If he knows enough to shoulder a musket and fight for the flag, fight for the government, he knows enough to vote. If he knows as much when he is sober as an Irishman knows when drunk, he knows enough to vote, on good American principles. [Laughter and applause.]. . . .

. . . Let me not be misunderstood here. I am not asking for sympathy at the hands of abolitionists, sympathy at the hands of any. I think the American people are disposed often to be generous rather than just. I look over this country at the present time, and I see Educational Societies, Sanitary Commissions, Freedmen's Associations, and the like,—all very good: but in regard to the colored people there is always more that is benevolent, I perceive, than just, manifested towards us. What I ask for the Negro is not benevolence, not pity, not sympathy, but simply *justice*. [Applause.] The American people have always been anxious to know what they shall do with us. Everybody has asked the question, and they learned to ask it early of the abolitionists, "What shall we do with the Negro?" I have had but one answer from the beginning. Do nothing with us! Your doing with us has already played the mischief with us. Do nothing with us! If the apples will not remain on the tree of their own strength, if they are worm-eaten at the core, if they are early ripe and disposed to fall, let them fall! I am not for tying or fastening them on the tree in any way, except by nature's plan, and if they will not stay there, let them fall. And if the Negro cannot stand on his own legs, let him fall also. All I ask is, give him a chance to stand on his own legs!

The Reconstruction Amendments
(1865–1870)

The thirteenth, fourteenth, and fifteenth amendments to the United States Constitution, ratified between 1865 and 1870, abolished slavery, admitted African-Americans to membership in the American nation by basing citizenship on birth or naturalization, and guaranteed the franchise to all adult males. But enforcement of the amendments turned out to depend on the presence of federal troops in the Southern states. By the time the last of those troops were withdrawn in 1877, Southern states were already enacting laws designed to enforce racial segregation and prevent African-Americans from exercising their constitutional rights.

Amendment XIII.

Section 1. Neither slavery nor involuntary servitude, except as a punishment for crime whereof the party shall have been duly convicted, shall exist within the United States, or any place subject to their jurisdiction.

Section 2. Congress shall have power to enforce this article by appropriate legislation. (Ratified December 6, 1865.)

Amendment IV.

Section 1. All persons born or naturalized in the United States and subject to the jurisdiction thereof, are citizens of the United States and of the State wherein they reside. No State shall make or enforce any law which shall abridge the privileges or immunities of citizens of the United States; nor shall any State deprive any person of life, liberty, or property, without due process of law; nor deny to any person within its jurisdiction the equal protection of the laws.

Section 2. Representatives shall be apportioned among the several States according to their respective numbers, counting the whole number of persons in each State, excluding Indians not taxed. But when the right to vote at any election for the choice of electors for President and Vice President of the United States, Representatives in Congress, the Executive and Judicial officers of a State, or the members of the Legislature thereof, is denied to any of the male inhabitants of such State, being twenty-one years of age, and citizens of the United States, or in any way abridged, except for participation in rebellion, or other crime, the basis of representation therein shall be reduced in the proportion which the number of such male citizens shall bear to the whole number of male citizens twenty-one years of age in such State.

Section 3. No person shall be a Senator or Representative in Congress, or elector of President and Vice President, or hold any office, civil or military, under the United States, or any State, who, having previously taken an oath, as a member of Congress, or as an officer of the United States, or as a member of any State legislature, or as an executive or judicial officer of any State, to support the Constitution of the United States, shall have engaged in insurrection or rebellion against the same, or given aid or comfort to the enemies thereof. But Congress may by a vote of two-thirds of each House, remove such disability.

Section 4. The validity of the public debt of the United States, authorized by law, including debts incurred for payment of pensions and bounties for services in suppressing insurrection or rebellion, shall not be questioned. But neither the United States nor any State shall assume or pay any debt or obligation incurred in aid of insurrection or rebellion against the United States, or any claim for the loss or emancipation of any slave; but all such debts, obligations and claims shall be held illegal and void.

Section 5. The Congress shall have power to enforce, by appropriate legislation, the provisions of this article. (Ratified July 9, 1868.)

Amendment XV.

Section 1. The right of citizens of the United States to vote shall not be denied or abridged by the United States or by any State on account of race, color, or previous condition of servitude.

Section 2. The Congress shall have power to enforce this article by appropriate legislation. (Ratified February 3, 1870).

Plessy v. Ferguson (1896)

Attempts to use the courts to re-assert African-American rights were usually unsuccessful during the nineteenth century. In 1896 the United States Supreme Court decided that legal equality did not imply social equality. The Plessy v. Ferguson *decision established a "separate but equal" interpretation of the Constitution, thereby legalizing segregation and ensuring the "second-class" status of African-American citizens.*

The constitutionality of this act is attacked upon the ground that it conflicts both with the Thirteenth Amendment of the Constitution, abolishing slavery, and the Fourteenth Amendment, which prohibits certain restrictive legislation on the part of the States.

1. That it does not conflict with the Thirteenth Amendment, which abolished slavery and involuntary servitude, except as a punishment for crime, is too clear for argument. . . .
2. By the Fourteenth Amendment, all persons born or naturalized in the United States, and subject to the jurisdiction thereof, are made citizens of the United States and of the State wherein they reside; and the States are forbidden from making or enforcing any law which shall abridge the privileges or immunities of citizens of the United States, or shall deprive any person of life, liberty, or property without due process of law, or deny to any person within their jurisdiction the equal protection of the laws. . . .

The object of the amendment was undoubtedly to enforce the absolute equality of the two races before the law, but in the nature of things it could not have been intended to abolish distinctions based upon color, or to enforce social, as distinguished from political equality, or a commingling of the two races upon terms unsatisfactory to either. Laws permitting, and even requiring, their separation in places where they are liable to be brought into contact do not necessarily imply the inferiority of either race to the other, and have been generally, if not universally, recognized as within the competency of the State legislatures in the exercise of their police power. The most common instance of this is connected with the establishment of separate schools for white and colored children, which has been held to be a valid exercise of

108

the legislative power even by courts of States where the political rights of the colored race have been longest and most earnestly enforced. . . .

The distinction between laws interfering with the political equality of the Negro and those requiring the separation of the two races in schools, theaters, and railway carriages has been frequently drawn by this court. . . .

We consider the underlying fallacy of the plaintiff's argument to consist in the assumption that the enforced separation of the two races stamps the colored race with a badge of inferiority. If this be so, it is not by reason of anything found in the act, but solely because the colored race chooses to put that construction upon it. The argument necessarily assumes that if, as has been more than once the case, and is not unlikely to be so again, the colored race should become the dominant power in the state legislature, and should enact a law in precisely similar terms, it would thereby relegate the white race to an inferior position. We imagine that the white race, at least, would not acquiesce in this assumption. The argument also assumes, that social prejudices may be overcome by legislation, and that equal rights cannot be secured to the Negro except by an enforced commingling of the two races. We cannot accept this proposition. If the two races are to meet upon terms of social equality, it must be the result of natural affinities, a mutual appreciation of each other's merits and a voluntary consent of individuals. . . . Legislation is powerless to eradicate racial instincts or to abolish distinctions based upon physical differences, and the attempt to do so can only result in accentuating the differences of the present situation. If the civil and political rights of both races be equal one cannot be inferior to the other civilly or politically. If one race be inferior to the other socially, the Constitution of the United States cannot put them upon the same plane. . .

The Edict of Closure (1635)

By 1603 Tokugawa Ieyasu (1542–1616) had crushed all opposition to his rule and assumed the post of Shogun (military dictator) in Japan. His heirs kept the Emperor powerless, persecuted Japanese Christians, and kept their feudal state as free of Western contamination as possible. The Edict of Closure (1635) shows the lengths they took to keep their culture "pure." The word "Namban" used by the Japanese for Europeans translates roughly to "barbarian."

1. Japanese ships shall by no means be sent abroad.
2. No Japanese shall be sent abroad. Anyone violating this prohibition shall suffer the penalty of death, and the shipowner and crew shall be held up together with the ship.
3. All Japanese residing abroad shall be put to death when they return home.
4. All Christians shall be examined by official examiners.
5. Informers against Christians shall be rewarded.
6. The arrival of foreign ships must be reported to Edo, and watch kept over them.
7. The Namban people (Spaniards or Portuguese) and any other people with evil titles propagating Christianity shall be incarcerated in the Omura prison as before.
8. Even ships shall not be left untouched in the matter of exterminating Christians.
9. Everything shall be done in order to see that no Christian is survived by descendants, and anyone disregarding this injunction shall be put to death, while proper punishment shall be meted out to the other members of his family according to their deeds.
10. Children born of the Namban people (Spaniards or Portuguese) in Nagasaki and people adopting these Namban children into their family shall be put to death; capital punishment shall also be meted out to those Namban descendants if they return to Japan, and their relatives in Japan, who may communicate with them, shall receive suitable punishment. . . .

A Dutch Anatomy Lesson in Japan (1771)

SUGITA GEMPAKU

*The wall thrown up around Japan by the Tokugawa was not impene-
trable. The ban on importing foreign books was relaxed in 1720, allowing limited contact between Japanese and western cultures. The "Dutch
Anatomy Lesson" described by the traditionally trained surgeon Sugita
Gempaku (1733–1817) conveys both the impact of Western science and
the willingness of the Japanese elite to make use of some "Namban"
expertise.*

. . .At the night of the third day of the third month [in 1771], I received a
letter from a man by the name of Tokuno, who was in the service of the Town
Commissioner. Tokuno stated in his letter that "A post-mortem examination
of the body of a condemned criminal by a resident physician will be held
tomorrow at Senjukotsugahara. You are welcome to witness it if you so
desire."

The next day, when we arrived at the location . . . [my colleague] Ryotaku
reached under his kimono to produce a Dutch book and showed it to us.
"This is a Dutch book of anatomy called *Tabulae Anatomicae*. I bought this
a few years ago when I went to Nagasaki, and kept it." . . . Ryotaku continued by saying: "When I went to Nagasaki, I learned and heard," and opened
this book. "These are called *long* in Dutch, they are lungs," he taught us.
"This is *hart*, or the heart. When it says *maag* it is the stomach, and when it
says *milt* it is the spleen." However, they did not look like the heart given in
the Chinese medical books, and none of us were sure until we could actually
see the dissection.

Thereafter we went together to the place which was especially set for us
to observe the dissection. . . . We compared the body as dissected against the
[Dutch] charts both Ryotaku and I had, and could not find a single variance
from the charts. The *Chinese Book of Medicine* says that the lungs are like the
eight petals of the lotus flower, with three petals hanging in front, three in
back, and two petals forming like two ears and that the liver has three petals

to the left and four petals to the right. There were no such divisions, and the positions and shapes of intestines and gastric organs were all different from those taught by the old theories. The official physicians . . . had witnessed dissection seven or eight times. Whenever they witnessed the dissection, they found that the old theories contradicted reality. Each time they were perplexed and could not resolve their doubts. Every time they wrote down what they thought was strange. They wrote in their books, "The more we think of it, there must be fundamental differences in the bodies of Chinese and of the eastern barbarians." I could see why they wrote this way.

That day, after the dissection was over, we decided that we also should examine the shape of the skeletons left exposed on the execution ground. We collected the bones, and examined a number of them. Again, we were struck by the fact that they all differed from the old theories while conforming to the Dutch charts.

The three of us, Ryotaku, Junan, and I went home together. On the way home we spoke to each other and felt the same way. "How marvelous was our actual experience today. It is a shame that we were ignorant of these things until now. As physicians who serve their masters through medicine, we performed our duties in complete ignorance of the true form of the human body. How disgraceful it is. Somehow, through this experience, let us investigate further the truth about the human body. If we practice medicine with this knowledge behind us, we can make contributions for people under heaven and on this earth." Ryotaku spoke to us. "Indeed, I agree with you wholeheartedly." Then I spoke to my companion. "Somehow if we can translate anew this book called *Tabulae Anatomicae*, we can get a clear notion of the human body inside out. It will have great benefit in the treatment of our patients. . . ."

36

Japan Industrializes

SHIBUZAWA EIICHI

*The isolation imposed by the Tokugawa dynasty was finally broken
with the signing of the* Treaty of Kanagawa *(1854), which opened
trade between Japan and the United States. In the Treaty's aftermath
came a revolution that toppled the Shogunate and ushered in a period
of industrial modernization designed to prevent Japan from following
China into semi-colonial status. The memoirs of Shibuzawa Eiichi
(1840–1931), an industrialist who controlled over a hundred corporations, describe Japan's attempt during the Meiji Era (1868–1912) to
adapt Western methods while preserving the core elements of Japanese
culture.*

The business world around 1873, the year when I resigned my post from
the Ministry of Finance, was one filled with inertia. That condition is hard
to imagine from the standards we hold for the business world today. . . .
There was a tradition of respecting officials and despising common people.
All talented men looked to government service as the ultimate goal in their
lives, and ordinary students followed their examples. There was practically no
one who was interested in business. When people met, they discussed only
matters relating to the affairs of the nation and of the world. There was no
such thing as practical business education.

It was said that the Meiji Restoration was to bring about equality among
the four classes of people. However, in practice, those who engaged in commerce and industry were regarded as plain townspeople as before, and were
despised and had to remain subservient to government officials. I knew that
conditions such as this should not be allowed to persist. A rigid class structure should not be tolerated. We should be able to treat each other with
respect, and make no differentiation between government officials and
townspeople. This was essential to our national welfare, as we looked forward
to strengthening the country which required wealth to back it up. We needed
commerce and industry to attain the goal of becoming a rich nation. Unworthy as I was, I thought of engaging in commerce and industry to help promote the prosperity of our nation. I might not have talent to become a good

politician, but I was confident that I could make a contribution in the fields of commerce and industry. . . .

As to the question of development of commerce and industry, I felt that to engage in an individually managed shop would be going against the tide of the times, and it was necessary for small business firms to be incorporated into larger ones. In other words, it was necessary to incorporate them, and I decided to devote my energy in this endeavor. As to the laws governing incorporation, I thought about them while studying in France. After my return from France and before my entering into government service, I orga-nized a chamber of commerce in Shizuoka to serve as a model for incorpo-ration in this country. Since that time, I have consistently advocated the advantages of incorporation. . . .

I also felt that it was necessary to raise the social [status of businessmen] and by way of setting an example, I began studying and practicing the teach-ings of the *Analects* of Confucius. It contains teachings first given more than 2,400 years ago. Yet it supplies the ultimate in practical ethics for all of us to follow in our daily life, and has many golden rules for businessmen to follow. For example there is a saying: "Wealth and respect are what men desire, but unless there be the right way, they are not to be obtained; poverty and lowly position are what men despise, but unless there be the right way, once they are obtained they cannot be abandoned." It shows very clearly how a busi-nessman must act in this world. Thus when I entered the business world, I engaged in commerce and industry in the way consistent with the teachings of the *Analects,* and practiced the doctrine of unity of knowledge and action.

37

Mitsubishi Letter to Employees (1876)

IWASAKI YATARŌ

*Japan's decision to modernize during the Meiji Era (1868–1912) did
not automatically do away with the concessions granted western companies in their "unequal" trade treaties. British and American shipping
lines controlled the trade between the islands that made up Japan as
well as between Japan and the rest of the world. Iwasaki Yatarō (1834-
1885), the son of an impoverished samurai family, set out to change
that by creating his own shipping line. When its success was threatened
by foreign competition, he cut prices by 50% and wages by 1/3 to make
his company (the core of today's Mitsubishi) more competitive. In this
letter, he appeals to his workers' patriotism to win their support for his
measures. A key element of the samurai's code of bushido was putting the
good of the whole before that of the individual. Two years later, Mitsubishi controlled almost three-quarters of all the shipping in Japan.*

Many people have expressed differing opinions concerning the principles
to be followed and advantages to be obtained in engaging foreigners or Japanese in the task of coastal trade. Granted, we may permit a dissenting voice,
which suggests that in principle both foreigners and Japanese must be permitted to engage in coastal trade, but once we look into the question of advantages, we know that coastal trade is too important a matter to be given over to
the control of foreigners. If we allow the right of coastal navigation to fall into
the hands of foreigners in peacetime, it means a loss of business and employment opportunities for our own people, and in wartime it means yielding the
vital right of gathering information to foreigners. In fact, this is not too different from abandoning the rights of our country as an independent nation.

Looking back into the past, at the time when we abandoned the policy of
seclusion and entered into an era of friendly intercourse and commerce with
foreign nations, we should have been prepared for this very task. However,
due to the fact that our people lack knowledge and wealth, we have yet to
assemble a fleet sufficient to engage in coastal navigation. Furthermore, we
have neither the necessary skills for navigation nor a plan for developing a
maritime transportation industry. This condition has attracted foreign ship-

ping companies to occupy our maritime transport lines. Yet our people show not a sense of surprise at it. Some people say that our treaties with foreign powers contain an express provision allowing foreign ships to proceed from Harbor A to Harbor B, and others claim that such a provision must not be regarded as granting foreign ships the right to coastal navigation inasmuch as it is intended not to impose unduly heavy taxes, on them. I am not qualified to discuss its legal merit, but the issue remains an important one.

I now propose to do my utmost, and along with my 35 million compatriots, perform my duty as a citizen of this country. That is to recover the right of coastal trade in our hands and not to delegate that task to foreigners. Unless we propose to do so, it is useless for our government to revise the unequal treaties or to change our entrenched customs. We need people who can respond, otherwise all the endeavors of the government will come to naught. This is the reason why the government protects our company, and I know that our responsibilities are even greater than the full weight of Mt. Fuji thrust upon our shoulders. There have been many who wish to hinder our progress in fulfilling our obligations. However, we have been able to eliminate one of our worst enemies, the Pacific Mail Company of the United States, from contention by applying appropriate means available to us. Now another rival has emerged. It is the Peninsula & Oriental Team Navigation Company of Great Britain, which is setting up a new line between Yokohama and Shanghai and is attempting to claim its rights over the ports of Nagasaki, Kobe, and Yokohama. The P & O Company is backed by its massive capital, its large fleet of ships, and by its experiences of operating in Oriental countries. In competing against this giant, what methods can we employ?

I have thought about this problem very carefully and have come to one conclusion. There is no other alternative but to eliminate unnecessary positions and unnecessary expenditures. This is a time-worn solution and no new wisdom is involved. Even though it is a familiar saying, it is much easier said than done, and this indeed has been the root cause of difficulties in the past and present times. Therefore, starting immediately, I propose that we engage in this task. By eliminating unnecessary personnel from the payroll, eliminating unnecessary expenditures, and engaging in hard and arduous tasks, we shall be able to solidify the foundation of our company. If there is a will, there is a way. Through our own efforts, we shall be able to repay the government for its protection and answer our nation for its confidence shown in us. Let us work together in discharging our obligations and let us not be ashamed of ourselves. Whether we succeed or fail, whether we can gain profit or sustain loss, we cannot anticipate at this time. Hopefully, all of you will join me in a singleness of heart to attain this cherished goal, forbearing and undaunted by setbacks, to restore to our own hands the right to our own coastal trade. If we succeed it will not only be an accomplishment for our company but also a glorious event for our Japanese Empire, which shall let its light shine to all four corners of the earth. We may succeed and we may fail, and it depends on your effort or lack of it. Do your utmost in this endeavor!

38

Article 27, The Mexican Constitution (1917)

Mexico's independence from Spain ushered in a century of conflict and misrule. The Mexican government failed to harness the country's rich resources or achieve any equity between its ethnic factions. The failure of La Reforma during the nineteenth century only led to further conflicts. Yet another Civil War (1910–1917) produced yet another Constitution in 1917, which attempted to safeguard Mexico's land and resources from foreign exploitation. To that end, the Mexican government used the authority of Article 27 to expropriate all foreign oil properties in 1938.

Article 27. The ownership of lands and waters comprised within the limits of the national territory is vested originally in the Nation, which has had and has the right to transmit title thereof to private persons, thereby constituting private property.

Private property shall not be expropriated except for reasons of public utility and by means of indemnification.

The Nation shall have at all times the right to impose on private property such limitations as the public interest may demand as well as the right to regulate the development of natural resources, which are susceptible of appropriation, in order to conserve them and equitably to distribute the public wealth. For this purpose necessary measures shall be taken to divide large landed estates; to develop small landed holdings; to establish new centers of agricultural population, with such lands and waters as may be indispensable to them; to encourage agriculture, to prevent the destruction of natural resources, and to protect property from damage detrimental to society. The villages, hamlets situated on private property, and communities that lack lands and water or do not possess them in sufficient quantities for their needs shall have the right to be provided with them from the adjoining properties, always having due regard for small landed holdings. . . . Private property acquired for the said purposes shall be considered as taken for public utility.

In the Nation is vested direct ownership of all minerals or substances that in veins, layers, masses, or beds constitute deposits whose nature is different from the components of the land, such as minerals from which metals and metalloids used for industrial purposes are extracted; beds of precious stones, rock salt, and salt lakes formed directly by marine waters; products derived from the decomposition of rocks, when their exploitation requires underground work; phosphates that may be used for fertilizers; solid mineral fuels; petroleum and all hydrocarbons—solid, liquid, or gaseous. . . .

The ownership of the Nation is inalienable and may not be lost by prescription; concessions shall be granted by the Federal Government to private parties or civil or commercial corporations organized under the laws of Mexico, only on condition that the said resources be regularly developed, and on the further condition that the legal provisions be observed.

Legal capacity to acquire ownership of lands and waters of the Nation shall be governed by the following provisions:

1. Only Mexicans by birth or naturalization and Mexican companies have the right to acquire ownership in lands, waters, and their appurtenances, or to obtain concessions to develop mines, waters, or mineral fuels in the Republic of Mexico. The Nation may grant the same right to foreigners, provided they agree before the Ministry of Foreign Relations to be considered Mexican in respect to such property, and accordingly not to invoke the protection of their Governments in respect to the same, under penalty, in case of breach, of forfeiture to the Nation of property so acquired.

Topic V

The New Imperialism

The Economic History of India under British Rule (1901)

ROMESH C. DUTT

India was the "crown jewel" of the British Empire, a vast sub-continent of enormous wealth that England had torn from French control in 1757. While few in Britain questioned the contributions of India to British wealth and prestige, by the end of the nineteenth century a series of crop failures and famines led many Indians to question the contributions of Britain to Indian well-being. In 1901 Romesh C. Dutt (1848–1909), a successful Indian civil servant, published The Economic History of India Under Early British Rule *that lay the blame for India's poverty on Britain's doorstep.*

The poverty of the Indian population at the present day is unparalleled in any civilised country; the famines which have desolated India within the last quarter of the nineteenth century are unexampled in their extent and intensity in the history of ancient or modern times. By a moderate calculation, the famines of 1877 and 1878, of 1889 and 1892, of 1897 and 1900, have carried off fifteen millions of people. The population of a fair-sized European country has been swept away from India within twenty-five years. A population equal to half of that of England has perished in India within a period which men and women, still in middle age, can remember.

What are the causes of this intense poverty and these repeated famines in India? Superficial explanations have been offered one after another, and have been rejected on close examination. It was said that the population increased rapidly in India, and that such increase must necessarily lead to famines; it is found on inquiry that the population has never increased in India at the rate of England, and that during the last ten years it has altogether ceased to increase. It was said that the Indian cultivators were careless and improvident, and that those who did not know how to save when there was plenty, must perish when there was want; but it is known to men who have lived all their lives among these cultivators, that there is not a more abstemious, a more thrifty, a more frugal race of peasantry on earth. It was said that the

Indian moneylender was the bane of India, and by his fraud and extortion kept the tillers of the soil in a chronic state of indebtedness; but the inquiries of the latest Famine Commission have revealed that the cultivators of India are forced under the thraldom of money-lenders by the rigidity of the Government revenue demand. It was said that in a country where the people depended almost entirely on their crops, they must starve when the crops failed in years of drought; but the crops in India, as a whole, have never failed, there has never been a single year when the food supply of the country was insufficient for the people, and there must be something wrong, when failure in a single province brings on a famine, and the people are unable to buy their supplies from neighboring provinces rich in harvests. . . .

It is, unfortunately, a fact which no well-informed Indian official will ignore, that, in many ways, the sources of national wealth in India have been narrowed under British rule. India in the eighteenth century was a great manufacturing as well as a great agricultural country, and the products of the Indian loom supplied the markets of Asia and of Europe. It is, unfortunately, true that the East India Company and the British Parliament, following the selfish commercial policy of a hundred years ago, discouraged Indian manufacturers in the early years of British rule in order to encourage the rising manufactures of England. Their fixed policy, pursued during the last decades of the eighteenth century and the first decades of the nineteenth, was to make India subservient to the industries of Great Britain, and to make the Indian people grow raw produce only, in order to supply material for the looms and factories of Great Britain. This policy was pursued with unwavering resolution and with fatal success; orders were sent out, to force Indian artisans to work in the Company's factories; commercial residents were legally vested with extensive powers over villages and communities of Indian weavers; prohibitive tariffs excluded Indian silk and cotton goods from England; English goods were admitted into India free of duty or on payment of a nominal duty. . . .

Agriculture is now virtually the only remaining source of national wealth in India, and four-fifths of the Indian people depend on agriculture. But the Land Tax levied by the British Government is not only excessive, but, what is worse, it is fluctuating and uncertain in many provinces. . . .

In Madras and Bombay things are worse. There the Land Tax is paid generally by the cultivators of the soil, there being, in most parts of those provinces, no intervening landlords. The British Government declared its intention in 1864 of realizing as Land Tax about one-half of the economic rent. But what the British Government does take as Land Tax at the present day sometimes approximates to the whole of the economic rent, leaving the cultivators little beyond the wages of their labor and the profits of their agricultural stock. The Land Tax is revised once every thirty years; the cultivator does not know on what grounds it is enhanced; he has to submit to each renewed assessment, or to leave his ancestral fields and perish. This uncertainty of the Land Tax paralyzes agriculture, prevents saving, and keeps the tiller of the soil in a state of poverty and indebtedness. . . .

Taxation raised by a king, says the Indian poet, is like the moisture of the earth sucked up by the sun, to be returned to the earth as fertilizing rain; but the moisture raised from the Indian soil now descends as fertilizing rain largely on other lands, not on India. Every nation reasonably expects that the proceeds of taxes raised in the country should be mainly spent in the country. Under the worst governments that India had in former times, this was the case. The vast sums which Afghan and Mughal Emperors spent on their armies went to support great and princely houses, as well as hundreds of thousands of soldiers and their families. The gorgeous palaces and monuments they built, as well as the luxuries and displays in which they indulged, fed and encouraged the manufacturers and artisans of India. Nobles and Commanders of the army, Subadars, Dewans, and Kazis, and a host of inferior officers in every province and every district, followed the example of the Court; and mosques and temples, roads, canals and reservoirs, attested to their wide liberality, or even to their vanity. Under wise rulers, as under foolish kings, the proceeds of taxation flowed back to the people and fructified their trade and industries.

But a change came over India under the rule of the East India Company. They considered India as a vast estate or plantation, the profits of which were to be withdrawn from India and deposited in Europe. They reserved all the high appointments in India for their own nominees seeking a lucrative career in the East. They bought their merchandise out of the revenues of India, and sold it in Europe for their own profit. They vigorously exacted from India a high interest on their stock-in-trade. In one shape or another all that could be raised in India by an excessive taxation flowed to Europe, after paying for a starved administration.

The East India Company's trade was abolished in 1833, and the Company was abolished in 1858, but their policy remains. Their capital was paid off by loans which were made into an Indian Debt, on which interest is paid from Indian taxes. The empire was transferred from the Company to the Crown, but the people of India paid the purchase-money. . . . One-half of the net revenues of India, which are now forty-four millions sterling, flows annually out of India. Verily the moisture of India blesses and fertilizes other lands.

. . . Place any other country under the same condition, with crippled industries, with agriculture subject to a heavy and uncertain Land Tax, and with financial arrangements requiring one-half of its revenues to be annually remitted out of the country, and the most prosperous nation on earth will soon know the horrors of famine.

Emperor Ch'ien Lung to George III (1793)

Emperor Ch'ien Lung (r. 1735–1796) led a series of military cam-paigns against the Mongols and Turks that successfully enlarged China's empire in the north and west by some 600,000 square miles. He also subdued a Tibetan revolution and succeeded in winning tribute from Burma and Vietnam to the south. Approached by an embassy from George III (r. 1760–1820) of Great Britain in 1793 requesting wider British access to China, Ch'ien saw no reason to reverse the Imperial Decree of 1757 restricting all European traders to a small section of Canton. Thirty-nine years later, China, defeated by Britain in the First Opium War (1839–1842), found itself forced to grant many more concessions than those Ch'ien Lung rejected in this reply to George III.

You, O King, live beyond the confines of many seas, nevertheless, impelled by your humble desire to partake of the benefits of our civilization, you have dispatched a mission respectfully bearing your memorial. Your Envoy has crossed the seas and paid his respects at my Court on the anniversary of my birthday. To show your devotion, you have also sent offerings of your country's produce.

I have perused your memorial: the earnest terms in which it is couched reveal a respectful humility on your part, which is highly praiseworthy. In consideration of the fact that your Ambassador and his deputy have come a long way with your memorial and tribute, I have shown them high favor and have allowed them to be introduced into my presence. To manifest my indulgence, I have entertained them at a banquet and made them numerous gifts. I have also caused presents to be forwarded to the Naval Commander and six hundred of his officers and men, although they did not come to Peking, so that they too may share in my all-embracing kindness.

As to your entreaty to send one of your nationals to be accredited to my Celestial Court and to be in control of your country's trade with China, this request is contrary to all usage of my dynasty and cannot possibly be entertained. It is true that Europeans, in the service of the dynasty, have been permitted to live at Peking, but they are compelled to adopt Chinese dress, they are strictly confined to their own precincts and are never permitted to return home. You are presumably familiar with our dynastic regulations. . . .

Besides, supposing I sent an Ambassador to reside in your country, how could you possibly make for him the requisite arrangements? Europe consists of many other nations besides your own: if each and all demanded to be represented at our Court, how could we possibly consent? The thing is utterly impracticable. How can our dynasty alter its whole procedure and system of etiquette, established for more than a century, in order to meet your individual views? . . .

If you assert that your reverence for Our Celestial dynasty fills you with a desire to acquire our civilization, our ceremonies and code of laws differ so completely from your own that, even if your Envoy were able to acquire the rudiments of our civilization, you could not possibly transplant our manners and customs to your alien soil. Therefore, however adept the Envoy might become, nothing would be gained thereby.

Swaying the wide world, I have but one aim in view, namely, to maintain a perfect governance and to fulfill the duties of the State: strange and costly objects do not interest me. If I have commanded that the tribute offerings sent by you, O King, are to be accepted, this was solely in consideration for the spirit which prompted you to dispatch them from afar. Our dynasty's majestic virtue has penetrated unto every country under Heaven, and Kings of all nations have offered their costly tribute by land and sea. As your Ambassador can see for himself, we possess all things. I set no value on objects strange or ingenious, and have no use for your country's manufactures. This then is my answer to your request to appoint a representative at my Court, a request contrary to our dynastic usage, which would only result in inconvenience to yourself. I have expounded my wishes in detail and have commanded your tribute Envoys to leave in peace on their homeward journey. It behoves you, O King, to respect my sentiments and to display even greater devotion and loyalty in future, so that, by perpetual submission to our Throne, you may secure peace and prosperity for your country hereafter. . . .

Hitherto, all European nations, including your own country's barbarian merchants, have carried on their trade with our Celestial Empire at Canton. Such has been the procedure for many years, although our Celestial Empire possesses all things in prolific abundance and lacks no product within its own borders. There was therefore no need to import the manufactures of outside barbarians in exchange for our own produce. But as the tea, silk and porcelain which the Celestial Empire produces, are absolute necessities to European nations and to yourselves, we have permitted, as a signal mark of favor, that foreign *hongs* [trading companies] should be established at Canton, so that your wants might be supplied and your country thus participate in our beneficence. But your Ambassador has now put forward new requests which completely fail to recognize the Throne's principle to "treat strangers from afar with indulgence," and to exercise a pacifying control over barbarian tribes, the world over. . . .

Regarding your nation's worship of the Lord of Heaven, it is the same religion as that of other European nations. Ever since the beginning of history, sage Emperors and wise rulers have bestowed on China a moral system and inculcated a code, which from time immemorial has been religiously observed by the myriads of my subjects. There has been no hankering after heterodox doctrines. Even the European (missionary) officials in my capital are forbidden to hold intercourse with Chinese subjects; they are restricted within the limits of their appointed residences, and may not go about propagating their religion. The distinction between Chinese and barbarian is most strict, and your Ambassador's request that barbarians shall be given full liberty to disseminate their religion is utterly unreasonable. . . .

The Treaty of Tientsin (1858)

A Second Opium War (1856–1858) between China and Great Britain ended in a second Chinese defeat. Forced to sign the Treaty of Tientsin *(1858), the Chinese agreed to increase opportunities for the British to trade with China, protect Christian missions, and grant extraterritoriality to British nationals on Chinese soil. This last provision, eventually extended to all foreigners, exempted the British from prosecution by Chinese authorities. Instead, they were subject only to British authority.*

Article VIII. The Christian religion as professed by Protestants or Roman Catholics, inculcates the practice of virtue and teaches man to do as he would be done by. Persons teaching it, or professing it, therefore, shall alike be entitled to the protection of the Chinese authorities, nor shall any such, peaceably pursuing their calling, and not offending against the laws, be persecuted or interfered with.

Article IX. British subjects are hereby authorized to travel for their pleasure or for purposes of trade, to all parts of the Interior, under Passports, which will be issued by their Consuls and countersigned by the Local Authorities. . . .

Article XI. In addition to the Cities and Towns of Canton, Amoy, Foochow, Ningpo and Shanghai, opened by the Treaty of Nanking, it is agreed that British subjects may frequent the Cities and Ports of Newchwang, Tangehow, Taiwan, Chawchow, and Kiungchow. . . .

Article XV. All questions in regard to rights, whether of property or person, arising between British subjects, shall be subject to the jurisdiction of the British authorities.

Article XVI. Chinese subjects who may be guilty of any criminal act towards British subjects shall be arrested and punished by the Chinese authorities according to the Laws of China. British subjects who may commit any crime in China shall be tried and punished by the Consul or other Public Functionary authorized thereto according to the Laws of Great Britain. . . .

Letter to Sir George Grey (1858) from Moshweshwe I

Moshweshwe I (c. 1785–1878) was the founder-king of Lesotho (then called Basutoland), a small state caught up in the struggle between British, Boers, and African peoples for what is now the Republic of South Africa. Despite aggressive pressure from Boer settlers, Moshweshwe worked to maintain peace with these intruders even as his domain dwindled. After several run-ins with the Boer Orange Free State, Moshweshwe petitioned Sir George Grey (1812–1898), governor of the British-controlled Cape Colony, to personally draw a new boundary. Grey's efforts ended Boer-Sotho fighting for a decade, but when the Boer advance resumed, Moshweshwe formally accepted British "protection." Lesotho did not regain its independence for another century.

Your Excellency—it may scarcely appear necessary to lay before Your Excellency any lengthened details of what has taken place between the Orange Free State and myself. I know that you have followed with interest the transactions which have led to the commencement of hostilities, and you have heard with pain of the horrors occasioned by the war, at present suspended in the hopes that peace may be restored by Your Excellency's mediation.

Allow me, however, to bring to your remembrance the following circumstances: About twenty-five years ago my knowledge of the White men and their laws was very limited. I knew merely that mighty nations existed, and among them was the English. These, the blacks who were acquainted with them, praised for their justice. Unfortunately it was not with the English Government that my first intercourse with the whites commenced. People who had come from the Colony first presented themselves to us, they called themselves Boers. I thought all white men were honest. Some of these Boers asked permission to live upon our borders. I was led to believe they would live with me as my own people lived, that is, looking to me as to a father and a friend.

About sixteen years since, one of the Governors of the Colony, Sir George Napier, marked down my limits on a treaty he made with me. I was to be ruler within those limits. A short time after, another Governor came, it was Sir P. Maitland. The Boers then began to talk of their right to places I had then lent to them. Sir P. Maitland told me those people were subjects of the Queen, and should be kept under proper control; he did not tell me that he recognized any right they had to land within my country, but as it was difficult to take them away, it was proposed that all desiring to be under the British rule should live in that part near the meeting of the Orange and Caledon rivers.

Then came Sir Harry Smith, and he told me not to deprive any chief of their lands or their rights, he would see justice done to all, but in order to do so, he would make the Queen's Laws extend over every white man. He said the Whites and Blacks were to live together in peace. I could not understand what he would do. I thought it would be something very just, and that he was to keep the Boers in my land under proper control, and that I should hear no more of their claiming the places they lived on as their exclusive property. But instead of this, I now heard that the Boers consider all those farms as their own, and were buying and selling them one to the other, and driving out by one means or another my own people.

In vain I remonstrated. Sir Harry Smith had sent Warden to govern in the Sovereignty. He listened to the Boers, and he proposed that all the land in which those Boers' farms were should be taken from me. I was at that time in trouble, for Sikonyela and the Korannas were tormenting me and my people by stealing and killing; they said openly the Major gave them orders to do so, and I have proof he did so. One day he sent me a map and said, sign that, and I will tell those people (Mantatis and Korannas) to leave off fighting: if you do not sign the map, I cannot help you in any way. I thought the Major was doing very improperly and unjustly. I was told to appeal to the Queen to put an end to this injustice. I did not wish to grieve Her Majesty by causing a war with her people. I was told if I did not sign the map, it would be the beginning of a great war. I signed, but soon after I sent my cry to the Queen. I begged Her to investigate my case and remove "the line," as it was called, by which my land was ruined. I thought justice would soon be done, and Warden put to rights.

I tried my utmost to satisfy them and avert war. I punished thieves, and sent my son Nehemiah and others to watch the part of the country near the Boers, and thus check stealing. In this he was successful, thieving did cease. We were at peace for a time. In the commencement of the present year my people living near farmers received orders to remove from their places. This again caused the fire to burn, still we tried to keep all quiet, but the Boers went further and further day by day in troubling the Basutos [*i.e.*, the Sotho] and threatening war. The President (Boshof) spoke of Warden's line, this was as though he had really fired upon us with his guns. Still I tried to avert war.

It was not possible, it was commenced by the Boers in massacring my people of Beersheba, and ruining that station, against the people of which there was not a shadow of a complaint ever brought forward. Poor people, they thought their honesty and love for Christianity would be a shield for them, and that the white people would attack in the first place, if they attacked at all, those who they said were thieves. I ordered my people then all to retreat towards my residence, and let the fury of the Boers be spent upon an empty land; unfortunately some skirmishes took place, some Boers were killed, some of my people also. We need not wonder at this, such is war! But I will speak of many Basutos who were taken prisoners by the Whites and then killed, most cruelly. If you require me to bring forward these cases, I will do so. I will however speak of the horrible doings of the Boers at Morija, they there burnt down the Missionary's house, carried off much goods belonging to the Mission, and pillaged and shamefully defiled the Church Buildings.

I had given orders that no farms should be burnt, and my orders were obeyed till my people saw village after village burnt off, and the corn destroyed, they then carried destruction among the enemy's homes. On coming to my mountain, the Boers found I was prepared to check their progress, and they consequently retired. My intention was then to have followed them up, and to have shown them that my people could also carry on offensive operations, believing that having once experienced the horrors of war in their midst, I should not soon be troubled by them again. My bands were getting ready to make a descent upon them, when the Boers thought proper to make request for a cessation of hostilities. I knew what misery I should bring upon the country by leaving the Basutos to ravage the Boer places, and therefore I have agreed to the proposal of Mr. J. P. Hoffman. I cannot say that I do so with the consent of my people, for many of those who suffered by the enemy were anxious to recover their losses. If they have remained quiet, it has been owing to my persuasions and my promises that they might have good hope of justice—Your Excellency having consented to act as arbitrator between the Boers and Basutos. With the expectation of soon meeting you, I remain, etc., etc.,

X [Mark of Moshweshwe, Chief of the Basutos]

43

A School Examination in German Togo (1909)

The missionary effort in Africa was not limited to converting the indigenous peoples. In French, British, and German colonies alike, Christians saw themselves as having a sacred "civilizing" mission that led to the creation of networks of "native" schools. Africans who went to these schools gained the skills necessary to make their way in the "new" Africa, but learned (as this school examination makes perfectly clear) more about European attitudes and culture than about their own.

Saturday, 20.xi.09.

10–10 1/2 A.M. *Calligraphy.* A passage was written on the blackboard and the pupils had to copy it.

10 1/2–11 A.M. *Spelling.* The chairman of the commission dictated a simple passage from a short story, with which none of them were acquainted.

11–12 A.M. *Geography.* The following questions had been set as a task:

(a) The large states of Europe and their capitals.

(b) What are the names of Germany's most important mountains?

(c) What are the names of the most important rivers in Germany and in what direction do they run?

The last question was intended to show whether the pupils could not only reproduce the names mechanically, but could also visualize a map.

3–4 1/2 P.M. *An Essay.* The subject set was: 'What good things have the Europeans brought us?'

5 1/2–6 P.M. *Reading.* In addition to passages known to the pupils, they had to read aloud an unfamiliar article from a little book, called "Drei Kaiserbuchlein", out of the bookshop of the North German Mission.

Monday, 22.xi.09

7 1/2–9 A.M. *Oral Arithmetic.* The questions were asked by the teachers themselves.

10–11. *Written Arithmetic.* One question each was chosen from amongst those proposed by the school associations:

(1) Multiply 118.92 by 67 1/4 and then divide the number obtained by 3,964.

(2) In 1906 Togo exported copra worth 8,000 marks, in 1907 11,000 marks' worth. What was the increase per cent on the export of 1907?

(3) A labourer drinks brandy worth 0.25m a day. (a) How much does he pay for the brandy in a year? (b) How many days must he work for the brandy, if he earns 2m a day? (c) How many kgs of pork could he have bought with this sum, if pork costs 65 pfennige a kg?

From 11–12 and from 3–6 in the afternoon, useful knowledge, grammar and translation were examined.

Tuesday, 23.xi.09

7–8 A.M. *History.* The task set was:

The reign of emperor William I and the wars he had waged. Name those men who had specially supported his government.

From 8–11 1/2 A.M., the examinations in translation were completed.

44

"The White Man's Burden" (1899)

RUDYARD KIPLING

The most widely read novelist of his day and the first Englishman to win a Nobel Prize for Literature, Rudyard Kipling (1865–1936) was born in British India and made the history of the Raj a constant theme in his works. Despite his firsthand experience of the excesses of imperialism, he saw it overall as a mechanism whereby advanced states served the common good. His poem, "The White Man's Burden" emphasized responsibility rather than oppression, but it also mocked the excessive expectations of an imperialist public. The poem was written to warn Americans of what they could expect in the new colonies they had won as a result of the Spanish-American War (1898).

Take up the White Man's burden—
Send forth the best ye breed—
Go bind your sons to exile
To serve your captives' need;
To wait in heavy harness
On fluttered folk and wild—
Your new-caught, sullen peoples,
Half devil and half child.

Take up the White Man's burden—
In patience to abide,
To veil the threat of terror
And check the show of pride;
By open speech and simple,
An hundred times made plain,
To seek another's profit,
And work another's gain.

Take up the White Man's burden—
The savage wars of peace—
Fill full the mouth of Famine

And bid the sickness cease;
And when your goal is nearest
The end for others sought,
Watch Sloth and heathen Folly
Bring all your hope to nought.

Take up the White Man's burden—
No tawdry rule of kings,
But toil of serf and sweeper—
The tale of common things.
The ports ye shall not enter,
The roads ye shall not tread,
Go make them with your living,
And mark them with your dead!

Take up the White Man's burden—
And reap his old reward:
The blame of those ye better,
The hate of those ye guard—
The cry of hosts ye humour
(Ah, slowly!) Toward the light:—
"Why brought ye us from bondage,
"Our loved Egyptian night?"

Take up the White Man's burden—
Ye dare not stoop to less—
Nor call too loud on Freedom
To cloak your weariness;
By all ye cry or whisper,
By all ye leave or do,
The silent, sullen peoples
Shall weigh your Gods and you.

Take up the White Man's burden—
Have done with childish days—
The lightly proffered laurel,
The easy, ungrudged praise.
Comes now, to search your manhood
Through all the thankless years,
Cold-edged with dear-bought wisdom,
The judgment of your peers!

45

"The Brown Man's Burden" (1899)

HENRY DU PRÉ LABOUCHÈRE

Henry du Pré Labouchère (1831–1912) came from a British banking family of Huguenot origin. Rejecting the family business, Henry moved from circus troupes in Mexico to a Chippeway Indian camp before his family tracked him down and set him up, ultimately unsuccessfully, in the diplomatic service. A Parliamentary career in perpetual opposition to each succeeding government proved more enduring, but Labouchère won his greatest renown as the founder of Truth *(est. 1876), a weekly journal devoted to muckraking. An answer to Kipling, Labouchère's "The Brown Man's Burden" took a far more cynical view of western imperial pretensions.*

Pile on the brown man's burden
To gratify your greed;
Go, clear away the "niggers"
Who progress would impede;
Be very stern, for truly
'Tis useless to be mild
With new-caught, sullen peoples,
Half devil and half child.

Pile on the brown man's burden;
And, if ye rouse his hate,
Meet his old-fashioned reasons
With Maxims up to date.
With shells and dumdum bullets
A hundred times made plain
The brown man's loss must ever
Imply the white man's gain.

Pile on the brown man's burden,
compel him to be free;
Let all your manifestoes

Reek with philanthropy.
And if with heathen folly
He dares your will dispute,
Then, in the name of freedom,
Don't hesitate to shoot.

Pile on the brown man's burden,
And if his cry be sore,
That surely need not irk you—
Ye've driven slaves before.
Seize on his ports and pastures,
The fields his people tread;
Go make from them your living,
And mark them with his dead.

Pile on the brown man's burden,
And through the world proclaim
That ye are Freedom's agent—
There's no more paying game!
And, should your own past history
Straight in your teeth be thrown,
Retort that independence
Is good for whites alone.

Imperialism (1902)

JOHN A. HOBSON

If few Europeans questioned whether Africa and Asia benefitted from European imperialism, fewer still doubted the benefits European states received from their empires. But English economist John Atkinson Hobson (1858–1940) believed that, in the end, imperialism did Europe more harm than good. His Imperialism *(1902) was a systematic attempt to show that finance capitalists, hungry for the profit windfalls of early industrialization, were cynically manipulating British public sentiment in order to fatten their own pockets. All the British public really got from imperialism was a higher tax bill and a contamination of their own democratic spirit. Hobson's argument made a significant contribution to the thinking of Lenin, leader of the Russian socialist movement, who argued that imperialism was the last stage of capitalism.*

First-Almost the whole of recent imperial expansion is occupied with the political absorption of tropical or sub-tropical lands in which white men will not settle with their families.

Second-Nearly all the lands are thickly peopled by "lower races."

Thus this recent imperial expansion stands entirely distinct from the colonization of sparsely peopled lands in temperate zones, where white colonists carry with them the modes of government, the industrial and other arts of the civilization of the mother country. The "occupation" of these new territories is comprised in the presence of a small minority of white men, officials, traders, and industrial organizers, exercising political and economic sway over great hordes of population regarded as inferior and as incapable of exercising any considerable rights of self-government, in politics or industry. . . .

Seeing that the Imperialism of the last three decades is clearly condemned as a business policy, in that at enormous expense it has procured a small, bad, unsafe increase of markets, and has jeopardized the entire wealth of the nation in rousing the strong resentment of other nations, we may ask, "How is the British nation induced to embark upon such unsound business?" The only possible answer is that the business interests of the nation as a whole are subordinated to those of certain sectional interests that usurp control of the

137

national resources and use them for their private gain. This is no strange or monstrous charge to bring; it is the commonest disease of all forms of government. The famous words of Sir Thomas More are as true now as when he wrote them: "Everywhere do I perceive a certain conspiracy of rich men seeking their own advantage under the name and pretext of the commonwealth."

Although the new Imperialism has been bad business for the nation, it has been good business for certain classes and certain trades within the nation. The vast expenditure on armaments, the costly wars, the grave risks and embarrassments of foreign policy, the stoppage of political and social reforms within Great Britain, though fraught with great injury to the nation, have served well the present business interests of certain industries and professions. . . .

What is the direct economic outcome of Imperialism? A great expenditure of public money upon ships, guns, military and naval equipment and stores, growing and productive of enormous profits when a war, or an alarm of war, occurs; new public loans and important fluctuations in the home and foreign *Bourses* [stock markets]; more posts for soldiers and sailors and in the diplomatic and consular services; improvement of foreign investments by the substitution of the British flag for a foreign flag; acquisition of markets for certain classes of exports, and some protection and assistance for trades representing British houses in these manufactures; employment for engineers, missionaries, speculative miners, ranchers and other emigrants.

Certain definite business and professional interests feeding upon imperialistic expenditure, or upon the results of that expenditure, are thus set up in opposition to the common good, and, instinctively feeling their way to one another, are found united in strong sympathy to support every new imperialist exploit. . . .

The services are, of course, imperialist by conviction and by professional interest, and every increase of the army and navy enhances their numerical strength and the political power they exert. The abolition of purchase in the army, by opening the profession to the upper middle classes, greatly enlarged this most direct feeder of imperial sentiment. The potency of this factor is, of course, largely due to the itch for glory and adventure among military officers upon disturbed or uncertain frontiers of the Empire. This has been a most prolific source of expansion in India. The direct professional influence of the services carries with it a less organized but powerful sympathetic support on the part of the aristocracy and the wealthy classes, who seek in the services careers for their sons.

To the military services we may add the Indian Civil Service and the numerous official and semi-official posts in our colonies and protectorates. Every expansion of the Empire is also regarded by these same classes as affording new openings for their sons as ranchers, planters, engineers, or missionaries. This point of view is aptly summarized by a high Indian official, Sir Charles Crossthwaite, in discussing British relations with Siam. "The real question was who was to get the trade with them, and how we could make the most of them, so as to find fresh markets for our goods and also employment for those superfluous articles of the present day, our boys."

From this standpoint our colonies still remain what James Mill cynically described them as being, "a vast system of outdoor relief for the upper classes." . . .

Analysis of the actual course of modem Imperialism has laid bare the combination of economic and political forces which fashions it. These forces are traced to their sources in the selfish interests of certain industrial, financial, and professional classes, seeking private advantages out of a policy of imperial expansion, and using this same policy to protect them in their economic, political, and social privileges against the pressure of democracy. It remains to answer the question, "Why does Imperialism escape general recognition for the narrow, sordid thing it is?" Each nation, as it watches from outside the Imperialism of its neighbors, is not deceived; the selfish interests of political and commercial classes are seen plainly paramount in the direction of the policy. So every other European nation recognizes the true outlines of British Imperialism and charges us with hypocrisy in feigning blindness. This charge is false; no nation sees its own shortcomings; the charge of hypocrisy is seldom justly brought against an individual, against a nation never. Frenchmen and Germans believe that our zeal in promoting foreign missions, putting down slavery, and in spreading the arts of civilization is a false disguise conveniently assumed to cover naked national self-assertion. The actual case is somewhat different.

There exists in a considerable though not a large proportion of the British nation a genuine desire to spread Christianity among the heathen, to diminish the cruelty and other sufferings which they believe exist in countries less fortunate than their own, and to do good work about the world in the cause of humanity. Most of the churches contain a small body of men and women deeply, even passionately, interested in such work, and a much larger number whose sympathy, though weaker, is quite genuine. Ill-trained for the most part in psychology and history, these people believe that religion and other arts of civilization are portable commodities which it is our duty to convey to the backward nations, and that a certain amount of compulsion is justified in pressing their benefits upon people too ignorant at once to recognize them. . . .

It is precisely in this falsification of the real import of motives that the gravest vice and the most signal peril of Imperialism reside. When, out of a medley of mixed motives, the least potent is selected for public prominence because it is the most presentable, when issues of a policy which was not present at all to the minds of those who formed this policy are treated as chief causes, the moral currency of the nation is debased. The whole policy of Imperialism is riddled with this deception. Although no candid student of history will maintain for a moment that the entrance of British power into India, and the chief steps leading to the present British Empire there, were motived by considerations other than our own political and commercial aggrandizement, nothing is more common than to hear the gains which it is alleged the natives of the country have received from British rule assigned as the moral justification of our Indian Empire. . . .

Thus do the industrial and financial forces of Imperialism, operating through the party, the press, the church, the school, mold public opinion and public policy by the false idealization of those primitive lusts of struggle, domination, and acquisitiveness which have survived throughout the eras of peaceful industrial order and whose stimulation is needed once again for the work of imperial aggression, expansion, and the forceful exploitation of lower races. For these business politicians biology and sociology weave thin convenient theories of a race struggle for the subjugation of the inferior peoples, in order that we, the Anglo-Saxon, may take their lands and live upon their labors; while economics buttresses, the argument by representing our work in conquering and ruling them as our share in the division of labor among nations, and history devises reasons why the lessons of past empire do not apply to ours, while social ethics paints the motive of "Imperialism" as the desire to bear the "burden" of educating and elevating races of "children." Thus are the "cultured" or semi-cultured classes indoctrinated with the intellectual and moral grandeur of Imperialism. For the masses there is a cruder appeal to hero-worship and sensational glory, adventure and the sporting spirit: current history falsified in coarse flaring colors, for the direct stimulation of the combative instincts.

47

Confession of Faith

CECIL RHODES

Most Englishman were far more optimistic than Hobson about the beneficial effects of British imperialism. Cecil Rhodes (1853–1902), a vicar's son sent to Africa for his health, became an imperial legend. He held extensive gold mining interests and eventually controlled 90% of the world's diamonds. Rhodesia was named for him. Rhodes continues to influence the contemporary world through the De Beers diamond syndicate he founded and the famed "Rhodes" scholarships supported by his wealth. The "Confession of Faith" he lived by exalted Anglo-Saxons as "the finest race in the world."

It often strikes a man to inquire what is the chief good in life; to one the thought comes that it is a happy marriage, to another great wealth, and as each seizes on his idea, for that he more or less works for the rest of his existence. To myself thinking over the same question the wish came to render myself useful to my country. I then asked myself how could I and after reviewing the various methods I have felt that at the present day we are actually limiting our children and perhaps bringing into the world half the human beings we might owing to the lack of country for them to inhabit that if we had retained America there would at this moment be millions more of English living. I contend that we are the finest race in the world and that the more of the world we inhabit the better it is for the human race. Just fancy those parts that are at present inhabited by the most despicable specimens of human beings what an alteration there would be if they were brought under Anglo-Saxon influence, look again at the extra employment a new country added to our dominions gives. I contend that every acre added to our territory means in the future birth to some more of the English race who otherwise would not be brought into existence. Added to this the absorption of the greater portion of the world under our rule simply means the end of all wars. . . .

The idea gleaming and dancing before ones eyes like a will-of-the-wisp at last frames itself into a plan. Why should we not form a secret society with but one object the furtherance of the British Empire and the bringing of the whole uncivilized world under British rule for the recovery of the United States for the making the Anglo-Saxon race but one Empire. What a dream, but yet it is probable, it is possible. I once heard it argued by a fellow in my own college, I am sorry to own it by an Englishman, that it was a good thing for us that we have lost the United States. There are some subjects on which there can be no arguments, and to an Englishman this is one of them, but even from an American's point of view just picture what they have lost, look at their government. Are not the frauds that yearly come before the public view a disgrace to any country and especially their's which is the finest in the world? Would they have occurred had they remained under English rule? Great as they have become, how infinitely greater they would have been with the softening and elevating influences of English rule? Think of those countless thousands of Englishmen that during the last 100 years would have crossed the Atlantic and settled and populated the United States. Would they have not made without any prejudice a finer country of it than the low class Irish and German emigrants? All this we have lost, and that country loses, owing to whom? Owing to two or three ignorant pig-headed statesmen of the last century; at their door lies the blame. Do you ever feel mad? Do you ever feel murderous. I think I do with those men. . . .

. . .We learn from having lost to cling to what we possess. We know the size of the world. We know the total extent. Africa is still lying ready for us; it is our duty to take it. It is our duty to seize every opportunity of acquiring more territory, and we should keep this one idea steadily before our eyes: that more territory simply means more of the Anglo-Saxon race, more of the best, the most human, most honorable race the world possesses.

48

Annual Message to Congress (1823)

JAMES MONROE

Separated from the Old World by the Atlantic and Pacific Oceans, the new United States of America took a stand against European intervention in the New World. In his 1823 Annual Message to Congress, President James Monroe (1758–1831) proclaimed America's willingness to defend the new Latin American republics against their former rulers. For most of the nineteenth century, conditions in Europe had more to do with the failure of France, Spain, or Portugal to reclaim their colonies than did this "Monroe Doctrine," but a rapidly industrializing United States was quick to take advantage of the peace to invest in its southern neighbors.

[The] American continents, by the free and independent condition which they have assumed and maintain, are henceforth not to be considered as subjects for future colonization by any European powers. . . .

In the wars of the European powers in matters relating to themselves we have never taken any part, nor does it comport with our policy so to do. It is only when our rights are invaded or seriously menaced that we resent injuries or make preparation for our defense. With the movements in this hemisphere we are of necessity more immediately connected, and by causes which must be obvious to all enlightened and impartial observers. . . . We owe it, therefore, to candor and to the amicable relations existing between the United States and those [European] powers to declare that we should consider any attempt on their part to extend their system to any portion of this hemisphere as dangerous to our peace and safety. With the existing colonies or dependencies of any European power we have not interfered and shall not interfere. But with the governments who have declared their independence and maintained it, and whose independence we have, on great consideration and on just principles, acknowledged, we could not view any interposition for the purpose of oppressing them, or controlling in any other manner their destiny, by any European power in any other light than as the manifestation of an unfriendly disposition toward the United States. . . .

Our policy in regard to Europe, which was adopted at an early stage of the wars which have so long agitated that quarter of the globe, nevertheless remains the same, which is, not to interfere in the internal concerns of any of its powers; to consider the government *de facto* as the legitimate government for us; to cultivate friendly relations with it, and to preserve those relations by a frank, firm, and manly policy, meeting in all instances the just claims of every power, submitting to injuries from none. But in regard to . . .[the Americas] circumstances are eminently and conspicuously different. It is impossible that the allied powers should extend their political system to any portion of either continent without endangering our peace and happiness; nor can anyone believe that our southern brethren, if left to themselves, would adopt it of their own accord. It is equally impossible, therefore, that we should behold such interposition in any form with indifference. . . .

49

Annual Message to Congress (1904)

THEODORE ROOSEVELT

As America's might increased, so did the frequency and force of its intervention in Latin America. The United States gained control over Puerto Rico and Cuba (and the Pacific territories of Guam and the Philippines) as a result of its victory in the Spanish-American War (1898). Cuba was granted independence in 1901, but not before a special amendment was written into its constitution guaranteeing the right of American intervention; the other territories ceded by Spain remained under American control. In 1903, the United States helped Panama break away from Colombia in exchange for a wide swath of land in which to build a canal. In his 1904 Annual Message to Congress, President Theodore Roosevelt (1858–1919) clarified the changed relationship between the United States and Latin America. Often called the "Roosevelt Corollary" to the "Monroe Doctrine," the message stressed America's intention to protect its now sizable investment in Latin America by armed force if necessary.

It is not true that the United States feels any land hunger or entertains any projects as regards the other nations of the Western Hemisphere save such as are for their welfare. All that this country desires is to see the neighboring countries stable, orderly, and prosperous. Any country whose people conduct themselves well can count upon our hearty friendship. If a nation shows that it knows how to act with reasonable efficiency and decency in social and political matters, if it keeps order and pays its obligations, it need fear no interference from the United States. Chronic wrongdoing, or an impotence which results in a general loosening of the ties of civilized society, may in America, as elsewhere, ultimately require intervention by some civilized nation, and in the Western Hemisphere the adherence of the United States to the Monroe Doctrine may force the United States, however reluctantly, in flagrant cases of such wrongdoing or impotence, to the exercise of an international police power. If every country washed by the Caribbean Sea would show the progress in stable and just civilization which with the aid of the Platt Amendment Cuba has shown since our troops left the island, and which so many of the republics in both Americas are constantly and brilliantly showing, all question of interference by this Nation with their affairs would be at an end. Our interests and those of our southern neighbors are in reality identical. They have great natural riches, and if within their borders the reign of law and justice obtains, prosperity is sure to come to them. While they thus obey the primary laws of civilized society they may rest assured that they will be treated by us in a spirit of cordial and helpful sympathy. We would interfere with them only in the last resort, and then only if it became evident that their inability or unwillingness to do justice at home and abroad had violated the rights of the United States or had invited foreign aggression to the detriment of the entire body of American nations. . . .

In asserting the Monroe Doctrine, in taking such steps as we have taken in regard to Cuba, Venezuela, and Panama, and in endeavoring to circumscribe the theater of war in the Far East, and to secure the "Open Door" in China, we have acted in our own interest as well as in the interest of humanity at large. . . .

Letter to the Editor, New York Evening Post, March 25, 1889

JOSÉ MARTI

José Julian Marti y Pérez (1853–1895), Cuba's most famous poet, was sentenced to six years' hard labor for revolutionary activities at the age of sixteen. Exiled to Spain in 1871, he spent much of his life far from home trying to raise support for Cuba's efforts to free itself from Spanish rule: he and his family moved from Spain to Mexico, Guatemala, and New York City. This letter was written nine years before the Spanish-American War (1898) that ended with the United States in temporary control of Cuba, but it demonstrates that there was already support for the United States to take permanent control of the island to protect American investment in the sugar industry. Killed in Cuba's 1895 rebellion, Marti never lived to see the island's eventual independence.

Sir:

I beg to be allowed the privilege of referring in your columns to the injurious criticism of the Cubans printed in the *Manufacturer* of Philadelphia, and reproduced in your issue of yesterday.

This is not the occasion to discuss the question of the annexation of Cuba. It is probable that no self-respecting Cuban would like to see his country annexed to a nation where the leaders of opinion share awards him the prejudices excusable only to vulgar jingoism or rampant ignorance. No honest Cuban will stoop to be received as a moral pest for the sake of the usefulness of his land in a community where his ability is denied, his morality insulted, and his character despised. There are some Cubans who, from honorable motives, from an ardent admiration for progress and liberty, from a prescience of their own powers under better political conditions, from an unhappy ignorance of the history and tendency of annexation, would like to see the island annexed to the United States. But those who have fought in war and learned in exile, who have built, by the work of hands and mind, a virtuous home in the heart of an unfriendly community; who by their successful efforts as scientists and merchants, as railroad builders and engineers, as teachers, artists, lawyers, journalists, orators, and poets, as men of alert intelligence and uncommon activity, are honored wherever their powers have been called into action and the people are just enough to understand them; those who have raised, with their less prepared elements, a town of working-men where the United States had previously a few huts in a barren cliff; those, more numerous than the others, do not desire the annexation of Cuba to the United States. They do not need it. They admire this nation, the greatest ever built by liberty, but they dislike the evil conditions that, like worms in the heart, have begun in this mighty republic their work of destruction. They have made of the heroes of this country their own heroes, and look to the success of the American commonwealth as the crowning glory of mankind; but they cannot honestly believe that excessive individualism, reverence for wealth, and the protracted exultation of a terrible victory are preparing the United States to be the typical nation of liberty, where no opinion is to be based in greed, and no triumph or acquisition reached against charity and justice. We love the country of Lincoln as much as we fear the country of Cutting [William Bayard Cutting (1850–1912), American financier active in the sugar industry and a supporter of annexing Cuba].

We are not the people of destitute vagrants or immoral pygmies that the *Manufacturer* is pleased to picture; nor the country of petty talkers, incapable of action, hostile to hard work, that, in a mass with the other countries of Spanish America, we are by arrogant travelers and writers represented to be. We lave suffered impatiently under tyranny; we have fought like men, sometimes like giants, to be freemen; we are passing that period of stormy repose, full of germs of revolt, that naturally follows a period of excessive and unsuccessful action. . . . we deserve in our misfortune the respect of those who did not help us in our need.

Because the healthier farmer, ruined by a war seemingly useless, turns in silence to the plough that he knew well how to exchange for the machete; because thousands of exiles, profiting by a period of calm that no human power can quicken until it is naturally exhausted, are practicing in the battle of life in the free countries the art of governing themselves and of building a nation; because our half-breeds and city-bred young men are generally of delicate physique, of suave courtesy, and ready words, hiding under the glove that polishes the poem the hand that fells the foe—are we to be considered as the *Manufacturer* does consider us, an "effeminate" people? These city-bred young men and poorly built half-breeds knew in one day how to rise against a cruel government, to pay their passages to the seat of war with the pawning of their watches and trinkets, to work their way in exile while their vessels were being kept from them by the country of the free in the interest of the foes of freedom, to obey as soldiers, sleep in the mud, eat roots, fight ten years without salary, conquer foes with the branch of a tree, die—these men of eighteen, these heirs of wealthy estates, these dusky striplings—a death not to be spoken of without uncovering the head. . . . These "effeminate" Cubans had courage enough, in the face of a hostile government, to carry on their left arms for a week the mourning-band for Lincoln.

The Cubans have, according the *Manufacturer*, "a distaste for exertion"; they are "helpless," "idle." These "helpless," "idle" men came here twenty years ago empty-handed, with very few exceptions; fought against the climate; mastered the language; lived by their honest labor, some in affluence, a few in wealth, rarely in misery; they bought or built homes; they raised families and fortunes; they loved luxury, and worked for it; they were not frequently seen in the dark roads of life; proud and self-sustaining, they never feared competition as to intelligence or diligence. . . . In Philadelphia the *Manufacturer* has a daily opportunity to see a hundred Cubans, some of them of heroic history and powerful build, who live by their work in easy comfort. In New York the Cubans are directors in prominent banks, substantial merchants, popular brokers, clerks of recognized ability, physicians with a large practice. . . the "senora" went to work; from a slave-owner she became a slave, took a seat behind the counter, sang in the churches, worked button-holes by the hundred, sewed for a living, curled feathers, gave her soul to duty, withered in work her body. This is the people of "defective morals."

We are "unfitted by nature and experience to discharge the obligations of citizenship in a great and free country" (From the *Manufacturer*). This cannot be justly said of a people who possess, besides the energy that built the first railroad in Spanish dominions and established against the opposition of the government all the agencies of civilization, a truly remarkable knowledge of the body politic. . . . The political knowledge of the average Cuban compares well with that of the average American citizen. Absolute freedom from religious intolerance, the love of man for the work he creates by his industry, and theoretical and practical familiarity with the laws and processes of liberty, will enable the Cuban to rebuild his country from the ruins in which he will receive it from its oppressors. It is not to be expected, for the honor of mankind, that the nation that was rocked in freedom, and received for three centuries the best blood of liberty-loving men, will employ the power thus acquired in depriving a less fortunate neighbor of its liberty.

It is, finally, said that "our lack of manly force and of self-respect is demonstrated by the supineness with which we have so long submitted to Spanish oppression, and even our attempts at rebellion have been so pitifully ineffective that they have risen little above the dignity of farce." Never was ignorance of history and character more pitifully displayed than in this wanton assertion. . . . A farce! The war that has been by foreign observers compared to an epic, the upheaval of a whole country, the voluntary abandonment of wealth, the abolition of slavery in our first moment of freedom, the burning of our cities by our own hands, the erection of villages and factories in the wild forests. . . . The struggle has not ceased. The exiles do not want to return. The new generation is worthy of its sires. Hundreds of men have died in darkness since the war in the misery of prisons. With life only will this fight for liberty cease among us. And it is the melancholy truth that our efforts would have been, in all probability, successfully renewed, were it not, in some of us, for the unmanly hopes of the annexationists of securing liberty without paying its price; and the just fears of others that our dead, our sacred memories, our ruins drenched in blood would be but the fertilizers of the soil for the benefit of a foreign plant, or the occasion for a sneer from the *Manufacturer* of Philadelphia.

With sincere thanks for the space you have kindly allowed me, I am, sir, yours very respectfully,

José Marti

Topic VI

The Evolution of Liberalism in Nineteenth Century Society

On Liberty (1859)

JOHN STUART MILL

Whether considered as economist or philosopher, John Stuart Mill (1806–1873) represents the birth of a new kind of liberal thought in the nineteenth century. His "New Liberalism" rejected strict laissez-faire in favor of government activism on behalf of needy citizens. At the same time he warned against the ability of overgrown government, predatory business, and the newly powerful "public" opinion to threaten human freedom. In On Liberty *(1859), Mill defended the right of even the most contrary individual to be different, because freedom of choice was essential for the development of the rationality that made us truly human.*

The object of this Essay is to assert one very simple principle, as entitled to govern absolutely the dealings of society with the individual in the way of compulsion and control, whether the means used be physical force in the form of legal penalties, or the moral coercion of public opinion. That principle is, that the sole end for which mankind are warranted, individually or collectively, in interfering with the liberty of action of any of their number, is self-protection. That the only purpose for which power can be rightfully exercised over any member of a civilized community, against his will, is to prevent harm to others. His own good, either physical or moral, is not a sufficient warrant. He cannot rightfully be compelled to do or forbear because it will be better for him to do so, because it will make him happier, because, in the opinions of others, to do so would be wise, or even right. These are good reasons for remonstrating with him, not for compelling him, or visiting him with any evil in case he do otherwise. To justify that, the conduct from which it is desired to deter him must be calculated to produce evil to some one else. The only part of the conduct of any one, for which he is amenable to society, is that which concerns others. In the part which merely concerns himself, his independence is, of right, absolute. . . .

This, then, is the appropriate region of human liberty. It comprises, first, the inward domain of consciousness; demanding liberty of conscience in the most comprehensive sense; liberty of thought and feeling; absolute freedom of opinion and sentiment on all subjects, practical or speculative, scientific, moral, or theological. The liberty of expressing and publishing opinions may seem to fall under a different principle, since it belongs to that part of the conduct of an individual which concerns other people; but, being almost of as much importance as the liberty of thought itself, and resting in great part on the same reasons, is practically inseparable from it. Secondly, the principle requires liberty of tastes and pursuits; of framing the plan of our life to suit our own character; of doing as we like, subject to such consequences as may follow: without impediment from our fellow-creatures, so long as what we do does not harm them, even though they should think our conduct foolish, perverse, or wrong. Thirdly, from this liberty of each individual, follows the liberty, within the same limits, of combination among individuals; freedom to unite, for any purpose not involving harm to others: the persons combining being supposed to be of full age, and not forced or deceived.

No society in which these liberties are not on the whole respected, is free, whatever may be its form of government; and none is completely free in which they do not exist absolute and unqualified. The only freedom which deserves the name, is that of pursuing our own good in our own way, so long as we do not attempt to deprive others of theirs, or impede their efforts to obtain it. Each is the proper guardian of his own health, whether bodily, or mental and spiritual. Mankind are greater gainers by suffering each other to live as seems good to themselves, than by compelling each to live as seems good to the rest. . . .

We have now recognized the necessity to the mental well-being of mankind (on which all their other well-being depends) of freedom of opinion, and freedom of the expression of opinion, on four distinct grounds; which we will now briefly recapitulate.

First, if any opinion is compelled to silence, that opinion may, for aught we can certainly know, be true. To deny this is to assume our own infallibility.

Secondly, though the silenced opinion be an error, it may and very commonly does, contain a portion of the truth; and since the general or prevailing opinion on any subject is rarely or never the whole truth, it is only by the collision of adverse opinions that the remainder of the truth has any chance of being supplied.

Thirdly, even if the received opinion be not only true, but the whole truth; unless it is suffered to be, and actually is, vigorously and earnestly contested, it will, by most of those who receive it, be held in the manner of a prejudice, with little comprehension or feeling of its rational grounds. And not only this, but, fourthly, the meaning of the doctrine itself will be in danger of being lost, or enfeebled, and deprived of its vital effect on the character and conduct. . . .

He who lets the world, or his own portion of it, choose his plan of life for him, has no need of any other faculty than the ape-like one of imitation. He who chooses his plan for himself, employs all his faculties. He must use observation to see, reasoning and judgment to foresee, activity to gather materials for decision, discrimination to decide, and when he has decided, firmness and self-control to hold to his deliberate decision. And these qualities he requires and exercises exactly in proportion as the part of his conduct which he determines according to his own judgment and feelings is a large one. It is possible that he might be guided in some good path, and kept out of harm's way, without any of these things. But what will be his comparative worth as a human being? . . . Human nature is not a machine to be built after a model, and set to do exactly the work prescribed for it, but a tree, which requires to grow and develop itself on all sides, according to the tendency of the inward forces which make it a living thing. . . .

But society has now fairly got the better of individuality; and the danger which threatens human nature is not the excess, but the deficiency, of personal impulses and preferences. . . . In our times, from the highest class of society down to the lowest, every one lives as under the eye of a hostile and dreaded censorship. . . . [People] live in crowds; they exercise choice only among things commonly done: peculiarity of taste, eccentricity of conduct, are shunned equally with crimes: until by dint of not following their own nature they have no nature to follow . . . . [they all] read the same things, listen to the same things, see the same things, go to the same places, have their hopes and fears directed to the same objects, have the same rights and liberties, and the same means of asserting them. Great as are the differences of position which remain, they are nothing to those which have ceased. And the assimilation is still proceeding. All the political changes of the age promote it, since they all tend to raise the low and to lower the high. Every extension of education promotes it, because education brings people under common influences, and gives them access to the general stock of facts and sentiments. Improvement in the means of communication promotes it, by bringing the inhabitants of distant places into personal contact, and keeping up a rapid flow of changes of residence between one place and another. The increase of commerce and manufactures promotes it, by diffusing more widely the advantages of easy circumstances, and opening all objects of ambition, even the highest, to general competition, whereby the desire of rising becomes no longer the character of a particular class, but of all classes. A more powerful agency than even all these, in bringing about a general similarity among mankind, is the complete establishment, in this and other free countries, of the ascendancy of public opinion in the State. As the various social eminences which enabled persons entrenched on them to disregard the opinion of the multitude gradually become levelled; as the very idea of resisting the will of the public, when it is positively known that they have a will, disappears more and more from the minds of practical politicians; there ceases to be any social support for nonconformity—any substantive power in society which, itself opposed to the ascendancy of numbers, is interested in taking under its protection opinions and tendencies at variance with those of the public.

The combination of all these causes forms so great a mass of influences hostile to Individuality, that it is not easy to see how it can stand its ground.

It will do so with increasing difficulty, unless the intelligent part of, the public can be made to feel its value—to see that it is good there should be differences, even though not for the better, even though, as it may appear to them, some should be for the worse. If the claims of Individuality are ever to be asserted, the time is now, while much is still wanting to complete the enforced assimilation. It is only in the earlier stages that any stand can be successfully made against the encroachment. The demand that all other people shall resemble ourselves grows by what it feeds on. If resistance waits till life is reduced nearly to one uniform type, all deviations from that type will come to be considered impious, immoral, even monstrous and contrary to nature. Mankind speedily become unable to conceive diversity, when they have been for some time unaccustomed to see it. . . .

A government cannot have too much of the kind of activity which does not impede, but aids and stimulates, individual exertion and development. The mischief begins, when, instead of calling forth the activity and powers of individuals and bodies, it substitutes its own activity for theirs; when, instead of informing, advising, and, upon occasion, denouncing, it makes them work in fetters, or bids them stand aside and does their work instead of them. The worth of a State, in the long run, is the worth of the individuals composing it; and a State which postpones the interests of *their* mental expansion and elevation to a little more of administrative skill, or of that semblance of it which practice gives, in the details of business; a State which dwarfs its men, in order that they may be more docile instruments in its hands even for beneficial purposes—will find that with small men no great thing can really be accomplished; and that the perfection of machinery to which it has sacrificed everything will in the end avail it nothing, for want of the vital power which, in order that the machine might work more smoothly, it has preferred to banish.

Declaration of Sentiments (1848)

ELIZABETH CADY STANTON

*The relegation of female volunteers to subsidiary roles in the abolition-
ist movement in the first half of the nineteenth century sparked a campaign for women's rights in the United States. Among the movement's
"founding mothers" was Elizabeth Cady Stanton (1815–1902), orga-
nizer of the first women's rights convention. Some 300 delegates
(including 40 men) attended that meeting at Seneca Falls, New York,
in July 1848. Drafted largely by Stanton, the meeting produced a Declaration of Sentiments deliberately modeled on the U.S.* Declaration of
Independence. *Despite her comfortable upper-middle class life, Stanton knew well the discrimination women faced: although she had studied law with her father, her sex made her ineligible for admission to the
profession.*

When, in the course of human events, it becomes necessary for one portion of the family of man to assume among the people of the earth a position different from that which they have hitherto occupied, but one to which
the laws of nature and of nature's God entitle them, a decent respect to the
opinions of mankind requires that they should declare the causes that impel
them to such a course.

We hold these truths to be self-evident: that all men and women are created equal; that they are endowed by their Creator with certain inalienable
rights; that among these are life, liberty, and the pursuit of happiness; that to
secure these rights governments are instituted, deriving their just powers
from the consent of the governed. Whenever any form of government
becomes destructive of these ends, it is the right of those who suffer from it
to refuse allegiance to it, and to insist upon the institution of a new government, laying its foundation on such principles, and organizing its powers in
such form, as to them shall seem most likely to effect their happiness. Prudence, indeed, will dictate that governments long established should not be
changed for light and transient causes; and accordingly all experience hath
shown that mankind are more disposed to suffer, while evils are sufferable,
than to right themselves by abolishing the forms to which they were accus-

tomed. But when a long train of abuses and usurpations, pursuing invariably the same object evinces a design to reduce them under absolute despotism, it is their duty to throw off such government, and to provide new guards for their future security. Such has been the patient sufferance of the women under this government, and such is now the necessity which constrains them to demand the equal station to which they are entitled.

The history of mankind is a history of repeated injuries and usurpations on the part of man toward woman, having in direct object the establishment of an absolute tyranny over her. To prove this, let facts be submitted to a candid world.

He has compelled her to submit to laws, in the formation of which she had no voice.

He has withheld from her rights which are given to the most ignorant and degraded men—both natives and foreigners.

Having deprived her of this first right of a citizen, the elective franchise, thereby leaving her without representation in the halls of legislation, he has oppressed her on all sides.

He has made her, if married, in the eye of the law, civilly dead.

He has taken from her all right in property, even to the wages she earns.

He has made her, morally, an irresponsible being, as she can commit many crimes with impunity, provided they be done in the presence of her husband. In the covenant of marriage, she is compelled to promise obedience to her husband, he becoming, to all intents and purposes, her master—the law giving him power to deprive her of her liberty, and to administer chastisement.

He has so framed the laws of divorce, as to what shall be the proper causes, and in case of separation, to whom the guardianship of the children shall be given, as to be wholly regardless of the happiness of women—the law, in all cases, going upon a false supposition of the supremacy of man, and giving all power into his hands.

After depriving her of all rights as a married woman, if single, and the owner of property, he has taxed her to support a government which recognizes her only when her property can be made profitable to it.

He has monopolized nearly all the profitable employments, and from those she is permitted to follow, she receives but a scanty remuneration. He closes against her all the avenues to wealth and distinction which he considers most honorable to himself. As a teacher of theology, medicine, or law, she is not known.

He has denied her the facilities for obtaining a thorough education, all colleges being closed against her.

He allows her in Church, as well as State, but a subordinate position, claiming Apostolic authority for her exclusion from the ministry, and, with some exceptions, from any public participation in the affairs of the Church.

He has created a false public sentiment by giving to the world a different code of morals for men and women, by which moral delinquencies which exclude woman from society, are not only tolerated, but deemed of little account in man.

He has usurped the prerogative of Jehovah himself, claiming it as his right to assign for her a sphere of action, when that belongs to her conscience and to her God.

He has endeavored, in every way that he could, to destroy her confidence in her own powers, to lessen her self-respect, and to make her willing to lead a dependent and abject life.

Now, in view of this entire disfranchisement of one-half the people of this country, their social and religious degradation,—in view of the unjust laws above mentioned, and because women do feel themselves aggrieved, oppressed, and fraudulently deprived of their most sacred rights, we insist that they have immediate admission to all the rights and privileges which belong to them as citizens of these United States.

In entering upon the great work before us, we anticipate no small amount of misconception, misrepresentation, and ridicule; but we shall use every instrumentality within our power to effect our object. We shall employ agents, circulate tracts, petition the State and national Legislatures, and endeavor to enlist the pulpit and the press in our behalf. We hope this Convention will be followed by a series of Conventions, embracing every part of the country.

Wages and the Franchise (1870)

SUSAN BROWNELL ANTHONY

What set the Declaration of Sentiments *(1848) apart from earlier feminist manifestoes was the organized movement that sprang from it. One of the movement's key organizers was Susan Brownell Anthony (1820–1906), the Quaker teacher who co-founded the National Women's Suffrage Association (1869) with Stanton. The NWSA lobbied Congress for a national right to vote and coordinated the campaigns of local chapters for the vote in individual states. As this speech makes clear, however, Anthony was as ardent a fighter for women's economic rights as she was for a truly universal franchise.*

My purpose tonight is to demonstrate the great historical fact that disfranchisement is not only political degradation, but also moral, social, educational and industrial degradation; and that it does not matter whether the disfranchised class live under a monarchial or a republican form of government, or whether it be white workingmen of England, Negroes on our southern plantations, serfs of Russia, Chinamen on our Pacific coast, or native born, tax-paying women of this republic. Wherever, on the face of the globe or on the page of history, you show me a disfranchised class, I will show you a degraded class of labor. Disfranchisement means inability to make, shape or control one's own circumstances. The disfranchised must always do the work, accept the wages, occupy the position the enfranchised assign to them. The disfranchised are in the position of the pauper. You remember the old adage, "Beggars must not be choosers;" they must take what they can get or nothing! That is exactly the position of women in the world of work today; they can not choose. If they could, do you for a moment believe they would take the subordinate places and the inferior pay? . . .

It is said women do not need the ballot for their protection because they are supported by men. Statistics show that there are 3,000,000 women in this nation supporting themselves. In the crowded cities of the East they are compelled to work in shops, stores and factories for the merest pittance. In New York alone, there are over 50,000 of these women receiving less than fifty cents a day. . . .

The law of capital is to extort the greatest amount of work for the least amount of money; the rule of labor is to do the smallest amount of work for the largest amount of money. Hence there is, and in the nature of things must continue to be, antagonism between the two classes; therefore, neither should be left wholly at the mercy of the other.

It was cruel, under the old regime, to give rich men the right to rule poor men. It was wicked to allow white men absolute power over black men. It is vastly more cruel, more wicked to give to all men—rich and poor, white and black, native and foreign, educated and ignorant, virtuous and vicious—this absolute control over women. Men talk of the injustice of monopolies. There never was, there never can be, a monopoly so fraught with injustice, tyranny and degradation as this monopoly of sex, of all men over all women. Therefore I not only agree with Abraham Lincoln that, "No man is good enough to govern another man without his consent;" but I say also that no man is good enough to govern a woman without her consent, and still further, that all men combined in government are not good enough to govern all women without their consent. There might have been some plausible excuse for the rich governing the poor, the educated governing the ignorant, the Saxon governing the African; but there can be none for making the husband the ruler of the wife, the brother of the sister, the man of the woman, his peer in birth, in education, in social position, in all that stands for the best and highest in humanity. . . .

The principle of self-government can not be violated with impunity. The individual's right to it is sacred—regardless of class, caste, race, color, sex or any other accident or incident of birth. What we ask is that you shall cease to imagine that women are outside this law, and that you shall come into the knowledge that disenfranchisement means the same degradation to your daughter as to your sons.

Governments can not afford to ignore the rights of those holding the ballot, who make and unmake every law and law-maker. It is not because the members of Congress are tyrants that women receive only half pay and are admitted only to inferior positions in the departments. It is simply in obedience to a law of political economy which makes it impossible for a government to do as much for the disfranchised as for the enfranchised. . . .

There are many women equally well qualified with men for principals and superintendents of schools, and yet, while three-fourths of the teachers are women, nearly all of them are relegated to subordinate positions on half or at most two-thirds the salaries paid to men. The law of supply and demand is so ignored, and that of sex alone settles the question. If a business man should advertise for a book-keeper and ten young men, equally well qualified, should present themselves and, after looking them over, he should say, "To you who have red hair, we will pay full wages, while to you with black hair we will pay half the regular price;" that would not be a more flagrant violation of the law of supply and demand than is now perpetrated upon women because of their sex. . . .

. . . .When women vote, they will make a new of balance of power that must be weighed and measured and calculated in its effect upon every social and moral question which goes to the arbitrament of the ballot-box. Who can doubt that when the representative women of thought and culture, who are today the moral backbone of our nation, sit in counsel with the best men of the country, higher conditions will be the result? . . .

If men possessing the power of the ballot are driven to desperate means to gain their ends, what shall be done by disfranchised women? . . . Women's crusades against saloons, brothels and gambling-dens, emptying kegs and bottles into the streets, breaking doors and windows and burning houses, all go to prove that disfranchisement, the denial of lawful means to gain desired ends, may drive even women to violations of law and order. Hence to secure both national and "domestic tranquillity," to "establish justice," to carry out the spirit of our Constitution, put into the hands of all women, as you have into those of all men, the ballot, that symbol of perfect equality, that right protective of all other rights.

Speeches on Women's Rights
(1851 & 1867)

SOJOURNER TRUTH

In the United States, Abolitionist and Feminist movements split over the fact that the Fifteenth Amendment did not grant women the right to vote. African-American feminists were left with a double burden. Those who fought for their rights as women were accused of abandoning the "greater" cause of Negro rights. Sojourner Truth (1797–1883), a field hand on her master's farm until New York State abolished slavery in 1837, was among those who refused to choose between their sex and their race. She campaigned as ardently for her rights as a woman after the Civil War (1861-1865) as she had for abolition before the war.

Speech in 1851:

That man over there states that women need to be helped into carriages, and lifted over ditches, and to have the best place everywhere. Nobody ever helps me into carriages, or over mud-puddles, or gives me any best place! And ain't I a woman? Look at me! Look at my arm! I have ploughed and planted, and gathered into barns, and no man could head me! And ain't I a woman? I could work as much and eat as much as a man—when I could get it—and bear the lash as well! And ain't I a woman? I have borne thirteen children, and seen them most all sold off to slavery, and when I cried out with my mother's grief, none but Jesus heard me! And ain't I a woman?

Then they talk about this thing in the head; what's this they call it? [Intellect, someone whispers.] That's it, honey. What's that got to do with women's rights or negro's rights? If my cup won't hold but a pint, and yours holds a quart, wouldn't you be mean not to let me have my little half-measure full?

Then that little man in black there, he says women can't have as much rights as men, 'cause Christ wasn't a woman! Where did your Christ come from? Where did your Christ come from? From God and a woman! Man had nothing to do with Him.

If the first woman God ever made was strong enough to turn the world upside down all alone, these women together ought to be able to turn it back, and get it right side up again! And now they is asking to do it, the men better let them.

Obliged to you for hearing me, and now old Sojourner ain't got nothing more to say.

Speech in 1867:

I want women to have their rights. In the courts women have no right, no voice; nobody speaks for them. I wish women to have her voice there among the pettifoggers. If it is not a fit place for women, it is unfit for men to be there.

I am above eighty years old; it is about time for me to be going. I have been forty years a slave and forty years free, and would be here forty years more to have equal rights for all. I suppose I am kept here because something remains for me to do; I suppose I am yet to help to break the chain. I have done a great deal of work; as much as a man, but did not get so much pay. I used to work in the field and bind grain, keeping up with the cradler; but men doing no more, got twice as much pay. . . . We do as much, we eat as much, we want as much. I suppose I am about the only colored woman that goes about to speak for the rights of the colored women. I want to keep the thing stirring, now that the ice is cracked. What we want is a little money. You men know that you get as much again as women, when you write, or for what you do. When we get our rights, we shall not have to come to you for money, for then we shall have money enough in our own pockets; and maybe you will ask us for money. But help us now until we get it. It is a good consolation to know that when we have got this battle once fought we shall not be coming to you any more. . . .

I am glad to see that men are getting their rights, but I want women to get theirs, and while the water is stirring I will step into the pool. Now that there is a great stir about colored men's getting their rights is the time for women to step in and have theirs. I am sometimes told that "Women ain't fit to vote. What, don't you know that a woman had seven devils in her; and do you suppose a woman is fit to rule the nation?" Seven devils ain't no account; a man had a legion in him.

"Why We Are Militant" (1913)

EMMELINE PANKHURST

The Reform Acts of 1832, 1867, and 1884 created a nearly universal male suffrage in Britain, but when John Stuart Mill challenged Parliament to extend that right to women, his bill failed by a vote of 196 to 73. Such defeats brought on a change in tactics in one wing of the British women's movement. Emmeline Pankhurst (1858–1928) formed the Women's Social and Political Union (1893) and turned to violence to win attention, enduring repeated imprisonment for the broken windows, disrupted sessions of Parliament, and assaults on its Members. In this speech to America's feminists in 1913, Pankhurst explained the logic of militancy.

I know that in your minds there are questions like these; you are saying, "Woman Suffrage is sure to come; the emancipation of humanity is an evolutionary process, and how is it that some women, instead of trusting to that evolution, instead of educating the masses of people of their country, instead of educating their own sex to prepare them for citizenship, how is it that these militant women are suing violence and upsetting the business arrangements of the country in their undue impatience to attain their end?"

Let me try to explain to you the situation. . . .

The extensions of the franchise to the men of my country have been preceded by very great violence, by something like a revolution, by something like civil war. In 1832, you know we were on the edge of a civil war and on the edge of a revolution, and it was at the point of the sword—no, not at the point of the sword—it was after the practice of arson on so large a scale that half the city of Bristol was burned down in a single night, it was because more and greater violence and arson were feared that the Reform Bill of 1832 was allowed to pass into law. [In 1867] rioting went on all over the country, and as the result of that rioting, as the result of the unrest, . . . the Reform Act of 1867 was put upon the statute books.

[In 1884] rioting was threatened and feared, and so the agricultural laborers go the vote.

Meanwhile, during the '80's women, like men, were asking for the franchise. Appeals, larger and more numerous that for any other reform, were presented in support of Woman's Suffrage. . . . and yet the women did not get it. Men got the vote because they were and would be violent. The women did not get it because they were constitutional and law abiding. . . .

I believed, as many women still in England believe, that women could get their way in some mysterious manner, by purely peaceful methods. We have been so accustomed, we women, to accept one standard for men and another standard for women, that we have even applied that variation of standard to the injury of our political welfare. . . .

Two women changed that in twinkling of an eye at a great Liberal demonstration in Manchester, where a Liberal leader, Sir Edward Grey, was explaining the program to be carried out during the Liberals' next turn of office. The two women put the fateful question, "When are you going to give votes to women?" and refused to sit down until they had been answered. These two women were sent to gaol [jail], and from that day to this the women's movement, both militant and constitutional has never looked back. We had little more than one moribund society for Women Suffrage in those days. Now we have nearly 50 societies for Woman Suffrage, and they are large in membership, they are rich in money, and their ranks are swelling every day that passes. That is how militancy has put back the clock of Woman Suffrage in Great Britain. . . .

I want to say here and now that the only justification for violence, the only justification for damage to property, the only justification for risk to the comfort of other human beings is the fact that you have tried all other available means and have failed to secure justice, and as a law-abiding person—and I am by nature a law abiding person, as one hating violence, hating disorder— I want to say that from the moment we began our militant agitation to this day I have felt absolutely guiltless in this matter. . . .

Patience is something akin to crime when our patience involves continued suffering on the part of the oppressed. . . .

. . .if you were talking of the men of any other nation you would not hesitate to reply in the affirmative. There is not a man in this meeting who has not felt sympathy with the uprising of the men of other lands when suffering from intolerable tyranny, when deprived of all representative rights. You are full of sympathy with men in Russia. You are full of sympathy with nations that rise against the domination of the Turk. You are full of sympathy with all struggling people striving for independence. How is it, that some of you have nothing but ridicule and contempt and (condemnation) for women who are fighting for exactly the same thing?

All my life I have tried to understand why it is that men who value their citizenship as their dearest possession seem to think citizenship ridiculous when it is to be applied to the women of their race. And I find an explanation, and it is the only one I can think of. It came to me when I was in a prison cell, remembering how I had seen men laugh at the idea of women going to prison. . . . A thought came to me in my prison cell, and it was this; that to men women are not human beings like themselves. Some men think we are superhuman; they put us on pedestals; they revere us; they think we are too fine and too delicate to come down into the hurly-burly of life. Other men think us sub-human; they think we are a strange species unfortunately having to exist for the perpetuation of the race. They think that we are fit for drudgery, but that in some strange way our minds are not like theirs, and so we are a sort of sub-human species.

We are neither superhuman nor are we sub-human. We are just human beings like yourselves.

When we were patient, when we believed in argument and persuasion, they [men] said, "You don't really want it because, if you did, you would do something unmistakable to show you were determined to have it." And then when we did something unmistakable they said, "You are behaving so badly that you show you are not fit for it."

Now, gentlemen, in your heart of hearts you do not believe that. You know perfectly well that there never was a thing worth having that was not worth fighting for. You know perfectly well that if the situation were reversed, if you had no constitutional rights and we had all of them, if you had the duty of paying and obeying and trying to look as pleasant, and we were the proud citizens who could decide our fate and yours, because we knew what was good for you better than you knew yourselves, you know perfectly well that you would be perfectly justified in rebelling against such intolerable conditions.

Nineteenth-Century
Chinese Marriage Contracts

Women in Asia lived under far greater restraints than did women in Western Europe or the United States. In China, family life and marriage practices followed laws and customs that had existed for thousands of years: all children belonged to the husband's family, and daughters were easily discarded as "child-brides" or concubines. Even female infanticide was not uncommon in times of economic hardship. The marriage contracts below were all too typical of an agricultural society in which daughters left their parents' household to become workers in their husbands' families, while sons brought in wives to work for the son's parents.

This "getting a husband to support a husband" contract is drawn up for and signed by Wang Yün-fa.

Years ago, I married Li San's daughter, Li Hsiu-liang, who is now twenty years old. We have lived together for four years. Hsiu-liang is very filial to my parents and she takes care of the household without creating trouble or stirring up quarrels. It makes one very content to have such a good wife.

Unfortunately, some time ago I contracted a disease and have become paralyzed. We are poor and have no source of income to meet our expenses. Although at the present time we are not starving, we have considered the fact that the most unfilial thing one can do is not to have heirs. When my wife's youth expires, it will be impossible to have a son. After long discussions, we have decided that there is no other alternative: if we insist that Hsiu-liang be faithful to me, the whole family will be without support. The only solution is to "get a husband to support a husband." We have, therefore, consulted a matchmaker, and it has been arranged for Hsiu-liang to be married to Wu Chiu-sheng's first-born son, Wu Chin-wen, who will come to live with us. We have, on this day, agreed that there will be no betrothal presents, but that Wu Chin-wen should provide the family with twenty dollars a month to help with expenses. Regardless of how many sons and grandsons Wu and Hsiu-liang may have, they will be heirs to the Wang family as well as to the Wu family.

This document is written evidence of the irrevocable agreement reached by both parties.

Signed, Wang Yün-fa, in the third month of 1869
  Preparer of document: Cheng Ju-shui
  Matchmaker: Mrs. Ch'en (née Hsü)
Witnesses: Wang Chin-fa and Wang T'ien-fu

※

This document is drawn up for and signed by Lin Yuchang.

My wife (whose maiden name is Ch'en) and I have a first-born daughter by the name of Wang-lien, who is now fifteen years old. Although she is of age, we have not yet promised her to anyone. Pressed by extreme poverty, we now wish to give her away to become a concubine.

We have entrusted the matter to a matchmaker, and it has been arranged that she should become the concubine of Wu Min-kuan. The two parties and the matchmaker have discussed the matter and agreed on the price of 200 silver dollars. The money has been received in full by me, Lin Yu-chang, and the matchmaker. Now Wu Min-kuan is free to select an auspicious day for the marriage. I hereby swear that this girl is the first-born daughter of me and my wife; that she has not been engaged to anyone else; and that she is not a kidnaped child or of suspicious origin. If any question concerning the girl's birth should arise, I am solely responsible, and the buyer will not be involved. I sincerely hope my daughter will give birth to many sons for the Wu family. Once she is sold, all her ties with me are cut.

This written evidence of the sale is to be kept by the buyer for later purposes.

It is clearly recorded here that, on this day, Lin Yu-chang and the matchmaker have personally received in full 200 silver dollars.

Signed, the father of the girl, Lin Yu-chang in the twelfth month of 1886
  Preparer of document: Ts'ai Wen-ping
  Matchmaker: K'ang A-hsiu
Witness: (the girl's mother) Ch'en

"An Address to Two Hundred Million Fellow Countrywomen"

CH'IU CHIN

The westerners pouring into China after its defeat in the Opium Wars, brought western ideals with them. Born in the Treaty Port of Amoy, Ch'iu Chin (1875–1907) moved to Beijing shortly before the Boxer Rebellion (1898–1900) that convinced her to join China's infant nationalist movement. A trip to Japan in 1903 exposed her to feminist ideology. Returning to Shanghai as a teacher in 1906, she participated in a failed attempt to establish a republic and was executed in 1907. In this article for a modernizing magazine, she advised Chinese women to take their emancipation into their own hands.

Alas! The greatest injustice in this world must be the injustice suffered by our female population of two hundred million. If a girl is lucky enough to have a good father, then her childhood is at least tolerable. But if by chance her father is an ill-tempered and unreasonable man, he may curse her birth: "What rotten luck: another useless thing." Some men go as far as killing baby girls while most hold the opinion that "girls are eventually someone else's property" and treat them with coldness and disdain. In a few years, without thinking about whether it is right or wrong, he forcibly binds his daughter's soft, white feet with white cloth so that even in her sleep she cannot find comfort and relief until the flesh becomes rotten and the bones broken. What is all this misery for? Is it just so that on the girl's wedding day friends and neighbors will compliment him, saying, "Your daughter's feet are really small"? Is that what the pain is for?

But that is not the worst of it. When the time for marriage comes, a girl's future life is placed in the hands of a couple of shameless matchmakers and a family seeking rich and powerful in-laws. A match can be made without anyone ever inquiring whether the prospective bridegroom is honest, kind, or educated. On the day of the marriage the girl is forced into a red and green bridal sedan chair, and all this time she is not allowed to breathe one word about her future. After her marriage, if the man doesn't do her any harm, she is told that she should thank Heaven for her good fortune. But if the man is bad or he ill-treats her, she is told that her marriage is retribution for some sin committed in her previous existence. If she complains at all or tries to reason with her husband, he may get angry and beat her. When other people find out they will criticize, saying, "That woman is bad; she doesn't know how to behave like a wife." . . . When Heaven created people it never intended such injustice because if the world is without women, how can men be born? Why is there no justice for women? We constantly hear men say, "The human mind is just and we must treat people with fairness and equality." Then why do they greet women like black slaves from Africa? How did inequality and injustice reach this state?

Dear sisters, you must know that you'll get nothing if you rely upon others. You must go out and get things for yourselves. In ancient times when decadent scholars came out with such nonsense as "men are exalted, women are lowly," "a virtuous woman is one without talent," and "the husband guides the wife," ambitious and spirited women should have organized and opposed them. . . . It seems clear now that it was we women who abandoned our responsibilities to ourselves and felt content to let men do everything for us. As long as we could live in comfort and leisure, we let men make all the decisions for us. When men said we were useless, we became useless; when they said we were incapable, we stopped questioning them even when our entire female sex had reached slave status. . . . And as slaves, how can we escape repression? Whom can we blame but ourselves since we have brought this on ourselves? I feel very sad talking about this, yet I feel that there is no need for me to elaborate since all of us are in the same situation.

I hope that we all shall put aside the past and work hard for the future. Let us all put aside our former selves and be resurrected as complete human beings. Those of you who are old, do not call yourselves old and useless. If your husbands want to open schools, don't stop them; if your good sons want to study abroad, don't hold them back. Those among us who are middle-aged, don't hold back your husbands lest they lose their ambition and spirit and fail in their work. After your sons are born, send them to schools. You must do the same for your daughters and, whatever you do, don't bind their feet. As for you young girls among us, go to school if you can. If not, read and study at home. Those of you who are rich, persuade your husbands to open schools, build factories, and contribute to charitable organizations. Those of you who are poor, work hard and help your husbands. Don't be lazy, don't eat idle rice. These are what I hope for you. You must know that when a country is near destruction, women cannot rely on the men any more because they aren't even able to protect themselves. If we don't take heart now and shape up, it will be too late when China is destroyed.

Sisters, we must follow through on these ideas!

Natural Selection

CHARLES DARWIN

The British naturalist Charles Darwin (1809–1882) produced the single most influential scientific work of the nineteenth century. On the Origin of Species by Means of Natural Selection *(1859) laid out a theory of evolution that had as great an impact outside the scientific community as within it. Drawing on Lyell's theories of the evolution of the earth itself, the population principles of Malthus, and his own observations as a naturalist aboard H.M.S. Beagle, Darwin presented a picture of life forms constantly changing in response to the mechanical forces of nature. In the face of mounting controversy, Darwin published the* Descent of Man *(1871), specifically incorporating humanity into this picture. The cornerstone of modern biology, Darwin's theory of Natural Selection remains controversial outside the scientific community for the challenges it poses to humanity's traditional view of its origins.*

The Origin of Species (1859)

In considering the Origin of Species, it is quite conceivable that a naturalist, reflecting on the mutual affinities of organic beings, on their embryological relations, their geographical distribution, geological succession, and other such facts, might come to the conclusion that species had not been independently created, but had descended, like varieties, from other species. Nevertheless, such a conclusion, even if well founded, would be unsatisfactory, until it could be shown how the innumerable species inhabiting this world would have been modified, so as to acquire that perfection of structure and co-adaptation which justly excites our admiration. . . .

Variation under Nature

Any variation which is not inherited is unimportant for us. But the number and diversity of inheritable deviations of structure, both those of slight and those of considerable physiological importance, are endless. . . . Every one must have heard of cases of albinism, prickly skin, hairy bodies, &c., appearing in several members of the same family. If strange and rare deviations of structure are really inherited, less strange and commoner deviations may be freely admitted to be inheritable. Perhaps, the correct way of viewing the whole subject would be, to look at the inheritance of every character whatever as the rule, and non-inheritance as the anomaly. . . .

The many slight differences which appear in the offspring from the same parents, or which it may be presumed have thus arisen, from being observed in the individuals of the same species inhabiting the same confined locality, may be called individual differences. No one supposes that all the individuals of the same species are cast in the same actual mold. These individual differences . . . afford materials for natural selection to act on and accumulate. . . .

Struggle for Existence

. . . it may be asked, how is it that varieties [or variations], which I have called incipient species, become ultimately converted into good and distinct species which in most cases obviously differ from each other far more than do the varieties of the same species. . . . All these results . . . follow from the struggle for life. Owing to this struggle, variations, however slight and from whatever cause proceeding, if they be in any degree profitable to the individuals of a species, in their infinitely complex relations to other organic beings and to their physical conditions of life, will tend to the preservation of such individuals, and will generally be inherited by their offspring. The offspring, also, will thus have a better chance of surviving, for, of the many individuals of any species which are periodically born, but a small number can survive. I have called this principle, by which each slight variation, if useful, is preserved, by the term Natural Selection. . . . But the expression often used by Mr. Herbert Spencer of the Survival of the Fittest, is more accurate, and is sometimes equally convenient. . . .

Geometrical Ratio of Increase

A struggle for existence inevitably follows from the high rate at which all organic beings tend to increase. Every being, which during its natural lifetime produces several eggs or seeds, must suffer destruction during some period of its life, and during some season or occasional year, otherwise, on the principal of geometrical increase, its numbers would quickly become so inordinately great that no country could support the product. Hence, as more individuals are produced than can possibly survive, there must in every case be a struggle for existence, either one individual with another of the same species, or with the individuals of distinct species, or with the physical conditions of life. It is the doctrine of Malthus applied with manifold force to the whole animal and vegetable kingdoms; for in this case there can be no artificial increase of food, and no prudential restraint from marriage. . . .

Nature of the Checks to Increase

The amount of food for each species of course gives the extreme limit to which each can increase; but very frequently it is not the obtaining food, but the serving as prey to other animals, which determines the average numbers of a species. . . .

The action of climate seems at first sight to be quite independent of the struggle for existence; but in so far as climate chiefly acts in reducing food, it brings on the most severe struggle between the individuals, whether of the same or of distinct species, which subsist on the same kind of food. . . .

When a species, owing to highly favorable circumstances, increases inordinately in numbers in a small tract, epidemics . . . often ensue; and here we have a limiting check independent of the struggle for life. But even some of these so-called epidemics appear to be due to parasitic worms . . . and here comes in a sort of struggle between the parasite and its prey. . . .

Natural Selection

Several writers have misapprehended or objected to the term Natural Selection. Some have even imagined that natural selection induces variability, whereas it implies only the preservation of such variations as arise and are beneficial to the being under its conditions of life. . . . Others have objected that the term selection implies conscious choice in the animals which become modified. . . . but I mean by Nature, only the aggregate action and product of many natural laws, and by laws the sequence of events as ascertained by us. . . .

On the Degree to Which Organization Tends to Advance

Natural Selection acts exclusively by the preservation and accumulation of variations, which are beneficial under the organic and inorganic conditions to which each creature is exposed at all periods of life. The ultimate result is that each creature tends to become more and more improved in relations to its conditions. This improvement inevitably leads to the gradual advancement of the organization of the greater number of living beings throughout the world. . . . If we take as the standard of high organization, the amount of differentiation and specialization of the several organs in each being when adult (and this will include the advancement of the brain for intellectual purposes), natural selection clearly leads towards this standard. . . .

But it may be objected that if all organic beings thus tend to rise in the scale, how is it that throughout the world a multitude of the lowest forms still exist. . . . On our theory the continued existence of lowly organisms offers no difficulty; for natural selection, or the survival of the fittest, does not necessarily include progressive development—it only takes advantage of such variations as arise and are beneficial to each creature under its complex relations of life. And it may be asked what advantage, as far as we can see, would it be

174

to an infusorian animalcule—to an intestinal worm—or even to an earth-worm, to be highly organized. . . .

The Geological Record

Geology assuredly does not reveal any such finely-graduated organic chain; and this, perhaps, is the most obvious and serious objection which can be urged against the theory. The explanation lies, as I believe, in the extreme imperfection of the geological record. . . .

Independently of our not finding fossil remains of such infinitely numer-ous connecting links, it may be objected that time cannot have sufficed for so great an amount of organic change, all changes having been effected slowly. It is hardly possible for me to recall to the reader who is not a practical geol-ogist, the facts leading the mind feebly to comprehend the lapse of time. He who can read Sir Charles Lyell's grand work on the Principles of Geology, which the future historian will recognize as having produced a revolution in natural science, and yet does not admit how vast have been the past periods of time, may at once close this volume. . . .

Recapitulation and Conclusion

The similar framework of bones in the hand of a man, wing of a bat, fin of the porpoise, and leg of the horse,—the same number of vertebrae forming the neck of the giraffe and of the elephant,—and innumerable other such facts, at once explain themselves on the theory of descent with slow and slight successive modifications. . . . Analogy would lead me one step farther, namely, to the belief that all animals and plants are descended from some one prototype. . . .

Authors of the highest eminence seem to be fully satisfied with the view that each species has been independently created. To my mind it accords bet-ter with what we know of the laws impressed on matter by the Creator, that the production and extinction of the past and present inhabitants of the world should have been due to secondary causes, like those determining the birth and death of the individual. When I view all beings not as special cre-ations, but as the lineal descendants of some few beings which lived long before the first bed of the Cambrian system was deposited, they seem to me to become ennobled. . . . As all the living forms of life are the lineal descen-dants of those which lived long before the Cambrian epoch [600 million years ago], we may feel certain that the ordinary succession by generation has never once been broken, and that no cataclysm has desolated the whole world. Hence we may look with some confidence to a secure future of great length. And as natural selection works solely by and for the good of each being, all corporeal and mental endowments will tend to progress towards perfection. . . . There is grandeur in this view of life, with its several powers, having been originally breathed by the Creator into a few forms or into one; and that, whilst this planet has gone cycling on according to the fixed law of gravity, from so simple a beginning endless forms most beautiful and most wonderful have been, and are being evolved.

❧

The Descent of Man (1871)

He who is not content to look . . . at the phenomena of nature as disconnected, cannot any longer believe that man is the work of a separate act of creation. . . .

We have seen that man incessantly presents individual differences in all parts of his body and in his mental faculties. These differences or variations seem to be induced by the same general causes, and to obey the same laws as with the lower animals. In both cases similar laws of inheritance prevail. Man tends to increase at a greater rate than his means of subsistence; consequently he is occasionally subjected to a severe struggle for existence, and natural selection will have affected whatever lies within its scope. . . .

By considering the embryological structure of man—the homologies which he presents with the lower animals—the rudiments which he retains—and the reversions to which he is liable, we can partly recall in imagination the former condition of our early progenitors; and can approximately place them in their proper place in the zoological series. We thus learn that man is descended from a hairy, tailed quadruped, probably arboreal in its habits and an inhabitant of the Old World. This creature, if its whole structure had been examined by a naturalist, would have been classed among the Quadrumana [apes, baboons and monkeys having all four feet adapted to function as hands], as surely as the still more ancient progenitor of the Old and New World monkeys. The Quadrumana and all the higher mammals are probably derived from an ancient marsupial animal and this through a long line of diversified forms, from some amphibian-like creature, and this again from some fish-like animal. . . .

The high standard of our intellectual powers and moral disposition is the greatest difficulty which presents itself, after we have been driven to this conclusion on the origin of man. But every one who admits the principle of evolution must see that the mental powers of the higher animals, which are the same in kind with those of man, though so different in degree, are capable of advancement. . . . [and] No one doubts that they are of the utmost importance to animals in a state of nature. Therefore, the conditions are favorable for their development through natural selection. The same conclusion may be extended to man; the intellect must have been all-important to him, even at a very remote period, as enabling him to invent and use language, to make weapons, tools, traps, etc., whereby with the aid of his social habits he long ago became the most dominant of all living creatures. . . .

The main conclusion arrived at in this work, namely, that man is descended from some lowly organized form, will, I regret to think, be highly distasteful to many. But there can hardly be a doubt that we are descended from barbarians. . . . He who has seen a savage in his native land will not feel much shame, if forced to acknowledge that the blood of some more humble creature flows in his veins. For my own part I would as soon be descended from that heroic little monkey who braved his dreaded enemy in order to save the life of his keeper, or from that old baboon, who, descending from the mountains, carried away in triumph his young comrade from a crowd of astonished dogs—as from a savage who delights to torture his enemies, offers up bloody sacrifices, practices infanticide without remorse, treats his wives like slaves, knows no decency, and is haunted by the grossest superstitions.

On the Inequality of the Races (1853–1855)

JOSEPH ARTHUR, COMTE DE GOBINEAU

The misapplication of theories of biological evolution to the social sciences is most often referred to as "Social Darwinism" even though these ideas predated the publication of Darwin's Origin of Species *(1859). According to "Social Darwinists," "success" was proof of superiority. While sympathizing with the plight of the "unfit," they dismissed attempts to "better" the unfortunate as being hopelessly unscientific, akin to trying to fight gravity. Transforming the idea of competition between species into competition between cultures (or races), Joseph Arthur, Comte de Gobineau (1816–1882) produced* On the Inequality of the Races *(1853–1855). He believed race mixing guaranteed the inevitable decline of the superior Aryan (white) race. Of little influence in his native France, de Gobineau's work later proved very popular with German nationalists. Similar theories of racial superiority were used to justify European imperialism.*

I think that the word *degenerate*, when applied to a people, should mean and does mean that the people no longer has the same intrinsic value as it once before had, because it no longer has the same blood in its veins, continual adulteration having gradually affected the quality of that blood, In other words, though the nation bears the name given by its founders, the name no longer connotes the same race. . . . [The *degenerate* man] is only a very distant kinsman of those he still calls his ancestors. He, and his civilization with him, will certainly die on the day when the primordial race-unit is so broken up and swamped by the influx of foreign elements, that its effective qualities no longer have a sufficient freedom of action. . . .

I have been able to distinguish, on physiological grounds alone, three great and clearly marked types, the black, the yellow and the white. . . .

The Negroid variety is the lowest, and stands at the foot of the ladder. The animal character, that appears in the shape of the pelvis, is stamped on the Negro from birth, and foreshadows his destiny. His intellect will always move within a very narrow orbit. He is not however a mere brute, for behind his low receding brow, in the middle of his skull, we can see signs of a powerful energy, however crude its objects. If his mental faculties are dull or even non-existent, he often has an intensity of desire, and so of will, which may be called terrible. Many of his senses, especially taste and smell, are developed to an extent unknown to the other two races. . . .

The yellow man has little physical energy, and is inclined to apathy; he commits none of the strange excesses so common among Negroes. His desires are feeble, his will-power obstinate rather than violent . . . He is practical, in the narrowest sense of the word. He does not dream or theorize; he invents little, but can appreciate and take over what is useful to him. His whole desire is to live in the easiest and most comfortable way possible. Every founder of a civilization would wish the backbone of his society, his middle class, to consist of such men. But no civilized society could be created by them; they could not supply its nerve force, or set in motion the springs of beauty and action.

We come now to the white peoples. These are gifted with reflective energy, or rather with an energetic intelligence. They have a feeling for utility, but in an sense far wider and higher, more courageous and ideal, than the yellow races; a perseverance that takes account of obstacles and ultimately finds a means of overcoming them; a greater physical power, an extraordinary instinct for order, not merely as a guarantee of peace and tranquility, but as an indispensable means of self-preservation. At the same time, they have a remarkable, and even extreme, love of liberty, and are openly hostile to the formalism under which the Chinese are glad to vegetate, as well as to the strict despotism which is the only way of governing the Negro. . . .

It would be unjust to assert that every [racial] mixture is bad and harmful. . . . Artistic genius, which is equally foreign to each of the three great types, arose only after the intermarriage of white and black. . . .

I do not deny that these are good results. The world of art and great literature that comes from the mixture of blood, the improvement and ennoblement of inferior races—all these are wonders for which we must needs be thankful. The small have been raised. Unfortunately, the great have been lowered by the same process; and this is an evil that nothing can balance or repair. . . . The white race originally possessed a monopoly of beauty, intelligence and strength. By its union with other races, hybrids were created that were beautiful without strength, strong without intelligence, or, if intelligent, both weak and ugly.

On the Concentration of Wealth

WILLIAM GRAHAM SUMNER

American Professor William Graham Sumner (1840–1910) of Yale University was among those Social Darwinists who stressed the competition between individuals in each society (a variation on the biological competition between individual members of each species). He argued that monetary success or failure was, by itself, proof of an individual's "fitness" or lack thereof. Such arguments were not only being used to dismiss welfare programs but to campaign, as did members of the Eugenics movement, for the forced sterilization of the alcoholic, the prostitute, the mentally ill, and the destitute, all of whom, in this way of thinking, were polluting the societal gene pool.

I often see statements published, in which the objectors lay stress upon the great inequalities of fortune, and, having set forth the contrast between rich and poor, they rest their case. What law of nature, religion, ethics, or the state is violated by inequalities of fortune? The inequalities prove nothing. Others argue that great fortunes are won by privileges created by law and not by legitimate enterprise and ability. This statement is true, but it is entirely irrelevant; we have to discuss the concentration of wealth within the facts of the institutions, laws, usages, and customs which our ancestors have bequeathed to us and which we allow to stand. If it is proposed to change any of these parts of the societal order, that is a proper subject of discussion, but it is aside from the concentration of wealth. So long as tariffs, patents, etc., are part of the system in which we live, how can it be expected that people will not take advantage of them; what else are they for? As for franchises, a franchise is only an *x* until it has been developed. It never develops itself; it requires capital and skill to develop it. When the enterprise is in the full bloom of prosperity the objectors complain of it, as if the franchise, which never was anything but an empty place where something might be created, had been the completed enterprise. . . . modern methods offer very great opportunities, and the rewards of those men who can "size up" a situation and develop its controlling elements with sagacity and good judgment, are very great. It is well that they are so, because these rewards stimulate to the utmost all the ambitious and able men, and they make it certain that great and useful inventions will not long remain unexploited as they did formerly. . . . No man can acquire a million without helping a million men to increase their little fortunes all the way down through all the social grades. . . .

What matters it then that some millionaires are idle, or silly, or vulgar; that their ideas are sometimes futile and their plans grotesque, when they turn aside from money-making? How do they differ in this from any other class? The millionaires are a product of natural selection, acting on the whole body of men to pick out those who can meet the requirement of certain work to be done. In this respect they are just like the great statesmen, or scientific men, or military men. It is because they are thus selected that wealth—both their own and that intrusted to them—aggregates under their hands. Let one of them make a mistake and see how quickly the concentration gives way to dispersion. They may fairly be regarded as the naturally selected agents of society for certain work. They get high wages and live in luxury, but the bargain is a good one for society. There is the intensest competition for their place and occupation. This assures us that all who are competent for this function will be employed in it, so that the cost of it will be reduced to the lowest terms. . . .

The "Will to Power" and the Self-Evolution of the Superior Man

FRIEDRICH NIETZSCHE

The German philosopher Friedrich Nietzsche (1844–1900) rejected both the mechanical determinism of much evolutionary theory and the "mass" culture being created by nineteenth-century urbanization and technology. He used his training in ancient Greek civilization to propose a new departure for humanity. Rejecting the "slave mentality" he saw at the heart of Christianity and modern culture, he argued for a heroic self-transformation of humankind into übermenschen *(supermen), creative individuals able to bring joyous purpose to life in the face of the meaninglessness of the universe. Although Nietzsche did not advocate brute force, the Nazis cited his words to justify their aggressions, and he was reputed to be Adolf Hitler's favorite philosopher.*

Have you not heard of that madman who lit a lantern in the bright morning hours, ran to the market-place, and cried incessantly: "I am looking for God! I am looking for God!" As many of those who did not believe in God were standing together there, he excited considerable laughter. Have you lost him, then? said one. Did he lose his way like a child? said another. Or is he hiding? Is he afraid of us? Has he gone on a voyage? or emigrated? Thus they shouted and laughed. The madman sprang into their midst and pierced them with his glances.

"Where has God gone?" he cried. "I shall tell you. *We have killed him—you and I.* We are his murderers. But how have we done this? How were we able to drink up the sea? Who gave us the sponge to wipe away the entire horizon? What did we do when we unchained this earth from its sun? Whither is it moving now? Whither are we moving now? Away from all suns? Are we not perpetually falling? Backward, sideward, forward, in all directions? Is there any up or down left? Are we not straying as through an infinite nothing? Do we not feel the breath of empty space? Has it not become colder? Is not more and more night coming on all the time? Must not lanterns be lit in the morning? Do we not hear anything yet of the noise of the grave-diggers who are burying God? Do we not smell anything yet of God's decomposition? Gods too decompose. God is dead. God remains dead. And we have killed him. *How shall we, the murderers of all murderers, console ourselves?* That which was holiest and mightiest of all that the world has yet possessed has bled to death under our knives. Who will wipe this blood off us? With what water could we purify ourselves? What festivals of atonement, what sacred games shall we need to invent? Is not the greatness of this deed too great for us? *Must not we ourselves become gods simply to seem worthy of it?* There has never been a greater deed; and whoever shall be born after us-for the sake of this deed he shall be part of a higher history than all history hitherto."

There is a universal need to exercise some kind of power, or to create for one's self the appearance of some power, if only temporarily, in the form of intoxication.

There are men who desire power simply for the sake of the happiness it will bring; these belong chiefly to political parties. Other men have the same yearning, even when power means visible disadvantages, the sacrifice of their happiness, and well-being; they are the ambitious. Other men, again, are only like dogs in a manger, and will have power only to prevent its falling into the hands of others on whom they would then be dependent.

In this age of universal suffrage, in which everybody is allowed to sit in judgment upon everything and everybody, I feel compelled to re-establish the order of rank.

Man has one terrible and fundamental wish; he desires power, and this impulse, which is called freedom, must be the longest restrained. Hence ethics has instinctively aimed at such an education as shall restrain the desire for power; thus our morality slanders the would-be tyrant, and glorifies charity, patriotism, and the ambition of the herd.

Impotence to power,—how it disguises itself and plays the hypocrite, as obedience, subordination, the pride of duty and morality, submission, devotion, love (the idolization and apotheosis of the commander is a kind of compensation, and indirect self-enhancement). It veils itself further under fatalism and resignation, objectivity, self-tyranny, stoicism, asceticism, self-abnegation, hallowing. Other disguises are: criticism, pessimism, indignation, susceptibility, "beautiful soul," virtue, self-deification, philosophic detachment, freedom from contact with the world (the realization of impotence disguises itself as disdain).

Quanta of power alone determine rank and distinguish rank: nothing else does. . . .

The modicum of power which you represent decides your rank; all the rest is cowardice.

The advantages of standing detached from one's age.—Detached from the two movements, that of individualism and that of collectivist morality; for even the first does not recognize the order of rank, and would give one indi-

183

vidual the same freedom as another. My thoughts are not concerned with the degree of freedom which should be granted to the one or to the other or to all, but with the degree of power which the one or the other should exercise over his neighbor or over all; and more especially with the question to what extent a sacrifice of freedom, or even enslavement, may afford the basis for the cultivation of a *superior* type. In plain words, *how could one sacrifice the development of mankind* in order to assist a higher species than man to come into being. . . .

It is necessary for *higher* men to declare war upon the masses! In all directions mediocre people are joining hands in order to make themselves masters. Everything that pampers, that softens, and that brings the "people" or "woman" to the front, operates in favor of universal suffrage—that is to say, the dominion of *inferior* men. But we must make reprisals, and draw the whole state of affairs (which commenced in Europe with Christianity) to the light of day and to judgment.

A teaching is needed which is strong enough to work in a *disciplinary* manner; it should operate in such a way as to strengthen the strong and to paralyze and smash up the world-weary.

The annihilation of declining races. The decay of Europe. The annihilation of slave-tainted valuations. The dominion of the world as a means to the rearing of a higher type. The annihilation of the humbug which is called morality (Christianity has a hysterical kind of honesty in this regard: Augustine, Bunyan). The annihilation of universal suffrage—that is to say, that system by means of which the lowest natures prescribe themselves as a law for higher natures. The annihilation of mediocrity and its prevalence. (The one-sided, the individuals—peoples; constitutional plenitude should be aimed at by means of the coupling of opposites; to this end race-combinations should be tried.) The new kind of courage—no *a priori* truths (those who were accustomed to believe in something sought such truths!), but *free* submission to a ruling thought, which has its time; for instance, time conceived as the quality of space, etc. . . .

The question, and at the same time the task, is approaching with hesitation, terrible as Fate, but nevertheless inevitable: how shall the earth as a whole be ruled? And to what end shall man as a whole—no longer as a people or as a race—be reared and trained? . . .

[Men must seek a new morality, one that] would rear man upwards instead of to comfort and mediocrity; such a morality, with the intention of producing a ruling caste—the future lords of the earth—must, in order to be taught at all, introduce itself as if it were in some way correlated to the prevailing moral law, and must come forward under the cover of the latter's words and forms. But seeing that, to this end, a host of transitional and deceptive measures must be discovered, and that the life of a single individual stands for almost nothing in view of the accomplishment of such lengthy tasks and aims, the first thing that must be done is to rear a *new kind* of man in whom the duration of the necessary will and the necessary instincts is guaranteed for many generations. This must be a new kind of ruling species and caste—this ought to be quite as clear as the somewhat lengthy and not easily expressed consequences of this thought. The aim should be to prepare a *transvaluation of values* for a particularly strong kind of man, most highly gifted in intellect and will, and, to this end, slowly and cautiously to liberate in him a whole host of slandered instincts hitherto held in check: whoever meditates about this problem belongs to us, the free spirits. . . .

The same applies to certain insatiably ambitious artists who courageously and unconditionally fight against the gregarious animal for the special rights of higher men, and subdue all herd-instincts and precautions of more exceptional minds by their seductive art. Thirdly and lastly, we should include in this group all those critics and historians by whom the discovery of the Old World, which has begun so happily—this was the work of the *new* Columbus, of German intellect—will be courageously *continued* (for we still stand in the very first stages of this conquest). . . .

I am writing for a race of men which does not yet exist: for "the lords of the earth." In Plato's *Theages* the following passage will be found: "Every one of us would like if possible to be master of mankind; if possible, a God." This *attitude* of mind must be reinstated in our midst.

Englishmen, Americans, and Russians.

Topic VII

World War I and Its Consequences

The Greatness of War (1897)

HEINRICH VON TREITSCHKE

A firm supporter of Bismarck's nationalism, Heinrich von Treitschke (1834–1896) was Germany's leading historian. His master work, five volumes covering German History in the Nineteenth Century *(1879–1894) argued that the "state was the basis of all national life" and that Prussia was Germany's natural leader. As can be seen in this selection from a posthumously published collection of his university lectures (*On Politics, *1897), Treitschke extolled the "sacred power" of war. He believed the British were "moneygrubbing," Jews "were of no further use to the world," and Germany was destined to dominate Europe. His influence extended far into the twentieth century, inspiring leaders from Kaiser Wilhelm II to Adolf Hitler.*

One must say with the greatest determination: War is for an afflicted people the only remedy. When the State exclaims: My very existence is at stake! Then social self-seeking must disappear and all party hatred be silent. The individual must forget his own *ego* and feel himself a member of the whole, he must recognize how negligible is his life compared with the good of the whole. Therein lies the greatness of war that the little man completely vanishes before the great thought of the State. The sacrifice of nationalities for one another is nowhere invested with such beauty as in war. At such a time the corn is separated from the chaff. All who lived through [the Franco-Prussian War in] 1870 will understand the saying of Neibuhr [a Prussian historian] with regard to [Napoleon's defeat in] 1813, that he then experienced the "bliss of sharing with all his fellow citizens, with the scholar and the ignorant, the one common feeling—no man who enjoyed this experience will to his dying day forget how loving, friendly and strong he felt."

It is indeed political idealism which fosters war, whereas materialism rejects it. What a perversion of morality to want to banish heroism from human life. The heroes of a people are the personalities who fill the youthful souls with delight and enthusiasm, and amongst authors we as boys and youths admire most those whose words sound like a flourish of trumpets. He who cannot take pleasure therein, is too cowardly to take up arms himself for his fatherland. All appeal to Christianity in this matter is perverted. The Bible states expressly that the man in authority shall wield the sword; it states likewise that: "Greater love hath no man than this that he giveth his life for his friend." Those who preach the nonsense about everlasting peace do no understand the life of the Aryan race, the Aryans are before all brave. They have always been men enough to protect by the sword what they had won by the intellect. . . .

To the historian who lives in the realm of the Will, it is quite clear that the furtherance of an everlasting peace is fundamentally reactionary. He sees that to banish war from history would be to banish all progress and becoming. It is only the periods of exhaustion, weariness and mental stagnation that have dallied with the dream of everlasting peace. . . . The living God will see to it that war returns again and again as a terrible medicine for humanity.

Austria's Ultimatum to Serbia
(July 23, 1914)

*On June 28, 1914, Gavrilo Princip (1895–1918), a member of Nar-
odna Odbrana (the Black Hand), a secret society of Bosnian Serb
nationalists, assassinated the heir to the Austrian throne in an attempt
to win Bosnia's independence from Austrian control. Austria's investigation of the crime revealed the complicity of members of the Serbian
government. Preparing to launch a punitive expedition against Serbia,
the Austrian government issued this ultimatum, certain that the Serbian government would refuse to meet its demands, but equally sure
that Germany would support Austria's planned attack on Serbia. What
Austria failed to anticipate was Serbia's successful bid for Russian support in rejecting the ultimatum.*

The results brought by the inquiry no longer permit the Imperial and
Royal Government to maintain the attitude of patient tolerance which it has
observed for years toward those agitations which center at Belgrade and are
spread thence into the territories of the Monarchy. Instead, these results
impose upon the Imperial and Royal Government the obligation to put an
end to those intrigues, which constitute a standing menace to the peace of
the Monarchy.

In order to attain this end, the Imperial and Royal Government finds itself
compelled to demand that the Serbian Government give official assurance
that it will condemn the propaganda directed against Austria-Hungary, that
is to say, the whole body of the efforts whose ultimate object it is to separate
from the Monarchy territories that belong to it; and that it will obligate itself
to suppress with all the means at its command this criminal and terroristic
propaganda.

In order to give these assurances a character of solemnity, the Royal
Serbian Government will publish on the first page of its official organ of
July 26/13, the following declaration:

> The Royal Serbian Government condemns the propaganda directed
> against Austria-Hungary, that is to say, the whole body of the efforts
> whose ultimate object it is to separate from the Austro-Hungarian

Monarchy territories that belong to it, and it most sincerely regrets the dreadful consequences of these criminal transactions.

The Royal Serbian Government regrets that Serbian officers and officials should have taken part in the above-mentioned propaganda and thus have endangered the friendly and neighborly relations, to the cultivation of which the Royal Government had most solemnly pledged itself by its declaration of March 31, 1909.

The Royal Government, which disapproves and repels every idea and every attempt to interfere in the destinies of the population of whatever portion of Austria-Hungary, regards it as its duty most expressly to call the attention of the officers, officials, and the whole population of the Kingdom to the fact that for the future it will proceed with the utmost rigor against any persons who shall become guilty of any such activities, activities to prevent and to suppress which, the Government will bend every effort.

This declaration shall be brought to the attention of the Royal army simultaneously by an order of the day from His Majesty the King, and by publication in the official organ of the army. The Royal Serbian Government will furthermore pledge itself:

1. to suppress every publication which shall incite to hatred and contempt of the Monarchy, and the general tendency of which shall be directed against the territorial integrity of the latter;

2. to proceed at once to the dissolution of the *Narodna Odbrana*, to confiscate all of its means of propaganda, and in the same manner to proceed against the other unions and associations in Serbia which occupy themselves with propaganda against Austria-Hungary; the Royal Government will take such measures as are necessary to make sure that the dissolved associations may not continue their activities under other names or in other forms;

3. to eliminate without delay from public instruction whether connected with the teaching corps or with the methods of teaching, that serves or may serve to nourish the propaganda against Austria-Hungary;

4. to remove from the military and administrative service in general all officers and officials who have been guilty of carrying on the propaganda against Austria-Hungary, whose names the Imperial and Royal Government reserves the right to make known to the Royal Government when communicating the material evidence now in its possession;

5. to agree to the cooperation in Serbia of the organs of the imperial and Royal Government in the suppression of the subversive movement directed against the integrity of the Monarchy;

6. to institute a judicial inquiry against every participant in the conspiracy of the twenty-eighth of June who may be found in Serbian territory; the organs of the Imperial and Royal Government delegated

for this purpose will take part in the proceedings held for this purpose;

7. to undertake with all haste the arrest of Major Voislav Tankositch and of one Milan Ciganovitch, a Serbian official, who have been compromised by the results of the inquiry;

8. by efficient measures to prevent the participation of Serbian authorities in the smuggling of weapons and explosives across the frontier; to dismiss from the service and to punish severely those members of the Frontier Service at Schabats and Losnitza who assisted the authors of the crime of Sarajevo to cross the frontier;

9. to make explanations to the Imperial and Royal Government concerning the unjustifiable utterances of high Serbian functionaries in Serbia and abroad, who, without regard for their official position, have not hesitated to express themselves in a manner hostile toward Austria-Hungary since the assassination of the twenty-eighth of June;

10. to inform the Imperial and Royal Government without delay of execution of the measures comprised in the foregoing points.

The Imperial and Royal Government awaits the reply of the Royal Government by Saturday, the twenty-fifth instant, at 6 P.M., at the latest. . . .

The "Willy-Nicky" Telegrams
(29 July–1 August, 1914)

The conflict between Austria (backed by Germany) and Serbia (backed by Russia) threatened to engulf Europe as each state called in promises of support made by allies in the Triple Alliance or the Triple Entente. Each government called up troops and struck threatening postures in a flood of diplomatic dispatches while attempting to find a way to avoid a European-wide war. This exchange of telegrams between Kaiser Wilhelm II of Germany and Tsar Nicholas II of Russia bears witness to the increasing frustration of the negotiators. Cousins by marriage (Nicholas' wife Alexandra and Wilhelm were both grandchildren of Britain's Queen Victoria), the Kaiser and the Tsar referred to each other as "Willy" and "Nicky," but their personal friendship could not prevent their countries from ending up on opposite sides in the coming World War.

Tsar Nicholas II to Kaiser Wilhelm II, July 29, 1:00 A.M: [K332]

Am glad you are back. An *ignoble* war has been declared to a *weak* country. The *indignation* in Russia *shared fully by me is enormous*. I foresee that very soon I shall be *overwhelmed* by the pressure forced upon me and be *forced* to take extreme measures which will *lead to war*. To try and avoid such a calamity as a European war I beg you in the name of our old friendship to do what you can to *stop* your allies from *going too far*.

Nicky

❀

Kaiser Wilhelm II to Tsar Nicholas II, July 29, 1:45 A.M.[This telegram dated July 28 and the previous telegraph crossed]: [K335]

It is with the gravest concern that I hear of the impression which the action of Austria against Serbia is creating in your country. The unscrupulous agitation that has been going on in Serbia for years has resulted in the outrageous crime, to which Archduke Francis Ferdinand fell a victim. The spirit that led Serbians to murder their own king and his wife still dominates the country. You will doubtless agree with me that we both, you and me, have a common interest as well as all Sovereigns to insist that all the persons

194

morally responsible for the dastardly murder should receive their deserved punishment. In this case politics plays no part at all.

On the other hand, I fully understand how difficult it is for you and your Government to face the drift of your public opinion. Therefore, with regard to the hearty and tender friendship which binds us both from long ago with firm ties, I am exerting my utmost influence to induce the Austrians to deal straightly to arrive to a satisfactory understanding with you. I confidently hope that you will help me in my efforts to smooth over difficulties that may still arise.

Your very sincere and devoted friend
and cousin, Willy.

❀

Kaiser Wilhelm II to Tsar Nicholas II, July 29, 6:30 P.M. [K359]

I received your telegram and share your wish that peace should be maintained. But as I told you in my first telegram, I cannot consider Austria's action against Serbia an "Ignoble" war. Austria knows by experience that Serbian promises on paper are wholly unreliable. I understand its action must be judged as trending to get full guarantee that the Serbian promises shall become real facts. This my reasoning is borne out by the statement of the Austrian cabinet that, Austria does not want to make any territorial conquests at the expense of Serbia. I therefore suggest that it would be quite possible for Russia to remain a spectator of the Austro-Serbian conflict without involving Europe in the most horrible war she ever witnessed. I think a direct understanding between your Government and Vienna possible and desirable, and as I already telegraphed to you, my Government is continuing its exercises to promote it. Of course military measures on the part of Russia would be looked upon by Austria as a calamity we both wish to avoid and jeopardize my position as mediator which I readily accepted on your appeal to my friendship and my help.

Willy

❀

Tsar Nicholas II to Kaiser Wilhelm II, July 29, 8:20 P.M. [K366]

Thanks for your telegram conciliatory and friendly. Whereas official message presented today by your ambassador to my minister was conveyed in a very different tone. Beg you to explain this divergency! It would be right to give over the Austro-Serbian problem to the Hague conference. Trust in your wisdom and friendship.

Your loving Nicky

❀

Tsar Nicholas II to Kaiser Wilhelm II, July 30, 1:20 A.M. [K390]

Thank you heartily for your quick answer. Am sending Tatischev this evening with instructions. The military measures which have now come into force were decided five days ago for reasons of defense on account of Austria's preparations. I hope from all my heart that these measures won't in any way interfere with your part as mediator which I greatly value. We need your strong pressure on Austria to come to an understanding with us.

Nicky

❧

Kaiser Wilhelm II to Tsar Nicholas II, July 30, 1:20 A.M. [K420]

Best thanks for telegram. It is quite out of the question that my ambassadors language could have been in contradiction with the tenor of my telegram. Count Pourtalès was instructed to draw the attention of your government to the danger & grave consequences involved by a mobilization; I said the same in my telegram to you. Austria has only mobilized against Serbia & only a part of her army. If, as it is now the case, according to the communication by you & your Government, Russia mobilizes against Austria, my role as mediator you kindly intrusted me with, & which I accepted at you[r] express prayer, will be endangered if not ruined. The whole weight of the decision lies solely on you[r] shoulders now, who have to bear the responsibility for Peace or War.

Willy

❧

Kaiser Wilhelm II to Tsar Nicholas II, July 31 [K480]

On your appeal to my friendship and your call for assistance began to mediate between your and the Austro-Hungarian Government. While this action was proceeding your troops were mobilized against Austro-Hungary, my ally. Thereby, as I have already pointed out to you, my mediation has been made almost illusory.

I have nevertheless continued my action. I now receive authentic news of serious preparations for war on my Eastern frontier. Responsibility for the safety of my empire forces preventive measures of defense upon me. In my endeavors to maintain the peace of the world I have gone to the utmost limit possible. The responsibility for the disaster which is now threatening the whole civilized world will not be laid at my door. In this moment it still lies in your power to avert it. Nobody is threatening the honour or power of Russia who can well afford to await the result of my mediation. My friendship for you and your empire, transmitted to me by my grandfather on his deathbed has always been sacred to me and I have honestly often backed up Russia when she was in serious trouble especially in her last war.

The peace of Europe may still be maintained by you, if Russia will agree to stop the military. measures which must threaten Germany and Austro-Hungary.

Willy

🏵

Tsar Nicholas II to Kaiser Wilhelm II, July 31, 2:52 pm [This and the previous telegram crossed]: [K487]

I thank you heartily for your mediation which begins to give one hope that all may yet end peacefully. It is *technically* impossible to stop our military preparations which were obligatory owing to Austria's mobilization. We are far from wishing war. As long as the negotiations with Austria on Serbia's account are taking place my troops shall not make any *provocative* action. I give you my solemn word for this. I put all my trust in God's mercy and hope in your successful mediation in Vienna for the welfare of our countries and for the peace of Europe.

Your affectionate Nicky

🏵

Tsar Nicholas II to Kaiser Wilhelm II, August 1, 2:06 pm: [K546]

I received your telegram. Understand you are obliged to mobilize but wish to have the same guarantee from you as I gave you, that these measures do not mean war and that we shall continue negotiating for the benefit of our countries and universal peace deal to all our hearts. Our long proved friendship must succeed, with God's help, in avoiding bloodshed. Anxiously, full of confidence await your answer.

Nicky

🏵

Kaiser Wilhelm II to Tsar Nicholas II, August 1: [K600]

Thanks for your telegram. I yesterday pointed out to your government the way by which alone war may be avoided. Although I requested an answer for noon today, no telegram from my ambassador conveying an answer from your Government has reached me as yet. I therefore have been obliged to mobilize my army. Immediate affirmative clear and unmistakable answer from your government is the only, way to avoid endless misery. Until I have received this answer alas, I am unable to discuss the subject of your telegram. As a matter of fact I must request you to immediately order your troops on no account to commit the slightest act of trespassing over our frontiers.

Willy

Count Johann von Bernstorff to the U.S. Secretary of State, January 31, 1917: Unrestricted Submarine Warfare

Officially neutral, the United States attempted to sell to both sides after war broke out in August 1914, but British control of the seas and a campaign of anti-German propaganda soon shifted most American sales to the allied side. A German counter attempt to isolate Britain via a submarine blockade backfired when 128 Americans lost their lives in the German submarine attack on the British liner Lusitania on May 7, 1915. Germany was forced to back off its threats to torpedo ships attempting to land in Britain, but by January 1917 a surrounded Germany decided to return to unrestricted submarine warfare. Aware this risked bringing in the United States, German Ambassador Johann von Bernstorff (1862–1939) argued that Great Britain was the first to violate sea law and Germany faced dismemberment if it did not act, but the United States declared war on Germany on April 6, 1917.

Washington, January 31, 1917. Mr. Secretary of State: Your excellency was good enough to transmit to the Imperial Government a copy of the message which the President of the United States of America addressed to the Senate on the 22 instant. The Imperial Government has given it the earnest consideration which the President's statements deserve, inspired as they are by a deep sentiment of responsibility. It is highly gratifying to the Imperial Government to ascertain that the main tendencies of this important statement correspond largely to the desires and principles professed by Germany. These principles especially include self-government and equality of rights for all nations. Germany would be sincerely glad if in recognition of this principle countries like Ireland and India, which do not enjoy the benefits of political independence, should now obtain their freedom. The German people also repudiate all alliances which serve to force the countries into a competition for might and to involve them in a net of selfish intrigues. On the other hand, Germany will gladly cooperate in all efforts to prevent future wars. The freedom of the seas, being a preliminary condition of the free existence of nations and the peaceful intercourse between them, as well as the open door for the commerce of all nations, has always formed part of the leading principles of Germany's political program. All the more the Imperial Government regrets that the attitude of her enemies who are so entirely opposed to peace makes it impossible for the world at present to bring about the realization of these lofty ideals. Germany and her allies were ready to enter now into a discussion of peace and had set down as a basis the guaranty of existence, honor, and free development of their peoples. Their aims, as has been expressly stated in the note of December 12, 1916, were not directed towards the destruction or annihilation of their enemies and were according to their conviction perfectly compatible with the rights of the other nations. As to Belgium for which such warm and cordial sympathy is felt in the United States, the Chancellor had declared only a few weeks previously that its annexation had never formed part of Germany's intentions. The peace to be signed with Belgium was to provide for such conditions in that country, with which Germany desires to maintain friendly neighborly relations, that Belgium should not be used again by Germany's enemies for the purpose of instigating continuous hostile intrigues. Such precautionary measures are all the more necessary, as Germany's enemies have repeatedly stated not only in speeches delivered by their leading men, but also in the statutes of the economical conference in Paris, that it is their intention not to treat Germany as an equal, even after peace has been restored, but to continue their hostile attitude and especially to wage a systematical economical war against her.

The attempt of the four allied powers to bring about peace has failed owing to the lust of conquest of their enemies, who desired to dictate the conditions of peace. Under the pretense of following the principle of nationality our enemies have disclosed their real aims in this war, viz. to dismember and dishonor Germany, Austria-Hungary, Turkey, and Bulgaria. To the wish of reconciliation they oppose the will of destruction. They desire a fight to the bitter end.

A new situation has thus been created which forces Germany to new decisions. Since two years and a half England is using her naval power for a criminal attempt to force Germany into submission by starvation. In brutal contempt of international law the group of powers led by England does not only curtail the legitimate trade of their opponents but they also by ruthless pressure compel neutral countries either to altogether forego every trade not agreeable to the Entente powers or to limit it according to their arbitrary decrees. The American Government knows the steps which have been taken to cause England and her allies to return to the rules of international law and to respect the freedom of the seas. The English Government, however, insists upon continuing its war of starvation, which does not at all affect the military power of its opponents, but compels women and children, the sick and the aged to suffer, for their country, pains and privations which endanger the vitality of the nation. Thus British tyranny mercilessly increases the sufferings of the world indifferent to the laws of humanity, indifferent to the protests of the neutrals whom they severely harm, indifferent even to the silent longing for peace among England's own allies. Each day of the terrible struggle causes new destruction, new sufferings. Each day shortening the war will, On both sides, preserve the life of thousands of brave soldiers and be a benefit to mankind.

The Imperial Government could not justify before its own conscience, before the German people, and before history the neglect of any means destined to bring about the end of the war. Like the President of the United States the Imperial Government had hoped to reach this goal by negotiations. After the attempts to come to an understanding with the Entente powers have been answered by the latter with the announcement of an intensified continuation of the war, the Imperial Government—in order to serve the welfare of mankind in a higher sense and not to wrong its own people— is now compelled to continue the fight for existence, again forced upon it, with the full employment of all the weapons which are at its disposal.

Sincerely trusting that the people and Government of the United States will understand the motives for this decision and its necessity, the Imperial Government hopes that the United States may view the new situation from the lofty heights of impartiality and assist, on their part, to prevent further misery and avoidable sacrifice of human life.

Enclosing two memoranda regarding the details of the contemplated military measures at sea, I remain [etc.]

J. Bernstorff

Memorandum:

After bluntly refusing Germany's peace offer, the Entente powers stated in their note addressed to the American Government that they are determined to continue the war in order to deprive Germany of German provinces in the West and the East, to destroy Austria-Hungary, and to annihilate Turkey. In waging war with such aims, the Entente allies are violating all rules of international law, as they prevent the legitimate trade of neutrals with the Central powers, and of the neutrals among themselves. Germany has, so far, not made unrestricted use of the weapon which she possesses in her submarines. Since the Entente powers, however, have made it impossible to come to an understanding based upon equality of rights of all nations, as proposed by the Central powers, and have instead declared only such a peace to be possible which shall be dictated by the Entente allies and shall result in the destruction and humiliation of the Central powers, Germany is unable further to forego the full use of her submarines. The Imperial Government, therefore, does not doubt that the Government of the United States will understand the situation thus forced upon Germany by the Entente allies' brutal methods of war and by their determination to destroy the Central powers, and that the Government of the United States will further realize that the now openly disclosed intentions of the Entente allies give back to Germany the freedom of action which she reserved in her note addressed to the Government of the United States on May 4, 1916.

Under these circumstances Germany will meet the illegal measures of her enemies by forcibly preventing after February 1, 1917, in a zone around Great Britain, France, Italy, and in the eastern Mediterranean all navigation, that of neutrals included, from and to England and from and to France, etc., etc. All ships met within that zone will be sunk.

The Imperial Government is confident that this measure will result in a speedy termination of the war and in the restoration of peace which the Government of the United States has so much at heart. Like the Government of the United States, Germany and her allies had hoped to reach this goal by negotiations. Now that the war, through the fault of Germany's enemies, has to be continued, the Imperial Government feels sure that the Government of the United States will understand the necessity of adopting such measures as are destined to bring about a speedy end of the horrible and useless bloodshed. The Imperial Government hopes all the more for such an understanding of her position, as the neutrals have under the pressure of the Entente powers, suffered, great losses, being forced by them either to give tip their entire trade or to limit it according to conditions arbitrarily determined by Germany's enemies in violation of international law.

"Dulce et Decorum est" (1917)

WILFRED OWEN

Wilfred Owen (1893–1918), a lieutenant in the British armed forces, won the Military Cross for heroism only a month before he died in battle during the last week of the war. His poems were published posthumously in 1920. This one, describing a poison gas attack, ends with the Latin motto "Dulce et Decorum est pro patria mori." It means "Pleasing and right it is to die for one's country."

Bent double, like old beggars under sacks,
Knock-kneed, coughing like hags, we cursed through sludge,
Till on the haunting flares we turned our backs
And towards our distant rest began to trudge.
Men marched asleep. Many had lost their boots
But limped on, blood-shod. All went lame; all blind;
Drunk with fatigue; deaf even to the hoots
Of tired, outstripped Five-Nines that dropped behind.

Gas! GAS! Quick, boys!—An ecstasy of fumbling,
Fitting the clumsy helmets just in time;
But someone was still yelling out and stumbling,
And flound'ring like a man in fire or lime. . .
Dim, through the misty panes and thick green light,
As under a green sea, I saw him drowning.
In all my dreams, before my helpless sight,
He plunges at me, guttering, choking, drowning.

If in some smothering dreams you too could pace
Behind the wagon that we flung him in,
And watch the white eyes writhing in his face,
His hanging face, like a devil's sick of sin;
If you could hear, at every jolt, the blood
Come gargling from the froth-corrupted lungs,

Obscene as cancer, bitter as the cud
Of vile, incurable sores on innocent tongues,
My friend, you would not tell with such high zest,
To children ardent for some desperate glory
The old lie: *Dulce et decorum est*
Pro patria mori.

The Fourteen Points (1918)

WOODROW WILSON

As an eventual Allied victory in "the Great War" became increasingly likely, Allied leaders began to construct their versions of the anticipated peace. President Woodrow Wilson (1856–1924) of the United States believed deeply that international cooperation could prevent all future wars and so "make the world safe for democracy." He laid out his vision of a settlement that would prevent future wars in Fourteen Points, a speech delivered to Congress on January 8, 1918. Wilson's program for peace brought Germany to the bargaining table and secured an armistice on November 18, but America's allies—France, Great Britain, and Italy—had different views of an appropriate settlement. French Premier Georges Clemenceau (1841–1929) quipped that "God gave us Ten Commandments—and we broke them. Wilson gave us Fourteen Points—we shall see!"

It will be our wish and purpose that the processes of peace, when they are begun, shall be absolutely open, and that they shall involve and permit henceforth no secret understandings of any kind. The day of conquest and aggrandizement is gone by; so is also the day of secret covenants entered into in the interest of particular Governments and likely at some unlooked-for moment to upset the peace of the world. It is this happy fact, now clear to the view of every public man whose thoughts do not still linger in an age that is dead and gone, which makes it possible for every nation whose purposes are consistent with justice and the peace of the world to avow now or at any other time the objects it has in view.

We entered this war because violations of right had occurred which touched us to the quick and made the life of our own people impossible unless they were corrected and the world secured once for all against their recurrence. What we demand in this war, therefore, is nothing peculiar to ourselves. It is that the world be made fit and safe to live in; and particularly that it be made safe for every peace-loving nation which, like our own, wishes to live its own life, determine its own institutions, be assured of justice and fair dealing by the other peoples of the world as against force and selfish aggression. All the peoples of the world are in effect partners in this interest, and for our own part we see very clearly that unless justice be done to others it will not be done to us. The program of the world's peace, therefore, is our program; and that program, the only possible program, as we see it, is this:

I. Open covenants of peace, openly arrived at, after which there shall be no private international understandings of any kind but diplomacy shall proceed always frankly and in the public view.

II. Absolute freedom of navigation upon the seas, outside territorial waters, alike in peace and in war, except as the seas may be closed in whole or in part by international action. . . .

III. The removal, so far as possible, of all economic barriers and the establishment of an equality of trade conditions among all the nations consenting to the peace and associating themselves for its maintenance.

IV. Adequate guarantees given and taken that national armaments will be reduced to the lowest point consistent with domestic safety.

V. A free, open-minded, and absolutely impartial adjustment of all colonial claims, based upon a strict observance of the principle that in determining all such questions of sovereignty the interests of the populations concerned must have equal weight with the equitable claims of the government whose title is to be determined.

VI. The evacuation of all Russian territory and such a settlement of all questions affecting Russia as will secure the best and freest cooperation of the other nations of the world in obtaining for her an unhampered and unembarrassed opportunity for the independent determination of her own political development and national policy and assure her of a sincere welcome into the society of free nations under institutions of her own choosing; and, more than a welcome, assistance also of every kind that she may need and may herself desire. The treatment accorded Russia by her sister nations in the months to come will be the acid test of their good will, of their comprehension of her needs as distinguished from their own interests, and of their intelligent and unselfish sympathy.

VII. Belgium, the whole world will agree, must be evacuated and restored, without any attempt to limit the sovereignty which she enjoys in common with all other free nations. No other single act will serve as this will serve to restore confidence among the nations in the laws which they have themselves set and determined for the government of their relations with one another. Without this healing act the whole structure and validity of international law is forever impaired.

VIII. All French territory should be freed and the invaded portions restored, and the wrong done to France by Prussia in 1871 in the matter of Alsace-Lorraine, which has unsettled the peace of the world for nearly fifty years, should be righted, in order that peace may once more be made secure in the interest of all.

IX. A readjustment of the frontiers of Italy should be effected along clearly recognizable lines of nationality.

X. The peoples of Austria-Hungary, whose place among the nations we wish to see safeguarded and assured, should be accorded the freest opportunity of autonomous development.

XI. Rumania, Serbia, and Montenegro should be evacuated; occupied territories restored; Serbia accorded free and secure access to the sea; and the relations of the several Balkan states to one another determined by friendly counsel along historically established lines of allegiance and nationality; and international guarantees of the political and economic independence and territorial integrity of the several Balkan states should be entered into.

XII. The Turkish portions of the present Ottoman Empire should be assured a secure sovereignty, but the other nationalities which are now under Turkish rule should be assured an undoubted security of life and an absolutely unmolested opportunity of autonomous development, and the Dardanelles should be permanently opened as a free passage to the ships and commerce of all nations under international guarantees.

XIII. An independent Polish state should be erected which should include the territories inhabited by indisputably Polish populations, which should be assured a free and secure access to the sea, and whose political and economic independence and territorial integrity should be guaranteed by international covenant.

XIV. A general association of nations must be formed under specific covenants for the purpose of affording mutual guarantees of political independence and territorial integrity to great and small states alike.

In regard to these essential rectifications of wrong and assertions of right we feel ourselves to be intimate partners of all the governments and peoples associated together against the Imperialists. We cannot be separated in interest or divided in purpose. We stand together until the end.

For such arrangements and covenants we are willing to fight and to continue to fight until they are achieved; but only because we wish the right to prevail and desire a just and stable peace such as can be secured only by removing the chief provocations to war, which this program does remove. We have no jealousy of German greatness, and there is nothing in this program that impairs it. We grudge her no achievement or distinction of learning or of pacific enterprise such as have made her record very bright and very enviable. We do not wish to injure her or to block in any way her legitimate influence or power. We do not wish to fight her either with arms or with hostile arrangements of trade if she is willing to associate herself with us and the other peace-loving nations of the world in covenants of justice and law and fair dealing. We wish her only to accept a place of equality among the peoples of the world—the new world in which we now live,—instead of a place of mastery.

Neither do we presume to suggest to her any alteration or modification of her institutions. But it is necessary, we must frankly say, and necessary as a preliminary to any intelligent dealings with her on our part, that we should know whom her spokesmen speak for when they speak to us, whether for the

Reichstag majority or for the military party and the men whose creed is imperial domination.

We have spoken now, surely, in terms too concrete to admit of any further doubt or question. An evident principle runs through the whole program I have outlined. It is the principle of justice to all peoples and nationalities, and their right to live on equal terms of liberty and safety with one another, whether they be strong or weak. Unless this principle be made its foundation no part of the structure of international justice can stand. The people of the United States could act upon no other principle; and to the vindication of this principle they are ready to devote their lives, their honor, and everything that they possess. The moral climax of this the culminating and final war for human liberty has come, and they are ready to put their own strength, their own highest purpose, their own integrity and devotion to the test.

The War Guilt Clause: Article 231, Treaty of Versailles (1919)

When the representatives of the new German Republic arrived at the Palace of Versailles on June 28, 1919, to sign the peace treaty formally ending World War I, they did not find an agreement based on the principles outlined by American President Woodrow Wilson in his "Fourteen Points" speech (1918), but a series of penalties imposed on Germany largely to satisfy France's desire to strip Germany of the power of ever attacking France again. Those penalties—an army limited to 100,000, a navy without submarines, no air force, loss of its colonies and some of its own territory, a demilitarized zone within its own boundaries, and massive reparations—were severe enough, but most resented by the German people was the clause in the Treaty of Versailles forcing Germany to agree that the whole war had been its fault.

Article 231. The Allied and Associated Governments affirm and Germany accepts the responsibility of Germany and her allies for causing all the loss and damage to which the Allied and Associated Governments and their nationals have been subjected as a consequence of the war imposed upon them by the aggression of Germany and her allies.

The Economic Consequences
of the Peace (1919)

JOHN MAYNARD KEYNES

British economist John Maynard Keynes (1883–1946) is best known for his General Theory (1936), the book that launched macroeconomics. But he was also one of the British Treasury officials who provided economic analysis for the writers of the Treaty of Versailles (1919) and the most prominent dissenter from the Treaty's harsh terms. Resigning his government post in disgust, he wrote The Economic Consequences of the Peace *(1919), predicting a cycle of hyperinflation, global depression, and global war set off by the exorbitant reparations imposed on Germany and the Allied failure to forgive war debts. Within twenty years, his predictions had come to pass. As yet unaware of the birth of Fascism, Keynes's only error in 1919 was to expect the next world war to be set off by a Communist revolution.*

The Treaty [of Versailles] includes no provisions for the economic rehabilitation of Europe,—nothing to make the defeated Central Empires into good neighbors, nothing to stabilize the new States of Europe, nothing to reclaim Russia; nor does it provide in any way a compact of economic solidarity amongst the Allies themselves; no arrangement was reached at Paris for restoring the disordered finances of France and Italy, or to adjust the systems of the Old World and the New.

The Council of Four paid no attention to these issues, being preoccupied with others,—Clemenceau to crush the economic life of his enemy, Lloyd George to do a deal and bring home something which would pass muster for a week, the [U.S.] President to do nothing that was not just and right. It is an extraordinary fact that the fundamental economic problems of a Europe starving and disintegrating before their eyes, was the one question in which it was impossible to arouse the interest of the Four. Reparation was their main excursion into the economic field, and they settled it as a problem of theology, of politics, of electoral chicane, from every point of view except that of the economic future of the States whose destiny they were handling. . . .

The essential facts of the situation, as I see them, are expressed simply. Europe consists of the densest aggregation of population in the history of the world. This population is accustomed to a relatively high standard of life, in which, even now, some sections of it anticipate improvement rather than deterioration. In relation to other continents Europe is not self-sufficient; in particular it cannot feed itself. Internally the population is not evenly distributed, but much of it is crowded into a relatively small number of dense industrial centers. This population secured for itself a livelihood before the war, without much margin of surplus, by means of a delicate and immensely complicated organization, of which the foundations were supported by coal, iron, transport, and an unbroken supply of imported food and raw materials from other continents. By the destruction of this organization and the interruption of the stream of supplies, a part of this population is deprived of its means of livelihood. . . . The danger confronting us, therefore, is the rapid depression of the standard of life of the European populations to a point which will mean actual starvation for some (a point already reached in Russia and approximately reached in Austria). Men will not always die quietly. For starvation, which brings to some lethargy and a helpless despair, drives other temperaments to the nervous instability of hysteria and to a mad despair. And these in their distress may overturn the remnants of organization, and submerge civilization itself in their attempts to satisfy desperately the overwhelming needs of the individual. This is the danger against which all our resources and courage and idealism must now co-operate. . . .

The final consideration influencing the reader's attitude to this proposal must, however, depend on his view as to the future place in the world's progress of the vast paper entanglements which are our legacy from war finance both at home and abroad. The war has ended with every one owing every one else immense sums of money. Germany owes a large sum to the Allies; the Allies owe a large sum to Great Britain; and Great Britain owes a large sum to the United States. The holders of war loan in every country are owed a large sum by the State; and the State in its turn is owed a large sum by these and other taxpayers. The whole position is in the highest degree artificial, misleading, and vexatious. We shall never be able to move again, unless we can free our limbs from these paper shackles. A general bonfire is so great a necessity that unless we can make of it an orderly and good tempered affair in which no serious injustice is done to any one, it will, when it comes at last, grow into a conflagration that may destroy much else as well. . . .

The only safeguard against [a Communist] Revolution in Central Europe is indeed the fact that, even to the minds of men who are desperate, Revolution offers no prospect of improvement whatever. There may, therefore, be ahead of us a long, silent process of semi-starvation, and of a gradual, steady lowering of the standards of life and comfort. The bankruptcy and decay of Europe, if we allow it to proceed, will affect every one in the long-run, but perhaps not in a way that is striking or immediate.

This has one fortunate side. We may still have time to reconsider our courses and to view the world with new eyes. For the immediate future events are taking charge, and the near destiny of Europe is no longer in the hands of any man. The events of the coming year will not be shaped by the deliberate acts of statesmen, but by the hidden currents, flowing continually beneath the surface of political history, of which no one can predict the outcome. In one way only can we influence these hidden currents,—by setting in motion those forces of instruction and imagination which change *opinion*. The assertion of truth, the unveiling of illusion, the dissipation of hate, the enlargement and instruction of men's hearts and minds, must be the means. . . .

. . .To the formation of the general opinion of the future I dedicate this book.

The Balfour Declaration (1917)

ARTHUR JAMES BALFOUR

Throughout World War I, Great Britain made overtures to subject groups within the Ottoman Empire in order to obtain post-war influence in a region vital to its imperial ambitions. The British government sent letters to Arab leaders promising them an independent Arab state if they rebelled against their Turkish overlords, while secretly negotiating a treaty with France (the Sykes-Picot Agreement of 1916) to carve up the Middle East into British and French spheres of influence at war's end. To gain support abroad for Britain's war effort and to secure a friendly presence in Palestine, which virtually overlooked Britain's Suez Canal, British Foreign Secretary Arthur James Balfour (1848–1930) sent this letter to Edmond James Rothschild (1845–1934), a prominent supporter of Jewish migration to Palestine.

Foreign Office
November 2, 1917

Dear Lord Rothschild,

I have much pleasure in conveying to you, on behalf of His Majesty's Government, the following declaration of sympathy with Jewish Zionist aspirations, which has been submitted to, and approved by, the Cabinet.

"His Majesty's Government view with favor the establishment in Palestine of a national home for the Jewish people, and will use their best endeavors to facilitate the achievement of this object, it being clearly understood that nothing shall be done which may prejudice the civil and religious rights of existing non-Jewish communities in Palestine, or the rights and political status enjoyed by Jews in any other country."

I should be grateful if you would bring this declaration to the knowledge of the Zionist Federation.

Yours sincerely,
Arthur James Balfour

The Mandate System: Article 22, League of Nations Charter (1919)

The Treaty of Versailles *included a Charter for the League of Nations called for by President Woodrow Wilson. Article 22 of the League's Charter consigned colonial possessions stripped from Germany and Turkey to a schooling in western political systems by the world's "advanced nations." Nations holding mandates were to report the progress of their pupil states annually to a League Commission holding the final authority to decide when the mandate states were ready for independence. The League Commission was filled by the same great powers—including Britain and France—that held the mandates.*

Article 22: To those colonies and territories which as a consequence of the late war have ceased to be under the sovereignty of the States which formerly governed them and which are inhabited by peoples not yet able to stand by themselves under the strenuous conditions of the modern world, there should be applied the principle that the well-being and development of such peoples form a sacred trust of civilization and that securities for the performance of this trust should be embodied in this Covenant.

The best method of giving practical effect to this principle is that the tutelage of such peoples should be entrusted to advanced nations who by reason of their resources, their experience or their geographical position can best undertake this responsibility, and who are willing to accept it, and that this tutelage should be exercised by them as Mandatories on behalf of the League.

The character of the mandate must differ according to the stage of the development of the people, the geographical situation of the territory, its economic conditions and other similar circumstances.

Certain communities formerly belonging to the Turkish Empire have reached a stage of development where their existence as independent nations can be provisionally recognized subject to the rendering of administrative advice and assistance by a Mandatory until such time as they are able to stand alone. The wishes of these communities must be a principal consideration in the selection of the Mandatory.

Other peoples, especially those of Central Africa, are at such a stage that the Mandatory must be responsible for the administration of the territory under conditions which will guarantee freedom of conscience and religion, subject only to the maintenance of public order and morals, the prohibition of abuses such as the slave trade, the arms traffic and the liquor traffic, and the prevention of the establishment of fortifications or military and naval bases and of military training of the natives for other than police purposes and the defense of territory, and will also secure equal opportunities for the trade and commerce of other Members of the League.

There are territories, such as South-West Africa and certain of the South Pacific Islands, which, owing to the sparseness of their population, or their small size, or their remoteness from the centers of civilization, or their geographical contiguity to the territory of the Mandatory, and other circumstances, can be best administered under the laws of the Mandatory as integral portions of its territory, subject to the safeguards above mentioned in the interests of the indigenous population.

In every case of mandate, the Mandatory shall render to the Council an annual report in reference to the territory committed to its charge.

The degree of authority, control, or administration to be exercised by the Mandatory shall, if not previously agreed upon by the Members of the League, be explicitly defined in each case by the council.

A permanent Commission shall be constituted to receive and examine the annual reports of the Mandatories and to advise the Council on all matters relating to the observance of the mandates.

The Jewish State (1896)

THEODOR HERZL

The rising force of nationalism created great tensions between the Mandate populations and the governing powers. In Palestine, Great Britain was simply unable to cope with the competing nationalist aims of Palestine's Jewish and Arab populations. Jewish aspirations to a homeland were given their modern shape by Theodor Herzl (1860–1904). Herzl first encountered anti-Semitism during law school in Vienna, and saw the power of its venom to corrupt even democratic states as a journalist covering the Dreyfus trial in France. Herzl turned to Zionism, making the creation of a Jewish State *(1896) a lifelong goal. In this pamphlet he outlined the case for a Jewish national (rather than merely religious) identity. Herzl was willing to resettle Jews almost anywhere in the world, but most of his followers believed Palestine (the site of ancient Israel, or "Zion") was the only possible place for a Jewish state.*

The idea which I have developed in this pamphlet is a very old one: it is the restoration of the Jewish State. . . .

The Jewish question still exists. It would be foolish to deny it. It is a remnant of the Middle Ages, which civilized nations do not even yet seem able to shake off, try as they will. They certainly showed a generous desire to do so when they emancipated us. The Jewish question exists wherever Jews live in perceptible numbers. . . . We naturally move to those places where we are not persecuted, and there our presence produces persecution. This is the case in every country, and will remain so, even in those highly civilized—for instance, France—until the Jewish question finds a solution on a political basis. . . .

We are a people—one people.

We have honestly endeavored everywhere to merge ourselves in the social life of surrounding communities and to preserve the faith of our fathers. We are not permitted to do so. In vain are we loyal patriots, our loyalty in some places running to extremes; in vain do we make the same sacrifices of life and property as our fellow-citizens; in vain do we strive to increase the fame of our native land in science and art, or her wealth by trade and commerce. In countries where we have lived for centuries we are still cried down as strangers. . . .

[It might] be objected that I am giving a handle to Anti-Semitism when I say we are a people—one people; that I am hindering the assimilation of Jews where it is about to be consummated, and endangering it where it is an accomplished fact. . . .

But the distinctive nationality of Jews neither can, will, nor must be destroyed. It cannot be destroyed, because external enemies consolidate it. It will not be destroyed; this is shown during two thousand years of appalling suffering. It must not be destroyed, and that, as a descendant of numberless Jews who refused to despair, I am trying once more to prove in this pamphlet. Whole branches of Judaism may wither and fall, but the trunk will remain. . . .

Let the sovereignty be granted us over a portion of the globe large enough to satisfy the rightful requirements of a nation; the rest we shall manage for ourselves. . . .

Should the [European] Powers declare themselves willing to admit our sovereignty over a neutral piece of land, then . . . [we] will enter into negotiations for the possession of this land. Here two territories come under consideration, Palestine and Argentine. In both countries important experiments in colonization have been made, though on the mistaken principle of a gradual infiltration of Jews. An infiltration is bound to end badly. It continues till the inevitable moment when the native population feels itself threatened, and forces the Government to stop a further influx of Jews. Immigration is consequently futile unless we have the sovereign right to continue such immigration. . . .

Shall we choose Palestine or Argentine? We shall take what is given us, and what is selected by Jewish public opinion. . . .

Argentine is one of the most fertile countries in the world, extends over a vast area, has a sparse population and a mild climate. The Argentine republic would derive considerable profit from the cession of a portion of its territory to us. . . .

Palestine is our ever-memorable historic home. The very name of Palestine would attract our people with a force of marvelous potency. If His Majesty the Sultan were to give us Palestine, we could in return undertake to regulate the whole finances of Turkey. We should there form a portion of a rampart of Europe against Asia, an outpost of civilization as opposed to barbarism. We should as a neutral State remain in contact with all Europe, which would have to guarantee our existence. The sanctuaries of Christendom would be safeguarded by assigning them an extra-territorial status such as is well-known to the law of nations. We should form a guard of honor about these sanctuaries, answering for the fulfilment of this duty with our existence. This guard of honor would be the great symbol of the solution of the Jewish Question after eighteen centuries of Jewish suffering. . . .

The land which the Society of Jews will have secured by international law must, of course, be privately acquired. . . .

We have cradles, we have graves, and we alone know how Jewish hearts cling to the graves. Our cradles we shall carry with us—they hold our future, rosy and smiling. Our beloved graves we must abandon—and I think this abandonment will cost us more than any other sacrifice. But it must be so.

Economic distress, political pressure, and social obloquy have already driven us from our homes and from our graves. We Jews are even now constantly shifting from place to place, a strong current carrying us westward over the sea to the United States, where our presence is also not desired. And where will our presence be desired, so long as we are a homeless nation?

But we shall give a home to our people. And we shall give it, not by dragging them ruthlessly out of their sustaining soil, but rather by transplanting them carefully to a better ground.

Resolutions of the
General Syrian Congress (July 2, 1919)

Zionists won a major diplomatic victory in 1917 when British Foreign Minister Arthur Balfour (1848–1930) announced his country's support for "a national home for the Jewish people" in Palestine. Though Balfour also promised nothing would be done to "prejudice the civil and religious rights of existing non-Jewish communities in Palestine," Arab leaders saw only betrayal of Britain's earlier promise of an Arab state in exchange for an Arab rebellion against the Ottoman Turks during World War I. The post-war imposition of the mandate system only heightened the Arab sense of betrayal as this Syrian resolution shows. Despite Syria's invocation of President Wilson's Fourteen Points, Palestine was taken from Syrian and put under a British mandate, while France used its Syrian mandate to break off Lebanon, a region of mostly Christian Arabs within Syria.

We, the undersigned, members of the General Syrian Congress assembled in Damascus on the 2nd of July, 1919, and composed of delegations from the three zones, namely the southern, eastern, and western, and furnished with credentials duly authorizing us to represent the Moslem, Christian and Jewish inhabitants of our respective districts, have resolved to submit the following as defining the aspirations of the people who have chosen us to place them before the American section of the Inter-Allied Commission. With the exception of the fifth clause, which was passed by a large majority, the Resolutions which follow were all adopted unanimously:—

(1) We desire full and absolute political independence for Syria. . . .

(2) We desire the Government of Syria to be a constitutional monarchy based on principles of democratic and broadly decentralized rule which shall safeguard the rights of minorities, and we wish that Amir Faisal who has striven so nobly for our liberation and enjoyed our full confidence and trust be our King.

(3) In view of the fact that the Arab inhabitants of Syria are not less fitted or gifted than were certain other nations (such as the Bulgarians, Serbs, Greeks and Rumanians) when granted independence, we

protest against Article XXII of the Covenant of the League of Nations which relegates us to the standing of insufficiently developed races requiring the tutelage of a mandatory power.

(4) If, for whatever reason that might remain undisclosed to us, the Peace Conference were to ignore this legitimate protest, we shall regard the mandate mentioned in the Covenant of the League of Nations as implying no more that the rendering of assistance in the technical and economic fields without impairment of our absolute independence. We rely on President Wilson's declaration that his object in entering the War was to put an end to acquisitive designs for imperialistic purposes. In our desire that our country should not be made a field for colonization, and in the belief that the American nation is devoid of colonial ambitions and has no political designs on our country, we resolve to seek assistance in the technical and economic fields from the United States of America on the understanding that the duration of such assistance shall not exceed twenty years.

(5) In the event of the United States finding herself unable to accede to our request for assistance, we would seek it from Great Britain, provided always that it will not be allowed to impair the unity and absolute independence of our country and that its duration should not exceed the period mentioned in the preceding clause.

(6) We do not recognize to the French Government any right to any part of Syria, and we reject all proposals that France should give us assistance or exercise any authority in any portion of the country.

(7) We reject the claims of the Zionists for the establishment of a Jewish commonwealth in that part of southern Syria which is known as Palestine, and we are opposed to Jewish immigration into any part of the country. We do not acknowledge that they have a title, and we regard their claims as a grave menace to our national, political and economic life. Our Jewish fellow-citizens shall continue to enjoy the rights and to bear the responsibilities which are ours in common.

(8) We desire that there should be no dismemberment of Syria and no separation of Palestine or the coastal region in the west or the Lebanon from the mother country; and we ask that the unity of the country be maintained under any circumstances. . . .

(10) The basic principles proclaimed by President Wilson in condemnation of secret treaties cause us to enter an emphatic protest against any agreement to provide for the dismemberment of Syria. . . .

The lofty principles proclaimed by President Wilson encourage us to believe that the determining consideration in the settlement of our own future will be the real desires of our people; and that we may look to President Wilson and the liberal American nation, who are known for their sincere and generous sympathy with the aspirations of weak nations, for help in the fulfilment of our hopes. . . .

Tenets of the New Party (January 2, 1907)

BAL GANGADHAR TILAK

Indian troops had done loyal service in support of Britain during World War I; some 90,000 died in the Allied cause. But India received few concessions from Britain in return. Bal Gangadhar Tilak (1856–1920) led a movement of radical nationalists seeking to impose a Hindu identity on India while freeing it from British control. This 1907 speech lays down the methods to be used by his "New Party": economic boycotts, tax boycotts, a job boycott of the civil service, and a boycott of imperial military service.

There is no empire lost by a free grant of concessions by the rulers to the ruled. History does not record any such event. Empires are lost by luxury, by being too much bureaucratic or overconfident or from other reasons. But an empire has never come to an end by the rulers conceding power to the ruled. . . .

We have come forward with a scheme which if you accept, shall better enable you to remedy this state of things than the scheme of the Old School. Your industries are ruined utterly, ruined by foreign rule; your wealth is going out of the country and you are reduced to the lowest level which no human being can occupy. In this state of things, is there any other remedy by which you can help yourself? The remedy is not petitioning but boycott. We say prepare your forces, organize your power, and then go to work so that they cannot refuse you what you demand. . . . Are you prepared in this way to fight if your demand is refused? If you are, be sure you will not be refused; but if you are not, nothing can be more certain than that your demand will be refused, and perhaps, for ever. We are not armed, and there is, no necessity for arms either. We have a stronger weapon, a political weapon, in boycott.

We have perceived one fact, that the whole of this administration, which is carried on by a handful of Englishmen, is carried on with our assistance. We are all in subordinate service. The whole Government is carried on with our assistance and they try to keep us in ignorance of our power of co-operation between ourselves by which that which is in our own hands at present can be claimed by us and administered by us. The point is to have the entire control in our bands. I want to have the key of my house, and not merely one stranger turned out of it. Self-Government is our goal; we want a control over our administrative machinery. . . . What the New Party wants you to do is to realize the fact that your future rests entirely in your own hands. If you mean to be free, you can be free; if you do not mean to be free, you will fall and be for ever fallen. So many of you need not like arms; but if you have not the power of active resistance, have you not the power of self-denial and self-abstinence in such a way as not to assist the foreign Government to rule over you? This is boycott and this is what is meant when we say, boycott is a political weapon. We shall not give them assistance to collect revenue and keep peace. We shall not assist them in fighting beyond the frontiers or outside India with Indian blood and money. We shall not assist them in carrying on the administration of justice. We shall have our own courts, and when time comes we shall not pay taxes. . . .

This is the advice of the New Party. . . . We may have a step in advance next year, so that within a few years our principles will be recognized, and recognized to such an extent that the generations who come after us may consider us Moderates. This is the way in which a nation progresses. . . .

Hind Swaraj (Indian Home Rule, 1921)

MOHANDAS KARAMCHAND GANDHI

Tilak's party collapsed during World War I, but many of his tactics were later adopted by other Indian nationalists. Responding to escalating tensions, the British imposed the Rowlatt Acts (1919), empowering authorities to imprison without trial individuals suspected of sedition. These acts galvanized Mohandas Karamchand Gandhi (1869–1948), an Indian attorney already famous for his work on behalf of the Indian community in South Africa, to resist British rule. He called his even more thoroughgoing brand of non-cooperation satyagraha ("devotion to truth" or "soul-force"). Gandhi explained his rejection of western rule and western values in this pamphlet cast as a interview with himself.

Reader: Is there any historical evidence as to the success of what you have called soul-force or truth-force? No instance seems to have happened of any nation having risen through soul-force. I still think that the evil-doers will not cease doing evil without physical punishment.

Gandhi: . . .Thousands, indeed tens of thousands, depend for their existence on a very active working of this force. Little quarrels of millions of families in their daily lives disappear before the exercise of this force. Hundreds of nations live in peace. History does not and cannot take note of this fact. History is really a record of every interruption of the even working of the force of love or of the soul. Two brothers quarrel; one of them repents and re-awakens the love that was lying dormant in him; the two again begin to live in peace; nobody takes note of this. But if the two brothers, through the intervention of solicitors or some other reason take up arms or go to law—which is another form of the exhibition of brute force,—their doings would be immediately noticed in the press, they would be the talk of their neighbors and would probably go down to history. And what is true of families and communities is true of nations. There is no reason to believe that there is one law for families and another for nations. History, then, is a record of an interruption of the course of nature. Soul-force, being natural, is not noted in history.

Reader: According to what you say, it is plain that instances of this kind of passive resistance are not to be found in history. It is necessary to understand this passive resistance more fully. It will be better, therefore, if you enlarge upon it.

Gandhi: Passive resistance is a method of securing rights by personal suffering; it is the reverse of resistance by arms. When I refuse to do a thing that is repugnant to my conscience, I use soul-force. For instance, the Government of the day has passed a law which is applicable to me. I do not like it. If by using violence I force the Government to repeal the law, I am employing what may be termed body-force. If I do not obey the law and accept the penalty for its breach, I use soul-force. It involves sacrifice of self.

Everybody admits that sacrifice of self is infinitely superior to sacrifice of others. Moreover, if this kind of force is used in a cause that is unjust, only the person using it suffers. He does not make others suffer for his mistakes. Men have before now done many things which were subsequently found to have been wrong. No man can claim that he is absolutely in the right or that a particular thing is wrong because he thinks so, but it is wrong for him so long as that is his deliberate judgment. It is therefore meet that he should not do that which he knows to be wrong, and suffer the consequence whatever it may be. This is the key to the use of soul-force. . . .

Reader: When you speak of driving out Western civilization, I suppose you will also say that we want no machinery.

Gandhi: By raising this question, you have opened the wound I have received. When I read Mr. Dutt's *Economic History of India*, I wept; and as I think of it again my heart sickens. It is machinery that has impoverished India. It is difficult to measure the harm that Manchester has done to us. It is due to Manchester that Indian handicraft has all but disappeared.

But I make a mistake. How can Manchester be blamed? We wore Manchester cloth and this is why Manchester wove it. . . .

Machinery has begun to desolate Europe. Ruination is now knocking at the English gates. Machinery is the chief symbol of modern civilization; it represents a great sin.

The workers in the mills of Bombay have become slaves. The condition of the women working in the mills is shocking. When there were no mills, these women were not starving. If the machinery craze grows in our country, it will become an unhappy land. It may be considered a heresy, but I am bound to say that it were better for us to send money to Manchester and to use flimsy Manchester cloth than to multiply mills in India. By using Manchester cloth we only waste our money; but by reproducing Manchester in India, we shall keep our money at the price of our blood, because our very moral being will be sapped, and I call in support of my statement the very mill-hands as witnesses. And those who have amassed wealth out of factories are not likely to be better than other rich men. It would be folly to assume that an Indian Rockefeller would be better than the American Rockefeller. Impoverished India can become free, but it will be hard for any India made rich through immorality to regain its freedom. . . .

Reader: Are the mills, then, to be closed down?

Gandhi: That is difficult. It is no easy task to do away with a thing that is established. We, therefore, say that the nonbeginning of a thing is supreme wisdom. We cannot condemn mill-owners; we can but pity them. It would be too much to expect them to give up their mills, but we may implore them not to increase them. If they would be good they would gradually contract their business. They can establish in thousands of households the ancient and sacred handlooms and they can buy out the cloth that may be thus woven. Whether the mill-owners do this or not, people can cease to use machine-made goods.

Reader: You have so far spoken about machine-made cloth, but there are innumerable machine-made things. We have either to import them or to introduce machinery into our country.

Gandhi: Indeed, our gods even are made in Germany. What need, then, to speak of matches, pins and glassware? My answer can be only one. What did India do before these articles were introduced? Precisely the same should be done today. As long as we cannot make pins without machinery so long will we do without them. The tinsel splendor of glassware we will have nothing to do with, and we will make wicks, as of old, with home-grown cotton and use handmade earthen saucers for lamps. So doing, we shall save our eyes and money and support Swadeshi and so shall we attain Home Rule. . . .

San Min Chu I (Three Principles of the People, 1924–1925)

SUN YAT-SEN

Although China was neither a colony nor a mandate, its wealth was steadily siphoned off by western merchants taking advantage of the advantages resulting from the trade treaties of the nineteenth century. In 1911 Dr. Sun Yat-sen (1866–1925), western educated yet intensely nationalistic, led a successful uprising that gave China a republican government. But the new Republic struggled to unite an unraveling China behind it. Sun believed "Three Principles"—Nationalism, Democracy and Livelihood—were the keys to China's unification. In the last years of his life, Sun delivered a series of lectures explaining his understanding of these principles as a fusion of western and Chinese values. The lectures were gathered into book form (as the San Min Chu I) and published by his successor, Chiang Kai-shek (1887-1975).

What is the Principle of Nationalism? I would say briefly that the Principle of Nationalism is equivalent to the "doctrine of the state". . . .

Considering the law of survival of ancient and modem races, we want to save China and to preserve the Chinese race, we must certainly promote Nationalism. To make this principle luminous for China's salvation, we must first understand it clearly. The Chinese race totals four hundred million people; for the most part, the Chinese people are of the Han or Chinese race with common blood, common language, common religion, and common customs—a single, pure race.

What is the standing of our nation in the world? In comparison with other nations we have the greatest population and the oldest culture, of four thousand years' duration. We ought to be advancing in line with the nations of Europe and America. But the Chinese people have only family and clan groups; there is no national spirit. Consequently, in spite of four hundred million people gathered together in one China, we are in fact but a sheet of loose sand. We are the poorest and weakest state in the world, occupying the lowest position in international affairs; the rest of mankind is the carving knife and the serving dish, while we are the fish and the meat. . . .

After the Chinese Revolution, the Powers realized that it would be exceedingly difficult to dismember China by political force. A China which had learned how to revolt against the control of the Manchus would be sure some day to oppose the political control of the Powers. As this would put them in a difficult position, they are now reducing their political activities against China and are using economic pressure instead to keep us down. Economic oppression is more severe than political oppression. Political oppression is an apparent thing. The common people are easily provoked by political oppression but are hardly conscious of economic oppression. China has already endured several tens of years of economic domination from the Powers and nobody has felt irritated at all.

The result is that China is everywhere becoming a colony of the Powers. The people of the nation still think we are only a "semi-colony" and comfort themselves with this term, but in reality we are being crushed by the economic strength of the Powers to a greater degree than if we were a full colony. China is not the colony of one nation but of all, and we are not the slaves of one country but of all. . . .

. . . the family and clan sentiment of the Chinese is very deep-rooted. For instance, when two Chinese meet each other on the road, they will chat together and ask each other's "honorable surname" and "great name;" if they happen to find that they are of the same clan, they become wonderfully intimate and cordial and look upon each other as uncle or brother of the same family. If this worthy clan sentiment could be expanded we might develop nationalism out of clanism. . . . But to reach the desired end, it will be necessary for all to cooperate; if we can secure this cooperation, it should be easier for the Chinese to revive their nationalism than for people of other countries. For in the West the individual is the unit, and laws regarding the rights of parents and children, brothers and sisters, husbands and wives, aim at the protection of the individual; in lawsuits, no questions are asked about family conditions, only the morals of the individual are considered. The individual expands immediately into the state; between the individual and the state there is no common, firm, social unit. So in welding the citizens together into a state, foreign countries do not have the advantage that China has. Because China lays emphasis upon the family as well as upon the individual, the family head has to be consulted on all matters, a system which some approve and some criticize. But I think that in the relation between the citizens of China and their state, there must first be family loyalty, then clan loyalty, and finally national loyalty. . . .

To-day I am speaking about the people's sovereignty and I want you all to understand clearly what it really means. Unless we do understand clearly, we can never get rid of imperial ambitions among us, ambitions which will make even brethren in a cause and citizens of the same country fight one another. The whole land will be torn year after year with civil strife and there will be no end to the sufferings of the people. Because I wanted us to avert such calamities, I lifted up the banner of democracy as soon as the revolution began and determined that we should found a republic. When we have a real republic, who will be king? The people, over four hundred millions, will be king. This will prevent everybody from struggling for power and will reduce the war evil in China. . . .

The government's own power to transact business may be called the power to work, to work on behalf of the people. If the people are very powerful, whether the government can work or not and what kind of work it does will depend entirely upon the will of the people. If the government is very powerful, as soon as it starts work it can display great strength, and whenever the people want it to stop, it will have to stop. In a nutshell, if the people are really to have direct control over the power of government they must be able to command at any time the actions of the government. . . .

. . .If we now want to combine the best from China and the best from other countries and guard against all kinds of abuse in the future, we must take the three Western governmental powers-the executive, legislative, and judicial; add to them the old Chinese powers of examination and censorship and make a finished wall, a quintuple-power government. Such a government will be the most complete and the finest in the world, and a state with such a government will indeed be of the people, by the people, and for the people.

The Principle of Livelihood which the Kuomintang advocates is not merely a high ideal; it is also a driving force in society, it is the center of all historical movements. Only as this principle is applied can our social problems be solved, and only as our social problems are solved can mankind enjoy the greatest blessings. . . .

. . .All of us have a share in the distressing poverty of the Chinese people. There is no especially rich class, there is only a general poverty. The "inequalities between rich and poor," which the Chinese speak of are only differences within the poor class, differences in degree of poverty. As a matter of fact, the great capitalists of China, in comparison with the great foreign capitalists, are really poor; the rest of the poor people are extremely poor. Since China's largest capitalists are poor men out in the world, then all the Chinese people must be counted as poor. There are no great rich among us, only differences between the fairly poor and the extremely poor. How can we equalize this condition so that there will be no more extreme poverty? . . .

If we want to solve the livelihood problem in China and "by one supreme effort win eternal ease," it will not be enough to depend upon the regulation of capital. The income tax levied in foreign countries is one method of regulating capital. But have these other countries solved the livelihood problem? China cannot be compared to foreign countries; it is not sufficient for us to regulate capital. Other countries are rich while China is poor; other countries have a surplus of production while China is not producing enough. So China must not only regulate private capital, but she must also develop state capital and promote industry. First, we must begin to build means of communication, railroads and waterways, on a large scale. Second, we must open up mines. China is rich in minerals, but alas, they are buried in the earth! Third, we must hasten to foster manufacturing. Although China has a multitude of workers, yet she has not machinery and so cannot compete with other nations. Goods used throughout China depend upon other countries for manufacture and transportation hither, and consequently our economic rights and interests are simply leaking away. If we want to recover these rights and interests, we must quickly employ state power to promote industry, use machinery in production, and give employment to the workers of the whole nation. When all the workers have employment and can use machinery in production, then China will have a great, new source of wealth. If we do not use state power to build up these enterprises but leave them in the hands of private Chinese or of foreign business men, the result will be simply the expansion of private capital and the emergence of a great wealthy class with the consequent inequalities in society. . . .

The youthful scholars to-day who are pinning their faith on Marxism, and who, as soon as socialism is mentioned, advocate Marx's way for the solution of China's social and economic problems. But they fail to realize that China now is suffering from poverty, not from unequal distribution of wealth. In seeking a solution for our livelihood problem, we are not going to propose some impracticable and radical method and then wait until industry is developed. We want a plan which will anticipate dangers and forearm us against emergencies, which will check the growth of large private capital and prevent the social disease of extreme inequality between the rich and the poor. Such a plan will rightly solve our immediate social problems and will not be like first wearing furs and then hoping for the north winds.

As I said a little while ago, the regulations of capital to-day in China will not be enough to solve our livelihood problem. It will also be necessary to build up state capital. What does this mean? Simply the development of state industries. . . . If these three great industries—communications, mining, and manufacturing—should all begin to thrive in China, our annual income from them would be very great. If the industries are carried on by the state, the rights and privileges which they bring will be enjoyed by all the people. The people of the whole nation will then have a share in the profits of capital and will not be injured by capital. In the solution of the social problem, we have the same object in view as that in foreign countries: to make everybody contented and happy, free from suffering caused by the unequal distribution of wealth and property.

Our Three Principles of the People mean government "of the people, by the people, and for the people"—that is, a state belonging to all the people, a government controlled by all the people, and rights and benefits for the enjoyment of all the people.

The Pan-African Congress of 1919

"Pan-African" was a term coined by in 1899 by Henry Sylvester Williams (1868–1910), a Trinidadian attorney and African activist living in London. A meeting between Williams and Booker Taliaferro Washington (1856–1915) led to Washington's agreeing to sponsor the world's first Pan-African Congress in London in 1900. Washington did not attend the conference, but a young speaker who gained prominence there was William Edward Burghardt Du Bois (1868–1963). While African independence seemed a remote possibility before World War I, Woodrow Wilson's "Fourteen Points" speech gave activists like Du Bois high hopes for Africa's treatment in any post-war settlement. Those hopes led Du Bois to convene a new Pan-African Congress in Paris in 1919, only to find no western leaders willing to listen to the Manifesto it issued. But this Pan-African Congress and the series of Congresses springing from it helped nurture the African leaders who would one day bring their nations from colonial to independent status.

The resolutions of the Congress asked in part:

A. That the Allied and Associated Powers establish a code of law for the international protection of the natives of Africa, similar to the proposed international code for labor.

B. That the League of Nations establish a permanent Bureau charged with the special duty of overseeing the application of these laws to the political, social, and economic welfare of the natives.

C. The Negroes of the world demand that hereafter the natives of Africa and the peoples of African descent be governed according to the following principles:

1. **The land:** the land and its natural resources shall be held in trust for the natives and at all times they shall have effective ownership of as much land as they can profitably develop.

2. **Capital:** the investment of capital and granting of concessions shall be so regulated as to prevent the exploitation of the natives and the exhaustion of the natural wealth of the country. Concessions shall always be limited in time and subject to State control. The growing

social needs of the natives must be regarded and the profits taxed for social and material benefit of the natives.

3. **Labor:** slavery and corporal punishment shall be abolished and forced labor except in punishment for crime; and the general conditions of labor shall be prescribed and regulated by the State.

4. **Education:** it shall be the right of every native child to learn to read and write his own language, and the language of the trustee nation, at public expense, and to be given technical instruction in some branch of industry. The State shall also educate as large a number of natives as possible in higher technical and cultural training and maintain a corps of native teachers.

5. **The State:** the natives of Africa must have the right to participate in the government as fast as their development permits, in conformity with the principle that the government exists for the natives, and not the natives for the government. They shall at once be allowed to participate in local and tribal government, according to ancient usage, and this participation shall gradually extend, as education and experience proceed, to the higher offices of State; to the end that, in time, Africa be ruled by consent of the Africans. . . . Whenever it is proven that African natives are not receiving just treatment at the hands of any State or that any State deliberately excludes its civilized citizens or subjects of Negro descent from its body politic and cultural, it shall be the duty of the League of Nations to bring the matter to the notice of the civilized World.

Topic VIII

Mass Politics, Mass Societies, and the Expansion of State Power

❀

Leninism

VLADIMIR ILYICH LENIN

*One key to Communism's success in Russia was the doctrinal and orga-
nizational innovation in Marxism made by Vladimir Ilyich Lenin
(1870–1924). In* What is to be Done? *(1902), Lenin argued that
only a small organization of professional revolutionaries had the discipline to topple capitalism and establish proletarian control.* State and
Revolution *(1917) was written while Lenin was in hiding after the
failure of his first attempt to gain control of the Russian Revolution. It
explored the nature of the "dictatorship of the proletariat" that Marx
had seen as a transitional stage between capitalism and true socialism.*

What is to be Done (1902)?

The history of all countries shows that the working class, exclusively by its
own effort, is able to develop only trade union consciousness, *i.e,* it may itself
realize the necessity for combining in unions, for fighting against the
employers and for striving to compel the government to pass necessary labor
legislation, etc. . . .

It is only natural that a Social-Democrat, who conceives the political
struggle as being identical with the "economic struggle against the employers and the government," should conceive of an "organization of revolutionaries" as being more or less identical with an "organization of workers." . . .

[But the] political struggle carried on by the Social-Democrats is far more
extensive and complex than the economic struggle the workers carry on
against the employers and the government. Similarly (and indeed for that
reason), the organization of a revolutionary Social-Democratic Party must
inevitably *differ* from the organizations of the workers designed for the latter
struggle. A workers' organization must the first place be a trade organization;
secondly, it must be as wide as possible; and thirdly, it must be as public as
conditions will allow (here, and further on, of course, I have only autocratic
Russia in mind). On the other hand, the organizations of revolutionaries

must consist first and foremost of people whose profession is that of a revolutionary (that is why I speak of organizations of *revolutionaries,* meaning revolutionary Social-Democrats). In view of this common feature of the members of such an organization, *all distinctions as between workers and intellectuals,* and certain distinctions of trade and profession must be obliterated. Such an organization must of necessity be not too extensive and as secret as possible. . . .

I assert: (1) that no movement can be durable without a stable organization of leaders to maintain continuity; (2) that the more widely the masses are spontaneously drawn into the struggle and form the basis of the movement and participate in it, the more necessary is it to have such an organization, and the more stable must it be (for it is much easier for demagogues to sidetrack the more backward sections of the masses); (3) that the organization must consist chiefly of persons engaged in revolutionary activities as a profession; (4) that in a country with an autocratic government, the more we *restrict* the membership of this organization to persons who are engaged in revolutionary activities as a profession and who have been professionally trained in the art of combating the political police, the more difficult will it be to catch the organization, and (5) the *wider* will be the circle of men and women of the working class or of other classes of society able to join the movement and perform active work in it. . . .

The active and widespread participation of the masses will not suffer; on the contrary, it will benefit by the fact that a "dozen" experienced revolutionaries, no less professionally trained than the police, will centralize all the secret side of the work—prepare leaflets, work out approximate plans and appoint bodies of leaders for each urban district, for each factory district and to each educational institution, etc. . . .

Let no active worker take offense at these frank remarks, for as far as insufficient training is concerned, I apply them first and foremost to myself. I used to work in a circle that set itself great and all-embracing tasks; and every member of that circle suffered to the point of torture from the realization that we were proving ourselves to be amateurs at a moment in history when we might have been able to say, paraphrasing a well-known epigram: "Give us an organization of revolutionaries, and we shall overturn the whole of Russia!"

❧

State and Revolution (1917)

Between capitalist and Communist society [Marx states] *lies the period of the revolutionary transformation of the former into the latter. To this also corresponds a political transition period, in which the state can be no other than the revolutionary dictatorship of the proletariat. . . .*

What, then, is the relation of this dictatorship to democracy?

We have seen that the *Communist Manifesto* simply places side by side the two ideas: the "transformation of the proletariat into the ruling class" and the "establishment of democracy." On the basis of all that has been said above, one can define more exactly how democracy changes in the transition from capitalism to Communism.

In capitalist society, under the conditions most favorable to its development, we have more or less complete democracy in the democratic republic. But this democracy is always bound by the narrow framework of capitalist exploitation, and consequently always remains, in reality, a democracy for the minority, only for the possessing classes, only for the rich. Freedom in capitalist society always remains just about the same as it was in the ancient Greek republics: freedom for the slave-owners. The modern wage-slaves, owing to the conditions of capitalist exploitation, are so much crushed by want and poverty that "democracy is nothing to them," "politics is nothing to them"; that, in the ordinary peaceful course of events, the majority of the population is debarred from participating in social and political life. . . .

Democracy for an insignificant minority, democracy for the rich—that is the democracy of capitalist society. . . .

But from this capitalist democracy—inevitably narrow, subtly rejecting the poor, and therefore hypocritical and false to the core—progress does not march onward, simply, smoothly and directly, to "greater and greater democracy," as the liberal professors and petty-bourgeois opportunists would have us believe. No, progress marches onward, *i.e.*, towards Communism, through the dictatorship of the proletariat; it cannot do otherwise, for there is no one else and no other way to *break the resistance* of the capitalist exploiters.

But the dictatorship of the proletariat—*i.e.*, the organization of the vanguard of the oppressed as the ruling class for the purpose of crushing the oppressors—cannot produce merely an expansion of democracy. *Together* with an immense expansion of democracy which *for the first time* becomes democracy for the poor, democracy for the people, and not democracy for the rich folk, the dictatorship of the proletariat produces a series of restrictions of liberty in the case of the oppressors, the exploiters, the capitalists. We must crush them in order to free humanity from wage-slavery; their resistance must be broken by force; it is clear that where there is suppression there is also violence, there is no liberty. . . .

[As Engels said] "as long as the proletariat still *needs* the state, it needs it not in the interests of freedom, but for the purpose of crushing its antagonists; and as soon as it becomes possible to speak of freedom, then the state, as such, ceases to exist."

Democracy for the vast majority of the people, and suppression by force, *i.e.*, exclusion from democracy, of the exploiters and oppressors of the people—this is the modification of democracy during the *transition* from capitalism to Communism.

Only in Communist society, when the resistance of the capitalists has been completely broken, when the capitalists have disappeared, when there are no classes (*i.e.,* there is no difference between the members of society in their relation to the social means of production), *only* then "the state ceases to exist," and *"it becomes possible to speak of freedom."* Only then a really full democracy, a democracy without any exceptions, will be possible and will be realized. And only then will democracy itself begin to *wither away* due to the simple fact that, freed from capitalist slavery, from the untold horrors, savagery, absurdities and infamies of capitalist exploitation, people will gradually *become accustomed* to the observance of the elementary rules of social life that have been known for centuries and repeated for thousands of years in all school books; they will become accustomed to observing them without force, without compulsion, without subordination, without the *special apparatus* for compulsion which is called the state. . . .

Finally, only Communism renders the state absolutely unnecessary, for there is *no one* to be suppressed—"no one" in the sense of a class, in the sense of a systematic struggle with a definite section of the population. We are not Utopians, and we do not in the least deny the possibility and inevitability of excesses on the part of *individual persons,* nor the need to suppress *such excesses.* But, in the first place, no special machinery, no special apparatus of repression is needed for this; this will be done by the armed people itself, as simply and as readily as any crowd of civilized people, even in modern society, parts a pair of combatants or does not allow a woman to be outraged. And, secondly, we know that the fundamental social cause of excesses which consist in violating the rules of social life is the exploitation of the masses, their want and their poverty. With the removal of this chief cause, excesses will inevitably begin to *"wither away."* We do not know how quickly and in what succession, but we know that they will wither away. With their withering away, the state will also *wither away.*

Stalin against the Kulaks (1933)

JOSEF STALIN

In order to rebuild the Soviet economy in the aftermath of revolution and civil war, Lenin's New Economic Policy allowed Russian peasants to keep some private property. Determined to complete the moderniza-tion of the Soviet Union in a thoroughly Socialist (collective) fashion, Stalin (1879–1953) mounted a military campaign against the wealth-iest peasants (kulaks) who resisted the state's confiscation of their land and livestock. Though millions died in the "offensive" and the ensuing famines, Stalin boasted of his campaign in this 1933 work. The "pood" referred to in the reading is a Russian unit of weight equal to 36.11 pounds.

The characteristic feature of our work during the past year is that we, as a Party, as the Soviet power, (a) have developed an offensive on the whole front against the capitalist elements in the countryside; and (b) that this offensive, as is known, has led and is leading to very palpable and *positive* results.

What does that mean? It means that we have gone over from the policy of *restricting* the exploiting tendencies of the kulaks to the policy of *liquidat-ing* the kulaks as a class. This means that we have carried out, and are still carrying out, one of the most decisive changes in our whole policy.

Up till quite lately the Party pursued the policy of *restricting* the exploit-ing tendencies of the kulak. . . .

Was this policy correct? Yes, it was indubitably correct. Could we have undertaken an offensive against the kulak five, or three, years ago? Could we have counted on such an attack being successful at that time? No, we could not. That would have been the most dangerous adventurism! That would have been playing a dangerous game. We would certainly have come to grief and thereby strengthened the position of the kulaks. Why? Because we had not yet at our disposal those strongholds in the countryside in the shape of a broad network of soviet and collective farms upon which to rely in the deci-sive attack on the kulaks. Because at that time it was not possible for us to *substitute* the capitalist production of the kulak by socialist production in the shape of the collective and soviet farms. . . .

In 1927, the kulak produced over 600,000,000 poods of grain, 130,000,000 of which he disposed of by exchange outside of the rural districts. That is a fairly serious force with which one must reckon. And how much did our soviet and collective farms produce at that time? About 80,000,000 poods, of which they brought a little over 35,000,000 (marketable grain) to the market. Judge for yourselves whether at that time we were in a position to *replace* the production and the marketable grain of the kulaks by the production and the marketable grain of our soviet and collective farms. It is clear that we could not have done so. What would undertaking a decisive attack on the kulak under such conditions have meant? It would have meant inviting failure, strengthening the position of the kulaks and remaining without grain. . . .

What is the position at present? We now have an adequate material basis from which to deliver a blow against the kulak, to break his resistance, to liquidate him as a class, and to *replace* his production by the production of the soviet and collective farms. . . .

That is the change that has taken place in the economics of the country.

That is the shift of class forces that has recently taken place.

As you see, the material basis exists today which enables us to *replace* kulak production by that of the collective and soviet farms. That is why our attack on the kulaks has now met with undeniable success. That is how one must attack the kulaks, when it is a question of a real attack and not empty declamations.

That is why we recently gave up the policy of *restricting* the exploiting tendencies of the kulaks and adopted the policy of *liquidating the kulaks as a class.*

Now how shall we approach the policy of dekulakizing the kulaks? Can we permit it in the regions of mass collectivization? This question is put from various sides. A ridiculous question! We could not permit it as long as we were pursuing the policy of restricting their exploiting tendencies, as long as we were unable to commence a determined offensive against them and as long as were unable to replace their production by the production of the collective and soviet farms. At that time a policy which did not permit dekulakization of the kulaks was correct and necessary. Now the position is different. Today we are able to make a decisive attack on the kulak, to break his resistance, to liquidate him as a class and replace his production by the production of the collective and soviet farms. Today, dekulakizing is being carried out by the masses of poor and middle peasants themselves, who are carrying through mass collectivization. In the regions of mass collectivization, dekulakization today is no longer a simple administrative measure; it forms an integral part of the formation and development of collective farms. Therefore, it is ridiculous and nonsensical to expiate on this now. "Weep not for the hair when the head is off."

The Nature of Fascism (1935)

BENITO MUSSOLINI

After briefly embracing socialism, journalism, and teaching, Benito Mussolini (1883–1945) found the inspiration he was seeking during his army service in World War I. His military career was undistinguished, but he came to see violence as a positive force and democracy as futile. Bitterly disappointed with the lack of opportunity in post-war Italy, he organized an ultra-nationalist Fascist Party (1919) and entered politics. Three years later, his supporters marched on Rome and made Mussolini premier. As the self-styled Il Duce explained his doctrine in Fascism (1935), individual freedoms and liberal democracy had no place in the coming "century of authority."

Anti-individualistic, the Fascist conception of life stresses the importance of the State and accepts the individual only in so far as his interests coincide with those of the State, which stands for the conscience and the universal will of man as a historic entity. It is opposed to classical liberalism which arose as a reaction to absolutism and exhausted its historical function when the State became the expression of the conscience and will of the people. Liberalism denied the State in the name of the individual; Fascism reasserts the rights of the State as expressing the real essence of the individual. And if liberty is to be the attribute of living men and not of abstract dummies invented by individualistic liberalism, then Fascism stands for liberty, and for the only liberty worth having, the liberty of the State and of the individual within the State. The Fascist conception of the State is all-embracing; outside of it no human or spiritual values can exist, much less have value. Thus understood, Fascism, is totalitarian, and the Fascist State—a synthesis and a unit inclusive of all values—interprets, develops, and potentiates the whole life of a people.

No individuals or groups (political parties, cultural associations, economic unions, social classes) [exist] outside the State. Fascism is therefore opposed to Socialism to which unity within the State (which amalgamates classes into a single economic and ethical reality) is unknown, and which sees in history nothing but the class struggle. Fascism is likewise opposed to trade-unionism as a class weapon. But when brought within the orbit of the State, Fascism recognizes the real needs which gave rise to socialism and trade-unionism, giving them due weight in the guild or corporative system in which divergent interests are coordinated and harmonized in the unity of the State.

Grouped according to their several interests, individuals form classes; they form trade-unions when organized according to their several economic activities; but first and foremost they form the State, which is no mere matter of numbers, the sum of the individuals forming the majority. Fascism is therefore opposed to that form of democracy which equates a nation to the majority, lowering it to the level of the largest number; but it is the purest form of democracy if the nation be considered—as it should be—from the point of view of quality rather than quantity, as an idea, the mightiest because the most ethical, the most coherent, the truest, expressing itself in a people as the conscience and will of the few, if not, indeed, of one, and tending to express itself in the conscience and the will of the mass, of the whole group ethnically molded by natural and historical conditions into a nation, advancing, as one conscience and one will, along the self-same line of development and spiritual formation. Not a race, nor a geographically defined region, but a people, historically perpetuating itself; a multitude unified by an idea and imbued with the will to live, the will to power, self-consciousness, personality.

In so far as it is embodied in a State, this higher personality becomes a nation. It is not the nation which generates the State; that is an antiquated naturalistic concept which afforded a basis for 19th century publicity in favor of national governments. Rather is it the State which creates the nation, conferring volition and therefore real life on a people made aware of their moral unity. . . .

. . .Fascism does not, generally speaking, believe in the possibility or utility of perpetual peace. It therefore discards pacifism as a cloak for cowardly supine renunciation in contra-distinction to self-sacrifice. War alone keys up all human energies to their maximum tension and sets the seal of nobility on those peoples who have the courage to face it. All other tests are substitutes which never place a man face to face with himself before the alternative of life or death. Therefore all doctrines which postulate peace at all costs are incompatible with Fascism. Equally foreign to the spirit of Fascism, even if accepted as useful in meeting special political situations—are all internationalistic or League superstructures which, as history shows, crumble to the ground whenever the heart of nations is deeply stirred by sentimental, idealistic or practical considerations. Fascism carries this anti-pacifistic attitude into the life of the individual. "I don't care a damn" *(me ne frego)*—the proud motto of the fighting squads scrawled by a wounded man on his bandages, is not only an act of philosophic stoicism, it sums up a doctrine which is not merely political: it is evidence of a fighting spirit which accepts all risks. It signifies a new style of Italian life. The Fascist accepts and loves life; he rejects and despises suicide as cowardly. Life as he understands it means duty,

240

elevation, conquest; life must be lofty and full, it must be lived for one-self but above all for others, both near by and far off, present and future. . . .

Such a conception of life makes Fascism the resolute negation of the doctrine underlying so-called scientific and Marxist socialism, the doctrine of historic materialism which would explain the history of mankind in terms of the class-struggle and by changes in the processes and instruments of production, to the exclusion of all else.

That the vicissitudes of economic life—discoveries of raw materials, new technical processes, scientific inventions—have their importance, no one denies; but that they suffice to explain human history to the exclusion of other factors is absurd. Fascism believes now and always in sanctity and heroism, that is to say in acts in which no economic motive—remote or immediate—is at work. Having denied historic materialism, which sees in men mere puppets on the surface of history, appearing and disappearing on the crest of the waves while in the depths the real directing forces move and work, Fascism also denies the immutable and irreparable character of the class struggle which is the natural outcome of this economic conception of history; above all it denies that the class struggle is the preponderating agent in social transformations. Having thus struck a blow at socialism in the two main points of its doctrine, all that remains of it is the sentimental aspiration—old as humanity itself—toward social relations in which the sufferings and sorrows of the humbler folk will be alleviated. But here again Fascism rejects the economic interpretation of felicity as something to be secured socialistically, almost automatically, at a given stage of economic evolution when all will be assured a maximum of material comfort. Fascism denies the materialistic conception of happiness as a possibility, and abandons it to the economists of the mid-eighteenth century. This means that Fascism denies the equation: well-being = happiness, which sees in men mere animals, content when they can feed and fatten, thus reducing them to a vegetative existence pure and simple.

After socialism, Fascism trains its guns on the whole block of democratic ideologies, and rejects both their premises and their practical applications and implements. Fascism denies that numbers, as such, can be the determining factor in human society; it denies the right of numbers to govern by means of periodical consultations; it asserts the irremediable and fertile and beneficent inequality of men who cannot be leveled by any such mechanical and extrinsic device as universal suffrage. Democratic regimes may be described as those under which the people are, from time to time, deluded into the belief that they exercise sovereignty, while all the time real sovereignty resides in and is exercised by other and sometimes irresponsible and secret forces. Democracy is a kingless regime infested by many kings who are sometimes more exclusive, tyrannical, and destructive than one, even if he be a tyrant. . . .

A party governing a nation "totalitarianly" is a new departure in history. There are no points of reference nor of comparison. From beneath the ruins of liberal, socialist, and democratic doctrines, Fascism extracts those elements which are still vital. It preserves what may be described as "the acquired facts" of history; it rejects all else. That is to say, it rejects the idea of a doctrine suited to all times and to all people. Granted that the 19th century was the century of socialism, liberalism, democracy, this does not mean that the 20th century must also be the century of socialism, liberalism, democracy. Political doctrines pass; nations remain. We are free to believe that this is the century of authority, a century tending to the "right," a Fascist century. If the 19th century was the century of the individual (liberalism implies individualism) we are free to believe that this is the "collective" century, and therefore the century of the State. . . .

The Fascist State expresses the will to exercise power and to command. Here the Roman tradition is embodied in a conception of strength. Imperial power, as understood by the Fascist doctrine, is not only territorial, or military, or commercial; it is also spiritual and ethical. An imperial nation, that is to say a nation which directly or indirectly is a leader of others, can exist without the need of conquering a single square mile of territory. Fascism sees in the imperialistic spirit—i.e., in the tendency of nations to expand—a manifestation of their vitality. In the opposite tendency, which would limit their interests to the home country, it sees a symptom of decadence. Peoples who rise or re-arise are imperialistic; renunciation is characteristic of dying peoples. The Fascist doctrine is that best suited to the tendencies and feelings of a people which, like the Italian, after lying fallow during centuries of foreign servitude, is now reasserting itself in the world.

Speech in Munich, April 17, 1923

ADOLF HITLER

The inability of Germany's many political parties to create a viable coalition government brought Adolf Hitler (1889–1945) to the position of Chancellor in 1933. Those who wished know his plans for Germany needed to look no further than this speech made in his first, failed attempt to gain power in 1923. Hitler's appeals to German "racial" pride, to national resentment of the penalties imposed by the Treaty of Versailles, and to a deep seated fear of a "Jewish peril" were constant themes in his plans to recreate the once great medieval German Empire (Reich).

With the armistice begins the humiliation of Germany. If the Republic on the day of its foundation had appealed to the country: "Germans, stand together! Up and resist the foe! The Fatherland, the Republic expects of you that you fight to your last breath," then millions who are now the enemies of the Republic would be fanatical Republicans. To-day they are the foes of the Republic not because it is a Republic but because this Republic was founded at the moment when Germany was humiliated, because it so discredited the new flag that men's eyes must turn regretfully towards the old flag.

It was no Treaty of Peace which was signed, but a betrayal of Peace. . . .

So long as this Treaty stands there can be no resurrection of the German people: no social reform of any kind is possible! The Treaty was made in order to bring 20 million Germans to their deaths and to ruin the German nation. But those who made the Treaty cannot set it aside. At its foundation our Movement formulated three demands:

1. Setting aside of the Peace Treaty
2. Unification of all Germans
3. Land and soil *(Grund und Boden)* to feed our nation.

Our Movement could formulate these demands, since it was not our Movement which caused the War, it has not made the Republic, it did not sign the Peace Treaty.

There is thus one thing which is the first task of this Movement: it desires to make the German once more National, that his Fatherland shall stand for him above everything else. It desires to teach our people to understand afresh the truth of the old saying: He who will not be a hammer must be an anvil. An anvil are we today, and that anvil will be beaten until out of the anvil we fashion once more a hammer, a German sword! . . . The German people was once clear thinking and simple: why has it lost these characteristics? Any inner renewal is possible only if one realizes that this is a question of race: America forbids the yellow peoples to settle there, but this is a lesser peril than that which stretches out its hand over the entire world—the Jewish peril. Many hold that the Jews are not a race, but is there a second people anywhere in the wide world which is so determined to maintain its race?

As a matter of fact the Jew can never become a German however often he may affirm that he can. If he wished to become a German, he must surrender the Jew in him. And that is not possible: he cannot, however much he try, become a German at heart, and that for several reasons: first because of his blood, second because of his character, thirdly because of his will, and fourthly because of his actions. His actions remain Jewish: he works for the "greater idea" of the Jewish people. Because that is so, because it cannot be otherwise, therefore the bare existence of the Jew as part of another State rests upon a monstrous lie. It is a lie when he pretends to the peoples to be a German, a Frenchman, &c.

What then are the specifically Jewish aims?

To spread their invisible State as a supreme tyranny over all other States in the whole world. The Jew is therefore a disintegrator of peoples. To realize his rule over the peoples he must work in two directions: in economics he dominates peoples when he subjugates them politically and morally; in politics he dominates them through the propagation of the principles of democracy and the doctrines of Marxism—the creed which makes a Proletarian a Terrorist in the domestic sphere and a Pacifist in foreign policy. Ethically the Jew destroys the peoples both in religion and in morals. He who wishes to see that can see it, and him who refuses to see it no one can help.

The Jew, whether consciously or unconsciously, whether he wishes it or not, undermines the platform on which alone a nation can stand.

We are now met by the question: Do we wish to restore Germany to freedom and power? If "yes": then the first thing to do is to rescue it from him who is ruining our country. Admittedly it is a hard fight that must be fought here. We National Socialists on this point occupy an extreme position: but we know only one people: it is for that people we fight and that is our own people. . . . We want to stir up a storm. Men must not sleep: they ought to know that a thunder-storm is coming up. We want to prevent our Germany from suffering, as Another did, the death upon the Cross.

We may be inhumane, but if we rescue Germany we have achieved the greatest deed in the world! We may work injustice, but if we rescue Germany then we have removed the greatest injustice in the world. We may be immoral, but if our people is rescued we have once more opened up the way for morality!

The Nuremberg Laws (1935)

The Nuremberg Laws of 1935 were a series of edicts unanimously approved by the Reichstag (Germany's national legislature) and announced to the nation at the Nazi Party's 1935 meeting in Nuremberg. Though unofficial attacks on Jews began as soon as the Nazis took office, these acts mark Hitler's first official step in removing German Jews from the life of the German nation by depriving them of the protection of citizenship.

The Reich Citizenship Law (September 15, 1935)

The Reichstag has adopted by unanimous vote the following law which is herewith promulgated:

Article 1

1. A subject of the State is a person who belongs to the protective union of the German Reich, and who therefore has specific obligations towards the Reich.
2. The status of subject is acquired in accordance with the provisions of the Reich and State Law of Citizenship.

Article 2

1. A citizen of the Reich is that subject only who is of German or kindred blood and who, through his conduct, shows that he is both desirous and fit to serve the German people and Reich faithfully.
2. The right to citizenship is acquired by the granting of Reich citizenship papers.
3. Only the citizen of the Reich enjoys full political rights in accordance with the provision of the laws.

Article 3

The Reich Minister of the Interior in conjunction with the Deputy of the *Führer* will issue the necessary legal and administrative decrees for carrying out and supplementing this law.

First Supplementary Decree of November 14, 1935

On the basis of Article 3 of the Reich Law of Citizenship of September 15, 1935, the following is hereby decreed:

Article 1

1. Until further provisions concerning citizenship papers, all subjects of German or kindred blood who possessed the right to vote in the Reichstag elections when the Law of Citizenship came into effect, shall continue to possess the rights of Reich citizens. The same shall be true of those upon whom the Reich Minister of the Interior and the Deputy of the *Führer* confer citizenship.

2. The Reich Minister of the Interior may revoke citizenship in conjunction with the Deputy of the *Führer.*

Article 2

1. The provisions of Article I also apply to subjects of mixed Jewish blood.

2. An individual of mixed Jewish blood is one descended from one or two grandparents who, racially, were full Jews, in so far that he is not a Jew according to Section 2 of Article 5. Full-blooded Jewish grandparents are those who belonged to the Jewish religious community.

Article 3

Only citizens of the Reich, as bearers of full political rights, can exercise the right of voting in political matters, and have the right to hold public office. The Reich Minister of the Interior, or any agency he empowers, can make exceptions during the transition period on the matter of holding public office. These measures do not apply to matters concerning religious organizations.

Article 4

1. A Jew cannot be a citizen of the Reich. He cannot exercise the right to vote; he cannot occupy public office.

2. Jewish officials will be retired as of December 31, 1935. In the event that such officials served at the front in the World War either for Germany or her allies, they shall receive as pension, until they reach the age limit, the full salary last received, on the basis of which their pension would have been computed. They shall not, however, be promoted according to their seniority in rank. When they reach the age limit, their pension will be computed again, according to the salary last received on which their pension was to be calculated.

3. These provisions do not concern the affairs of religious organizations.

4. The conditions regarding service of teachers in public Jewish schools will remain unchanged until the promulgation of new regulations on the Jewish school system.

Article 5

1. A Jew is an individual who is descended from at least three grand-parents who were, racially, full Jews. . . .
2. A Jew is also an individual who is descended from two full-Jewish grandparents if:
    (a) he was a member of the Jewish religious community when this law was issued, or who joined the community later;
    (b) when the law was issued he was married to a person who was a Jew, or was subsequently married to a Jew;
    (c) he is the issue from a marriage with a Jew, in the sense of Section 1, which was contracted after the coming into effect of the Law for the Protection of German Blood and Honor of September 15, 1935;
    (d) he is the issue of an extra-marital relationship with a Jew, according to Section 1, and will have been born out of wedlock after July 31, 1936. . . .

The Law for the Protection of German Blood and German Honor (September 15, 1935)

Entirely convinced that the purity of German blood is essential to the further existence of the German people, and inspired by the uncompromising determination to safeguard the future of the German nation, the Reichstag has unanimously resolved upon the following law, which is promulgated forthwith.

Section 1

1. Marriages between Jews and citizens of German or kindred blood are forbidden. Marriages concluded in defiance of this law are void, even if, for the purposes of evading this law, they were concluded abroad.
2. Proceeding for annulment may be initiated only by the Public Prosecutor.

Section 2

Sexual relations outside marriages between Jews and nationals of German or kindred blood are forbidden.

Section 3

Jews will not be permitted to employ female citizens of German or kindred blood as domestic servants.

Section 4

1. Jews are forbidden to display the Reich and national flag or the national colors.
2. On the other hand they are permitted to display the Jewish colors. The exercise of this right is protected by the State.

A Red Record (1895)

IDA BELL WELLS-BARNETT

Racism tainted the nationalism of many countries as the twentieth cen-
tury unfolded. In the United States, the Plessy decision (1896) legiti-
matized "separate but equal" spheres for whites and blacks, a policy
violently enforced by members of the Ku Klux Klan. Lynching became
increasingly common. Ida Bell Wells-Barnett (1862–1931), editor of
the Memphis Free Speech *and later a founder of the NAACP, cru-*
saded against the evil of lynching for 40 years. Her book, The Red
Record *(1895) chronicled these vicious crimes and urged an end to*
"outlawry in our land."

We plead not for the colored people alone, but for all the victims of the terrible injustice which puts men and women to death without form of law. During the year 1894, there were 132 persons executed in the United States by due form of law, while in the same year, 197 persons were put to death by mobs who gave the victims no opportunity to make a lawful defense....

Lynched Because the Jury Acquitted Him

The entire system of the judiciary of this country is in the hands of white people. To this add the fact of the inherent prejudice against colored people, and it will be clearly seen that a white jury is certain to find a Negro prisoner guilty if there is the least evidence to warrant such a finding.

Meredith Lewis was arrested in Roseland, La., in July of last year. A white jury found him not guilty of the crime of murder wherewith he stood charged. This did not suit the mob. A few nights after the verdict was rendered, and he declared to be innocent, a mob gathered in his vicinity and went to his house. He was allayed, and suspecting nothing, went outside. He was seized and hurried off to a convenient spot and hanged by the neck until he was dead for the murder of a woman of which the jury said he was innocent....

Lynched Because They Were Saucy

At Moberly, Mo. February 18ᵗʰ and at Fort Madison, S. C., Jund 2d, both in 1892, a record was made in the line of lynching which should certainly appeal to every humanitarian who has any regard for the sacredness of human life. John Hughes, of Moberly, and Isaac Lincoln, of Fort Madison, and Will Lewis in Tullahoma, Tenn., suffered death for no more serious charge than that they "were saucy to white people." . . .

Color Line Justice

. . .In Nashville, Tennessee, there was a white man, Pan Hanifan, who outraged a little colored girl, and from the physical injuries received she was ruined for life. He was jailed for six months, discharged, and is now a detective in that city. In the same city, last May, a white man outraged a colored girl in a drug store. He was arrested and released on bail at the trial. It was rumored that five hundred colored men had organized to lynch him. Two hundred and fifty citizens armed themselves with Winchesters and guarded him. A cannon was placed in front of his home, and the Buchanan Rifles (State Militia) ordered to the scene for his protection. The colored mob did not show up. Only two weeks before, Eph. Grizzard, who had been charged with rape upon a white woman, had been taken from the jail, with Governor Buchanan and the police and militia standing by, dragged through the streets in broad daylight, knives plunged into him at every step, and with every fiendish cruelty that a frenzied mob could devise, he was at last swung out on the bridge with hands cut to pieces as he tried to climb up the stanchions. A naked, bloody example of the bloodthirstiness of the nineteenth century civilization of the Athens of the South! No cannon nor military were called out in his defense. He dared to visit a white woman.

The remedy

. . . .What can you do, reader, to prevent lynching, to thwart anarchy and promote law and order throughout our land?

1st You can help disseminate the facts contained in this book by bringing them to the knowledge of everyone with whom you come into contact, to the end that public sentiment may be revolutionized. Let the facts speak for themselves, with you as a medium.

2nd You can be instrumental in having churches, missionary societies . . . pass resolutions of condemnation and protest every time a lunching takes place, and see that they are sent to the place where these outrages occur.

3rd Bring to the intelligent consideration of Southern people the refusal of capital to invest where lawlessness and mob violence hold sway. . . .

4th Think and act on independent lines in this behalf, remembering that after all, it is the white man's civilization and the white man's government which are on trial. . . .

"Tell the world the facts." When the Christian world knows the alarming growth and extent of outlawry in our land, some means will be found to stop it.

Topic IX

World War II

❀

84

The Appeasement Debate (1938)

During the 1930s, Adolf Hitler exploited Europe's fear of another war to successfully restore the German draft, re-occupy the Rhineland, and achieve Anschluss with Austria. France and Great Britain even accepted his seizure of the Czech Sudetenland in September 1938. The House of Commons debate between Prime Minister Neville Chamberlain (1869–1940) and Winston Churchill (1874–1965) in October was the first discussion of the implications of the Munich Agreement accepting Hitler's claim to the Sudetenland.

Neville Chamberlain:

Since I first went to Berchtesgaden [to confer with Hitler] more than 20,000 letters and telegrams have come to No. 10 Downing Street. Of course, I have only been able to look at a tiny fraction of them, but I have seen enough to know that the people who wrote did not feel that they had such a cause for which to fight, if they were asked to go to war in order that the Sudeten Germans might not join the Reich. That is how they are feeling. That is my answer to those who say that we should have told Germany weeks ago that, if her army crossed the border of Czechoslovakia, we should be at war with her. We had no treaty obligations and no legal obligations to Czechoslovakia and if we had said that, we feel that we should have received no support from the people. . . .

When we were convinced, as we became convinced, that nothing any longer would keep the Sudetenland within the Czechoslovakian State, we urged the Czech Government as strongly as we could to agree to the cession of territory, and to agree promptly. The Czech Government, through the wisdom and courage of President Benes, accepted the advice of the French Government and ourselves. It was a hard decision for anyone who loved his country to take, but to accuse us of having by that advice betrayed the Czechoslovakian State is simply preposterous. What we did was to save her from annihilation and give her a chance of new life as a new State, which involves the loss of territory and fortifications, but may perhaps enable her to enjoy in the future and develop a national existence under a neutrality and security comparable to that which we see in Switzerland to-day. Therefore, I think the Government deserve the approval of this House for their conduct of affairs in this recent crisis which has saved Czechoslovakia from destruction and Europe from Armageddon.

Does the experience of the Great War and of the years that followed it give us reasonable hope that, if some new war started, that would end war any more than the last one did? . . .

One good thing, at any rate, has come out of this emergency through which we have passed. It has thrown a vivid light upon our preparations for defence, on their strength and on their weakness. I should not think we were doing our duty if we had not already ordered that a prompt and thorough inquiry should be made to cover the whole of our preparations, military and civil, in order to see, in the light of what has happened during these hectic days, what further steps may be necessary to make good our deficiencies in the shortest possible time.

Winston Churchill:

I will begin by saying what everybody would like to ignore or forget but which must nevertheless be stated, namely, that we have sustained a total and unmitigated defeat, and that France has suffered even more than we have. . . . The German dictator, instead of snatching his victuals from the table, has been content to have them served to him course by course. . . .

I have always held the view that the maintenance of peace depends upon the accumulation of deterrents against the aggressor, coupled with a sincere effort to redress grievances. Herr Hitler's victory, like so many of the famous struggles that have governed the fate of the world, was won upon the narrowest of margins. After the seizure of Austria in March we faced this problem in our Debates. I ventured to appeal to the Government to go a little further than the Prime Minister went, and to give a pledge that in conjunction with France and other Powers they would guarantee the security of Czechoslovakia while the Sudeten-Deutsch question was being examined either by a League of Nations Commission or some other impartial body, and I still believe that if that course had been followed events would not have fallen into this disastrous state. . . .

It is quite true that such a policy in order to succeed demanded that Britain should declare straight out and a long time beforehand that she would, with others, join to defend Czechoslovakia against an unprovoked aggression. His Majesty's Government refused to give that guarantee when it would have saved the situation, yet in the end they gave it when it was too late, and now, for the future, they renew it when they have not the slightest power to make it good.

All is over. Silent, mournful, abandoned, broken, Czechoslovakia recedes into the darkness. She has suffered in every respect by her association with the Western democracies and with the League of Nations, of which she has always been an obedient servant. She has suffered in particular from her association with France, under whose guidance and policy she has been actuated for so long. . . .

We in this country, as in other Liberal and democratic countries, have a perfect right to exalt the principle of self-determination, but it comes ill out of the mouths of those in totalitarian States who deny even the smallest element of toleration to every section and creed within their bounds. But, however you put it, this particular block of land, this mass of human beings to be handed over, has never expressed the desire to go into the Nazi rule. I do not believe that even now—if their opinion could be asked, they would exercise such an option.

What is the remaining position of Czechoslovakia? Not only are they politically mutilated, but, economically and financially, they are in complete confusion. Their banking, their railway arrangements, are severed and broken, their industries are curtailed, and the movement of their population is most cruel. The Sudeten miners, who are all Czechs and whose families have lived in that area for centuries, must now flee into an area where there are hardly any mines left for them to work. It is a tragedy which has occurred. . . .

I venture to think that in future the Czechoslovak State cannot be maintained as an independent entity. You will find that in a period of time which may be measured by years, but may be measured only by months, Czechoslovakia will be engulfed in the Nazi regime. Perhaps they may join it in despair or in revenge. At any rate, that story is over and told. But we cannot consider the abandonment and ruin of Czechoslovakia in the light only of what happened only last month. It is the most grievous consequence which we have yet experienced of what we have done and of what we have left undone in the last five years—five years of futile good intention, five years of eager search for the line of least resistance, five years of uninterrupted retreat of British power, five years of neglect of our air defences. Those are the features which I stand here to declare and which marked an improvident stewardship for which Great Britain and France have dearly to pay. We have been reduced in those five years from a position of security so overwhelming and so unchallengeable that we never cared to think about it. We have been reduced from a position where the very word "war" was considered one which would be used only by persons qualifying for a lunatic asylum. We have been reduced from a position of safety and power—power to do good, power to be generous to a beaten foe, power to make terms with Germany, power to give her proper redress for her grievances, power to stop her arming if we chose, power to take any step in strength or mercy or justice which we thought right—reduced in five years from a position safe and unchallenged to where we stand now.

When I think of the fair hopes of a long peace which still lay before Europe at the beginning of 1933 when Herr Hitler first obtained power, and of all the opportunities of arresting the growth of the Nazi power which have been thrown away, when I think of the immense combinations and resources which have been neglected or squandered, I cannot believe that a parallel exists in the whole course of history. So far as this country is concerned the responsibility must rest with those who have the undisputed control of our political affairs. They neither prevented Germany from rearming, nor did they rearm ourselves in time. . . . They neglected to make alliances and combinations which might have repaired previous efforts, and thus they left us in the hour of trial without adequate national defence or effective international security. . . .

We are in the presence of a disaster of the first magnitude which has befallen Great Britain and France. Do not let us blind ourselves to that.

85

Treaty of Non-Aggression Between Germany and the Union of Soviet Socialist Republics (1939)

The failure of Great Britain and France to oppose German aggression convinced Hitler that they would never defend Poland. But Hitler could not move his armies into Poland until he had an agreement with Stalin, for the Soviet Union was also hoping to regain territories it had lost there in the wake of World War I. The 1939 treaty between Hitler and Stalin claimed to be a simple "non-aggression" pact, but its "secret" provisions divided up much of Eastern Europe (including Poland) between the two powers. The failure of Britain and France to stop Hitler's seizure of the Sudetenland had also convinced Stalin that he needed to make his own security arrangements with Hitler. Was Stalin as confident as Neville Chamberlain that Hitler would be satisfied with a partial victory?

The Government of the German Reich and the Government of the Union of Soviet Socialist Republics, desirous of strengthening the cause of peace between Germany and the U.S.S.R., and proceeding from the fundamental provisions of the Treaty of Neutrality, which was concluded between Germany and the U.S.S.R. in April 1926, have reached the following agreement:

Article I: The two Contracting Parties undertake to refrain from any act of violence, any aggressive action and any attack on each other either severally or jointly with other Powers.

Article II: Should one of the Contracting Parties become the object of belligerent action by a third Power, the other Contracting Party shall in no manner lend its support to this third Power.

Article III: The Governments of the two Contracting Parties will in future maintain continual contact with one another for the purpose of consultation in order to exchange information on problems affecting their common interests.

Article IV: Neither of the two Contracting Parties will join any grouping of Powers whatsoever which is aimed directly or indirectly at the other Party.

Article V: Should disputes or conflicts arise between the Contracting Parties over questions of one kind or another, both Parties will settle these disputes or conflicts by means of a friendly exchange of views or if necessary by the appointment of arbitration commissions.

Article VI: The present Treaty shall be concluded for a period of ten years with the proviso that, in so far as one of the Contracting Parties does not denounce it one year before the expiry of this period, the validity of this Treaty shall be deemed to be automatically prolonged for another five years.

Article VII: The present treaty shall be ratified within the shortest possible time. The instruments of ratification will be exchanged in Berlin. The treaty shall enter into force immediately upon signature.

Done in duplicate in the German and Russian languages. Moscow, August 23, 1939.

For the Government of the German Reich: V. Ribbentrop
With full power of the Government of the U.S.S.R.: V. Molotov

Secret Additional Protocol:

On the occasion of the signature of the Non-Aggression Treaty between the German Reich and the Union of Soviet Socialist Republics, the undersigned plenipotentiaries of the two Parties discussed in strictly confidential conversations the question of the delimitation of their respective spheres of interest in Eastern Europe. These conversations led to the following result:

1. In the event of a territorial and political transformation in the territories belonging to the Baltic States (Finland, Estonia, Latvia, Lithuania), the northern frontier of Lithuania shall represent the frontier of the spheres of interest both of Germany and the U.S.S.R. In this connection the interest of Lithuania in the Vilna territory is recognized by both Parties.

2. In the event of a territorial and political transformation of the territories belonging to the Polish State, the spheres of interest of both Germany and the U.S.S.R. shall be bounded approximately by the line of the rivers Narev, Vistula, and San.

   The question whether the interests of both Parties make the maintenance of an independent Polish State appear desirable and how the frontiers of this State should be drawn can be definitely determined only in the course of further political developments.

   In any case both Governments will resolve this question by means of a friendly understanding.

3. With regard to South-Eastern Europe, the Soviet side emphasizes its interest in Bessarabia. The German side declares complete political *désintéressement* in these territories.

4. This Protocol will be treated by both parties as strictly secret.

Moscow, August 23, 1939.

For the Government of the German Reich: V. Ribbentrop
With the full power of the Government of the U.S.S.R.: V. Molotov

86

The Four Freedoms (1941)

FRANKLIN DELANO ROOSEVELT

Hitler's invasion of Poland on August 31, 1939, set off World War II (1939–1945). Less than a year later, Britain stood alone as most of Western Europe fell to Nazi and Fascist control. The United States remained officially neutral, although an aid package for Britain was approved in 1940. Believing America would eventually have to enter the war, President Franklin Delano Roosevelt (1882–1945) used his Annual Message to Congress in January 1941 to help prepare the nation for war by universalizing America's definition of its basic "Four Freedoms."

Our national policy is this.

First, by an impressive expression of the public will and without regard to partisanship, we are committed to all-inclusive national defense.

Second, by an impressive expression of the public will and without regard to partisanship, we are committed to full support of all those resolute peoples, everywhere, who are resisting aggression and are thereby keeping war away from our Hemisphere. By this support, we express our determination that the democratic cause shall prevail; and we strengthen the defense and security of our own nation.

Third, by an impressive expression of the public will and without regard to partisanship we are committed to the proposition that principles of morality and considerations for our own security will never permit us to acquiesce in a peace dedicated by aggressors and sponsored by appeasers. We know that enduring peace cannot be bought at the cost of other people's freedom. . . .

Our most useful and immediate role is to act as an arsenal for them as well as for ourselves. They do not need man power. They do need billions of dollars worth of the weapons of defense. . . .

Let us say to the democracies: "We Americans are vitally concerned in your defense of freedom. We are putting forth our energies, our resources and our organizing powers to give you the strength to regain and maintain a free world. We shall send you, in ever-increasing numbers, ships, planes, tanks, guns. This is our purpose and our pledge." In fulfillment of this purpose we will not be intimidated by the threats of dictators that they will regard as a breach of international law and as an act of war our aid to the democracies which dare to resist their aggression. Such aid is not an act of war, even if a dictator should unilaterally proclaim it so to be. When the dictators are ready to make war upon us, they will not wait for an act of war on our part. They did not wait for Norway or Belgium or the Netherlands to commit an act of war. Their only interest is in a new one-way international law, which lacks mutuality in its observance, and, therefore, becomes an instrument of oppression.

The happiness of future generations of Americans may well depend upon how effective and how immediate we can make our aid felt. No one can tell the exact character of the emergency situations that we may be called upon to meet. The Nation's hands must not be tied when the Nation's life is in danger. We must prepare to make the sacrifices that the emergency—as serious as war itself—demands. Whatever stands in the way of speed and efficiency in defense preparations must give way to the national need.

A free nation has the right to expect full cooperation from all groups. A free nation has the right to look to the leaders of business, of labor, and of agriculture to take the lead in stimulating effort, not among other groups but within their own groups. The best way of dealing with the few slackers or trouble makers in our midst is, first, to shame them by patriotic example, and, if that fails, to use the sovereignty of government to save government.

As men do not live by bread alone, they do not fight by armaments alone. Those who man our defenses, and those behind them who build our defenses, must have the stamina and courage which come from an unshakable belief in the manner of life which they are defending. The mighty action which we are calling for cannot be based on a disregard of all things worth fighting for.

The Nation takes great satisfaction and much strength from the things which have been done to make its people conscious of their individual stake in the preservation of democratic life in America. Those things have toughened the fibre of our people, have renewed their faith and strengthened their devotion to the institutions we make ready to protect. Certainly this is no time to stop thinking about the social and economic problems which are the root cause of the social revolution which is today a supreme factor in the world.

There is nothing mysterious about the foundations of a healthy and strong democracy. The basic things expected by our people of their political and economic systems are simple. They are: equality of opportunity for youth and for others; jobs for those who can work; security for those who need it; the ending of special privilege for the few; the preservation of civil liberties for all; the enjoyment of the fruits of scientific progress in a wider and constantly rising standard of living.

These are the simple and basic things that must never be lost sight of in the turmoil and unbelievable complexity of our modern world. The inner and abiding strength of our economic and political systems is dependent upon the degree to which they fulfill these expectations. . . .

In the future days, which we seek to make secure, we look forward to a world founded upon four essential human freedoms.

The first is freedom of speech and expression—everywhere in the world.

The second is freedom of every person to worship God in his own way—everywhere in the world.

The third is freedom from want—which, translated into world terms, means economic understandings which will secure to every nation a healthy peacetime life for its inhabitants—everywhere in the world.

The fourth is freedom from fear—which, translated into world terms, means a world-wide reduction of armaments to such a point and in such a thorough fashion that no nation will be in a position to commit an act of physical aggression against any neighbor—anywhere in the world.

That is no vision of a distant millennium. It is a definite basis for a kind of world attainable in our time and generation. That kind of world is the very antithesis of the so-called new order of tyranny which the dictators seek to create with the crash of a bomb.

To that new order we oppose the greater conception—the moral order. A good society is able to face schemes of world domination and foreign revolutions alike without fear.

Since the beginning of our American history we have been engaged in change—in a perpetual peaceful revolution—a revolution which goes on steadily, quietly adjusting itself to changing conditions—without the concentration camp or the quick-lime in the ditch. The world order which we seek is the cooperation of free countries, working together in a friendly, civilized society. . . .

To that high concept there can be no end save victory.

Speech to SS Leaders, October 4, 1943

HEINRICH HIMMLER

Germany's occupation of Europe was only the first step in Hitler's dream of a new world order dominated by Aryans and purged of inferior races. Heinrich Himmler (1900–1945) led the SS (Schutzstaffel), the elite Nazi force in charge of the concentration camps. Here, he warns them not to let a natural but false human sympathy blind them to the need to wipe out Europe's entire Jewish population. True humanity required them to be as ruthless as a physician out to eliminate a deadly "germ."

I also want to make reference before you here, in complete frankness, to a really grave matter. Among ourselves, this once, it shall be uttered quite frankly; but in public we will never speak of it. Just as we did not hesitate on June 30, 1934, to do our duty as ordered, to stand up against the wall comrades who had transgressed, and shoot them, so we have never talked about this and never will. It was the tact which I am glad to say is a matter of course to us that made us never discuss it among ourselves, never talk about it. Each of us shuddered, and yet each one knew that he would do it again if it were ordered and if it were necessary.

I am referring to the evacuation of the Jews, the annihilation of the Jewish people. This is one of those things that are easily said. "The Jewish people is going to be annihilated," says every party member. "Sure, it's in our program, elimination of the Jews, annihilation—we'll take care of it." And then they all come trudging, 80 million worthy Germans, and each one has his one decent Jew. Sure, the others are swine, but this one is an A-1 Jew. Of all those who talk this way, not one has seen it happen, not one has been through it. Most of you must know what it means to see a hundred corpses lie side by side, or five hundred, or a thousand. To have stuck this out and—excepting cases of human weakness—to have kept our integrity, that is what has made us hard. In our history, this is an unwritten and never-to-be-written page of glory, for we know how difficult we would have made it for ourselves if today—amid the bombing raids, the hardships and the deprivations of war—we still had the Jews in every city as secret saboteurs, agitators, and demagogues. If the Jews were still ensconced in the body of the German nation, we probably would have reached the 1916–17 stage by now.

The wealth they had we have taken from them. I have issued a strict order, carried out by SS-Obergruppenführer Pohl, that this wealth in its entirety is to be turned over to the Reich as a matter of course. We have taken none of it for ourselves. Individuals who transgress will be punished in accordance with an order I issued at the beginning, threatening that whoever takes so much as a mark of it for himself is a dead man. A number of SS men—not very many—have transgressed, and they will die, without mercy. We had the moral right, we had the duty toward our people, to kill this people which wanted to kill us. But we do not have the right to enrich ourselves with so much as a fur, a watch, a mark, or a cigarette or anything else. Having exterminated a germ, we do not want, in the end, to be infected by the germ, and die of it. I will not stand by and let even a small rotten spot develop or take hold. Wherever it may form, we together will cauterize it. All in all, however, we can say that we have carried out this heaviest of our tasks in a spirit of love for our people. And our inward being, our soul, our character has not suffered injury from it.

The Death Camp at Treblinka

JEAN-FRANÇOIS STEINER

The campaign of extermination carried out by the Nazis destroyed two-thirds of Europe's pre-war Jewish population of almost nine million and took the lives of another five to six million Slavs, Gypsies, homosexuals, political and religious dissidents, and physically handicapped or mentally ill individuals. Jean-François Steiner (b. 1938), who lost most of his family in the gas chambers of Treblinka (an extermination camp in eastern Poland), compiled this account of the Nazi adaptation of the factory system to the complexities of mass murder from the memories of his fellow survivors.

[Kurt Franz, also known as Lalka] decided that better organization could save much time in the operations of undressing and recovery of the baggage. To do this you had only to rationalize the different operations, that is, to organize the undressing like an assembly line. But the rhythm of this assembly line was at the mercy of the sick, the old and the wounded, who, since they were unable to keep the pace, threatened to bog down the operation and make it proceed even more slowly than before. . . . Individuals of both sexes over the age of ten, and children under ten, at a maximum rate of two children per adult, were judged fit to follow the complete circuit, as long as they did not show serious wounds or marked disability. Victims who did not correspond to the norms were to be conducted to the "hospital" by members of the blue commando and turned over to the Ukrainians for special treatment. A bench was built all around the ditch of the "hospital" so that the victims would fall of their own weight after receiving the bullet in the back of the head. This bench was to be used only when Kurland was swamped with work. On the platform, the door which these victims took was surmounted by the Wolkowysk arrow. In the Sibylline language of Treblinka, "Wolkowysk" meant the bullet in the back of the neck or the injection. "Bialystok" meant the gas chamber.

Beside the "Bialystok" door stood a tall Jew whose role was to shout endlessly, "Large bundles here, large bundles here!" He had been nicknamed "Gröysse Päck." As soon as the victims had gone through, Gröysse Päck and

264

his men from the red commando carried the bundles at a run to the sorting square, where the sorting commandos immediately took possession of them. As soon as they had gone through the door came the order, "Women to the left, men to the right." This moment generally gave rise to painful scenes.

While the women were being led to the lefthand barracks to undress and go to the hairdresser, the men, who were lined up double file, slowly entered the production line. This production line included five stations. At each of these a group of "reds" shouted at the top of their lungs the name of the piece of clothing that it was in charge of receiving. At the first station the victim handed over his coat and hat. At the second, his jacket. (In exchange, he received a piece of string.) At the third he sat down, took off his shoes, and tied them together with the string he had just received. (Until then the shoes were not tied together in pairs, and since the yield was at least fifteen thousand pairs of shoes per day, they were all lost, since they could not be matched up again.) At the fourth station the victim left his trousers, and at the fifth his shirt and underwear. . . .

Meanwhile the women had been conducted to the barracks on the left. This barracks was divided into two parts: a dressing room and a beauty salon. "Put your clothes in a pile so you will be able to find them after the shower," they were ordered in the first room. The "beauty salon" was a room furnished with six benches, each of which could seat twenty women at a time. Behind each bench twenty prisoners of the red commando, wearing white tunics and armed with scissors, waited at attention until all the women were seated. Between hair-cutting sessions they sat down on the benches and, under the direction of a *kapo* who was transformed into a conductor, they had to sing old Yiddish melodies.

Lalka, who had insisted on taking personal responsibility for every detail, had perfected the technique of what he called the "Treblinka cut." With five well-placed slashes the whole head of hair was transferred to a sack placed beside each hairdresser for this purpose. It was simple and efficient. How many dramas did this "beauty salon" see? From the very beautiful young woman who wept when her hair was cut off, because she would be ugly, to the mother who grabbed a pair of scissors from one of the "hairdressers" and literally severed a Ukrainian's arm; from the sister who recognized one of the "hairdressers" as her brother, to the young girl, Ruth Dorfman, who, suddenly understanding and fighting back her tears, asked whether it was difficult to die and admitted in a small brave voice that she was a little afraid and wished it were all over.

When they had been shorn the women left the "beauty salon" double file. Outside the door, they had to squat in a particular way also specified by Lalka, in order to be intimately searched. Up to this point, doubt had been carefully maintained. Of course, a discriminating eye might have observed that the clock was made of wood and that the smell was the smell of rotting bodies. A thousand details proved that Treblinka was not a transient camp, and some realized this, but the majority had believed in the impossible for too long to begin to doubt at the last moment. The door of the barracks, which opened directly onto the "road to heaven," represented the turning point. Up to here the prisoners had been given a minimum of hope, from here on this policy was abandoned.

This was one of Lalka's great innovations. After what point was it no longer necessary to delude the victims? This detail had been the subject of rather heated controversy among the Technicians. At the Nuremberg trials, Rudolf Höss, Commandant of Auschwitz, criticized Treblinka where, according to him, the victims knew that they were going to be killed. Höss was an advocate of the towel distributed at the door to the gas chamber. He claimed that his system not only avoided disorder, but was more humane, and he was proud of it. . . .

[But Lalka's efficiency studies led him to observe] that winded victims died much more rapidly than the rest. This discovery had led him to make a clean sweep of accepted principles. Let us follow his industrialist's logic, keeping well in mind that his great preoccupation was the saving of time. A winded victim dies faster. Hence, a saving of time. The best way to wind a man is to make him run—another saving of time. Thus Lalka arrived at the conclusion that you must make the victims run. A new question had then arisen: at what point must you make the victims run and thus create panic (a further aid to breathlessness)? The question had answered itself: as soon as you have nothing more to make them do. Franz [Lalka] located the exact point, the point of no return: the door of the barracks.

The rest was merely a matter of working out the details. Along the "road to heaven" and in front of the gas chambers he stationed a cordon of guards armed with whips, whose function was to make the victims run, to make them rush into the gas chambers of their own accord in search of refuge. . . . There were still further elaborations later on, but from the first day, Lalka had only to pride himself on his innovation: it took no more than three quarters of an hour, by the clock, to put the victims through their last voyage, from the moment the doors of the cattle cars were unbolted to the moment the great trap doors of the gas chambers were opened to take out the bodies. Three quarters of an hour, door to door, compared to an hour and a quarter and sometimes even as much as two hours with the old system; it was a record. . . .

Since a string of twenty cars arrived at the platform every half hour, the Lalka system made it possible to fully process twelve trains of twenty cars each—or four convoys, or twenty-four thousand persons—between seven o'clock in the morning and one-fifteen in the afternoon.

The rest of the day was devoted to the sorting of the clothing in Camp Number One and the disposal of the bodies in Camp Number Two.

Transported by two prisoners on litterlike affairs, the bodies, after they were removed from the gas chambers, were carefully stacked, to save room, in immense ditches in horizontal layers, which alternated with layers of sand. In this realm, too, Lalka introduced a number of improvements.

Until the great reform, the "dentists" had extracted gold teeth and bridges from the corpses by rummaging through the big piles that accumulated during the morning in front of the trap doors of the gas chambers. It was not very efficient, as Lalka realized. Thus he got the idea of stationing a line of dentists between the gas chambers and the ditches, a veritable gold filter. As they came abreast of the dentists, the carriers of the bodies, without setting down their litters, would pause long enough for the "dentists" to examine the mouths of the corpses and extract what ever needed extracting. For a trained "dentist" the operation never required more than a minute. He placed his booty in a basin which another "dentist" came to empty from time to time. After the take had been washed in the well, it was brought to a barracks where other "dentists" sorted, cleaned and classified it.

Meanwhile, the carriers of the bodies resumed their race—all moving from one place to another was done on the double—to the ditch. Here Lalka had made another improvement: previously the body carriers had gone down and stacked their bodies themselves. Lalka, that maniac for specialization, created a commando of body stackers which never left the bottom of the ditch. When they arrived, the carriers heaved their burdens with a practiced movement, the role of personal initiative being reduced to the minimum, and returned to the trap doors of the gas chambers by a lower route, as on a gymnastic platform, so as not to disturb the upward movement. When all the corpses had been removed from the gas chambers, which was generally between noon and one o'clock, the ramp commando, in charge of removal of the bodies joined the carrier commando. The burial rites lasted all afternoon and continued even into the night. Lalka had made it a rule that nobody was to go to bed until the last corpse had been stacked in its place.

Burma under the Japanese, 1942–1945

U NU

The conquests of Japanese forces in Asia from 1937 to 1942 outpaced even those of their German ally in Europe and Africa. Japan sought aid from the colonized peoples it conquered by holding out the promise of freedom from British or French rule. When Burma (now Myanmar) eventually got its freedom from Britain, U Nu (1907–1995) became its first Prime Minister. Here, he tells the story of how the Burmese came to realize that the "freedom" from British rule offered by the Japanese imperial army during World War II was only another word for tyranny.

At last Burma was to be free. . . .

The whole air was breathing rumors. "The Japanese are our great friends." "When a Japanese meets a Burman he greets him with our own war cry." "The Japanese will die for Burma's freedom." "A Burman prince is coming as a leader in the Japanese army." They all firmly believed the messages scattered down from aeroplanes and broadcast on the wireless that the Japanese were coming to help Burma, and rumor had swollen a handful of hope until it overflowed the basket. Now they were off to welcome their great ally the Japanese, and although it was close on noon under the scorching sun of Mandalay, the poor people were so keen to greet their great ally that they did not even notice the heat.

We met them again in the afternoon about four o'clock. They were no longer marching in a procession but limping along in clumps of three or four. Their faces were no longer joyful and exultant as in the morning, and they seemed quite shy of facing the people who had stayed at home. When they came up to us, we asked what had happened. One of them replied in a surly tone. "Don't talk about it. We expected the Japanese commander to be very thankful for our bowls of rice, but all he did was to take his hand out of his trouser pocket and give us a hard slap in the face." And then he suddenly broke out laughing.

And another man chipped in, "Talk about rough treatment. After he had slapped our faces he made us drag logs and draw water; drag, draw; drag, draw. It almost broke our backs." Then they all burst out laughing. . . . And I thought to myself whatever one may say, there is nothing much wrong with Burmans who can see the funny side of things even in the most unpleasant circumstances. And from that time onwards the news spread like wildfire from one village to another that the Japanese were a tough crowd.

One had to be pretty careful not to make any mistakes. . . .

Suppose you exchanged cigarettes or a few sweetmeats with a Japanese. He may come along by himself and say there are a few things he does not understand very clearly. Or he may bring a friend and introduce him. One of them may remark that the *Kempeitai,* or the Japanese soldiers and traders, are a bad lot. You may be inclined to think that this Japanese is rather a decent sort. But don't go blurting out what you really think. For when you have met these men, you have not done with them. Suppose that the Japanese suspect you are a Communist. Some Japanese who say they are Communists will call on you. And they will fish for what they can find out. Someone will say that his younger brother has been arrested as a Communist. And they will tell you how badly the Japanese treat the Communists, giving them no more than a handful of rice and a cup of water a day, and how the government oppresses them. Or one of them will say that Communist ideas are very sound and that communism works to help the poor; that even the Japanese government has taken over many ideas from communism. So they tempt you with leading questions like digging a canal for water to run along.

And when you are looking at their stolid round faces, my friend, don't go thinking you are clever enough to deceive them. "Least said, soonest mended." There is always a chance of making a slip, and, even if what you have actually said may be all right, you may get into trouble because of some mistake by the interpreter, and everything that you say to the interpreter or the reporter or to that friend of yours or to the communists is reported to the police station. And any scrap of conversation with a Japanese spy who scrapes up acquaintance with you in the street or in the club or theater or market or opium den is reported to the police station. And the officer in charge compares it with all the other reports to check what you have said.

But they only take all these precautions, my friend, if you are an official of some standing. They don't take so much trouble to make up their mind about an ordinary man. A cup of boiling water, stripping the nails off three or four fingers, or a couple of turns with the machine round your testicles, and You will be ready to admit anything, true or false, in accordance with what they think.

Government Information Manual for the Motion Picture Industry (1942)

The United States government did not simply react to patriotism during World War II, it attempted to help shape that patriotism. These 1942 instructions to the Motion Picture Industry show how the government expected every American institution to do its part for the war effort. The power of the government to cut off supplies needed by film makers was just one of the hidden persuaders behind this curtailment of a First Amendment freedom.

The Government Information Program is predicated on the following basic premises:

1. The overwhelming majority of the people are behind the government in its war program but they do not have adequate knowledge and understanding of this program. In the United States we are not for "blind followers". Unless the people adequately understand this program a few military reverses can shatter the high morale of the American people. Unless they adequately understand the magnitude of the program the people will not willingly make the additional sacrifices that they shall be called upon to make in the prosecution of total war and total victory. . . . If we are to keep faith with the American people, we must not resort to any devious information tactics. We must meet lies with a frontal attack—with the weapons of truth. . . .

I. The Issues

Here are suggestions as to the type of footage, shorts or features that will make the issues clear to the people:

(1) Some people do not realize we are fighting for survival, that the actual existence of this nation as a politically independent state depends on winning the war.

(2) We are fighting for freedom and against slavery—for freedom of speech, freedom of religion, freedom from want, freedom from fear. The realization must be driven home that we cannot enjoy these freedoms exclusively. They must be established on a world-wide basis of they will always be in jeopardy in America. . . .

(3) We must emphasize that this country is a melting pot, a nation of many races and creeds, who have demonstrated that they can live together and progress.

(4) We must inject a strong note of tolerance every time we deal in terms of alien and minority groups—a note of understanding that they, too, are human beings, Americans.

(5) We must portray the American way of life. What is it? It is a 1942 version of 1776, of the day the Pilgrims landed on American shores. . . .

II. The Enemy

(1) Who is the enemy? The enemy is not just Hitler, Hirohito, Mussolini. The enemy is much bigger and older than the Nazi and Fascist parties. The enemy is militarism—the doctrine of force—the age-old idea that men can not co-inhabit the earth without a few men dominating others through physical force. . . .

(2) This war is the result of a scheme for world domination by men and parties that are dedicated to the doctrine of force.

(3) Those who subscribe to this doctrine have a cynical regard for the individual. The individual is merely a cipher within a military machine. The individual is a slave. This can be documented by the degradation and suffering in the conquered countries. This was the fate of the appeaser nations as well as the defeated ones.

(4) Overconfidence is dangerous. True, the United States has never lost a war, but neither has Japan. It is therefore dangerous to picture the enemy as weak, as stupid.

(5) The power, cruelty, treachery and complete cynicism of the enemy should be pictured but it is dangerous to try to picture that all Germans, all Italians and all Japanese are bestial barbarians. The people know that this is not true. They will resent efforts to mislead them. . . .

V. The Home Front

(1) Every civilian, too, must take his battle station. He is part of our war mobilization. . . .

(3) First let's show that sacrifice is worthwhile. The people should know what they can win out of this war, not merely that they want to defend certain cherished institutions, and a way of life. They should know certainly what they would lose if we do not win but they

should also know about the brave, new, exciting possibilities for them as individuals in a world that has the prospect of a permanent peace, in a world that will not continually impoverish the individual because of military and economic wars. Only by establishing in the minds of the people the legitimate, decent fruits of victory can they be expected to make the all-out sacrifices that are necessary to achieve total victory and total peace. Having established this, it is possible to point out:

A. The part that "going without" things will play in winning the war.

B. Going without is part of the war effort.

C. Every housewife, every child, can fight by cutting down, by spending less, by saving.

D. Going without is creating. A yard of wool saved is a yard of wool created.

E. Luxury is anything that is not needed.

F. Consumers must be prepared for rationing of many things.

G. Show that every penny invested in defense bonds and stamps is an anchor against inflation and that this is the democratic way of financing a war.

H. Picture and dramatize the tax program. If the people adequately understand this program they will pay their taxes more cheerfully. They should know how taxes are a brake against inflation.

I. Show that hoarding is useless and unpatriotic.

J. Show that every effort is being made to distribute civilian sacrifices evenly.

VI. The Fighting Forces

(1) The mortal realities of war must be realized. War means death in battle.

(2) The heroic sacrifice of individual soldiers can be exalted in dignified terms.

(3) This nation has been built upon the devotion of men who have been willing to die for their country. The work of the Navy, particularly its vital function of convoy and supply, can be dramatized.

(4) It is relatively easy to dramatize the more spectacular services of the Army. It is a more difficult but necessary job to dramatize such services as the Infantry and the service of Supply.

(5) The broad strategy of the war, the necessity of a unified command in a war on a world-wide scale. Show that just as American commanders have Allied troops and naval units under them in certain theatres, so it is necessary for American army and naval units to be under Allied commanders in other theatres.

(A) Many soldiers and sailors on leave are attending local moving picture theatres. We must tell them again and again what they are fighting for and that the country is behind them and appreciates the sacrifices that they are making.

(B) Let us bring the American soldier and sailor to our hearts when he sits before a motion picture screen.

(C) Life in the Army and Navy should not be ridiculed even in a friendly spirit

(D) Yes, glorify our military machine—we are proud of it. But let us not forget that theirs is a serious business.

(E) Let us show the Army in its true light, how the best medical care and sanitary conditions are theirs; how they are fed, how they are buoyed in spirit and determination.

(F) Remember, too, there is now a woman's army. It is not a lipstick, hairpin affair. It is also serious business. Remember the nurse.

(G) The Merchant Marine is also part of our fighting force. It, too, is making the supreme sacrifice to get the goods through.

Korematsu v. United States (1944)

The shock of the Japanese attack on Pearl Harbor led to a severe reaction on the part of many Americans against citizens of Japanese descent. The Supreme Court decision in Korematsu v. United States *approved internment of Japanese-Americans on a claim of "military necessity"— the possibility of a Japanese attack on America's West Coast. The Hirabayashi case referred to below involved imposing a curfew on Japanese citizens living on the West Coast, also in the name of national security.*

. . . In the light of the principles we announced in the Hirabayashi Case, we are unable to conclude that it was beyond the war power of Congress and the Executive to exclude those of Japanese ancestry from the West Coast war area at the time they did. True, exclusion from the area in which one's home is located is a far greater deprivation than constant confinement to the home from 8 p.m. to 6 a.m. Nothing short of apprehension by the proper military authorities of the gravest imminent danger to the public safety can constitutionally justify either. But exclusion from a threatened area, no less than curfew, has a definite and close relationship to the prevention of espionage and sabotage. The military authorities, charged with the primary responsibility of defending our shores, concluded that curfew provided inadequate protection and ordered exclusion. They did so, as pointed out in our Hirabayashi opinion, in accordance with congressional authority to the military to say who should, and who should not, remain in the threatened areas.

In this case the petitioner challenges the assumptions upon which we rested our conclusions in the Hirabayashi Case. He also urges that by May 1942, when Order No. 34 was promulgated, all danger of Japanese invasion of the West Coast had disappeared, After careful consideration of these contentions we are compelled to reject them. . . .

Like curfew, exclusion of those of Japanese origin was deemed necessary because of the presence of an unascertained number of disloyal members of the group, most of whom we have no doubt were loyal to this country. It was because we could not reject the finding of the military authorities that it was impossible to bring about an immediate segregation of the disloyal from the loyal that we sustained the validity of the curfew order as applying to the whole group. In the instant case, temporary exclusion of the entire group was rested by the military on the same ground. The judgment that exclusion of the whole group was for the same reason a military imperative answers the contention that the exclusion was in the nature of group punishment based on antagonism to those of Japanese origin. That there were members of the group who retained loyalties to Japan has been confirmed by investigations made subsequent to the exclusion. Approximately five thousand American citizens of Japanese ancestry refused to swear unqualified allegiance to the United States and to renounce allegiance to the Japanese Emperor, and several thousand evacuees requested repatriation to Japan.

We uphold the exclusion order as of the time it was made and when the petitioner violated it. . . . In doing so, we are not unmindful of the hardships imposed by it upon a large group of American citizens. . . . But hardships are part of war, and war is an aggregation of hardships. All citizens alike, both in and out of uniform, feel the impact of war in greater or lesser measure. Citizenship has its responsibilities as well as its privileges, and in time of war the burden is always heavier. Compulsory exclusion of large groups of citizens from their homes, except under circumstances of direst emergency and peril, is inconsistent with our basic governmental institutions. But when under conditions of modern warfare our shores are threatened by hostile forces, the power to protect must be commensurate with the threatened danger. . . .

It is said that we are dealing here with the case of imprisonment of a citizen in a concentration camp solely because of his ancestry, without evidence or inquiry concerning his loyalty and good disposition towards the United States. Our task would be simple, our duty clear, were this a case involving the imprisonment of a loyal citizen in a concentration camp because of racial prejudice. Regardless of the true nature of the assembly and relocation centers—and we deem it unjustifiable to call them concentration camps with all the ugly connotations that term implies—we are dealing specifically with nothing but an exclusion order. To cast this case into outlines of racial prejudice, without reference to the real military dangers which were presented, merely confuses the issue. Korematsu was not excluded from the Military Area because of hostility to him or his race. He was excluded because we are at war with the Japanese Empire, because the properly constituted military authorities feared an invasion of our West Coast and felt constrained to take proper security measures, because they decided that the military urgency of the situation demanded that all citizens of Japanese ancestry be segregated from the West Coast temporarily, and finally, because Congress, reposing its confidence in this time of war in our military leaders—as inevitably it must—determined that they should have the power to do just this. . . . We cannot—by availing ourselves of the calm perspective of hindsight—now say that at the time these actions were unjustified.

A Strategic Dilemma

Almost immediately after Allied Forces launched their main invasion of Europe in June 1944, the United States began receiving letters from Jewish organizations pressing it to bomb the extermination camps, or even the rail lines leading to them, to slow down the genocide. As this exchange of letters between the World Jewish Congress and the American Assistant Secretary of War make clear, the United States decided to put strategic considerations ahead of humanitarian ones, believing that the best way to end Hitler's crimes was to concentrate its firepower on targets designed to end the war as quickly as possible.

August 9, 1944

Hon. John J. McCloy
Under Secretary of War
War Department
Washington D. C.

My Dear Mr. Secretary:

I beg to submit to your consideration the following excerpt from a message which we received under the date of July 29 from Mr. Ernest Frischer of the Czechoslovak State Council through the War Refugee Board:

> "I believe that destruction of gas chambers and crematoria in Oswiecim by bombing would have a certain effect now. Germans are now exhuming and burning corpses in an effort to conceal their crimes. This could be prevented by destruction of crematoria and then the Germans might possibly stop further mass exterminations especially since so little time is left to them. Bombing of railway communications in this same are would also be of great importance and of military interest."

Sincerely yours,
A. Leon Kubowitzki
Head, Rescue Department
World Jewish Congress

14 August 1944

Dear Mr. Kubowitzki:

I refer to your letter of August 9 in which you request consideration of a proposal made by Mr. Ernest Frischer that certain installations and railroad centers be bombed.

The War Department has been approached by the War Refugee Board, which raised the question of the practicability of this suggestion. After a study it became apparent that such an operation could be executed only by the diversion of considerable air support essential to the success of our forces now engaged in decisive operations elsewhere and would in any case be of such doubtful efficacy that it would not warrant the use of our resources. There has been considerable opinion to the effect that such an effort, even if practicable, might provoke even more vindictive action by the Germans.

The War Department fully appreciates the humanitarian motives which prompted the suggested operation, but for the reasons stated above it has not been felt that it can or should be undertaken, at least at this time.

Sincerely,
John J. McCloy
Assistant Secretary of War.

The Yalta Protocols (February 1945)

The war against Fascism made allies of nations that had very different political and economic systems. By the time Britain's Churchill, America's Roosevelt, and the Soviet Union's Stalin met in February 1945 to shape the postwar world, the differences between their nations were tearing the Grand Alliance apart. Still, the three leaders agreed to create the United Nations, approved a division of Germany, and endorsed a Declaration on Liberated Europe that envisioned a democratic future. But instead of a world of international cooperation, the Yalta Conference ushered in a "Cold" War between Communism and Capitalism that lasted for 45 years.

The Crimea conference of the Heads of the Governments of the United States of America, the United Kingdom, and the Union of Soviet Socialist Republics which took place from February 4th to 11th came to the following conclusions.

I. World Organization

It was decided:

(1) that a United Nations Conference on the proposed world Organization should be summoned for Wednesday, 25th April, 1945, and should be held in the United States of America.

(2) the Nations to be invited to this Conference should be:

   (a) the Allied Nations as they existed on the 8th February, 1945 and

   (b) such of the Associated Nations as have declared war on the common enemy by 1st March, 1945. (For this purpose by the term "Associated Nation" was meant the eight Associated Nations and Turkey). When the Conference on World Organization, is held, the delegates of the United Kingdom and United States of America will support a proposal to admit to original membership two Soviet Socialist Republics, i.e. the Ukraine and White Russia.

(3) that the United States Government on behalf of the Three Powers should consult the Government of China and the French Provisional

Government in regard to the decisions taken at the present Conference concerning the proposed World Organization.

(4) that the text of the invitation to be issued to all the nations which would take part in the United Nations Conference should be as follows:

Invitation

"The Government of the United States of America, on behalf of itself and of the Governments of the United Kingdom, the Union of Soviet Socialist Republics, and the Republic of China and of the Provisional Government of the French Republic, invite the Government of _____ to send representatives to a Conference of the United Nations to be held on 25th April, 1945, or soon thereafter, at San Francisco in the United States of America to prepare a Charter for a General International Organization for the maintenance of international peace and security.

"The above named governments suggest that the Conference consider as affording a basis for such a Charter the Proposals for the Establishment of a General International Organization, which were made public last October as a result of the Dumbarton Oaks Conference, and which have now been supplemented by the following provisions for Section C of Chapter VI:

"C. Voting

'1. Each member of the Security Council should have one vote.

'2. Decisions of the Security Council on procedural matters should be made by an affirmative vote of seven members.

'3. Decisions of the Security Council on all other matters should be made by an affirmative vote of seven members including the concurring votes of the permanent members; provided that, in decisions under Chapter VIII, Section A and under the second sentence of paragraph 1 of Chapter VIII, Section C, a party to a dispute should abstain from voting.'

"Further information as to arrangements will be transmitted subsequently.

"In the event that the Government of _____ desires in advance of the Conference to present views or comments concerning the proposals, the Government of the United States of America will be pleased to transmit such views and comments to the other participating Governments."

Territorial Trusteeship

It was agreed that the five Nations which will have permanent seats on the Security Council should consult each other prior to the United Nations Conference on the question of territorial trusteeship.

The acceptance of this recommendation is subject to its being made clear that territorial trusteeship will only apply to (a) existing mandates of the League of Nations; (b) territories detached from the enemy as a result of the present war; (c) any other territory which might voluntarily be placed under trusteeship; and (d) no discussion of actual territories is contemplated at the forthcoming United Nations Conference or in the preliminary consultations, and it will be a matter for subsequent agreement which territories within the above categories will be placed under trusteeship.

II. Declaration on Liberated Europe

The following declaration has been approved:

"The Premier of the Union of Soviet Socialist Republics, the Prime Minister of the United Kingdom and the President of the United States of America have consulted with each other in the common interests of the peoples of their countries and those of liberated Europe. They jointly declare their mutual agreement to concert during the temporary period of instability in liberated Europe the policies of their three governments in assisting the peoples liberated from the domination of Nazi Germany and the peoples of the former Axis satellite states of Europe to solve by democratic means their pressing political and economic problems.

"The establishment of order in Europe and the re-building of national economic life must be achieved by processes which will enable the liberated peoples to destroy the last vestiges of Nazism and Fascism and to create democratic institutions of their own choice. This is a principle of the Atlantic Charter—the right of all peoples to choose the form of government under which they will live—the restoration of sovereign rights and self-government to those peoples who have been forcibly deprived of them by the aggressor nations.

"To foster the conditions in which the liberated peoples may exercise these rights, the three governments will jointly assist the people in any European liberated state or former Axis satellite state in Europe where in their judgment conditions require (a) to establish conditions of internal peace; (b) to carry out emergency measures for the relief of distressed peoples; (c) to form interim governmental authorities broadly representative of all democratic elements in the population and pledged to the earliest possible establishment through free elections of governments responsive to the will of the people; and (d) to facilitate where necessary the holding of such elections.

"The three governments will consult the other United Nations and provisional authorities or other governments in Europe when matters of direct interest to them are under consideration.

"When, in the opinion of the three governments, conditions in any European liberated state or any former Axis satellite state in Europe make such action necessary, they will immediately consult together on the measures necessary to discharge the joint responsibilities set forth in this declaration.

"By this declaration we reaffirm our faith in the principles of the Atlantic Charter, our pledge in the Declaration by the United Nations, and our determination to build in co-operation with other peace-loving nations world order under law, dedicated to peace, security, freedom and general well-being of all mankind.

"In issuing this declaration, the Three Powers express the hope that the Provisional Government of the French Republic may be associated with them in the procedure suggested."

III. Dismemberment of Germany

It was agreed that Article 12 (a) of the Surrender Terms for Germany should be amended to read as follows:

"The United Kingdom, the United States of America and the Union of Soviet Socialist Republics shall possess supreme authority with respect to Germany. In the exercise of such authority they will take such steps, including the complete disarmament, demilitarization and the dismemberment of Germany as they deem requisite for future peace and security."

The study of the procedure for the dismemberment of Germany was referred to a Committee, consisting of Mr. Eden (Chairman), Mr. Winant and Mr. Gousev. This body would consider the desirability of associating with it a French representative.

IV. Zone of Occupation for the French and Control Council for Germany

It was agreed that a zone in Germany, to be occupied by the French Forces, should be allocated to France. This zone would be formed out the British and American zones and its extent would be settled by the British and Americans in consultation with the French Provisional Government.

It was also agreed that the French Provisional Government should be invited to become a member of the Allied Control Council for Germany.

V. Reparation

The following protocol has been approved:

1. Germany must pay in kind for the losses caused by her to the Allied nations in the course of the war. Reparations are to be received in the first instance by those countries which have borne the main burden of the war, have suffered the heaviest losses and have organized victory over the enemy. . . .

VI. Major War Criminals

The Conference agreed that the question of the major war criminals should be the subject of enquiry by the three Foreign Secretaries for report in due course after the close of the Conference.

Topic X

The Cold War, 1945–1991

The Iron Curtain (1946)

WINSTON CHURCHILL

By the end of 1945, the Grand Alliance had fallen apart. The Soviet Union believed itself surrounded by capitalist states dismissive of its legitimate security. On the other side, the United States and Great Britain saw a new totalitarian threat in the Soviet Union's consolidation of its control over Eastern Europe. In a speech at Westminster College in Missouri, former British Prime Minister Winston Churchill (1874–1965) depicted Stalin's actions as creating an "Iron Curtain" across Europe and warned the West not to repeat the policy of appeasing dictators that had proved so disastrous only a decade before.

A shadow has fallen upon the scenes so lately lighted by the Allied victory. Nobody knows what Soviet Russia and its Communist international organization intends to do in the immediate future, or what are the limits, if any, to their expansive and proselytizing tendencies. I have a strong admiration and regard for the valiant Russian people and for my war-time comrade, Marshal Stalin. There is sympathy and good will in Britain—and I doubt not here also—toward the peoples of all the Russias and a resolve to persevere through many differences and rebuffs in establishing lasting friendships. We understand the Russian need to be secure on her western frontiers from all renewal of German aggression. We welcome her to her rightful place among the leading nations of the world. Above all we welcome constant, frequent and growing contacts between the Russian people and our own people on both sides of the Atlantic. It is my duty, however, to place before you certain facts about the present position in Europe—I am sure I do not wish to, but it is my duty, I feel, to present them to you.

From Stettin in the Baltic to Trieste in the Adriatic, an iron curtain has descended across the Continent. Behind that line lie all the capitals of the ancient states of central and eastern Europe. Warsaw, Berlin, Prague, Vienna, Budapest, Belgrade, Bucharest and Sofia, all these famous cities and the populations around them lie in the Soviet sphere and all are subject in one form or another, not only to Soviet influence but to a very high and increasing measure of control from Moscow. Athens alone, with its immortal glories, is free to decide its future at an election under British, American and French observation. The Russian-dominated Polish government has been encouraged to make enormous and wrongful inroads upon Germany, and mass expulsions of millions of Germans on a scale grievous and undreamed of are now taking place. The Communist parties, which were very small in all these eastern states of Europe, have been raised to pre-eminence and power far beyond their numbers and are seeking everywhere to obtain totalitarian control. Police governments are prevailing in nearly every case, and so far, except in Czechoslovakia, there is no true democracy. Turkey and Persia are both profoundly alarmed and disturbed at the claims which are made upon them and at the pressure being exerted by the Moscow government. An attempt is being made by the Russians in Berlin to build up a quasi-Communist party in their zone of occupied Germany by showing special favors to groups of Left-Wing German leaders. . . . Whatever conclusions may be drawn from these facts—and facts they are—this is certainly not the liberated Europe we fought to build up. Nor is it one which contains the essentials of permanent peace.

The safety of the world, ladies and gentlemen, requires a new unity in Europe from which no nation should be permanently outcast.

It is impossible not to comprehend—twice we have seen them drawn by irresistible forces in time to secure the victory but only after frightful slaughter and devastation have occurred. Twice the United States has had to send millions of its young men to fight a war, but now war can find any nation between dusk and dawn. Surely we should work within the structure of the United Nations and in accordance with our charter. That is an open course of policy. In front of the iron curtain which lies across Europe are other causes for anxiety. . . . in a great number of countries, far from the Russian frontiers and throughout the world, Communist fifth columns are established and work in complete unity and absolute obedience to the directions they receive from the Communist center. Except in the British Commonwealth and in this United States, where Communism is in its infancy, the Communist parties or fifth columns constitute a growing challenge and peril to Christian civilization. . . . The outlook is also anxious in the Far East and especially in Manchuria.

I do not believe that Soviet Russia desires war. What they desire is the fruits of war and the indefinite expansion of their power and doctrines. But what we have to consider here today while time remains, is the permanent prevention of war and the establishment of conditions of freedom and democracy as rapidly as possible in all countries. Our difficulties and dangers will not be removed by closing our eyes to them. They will not be removed by mere waiting to see what happens; nor will they be relieved by a policy of appeasement. What is needed is a settlement and the longer this is delayed the more difficult it will be and the greater our dangers will become. From what I have seen of our Russian friends and allies during the war, I am convinced that there is nothing they admire so much as strength, and there is nothing for which they have less respect than for military weakness. For that reason the old doctrine of a balance of power is unsound. We cannot afford, if we can help it, to work on narrow margins, offering temptations to a trial of strength. If the western democracies stand together in strict adherence to the principles of the United Nations Charter, their influence for furthering these principles will be immense and no one is likely to molest them. If, however, they become divided or falter in their duty, and if these all-important years are allowed to slip away, then indeed catastrophe may overwhelm us all.

Last time I saw it all coming, and cried aloud to my fellow countrymen and to the world, but no one paid any attention. Up till the year 1933 or even 1935, Germany might have been saved from the awful fate which has overtaken her and we might all have been spared the miseries Hitler let loose upon mankind. There never was a war in all history easier to prevent by timely action than the one which has just desolated such great areas of the globe. It could have been prevented without the firing of a single shot, and Germany might be powerful, prosperous and honored today, but no one would listen and one by one we were all sucked into the awful whirlpool. We surely must not let that happen again. This can only be achieved by reaching now, in 1946, a good understanding on all points with Russia under the general authority of the United Nations Organization and by the maintenance of that good understanding through many peaceful years by the world instrument, supported by the whole strength of the English-speaking world and all its connections. . . .

If we adhere faithfully to the charter of the United Nations and walk forward in sedate and sober strength, seeking no one's land or treasure, or seeking to lay no arbitrary control on the thoughts of men, if all British moral and material forces and convictions are joined with your own in fraternal association, the highroads of the future will be clear, not only for us but for all, not only for our time but for a century to come.

The "Long Telegram"
(February 22, 1946)

GEORGE FROST KENNAN

George Frost Kennan (1904–2005), a career diplomat with long experience in the Soviet Union, was particularly troubled by its refusal to cooperate with its former allies during a 1946 crisis in Iran. As chargé d'affaires in Moscow, he sent his superiors a "Long Telegram" tracing the USSR's "neurotic view of world affairs" to a tradition of Russian insecurity and fear, but pointing out how Marxism aggravated that tradition. Kennan's argument became the basis for the American policy of "containment" during the Cold War.

Basic Features of Postwar Soviet Outlook, as Put Forward by Official Propaganda Machine

(a) USSR still lives in antagonistic "capitalist encirclement" with which in the long run there can be no permanent peaceful coexistence. . . .

(b) Capitalist world is beset with internal conflicts, inherent in the nature of capitalist society. These conflicts are insoluble by means of peaceful compromise. . . .

(c) Internal conflicts of capitalism inevitably generate wars. Wars thus generated may be of two kinds: intra-capitalist wars between two capitalist states and wars of intervention against socialist world. Smart capitalists, vainly seeking escape from inner conflicts of capitalism, incline toward latter.

(d) Intervention against USSR, while it would be disastrous to those who undertook it, would cause renewed delay in progress of Soviet Socialism and must therefore be forestalled at all costs.

(e) Conflicts between capitalist states, though likewise fraught with danger for USSR, nevertheless hold out great possibilities for advancement of socialist cause. . . .

Background of outlook

...[The] premises on which this party line is based are for most part simply not true. ... [But the] Soviet party line is not based on any objective analysis of situation beyond Russia's borders; that it has, indeed, little to do with conditions outside of Russia; that it arises mainly from basic inner-Russian necessities which existed before recent war and exist today.

... Russian rulers have always invariably sensed that their rule was relatively archaic in form, fragile and artificial in its psychological foundations, unable to stand comparison or contact with political systems of Western countries. For this reason they have always feared foreign penetration, feared direct contact between Western world and their own, feared what would happen if Russians learned truth about world without or if foreigners learned truth about world within. And they have learned to seek security only in patient but deadly struggle for total destruction of rival power, never in compacts and compromises with it.

It was no coincidence that Marxism, which had smouldered ineffectively for half a century in Western Europe, caught hold and blazed for first time in Russia. Only in this land which had never known a friendly neighbor or indeed any tolerant equilibrium of separate powers, either internal or international, could a doctrine thrive which viewed economic conflicts of society as insoluble by peaceful means. ... It *[Marxism]* is *[the]* fig leaf of their moral and intellectual respectability. Without it they would stand before history, at best, as only the last of that long succession of cruel and wasteful Russian rulers who have relentlessly forced country on to ever new heights of military power in order to guarantee external security of their internally weak regimes. ... Basically this is only the steady advance of uneasy Russian nationalism, a centuries old movement in which conceptions of offense and defense are inextricably confused. But in new guise of international Marxism, with its honeyed promises to a desperate and war-torn outside world, it is more dangerous and insidious than ever before. ...

Projection of Soviet Outlook in Practical Policy on Official Level

(a) Internal policy devoted to increasing in every way strength and prestige of Soviet state: intensive military-industrialization; maximum development of armed forces; great displays to impress outsiders; continued secretiveness about internal matters, designed to conceal weaknesses and to keep opponents in the dark.

(b) Wherever it is considered timely and promising, efforts will be made to advance official limits of Soviet power. ...

(c) Russians will participate officially in international organizations where they see opportunity of extending Soviet power or of inhibiting or diluting power of others. Moscow sees in UNO [United Nations Organization] not the mechanism for a permanent and stable world society founded on mutual interest and aims of all nations, but an arena in which aims just mentioned can be favorably pursued. . . .

(d) Toward colonial areas and backward or dependent peoples, Soviet policy, even on an official plane, will be directed toward weakening of power and influence and contacts of advanced Western nations, on theory that insofar as this policy is successful, there will be created a vacuum which will favor Communist-Soviet penetration. . . .

What We May Expect by Way of Implementation of Basic Soviet Policies on Unofficial, or Subterranean Plane. . . .

Agencies utilized for promulgation of policies on this plane are following:

1. Inner central core of Communist parties in other countries. While many of persons who compose this category may also appear and act in unrelated public categories, they are in reality working closely together as an underground operating directorate of world communism, a concealed Comintern tightly coordinated and directed by Moscow. . . .

2. Rank and file of Communist parties. . . .

3. A wide variety of national organizations or bodies which can be dominated or influenced by such penetration. These include: labor unions, youth leagues, women's organizations, racial societies, religious societies, social organizations, cultural groups, liberal magazines, publishing houses, etc. . . .

It may be expected that component parts of this far-flung apparatus will be utilized, in accordance with their individual suitability, as follows:

(a) To undermine general political and strategic potential of major Western Powers. Efforts will be made in such countries to disrupt national self-confidence, to hamstring measures of national defense, to increase social and industrial unrest, to stimulate all forms of disunity. All persons with grievances, whether economic or racial, will be urged to seek redress not in mediation and compromise, but in defiant, violent struggle for destruction of other elements of society. Here poor will be set against rich, black against white, young against old, newcomers against established residents, etc. . . .

Practical Deductions from Standpoint of US Policy . . . .

(3) Much depends on health and vigor of our own society. World communism is like malignant parasite which feeds only on diseased tissue. This is point at which domestic and foreign policies meet. Every courageous and incisive measure to solve internal problems of our own society, to improve self-confidence, discipline, morale and community spirit of our own people, is a diplomatic victory over Moscow worth a thousand diplomatic notes and joint communiqués. If we cannot abandon fatalism and indifference in face of deficiencies of our own society, Moscow will profit— Moscow cannot help profiting by them in its foreign policies.

(4) We must formulate and put forward for other nations a much more positive and constructive picture of sort of world we would like to see than we have put forward in past. It is not enough to urge people to develop political processes similar to our own. Many foreign peoples, in Europe at least, are tired and frightened by experiences of past, and are less interested in abstract freedom than in security. They are seeking guidance rather than responsibilities. We should be better able than Russians to give them this. And, unless we do, Russians certainly will.

(5) Finally we must have courage and self-confidence to cling to our own methods and conceptions of human society. After all, the greatest danger than can befall us in coping with this problem of Soviet communism is that we shall allow ourselves to become like those with whom we are coping.

"Equal Opportunity" (1946)

VYACHESLAV MIKHAILOVICH MOLOTOV

Although the United States' Naval Base at Pearl Harbor had been attacked and some of its farthest flung Pacific territories invaded by the Japanese, the American mainland was untouched by the onslaught of war that had ravaged its European allies. In fact, the United States emerged from World War II even stronger economically than before. This October 1946 speech by Soviet Foreign Minister Vyacheslav Mikhailovich Molotov (1890–1986) shows the depth of Soviet fears of American economic and cultural domination of an Eastern Europe in virtual ruins after six years of world war.

We know that the United States made a very great effort in this war, in defence of its own interests and of our common aims, for which we are all very grateful to the United States. But for all that, it cannot be said that the United States is one of those states which suffered grave material damage in the Second World War, which were ruined and weakened in this war. We are glad that this did not happen to our ally, although we ourselves have had to go through trying times, the consequences of which will take us long years to heal.

Now that you know the facts, place side by side Rumania, enfeebled by the war, or Yugoslavia, ruined by the German and Italian fascists, and the United States of America, whose wealth has grown immensely during the war, and you will clearly see what the implementation of the principle of "equal opportunity" would mean in practice. Imagine, under these circumstances, that in this same Rumania or Yugoslavia, or in some other war-weakened state, you have this so-called "equal opportunity" for, let us say, American capital—that is, the opportunity for it to penetrate unhindered into Rumanian industry, or Yugoslav industry and so forth; what, then, will remain of Rumania's national industry, or of Yugoslavia's national industry?

It is surely not so difficult to understand that if American capital were given a free hand in the small states ruined and enfeebled by the war, as the advocates of the principle of "equal opportunity" desire, American capital would buy up the local industries, appropriate the more attractive Rumanian,

Yugoslav and all other enterprises, and would become the master in these small states. Given such a situation, we would probably live to see the day when in your own country, on switching on the radio, you would be hearing not so much your own language as one American gramophone record after another or some piece or other of British propaganda. The time might come when in your own country, on going to the cinema, you would be seeing American films sold for foreign consumption—and not those of the better quality, but those manufactured in greater quantity, and, circulated and imposed abroad by the agents of powerful firms and cinema companies which have grown particularly rich during the war.

Can anyone really fail to see that if, as a result of the application of the so-called "equal opportunity" in small states, unrestricted competition between the home products and the products poured out by the factories of the United States or Great Britain, nothing will remain of the sovereignty and independence of these states, especially considering the postwar conditions? Is it not clear that such unrestricted application of the principle of "equal opportunity" in the given conditions would in practice mean the veritable economic enslavement of the small states and their subjugation to the rule and arbitrary will of strong and enriched foreign firms, banks and industrial companies? Is it not clear that if such "principles of equality" are applied in international economic life, the smaller states will be governed by the orders, injunctions, instructions of strong foreign trusts and monopolies? Was this what we fought for when we battled the fascist invaders, the Hitlerite and Japanese imperialists?

Address to Congress (1947)

HARRY S. TRUMAN

By 1947 United States President Harry S. Truman (1884–1972) was convinced that the Soviet Union was an expansionist state. In order to resist advancing Communist forces in Greece and Turkey, Truman asked Congress for an expensive aid program to shore up the anti-Communist governments of those countries. Showing that he meant to use similar combinations of economic and military aid to stop the advance of Communism elsewhere, this strategy (called the "Truman Doctrine") became the foundation stone of America's Cold War "containment" policy.

The gravity of the situation which confronts the world today necessitates my appearance before a joint session of the Congress.

The foreign policy and the national security of this country are involved.

One aspect of the present situation, which I wish to present to you at this time for your consideration and decision, concerns Greece and Turkey. . . .

The very existence of the Greek state is today threatened by the terrorist activities of several thousand armed men, led by Communists, who defy the Government's authority at a number of points, particularly along the northern boundaries. A commission appointed by the United Nations Security Council is at present investigating disturbed conditions in northern Greece and alleged border violations along the frontier between Greece on the one hand and Albania, Bulgaria, and Yugoslavia on the other.

Meanwhile, the Greek Government is unable to cope with the situation. The Greek Army is small and poorly equipped. It needs supplies and equipment if it is to restore the authority of the Government throughout Greek territory. . . .

The British Government, which has been helping Greece, can give no further financial or economic aid after March 31. Great Britain finds itself under the necessity of reducing or liquidating its commitments in several parts of the world, including Greece.

We have considered how the United Nations might assist in this crisis. But the situation is an urgent one requiring immediate action, and the

United Nations and its related organizations are not in a position to extend help of the kind that is required.

It is important to note that the Greek Government has asked for our aid in utilizing effectively the financial and other assistance we may give to Greece, and in improving its public administration. It is of the utmost importance that we supervise the use of any funds made available to Greece, in such a manner that each dollar spent will count toward making Greece self-supporting, and will help to build an economy in which a healthy democracy can flourish.

No government is perfect. One of the chief virtues of a democracy, however, is that its defects are always visible and under democratic processes can be pointed out and corrected. The Government of Greece is not perfect. Nevertheless it represents 85 percent of the members of the Greek Parliament who were chosen in an election last year. Foreign observers, including 692 Americans, considered this election to be a fair expression of the views of the Greek people.

The Greek Government has been operating in an atmosphere of chaos and extremism. It has made mistakes. The extension of aid by this country does not mean that the United States condones everything that the Greek Government has done or will do. We have condemned in the past, and we condemn now, extremist measures of the right or the left. We have in the past advised tolerance, and we advise tolerance now.

Greece's neighbor, Turkey, also deserves our attention.

The future of Turkey as an independent and economically sound state is clearly no less important to the freedom-loving peoples of the world than the future of Greece. The circumstances in which Turkey finds itself today are considerably different from those of Greece. Turkey has been spared the disasters that have beset Greece. And during the war, the United States and Great Britain furnished Turkey with material aid.

Nevertheless, Turkey now needs our support. . . .

The British Government has informed us that, owing to its own difficulties, it can no longer extend financial or economic aid to Turkey.

As in the case of Greece, if Turkey is to have the assistance it needs, the United States must supply it. We are the only country able to provide that help.

I am fully aware of the broad implications involved if the United States extends assistance to Greece and Turkey, and I shall discuss these implications with you at this time.

One of the primary objectives of the foreign policy of the United States is the creation of conditions in which we and other nations will be able to work out a way of life free from coercion. This was a fundamental issue in the war with Germany and Japan. Our victory was won over countries which sought to impose their will, and their way of life, upon other nations.

To insure the peaceful development of nations, free from coercion, the United States has taken a leading part in establishing the United Nations. The United Nations is designed to make possible lasting freedom and independence for all its members. We shall not realize our objectives, however, unless we are willing to help free peoples to maintain their free institutions and their national integrity against aggressive movements that seek to impose upon them totalitarian regimes. This is no more than a frank recognition that totalitarian regimes imposed on free peoples, by direct or indirect aggression, undermine the foundations of international peace and hence the security of the United States.

The peoples of a number of countries of the world have recently had totalitarian regimes forced upon them against their will. The Government of the United States has made frequent protests against coercion and intimidation, in violation of the Yalta agreement, in Poland, Rumania, and Bulgaria. I must also state that in a number of other countries there have been similar developments.

At the present moment in world history nearly every nation must choose between alternative ways of life. The choice is too often not a free one.

One way of life is based upon the will of the majority, and is distinguished by free institutions, representative government, free elections, guaranties of individual liberty, freedom of speech and religion, and freedom from political oppression.

The second way of life is based upon the will of a minority forcibly imposed upon the majority. It relies upon terror and oppression, a controlled wireless and radio, fixed elections, and the suppression of personal freedoms.

I believe that it must be the policy of the United States to support free peoples who are resisting attempted subjugation by armed minorities or by outside pressures.

I believe that we must assist free peoples to work out their own destinies in their own way.

I believe that our help should be primarily through economic and financial aid, which is essential to economic stability and orderly political processes. . . .

I therefore ask the Congress to provide authority for assistance to Greece and Turkey in the amount of $400,000,000 for the period ending June 30, 1948. . . .

In addition to funds, I ask the Congress to authorize the detail of American civilian and military personnel to Greece and Turkey, at the request of those countries, to assist in the tasks of reconstruction, and for the purpose of supervising the use of such financial and material assistance as may be furnished. I recommend that authority also be provided for the instruction and training of selected Greek and Turkish personnel. . . .

This is a serious course upon which we embark.

I would not recommend it except that the alternative is much more serious.

The United States contributed $341,000,000,000 toward winning World War II. This is an investment in world freedom and world peace.

The assistance that I am recommending for Greece and Turkey amounts to little more than one-tenth of one percent of this investment. It is only common sense that we should safeguard this investment and make sure that it was not in vain.

The seeds of totalitarian regimes are nurtured by misery and want. They spread and grow in the evil soil of poverty and strife. They reach their full growth when the hope of a people [dies].

We must keep that hope alive.

The free peoples of the world look to us for support in maintaining their freedoms.

If we falter in our leadership, we may endanger the peace of the world—and we shall surely endanger the welfare of our own Nation.

Great responsibilities have been placed upon us by the swift movement of events.

I am confident that the Congress will face these responsibilities squarely.

NSC 68 (April 14, 1950)

PAUL H. NITZE

Created by the National Security Act of 1947, the National Security Council (NSC) was charged with advising the President of the United States on matters relating to the integration of domestic, foreign, and military policies affecting national security. In NSC 68, the National Security Council laid out a detailed outline of "Objectives and Programs" designed to maintain American economic and military superiority in the face of mounting Soviet competition. The high costs of the increased conventional forces it envisioned, however, led successive presidents to rely instead on a strategic nuclear weapons deterrent. The principal author of the report was Paul H. Nitze (1907–2004), a wealthy financier who served as an economic advisor to the government during World War II, helped draft the Marshall Plan in 1947, and advocated the development of the hydrogen bomb as a guarantee of American military superiority. After serving in the Department of Defense under Presidents Kennedy and Johnson, Nitze was appointed by President Nixon to head the American Strategic Arms Limitation Talks (SALT) delegation in 1969 and later served as principal arms control advisor to President Reagan before retiring from official service in 1989.

NSC 68: United States Objectives and Programs for National Security
April 14, 1950
A Report to the President Pursuant to the President's Directive of January 31, 1950
TOP SECRET
[by Paul Nitze]

. . . The issues that face us are momentous, involving the fulfillment or destruction not only of this Republic but of civilization itself. They are issues which will not await our deliberations. With conscience and resolution this

Government and the people it represents must now take new and fateful decisions. . . .

The fundamental design of those who control the Soviet Union and the international communist movement is to retain and solidify their absolute power, first in the Soviet Union and second in those areas now under their control. In the minds of the Soviet leaders, however, achievement of this design requires the dynamic extension of their authority and the ultimate elimination of any effective opposition to their authority.

The design, therefore, calls for the complete subversion or forcible destruction of the machinery of the government and structure of society in the countries of the non-soviet world and their replacement by an apparatus and structure subservient to and controlled from the Kremlin. To that end Soviet efforts are now directed toward the domination of the Eurasian land mass. The United States, as the principal center of power in the non-Soviet world and the bulwark of opposition to Soviet expansion, is the principal enemy whose integrity and vitality must be subverted or destroyed by one means or another if the Kremlin is to achieve its fundamental design. . . .

The United States now possesses the greatest military potential of any single nation in the world. The military weaknesses of the United States vis-à-vis the Soviet Union, however, include its numerical inferiority in forces in being and in total manpower. Coupled with the inferiority of forces in being, the United States also lacks tenable positions from which to employ its forces in event of war and munitions power in being and readily available.

It is true that the United States armed forces are now stronger than ever before in other times of apparent peace; it is also true that there exists a sharp disparity between our actual military strength and our commitments. The relationship of our strength to our present commitments, however, is not alone the governing factor. The world situation, as well as commitments, should govern; hence, our military strength more properly should be related to the world situation confronting us. When our military strength is related to the world situation and balanced against the likely exigencies of such a situation, it is clear that our military strength is becoming dangerously inadequate. . . .

The risks we face are of a new order of magnitude, commensurate with the total struggle in which we are engaged. For a free society there is never total victory, since freedom and democracy are never wholly attained, are always in the process of being attained. But defeat at the hands of the totalitarian is total defeat. These risks crowd in on us, in a shrinking world of polarized power, so as to give us no choice, ultimately, between meeting them effectively or being overcome by them. . . .

Politically, recognition of the military implications of a continuation of present trends will mean that the United States and especially other free countries will tend to shift to the defensive, or to follow a dangerous policy of bluff, because the maintenance of a firm initiative in the cold war is closely related to aggregate strength in being and readily available. . . .

A more rapid build-up of political, economic, and military strength and thereby of confidence in the free world than is now contemplated is the only course which is consistent with progress toward achieving our fundamental purpose. The frustration of the Kremlin design requires the free world to develop a successfully functioning political and economic system and a vigorous political offensive against the Soviet Union. These, in turn, require an adequate military shield under which they can develop. It is necessary to have the military power to deter, if possible, Soviet expansion, and to defeat, if necessary, aggressive Soviet or Soviet-directed actions of a limited or total character. The potential strength of the free world is great; its ability to develop these military capabilities and its will to resist Soviet expansion will be determined by the wisdom and will with which it undertakes to meet its political and economic problems. . . .

A program for rapidly building up strength and improving political and economic conditions will place a heavy demand on our courage and intelligence; it will be costly; it will be dangerous. But half-measures will be more costly and more dangerous, for they will be inadequate to prevent and may actually invite war. Budgetary considerations will need to be subordinated to the stark fact that our very independence as a nation may be at stake. . . .

. . .In particular, the United States now faces the contingency that within the next four or five years the Soviet Union will possess the military capability of delivering a surprise atomic attack of such weight that the United States must have substantially increased general air, ground, and sea strength, atomic capabilities, and air and civilian defenses to deter war and to provide reasonable assurance, in the event of war, that it could survive the initial blow and go on to the eventual attainment of its objectives.

99

100 Things You Should Know About Communism and Education (1950)

H.U.A.C.

In the early years of the Cold War (1945-1991), the United States expected as much patriotism from its people as it had during World War II (1939-1945). Both were seen as "total" wars, this new one against Communism as the previous one had been against Fascism and Nazism. 100 Things You Should Know About Communism and Education, the third in a series of pamphlets alerting citizens to "the Communist conspiracy and its influence...on religion, on education, on labor, and on government" was produced by the House Un-American Activities Committee. It provides an example of such propaganda in the form of "answers" to "commonly asked" questions. Other measures were also taken. Hollywood dissenters were blacklisted, professors were fired from university positions, and people sent to jail for "contempt of Congress" for refusing to say whether they and their friends were members of the Communist Party.

1. *What is Communism?*

   A Conspiracy to conquer and rule the world by any means, legal or illegal, in peace or war.

2. *Is it aimed at me?*

   Right between your eyes.

3. *What do the Communists want?*

   To rule your mind and your body from the cradle to the grave. . . .

10. *Are Communists really against education?*

    Yes, but don't take our word for it. Take theirs. The details here following are from their own stuff.

11. *What do they say?*

    Here's a quote from Lenin, founder of the Soviet state: "Give us the child for eight years and it will be a Bolshevik forever." . . .

17. *How?*

Here's a quote from an official 1946 guide to teachers of kinder-gartens in Soviet Russia, which handle children from 3 to 6 years of age: . . . . "Here the children play Red Army soldier; in their hands are little flags, on their uniforms and caps are the insignia of infantrymen, tankmen, sailors, and aviators. . . ."

18. *What's the purpose of all this?*

Again, that same teacher's handbook tells us the aim is—"prepara-tion for organized and disciplined labor in higher schools, in pro-duction, and in the service of the Red Army." . . .

32. *Who are these 'enemies' the Russian Communists train children to hate?*

Anybody and everybody who objects to being dominated all his life long by the Communists. Any loyal citizen of the United States, for instance.

And this training in hate is made twice as deadly by coupling it with formal military training for all children from the fourth grade up. . . .

37. *How can I tell a Communist?*

Compare his opinions of this or any other country with his opinions of Russia. A Communist will criticize the President of the United States of America, but not Stalin. . . .

42. *Are there many Communist fronts and fellow travelers in the United States school system?*

There are, and they are a deadly danger.

43. *Who says so?*

The Attorney General of the United States, and the United States Office of Education, to mention just two of many official sources.

44. *How do they work?*

Here is an example given by Dr. Harry Gideonese, president of Brooklyn College:

"A Communist group at an Ohio college recently tried very hard to bring into its ranks a young liberal who was a Phi Beta Kappa and an officer of the Student Council. When ideological arguments failed, he was invited to a house off the campus where drinks were served lavishly. He was then told he could bring a girl to the house any time he wanted to, provided he joined the group. If he didn't know any girls without bourgeois ideas of morality, he could be introduced to one.". . . .

47. *What are some of their other "war" tactics on the school campus?*

There are many Communist and Communist sympathizers among actors, actresses, authors, musicians, and other artists whose careers are interesting and attractive to young people.

One of the Communist Party's most powerful devices for catching youth is that of using these "big name" agents to spark a campus rally or meeting which has as its real purpose the planting of Party propaganda.

48. *Do they meddle in student activities?*

Says Dr. Gideonese: "Perhaps the most effective tactic they employ, however, is their practice of espousing popular causes and protesting militantly against anything which they can made appear as unfair practice, exploitation or discrimination."

49. *Do the students know what they're getting into, when they go to these things?*

Hardly ever. They go for the fun and excitement, usually, but then the loops and snares go out and catch all too many.

50. *What happens to them, then?*

The girl or boy who falls under Communist influence is in danger of losing his whole future as an independent, American citizen.

The same applies for teachers or anyone else.

51. *Why?*

Because nobody, man, woman or child, can be a Communist and a good citizen of the United States of America at the same time.

52. *Again, why?*

All Communists everywhere come under the same rule: Absolute obedience in all things to Party orders. Each and every one of those Party orders starts from the Kremlin in Moscow, Russia.

No good American can surrender to that.

53. *Do any teachers in our schools actually submit to such a Communist dictatorship?*

Here again, read what Dr. Gideonese has to say: "Communist professors and teachers play an important part, of course, in the broad-scale campaign to convert our youth to Stalinism."

54. *How do they work?*

By slipping propaganda into classroom work and textbooks and by leading gullible students into Red-sponsored campus activities.

55. *What's biting these people, anyhow?*

Here is at least one part of the answer given by John Hanna, a professor of Columbia University, who was formerly with the Farm Credit Administration and chief analyst with the United States Courts' Administration Office:

"The girls' schools and women's colleges contain some of the most loyal disciples of Russia. Teachers there are often frustrated females. They have gone through bitter struggles to obtain their positions. A political dogma based on hatred expresses their personal attitude."

Politics based on hatred and self-pity has the same appeal for men, too, who feel frustrated by life.

56. *Are they open in their hate?*

No. Says the same expert:

"They can manipulate admissions and scholarships to obtain radical students. They require courses that give a maximum of indoctrinations. They favor students who follow their leadership. At the same time, they are shrewd enough to avoid any open affiliation with Communism." . . .

60. *[Concerning a survey of possibly Communist–influenced textbooks used in American schools] What did the results show?*

That the success of the United States of America is played down in too many of our school books and its failures are played up. That the success of Soviet Russia is played up and its failures are played down. This is an important and much-used Communist device. . . .

100. *What can I do?*

FIRST, know the facts.

SECOND, work in your own community to get rid of Communists and Communist influences, whether in the school system or anywhere else.

THIRD, be prepared to face accusations of "witch-hunting," "Red-baiting," "textbook burning," and "strangling academic freedom."

These are all standard smears in the Communist propaganda routine.

ABOVE ALL, remember that whatever you do you must always keep the Constitution of the United States in one hand and common sense in the other. The object here is NOT to destroy academic freedom. It is to STOP COMMUNISM before it destroys us. The Communists CAN be stopped under our system of laws and MUST be.

100

A Marxist Condemns Stalin (1956)

NIKITA KHRUSHCHEV

Stalin's death in 1953 led to a two-year long power struggle within the Soviet Union's Communist leadership. To cement his final victory in that struggle, Nikita Khrushchev (1894–1971) decided to denounce the excesses of Stalin's rule at a meeting of the Twentieth Party Congress in February 1956. His speech, and the relaxation of censorship that followed it, increased his popularity at home and led to a temporary "thaw" in Soviet-American relations. However, as China's Communist leadership used the same tactics as Stalin, Khrushchev's speech also led to a split between the Soviet Union and China that divided the Communist world.

When we analyze the practice of Stalin in regard to the direction of the party and of the country, when we pause to consider everything which Stalin perpetrated, we must be convinced that Lenin's fears were justified. The negative characteristics of Stalin, which, in Lenin's time, were only incipient, transformed themselves during the last years into a grave abuse of power by Stalin, which caused untold harm to our party. . . .

Stalin acted not through persuasion, explanation, and patient cooperation with people, but by imposing his concepts and demanding absolute submission to his opinion. Whoever opposed this concept or tried to prove his viewpoint, and the correctness of his position—was doomed to removal from the leading collective and to subsequent moral and physical annihilation. This was especially true during the period following the 17th party congress, when many prominent party leaders and rank-and-file party workers, honest and dedicated to the cause of communism, fell victim to Stalin's despotism. . . .

Lenin's traits—patient work with people; stubborn and painstaking education of them; the ability to induce people to follow him without using compulsion, but rather through the ideological influence on them of the whole collective—were entirely foreign to Stalin. He (Stalin) discarded the Leninist method of convincing and educating; he abandoned the method of ideological struggle for that of administrative violence, mass repressions, and terror. He acted on an increasingly larger scale and more stubbornly through

305

punitive organs, at the same time often violating all existing norms of morality and of Soviet laws. . . .

Facts prove that many abuses were made on Stalin's orders without reckoning with any norms of party and Soviet legality. Stalin was a very distrustful man. . . . He could look at a man and say: "Why are your eyes so shifty today," or "Why are you turning so much today and avoiding to look me directly in the eyes?" The sickly suspicion created in him a general distrust even toward eminent party workers whom he had known for years. Everywhere and in everything he saw enemies, "two-facers" and spies.

Possessing unlimited power he indulged in great willfulness and choked a person morally and physically. A situation was created where one could not express one's own will.

When Stalin said that one or another should be arrested, it was necessary to accept on faith that he was an "enemy of the people." Meanwhile, Beriya's gang, which ran the organs of state security, outdid itself in proving the guilt of the arrested and the truth of materials which it falsified. And what proofs were offered? The confessions of the arrested, and the investigative judges accepted these confessions. And how is it possible that a person confesses to crimes which he had not committed? Only in one way, because of application of physical methods of pressuring him, tortures, bringing him to a state of unconsciousness, deprivation of his judgment, taking away of his human dignity. In this manner were confessions acquired. . . .

All the more monstrous are the acts whose initiator was Stalin and which are rude violations of the basic Leninist principles of the nationality policy of the Soviet state. We refer to the mass deportations from their native places of whole nations, together with all Communists and Komsomols without an exception; this deportation action was not dictated by any military considerations.

Thus, already at the end of 1943, when there occurred a permanent breakthrough at the fronts of the Great Patriotic War benefiting the Soviet Union, a decision was taken and executed concerning the deportation of the Karachai from the lands on which they lived. In the same period, at the end of December 1943, the same lot befell the whole population of the Autonomous Kalmyk Republic. In March 1944 all the Chechen and Ingush peoples were deported and the Chechen-Ingush Autonomous Republic was liquidated. In April 1944 all Balkars were deported to faraway places from the territory of the Kabardyno-Balkar Autonomous Republic and the Republic itself was renamed the Autonomous Kabardnian Republic. The Ukrainians avoided meeting this fate only because there were too many of them and there was no place to deport them. Otherwise, he would have deported them also. [Laughter and animation in the hall.] . . .

Some comrades may ask us: Where were the members of the Political Bureau of the Central Committee? Why did they not assert themselves against the cult of the individual in time? And why is this being done only now?

First of all we have to consider the fact that the members of the Political Bureau viewed these matters in a different way at different times. Initially, many of them backed Stalin actively because Stalin was one of the strongest Marxists and his logic, his strength, and his will greatly influenced the cadres and party work. . . . Later, however, abusing his power more and more [Stalin] began to fight eminent party and government leaders and to use terroristic methods against honest Soviet people. . . . And when we also consider the fact that in the last years the Central Committee plenary sessions were not convened, and that the sessions of the Political Bureau occurred only occasionally, from time to time, then we will understand how difficult it was for any member of the Political Bureau to take a stand against one or another unjust or improper procedure, against serious errors and shortcomings in the practices of leadership. . . .

Comrades, we must abolish the cult of the individual decisively, once and for all; we must draw the proper conclusions concerning both ideological-theoretical and practical work.

It is necessary for this purpose:

. . . in a Bolshevik manner to condemn and to eradicate the cult of the individual as alien to Marxism-Leninism and not consonant with the principles of party leadership and the norms of party life, and to fight inexorably all attempts at bringing back this practice. . . . [In order] to restore completely the Leninist principles of Soviet Socialist democracy, expressed in the constitution of the Soviet Union, to fight willfulness of individuals abusing their power. . . .

Comrades, the 20th Congress of the Communist Party of the Soviet Union has manifested with a new strength the unshakable unity of our party, its cohesiveness around the central committee, its resolute will to accomplish the great task of building communism. And the fact that we present in all their ramifications the basic problems of overcoming the cult of the individual which is alien to Marxism-Leninism, as well as the problem of liquidating its burdensome consequences, is an evidence of the great moral and political strength of our party.

The Military-Industrial Complex (1961)

DWIGHT DAVID EISENHOWER

United States President Dwight David Eisenhower (1890–1969) sought peace in international affairs because as Commander-in-Chief of Allied Forces during World War II he had seen the ravages of war. Having brought the Korean War (1950–1953) to a close, he met serious resistance to his cautious policies from America's "military-industrial complex," which prospered in direct relation to miliary spending. Fearful of the power of a "technological elite," Eisenhower used his "Farewell Address" to alert the nation to the possibility that its resources were being used to benefit the few at the expense of "our grandchildren."

. . . Crises there will continue to be. In meeting them, whether foreign or domestic, great or small, there is a recurring temptation to feel that some spectacular and costly action could become the miraculous solution to all current difficulties. A huge increase in newer elements of our defense; development of unrealistic programs to cure every ill in agriculture; a dramatic expansion in basic and applied research—these and many other possibilities, each possibly promising in itself, may be suggested as the only way to the road we wish to travel.

But each proposal must be weighed in the light of a broader consideration; the need to maintain balance in and among national programs—balance between the private and the public economy, balance between the cost and the hoped for advantages—balance between the clearly necessary and the comfortably desirable; balance between our essential requirements as a nation and the duties imposed by the nation upon the individual; balance between actions of the moment and the national welfare of the future. Good judgment seeks balance and progress; lack of it eventually finds imbalance and frustration.

The record of many decades stands as proof that our people and their Government have, in the main, understood these truths and have responded to them well in the face of threat and stress.

But threats, new in kind or degree, constantly arise. Of these I mention two only.

A vital element in keeping the peace is our military establishment. Our arms must be mighty, ready for instant action, so that no potential aggressor may be tempted to risk his own destruction.

Our military organization today bears little relation to that known of any of my predecessors in peace time—or, indeed, by the fighting men of World War II or Korea.

Until the latest of our world conflicts, the United States had no armaments industry. American makers of plowshares could, with time and as required, make swords as well.

But we can no longer risk emergency improvisation of national defense. We have been compelled to create a permanent armaments industry of vast proportions. Added to this, three and a half million men and women are directly engaged in the defense establishment. We annually spend on military security alone more than the net income of all United States corporations. . . .

In the councils of Government, we must guard against the acquisition of unwarranted influence, whether sought or unsought by the military-industrial complex. The potential for the disastrous rise of misplaced power exists and will persist.

We must never let the weight of this combination endanger our liberties or democratic processes. We should take nothing for granted. Only an alert and knowledgeable citizenry can compel the proper meshing of the huge industrial and military machinery of defense with our peaceful methods and goals, so that security and liberty may prosper together.

Akin to, and largely responsible for the sweeping changes in our industrial-military posture has been the technological revolution during recent decades.

In this revolution research has become central. It also becomes more formalized, complex and costly. A steadily increasing share is conducted for, by, or at the direction of the Federal Government.

Today the solitary inventor, tinkering in his shop, has been foreshadowed by task forces of scientists, in laboratories and testing fields. In the same fashion, the free university, historically the fountainhead of free ideas and scientific discovery has experienced a revolution in the conduct of research. Partly because of the huge costs involved, a Government contract becomes virtually a substitute for intellectual curiosity.

For every old blackboard there are now hundreds of new electronic computers.

The prospect of domination of the nation's scholars by Federal employment, project allocations and the power of money is ever present, and is gravely to be regarded.

Yet, in holding scientific research and discovery in respect, as we should, we must also be alert to the equal and opposite danger that public policy could itself become the captive of a scientific-technological elite.

It is the task of statesmanship to mold, to balance, and to integrate these and other forces, new and old, within the principles of our democratic system—ever aiming toward the supreme goals of our free society.

Another factor in maintaining balance involves the element of time. As we peer into society's future, we—you and I, and our Government—must avoid the impulse to live only for today, plundering, for our own ease and convenience, the precious resources of tomorrow.

We cannot mortgage the material assets of our grandchildren without risking the loss also of their political and spiritual heritage. We want democracy to survive for all generations to come, not to become the insolvent phantom of tomorrow. . . .

Speech at the United Nations (1988)

MIKHAIL GORBACHEV

In 1985 Mikhail Gorbachev (b.1931) assumed leadership of the Soviet Union, which had been made nearly bankrupt by the demands of fighting the Cold War. Gorbachev believed that if Communism were to survive, he must open up the Soviet political system (glasnost) and restructure its economy (perestroika). Appearing before the United Nations in December 1988, he pledged to work towards global stability, reduce Soviet military forces, and end Soviet incursion into Afghanistan. His subsequent decision to withdraw troops from Eastern Europe and concede full independence to the Soviet Union's "satellite" states won him the Nobel Peace Prize. Nothing, however, could prevent the disintegration of the USSR, which was officially dissolved in 1991.

The world in which we live today is radically different from what it was at the beginning or even in the middle of this century. And it continues to change as do all its components.

The advent of nuclear weapons was just another tragic reminder of the fundamental nature of that change. A material symbol and expression of absolute military power, nuclear weapons at the same time revealed the absolute limits of that power.

The problem of mankind's survival and self-preservation came to the fore.

It is obvious, for instance, that the use or threat of force no longer can or must be an instrument of foreign policy. This applies above all to nuclear arms, but that is not the only thing that matters. All of us, and primarily the stronger of us, must exercise self-restraint and totally rule out any outward-oriented use of force.

That is the first and the most important component of a nonviolent world as an ideal. . . .

The new phase also requires de-ideologizing relations among states. We are not abandoning our convictions, our philosophy or traditions, nor do we urge anyone to abandon theirs.

But neither do we have any intention to be hemmed in by our values. That would result in intellectual impoverishment, for it would mean rejecting a powerful source of development—the exchange of everything original that each nation has independently created.

In the course of such exchange, let everyone show the advantages of their social system, way of life or values and not just by words or propaganda, but by real deeds. . . .

Could this view be a little too romantic? Are we not overestimating the potential and the maturity of the world's social consciousness? We have heard such doubts and such questions both in our country and from some of our Western partners.

I am convinced that we are not floating above reality. . . .

In this specific historical situation we face the question of a new role for the United Nations.

We feel that states must to some extent review their attitude to the United Nations, this unique instrument without which world politics would be inconceivable today.

The recent reinvigoration of its peacemaking role has again demonstrated the United Nations' ability to assist its members in coping with the daunting challenges of our time and working to humanize their relations. . . .

Let us also think about setting up within the framework of the United Nations a center for emergency environmental assistance. Its function would be promptly to send international groups of experts to areas with badly deteriorating environment.

The Soviet Union is also ready to cooperate in establishing an international space laboratory or manned orbital station designed exclusively for monitoring the state of the environment.

In the general area of space exploration, the outlines of a future space industry are becoming increasingly clear.

The position of the Soviet Union is well known: activities in outer space must rule out the appearance of weapons there. Here again, there has to be a legal base. The groundwork for it—the provisions of the 1967 treaty and other agreements—is already in place. . . .

The whole world welcomes the efforts this organization and its Secretary General, Mr. Pérez de Cuéllar, and his representatives in untying knots of regional problems. . . .

I will single out only Afghanistan.

The Geneva accords, whose fundamental and practical significance has been praised throughout the world, provided a possibility for completing the process of settlement even before the end of this year. That did not happen.

This unfortunate fact reminds us again of the political, legal and moral significance of the Roman maxim *"pacta sunt servanda"*—treaties must observed.

I don't want to use this rostrum for recriminations against anyone.

But it is our view that, within the competence of the United Nations, the General Assembly Resolution adopted last November could be supplemented by some specific measures. . . .

A complete cease-fire effective everywhere as of Jan. 1, 1989, and the cessation of all offensive operations or shellings, with the opposing Afghan groups retaining, for the duration of the negotiations, all territories under their control;

Linked to that, stopping as of the same date any supplies of arms to all belligerents;

For the period of establishing a broad-based government, as provided in the General Assembly resolution, sending to Kabul and other strategic centres of the country a contingent of United Nations peacekeeping forces. . . .

I would like to join the voice of my country in the expressions of high appreciation of the significance of the Universal Declaration of Human Rights adopted 40 years ago, on Dec. 10, 1948.

Today, this document retains its significance. It, too, reflects the universal nature of the goals and objectives of the United Nations.

The most fitting way for a state to observe this anniversary of the declaration is to improve its domestic conditions for respecting and protecting the rights of its own citizens. . . .

Our country is going through a period of truly revolutionary uplifting.

The process of *perestroika* is gaining momentum. We began with the formulation of the theoretical concept of perestroika. We had to evaluate the nature and the magnitude of problems, to understand the lessons of the, past and express that in the form of political conclusions and programmes. This was done.

[But] For our society to participate in efforts to implement the plans of perestroika, it had to be democratized in practice. Under the sign of democratization, *perestroika* has now spread to politics, the economy, intellectual life and ideology. . . .

We intend to expand the Soviet Union's participation in the United Nations and Conference of Security and Cooperation in Europe human rights monitoring arrangements. We believe that the jurisdiction of the International Court of Justice at the Hague as regards the interpretation and implementation of agreements on human rights should be binding on all states.

We regard as part of the Helsinki process the cessation of jamming of all foreign radio broadcasts beamed at the Soviet Union.

Overall, this is our credo. Political problems must be solved only by political means; human problems, only in a humane way.

Now let me turn to the main issue—disarmament, without which none of the problems of the coming century can be solved.

Today, I can report to you that the Soviet Union has taken a decision to reduce its armed forces.

Within the next two years their numerical strength will be reduced by 500,000 men. The numbers of conventional armaments will also be substantially reduced. This will be done unilaterally, without relation to the talks on the mandate of the Vienna meeting.

313

By agreement with our Warsaw Treaty allies, we have decided to withdraw by 1991 six tank divisions from East Germany, Czechoslovakia and Hungary, and to disband them. . . .

And finally, since I am here on American soil, and also for other obvious reasons, I have to turn to the subject of our relations with this great country. . . .

The relations between the Soviet Union and the United States of America have a history of five and a half decades. As the world changed, so did the nature, role and place of those relations in world politics.

For too long a time they developed along the lines of confrontation and sometimes animosity—either overt or covert.

But in the last few years the entire world could breath a sigh of relief thanks to the changes for the better in the substance and the atmosphere of the relationship between Moscow and Washington.

No one intends to underestimate the seriousness of our differences and the toughness of outstanding problems. We have, however, already graduated from the primary school of learning to understand each other and seek solutions in both our own and common interests.

The Soviet Union and the United States have built the largest nuclear and missile arsenals. But it is those two countries that, having become specifically aware of their responsibility, were the first to conclude a treaty on the reduction and physical elimination of a portion of their armaments which posed a threat to both of them and to all others. . . .

I would like to believe that our hopes will be matched by our joint effort to put an end to an era of wars, confrontation and regional conflicts, to aggressions against nature, to the terror of hunger and poverty as well as to political terrorism.

This our common goal and we can only reach it together.

Topic XI

The End of Empire in Asia and the Middle East

Toward Freedom (1941)

JAWAHARLAL NEHRU

Jawaharlal Nehru (1889–1964), Gandhi's aide, confidant and co-architect of India's independence movement, spent years in British jails. He used that time to reflect on the historic relationship between the two peoples. In these excerpts from a work written in 1941, when the leaders of the Congress Party's World War II "Quit India" campaign were imprisoned, Nehru recognized that British rule had brought many benefits to India, but wondered if India might not have received much the same advantages through a fair and free trade relationship and at a far lower "price."

Reports of Nazi excesses in Germany had a curious effect on British officials and their press in India. They gave them a justification for all they had done in India, and it was pointed out to us, with a glow of conscious virtue, how much worse our lot would have been if the Nazis had had anything to do with us. New standards and records had been set up by the Nazis, and it was certainly not an easy matter to rival them. Perhaps our lot would have worse; it is difficult for me to judge, for I have not all the facts of the occurrences that have taken place in various parts of India during the past five years. The British Government in India believes in the charity that its right hand should not know what its left hand does, and so it has turned down every suggestion for an impartial inquiry, although such inquiries are always weighted on the official side. I think it is true that the average Englishman hates brutality, and I cannot conceive English people openly glorying in and repeating lovingly the word *Brutalitat* (or its English equivalent), as the Nazis do. Even when they indulge in the deed, they are a little ashamed of it. But whether we are Germans or English or Indians, I am afraid our veneer of civilized conduct is thin enough, and, when passions are aroused, it rubs off and reveals something that is not good to look at.

For many generations the British treated India as a kind of enormous country house (after the old English fashion) that they owned. They were the gentry owning the house and occupying the desirable parts of it, while the Indians were consigned to the servants' hall, the pantry, and the kitchen. As in every proper country house, there was a fixed hierarchy in those lower regions—butler, housekeeper, cook, valet, maid, footman, etc.—and strict precedence was observed among them. But between the upper and lower regions of the house there was, socially and politically, an impassable barrier. The fact that the British Government should have imposed this arrangement upon us was not surprising; but what does seem surprising is that we, or most of us, accepted it as the natural and inevitable ordering of our lives and destiny. We developed the mentality of a good country-house servant. Sometimes we were treated to a rare honor—we were given a cup of tea in the drawing room. The height of our ambition was to become respectable and to be promoted individually to the upper regions. Greater than any victory of arms or diplomacy was this psychological triumph of the British in India. The slave began to think as a slave, as the wise men of old had said.

Times have changed, and the country-house type of civilization is not accepted willingly now, either in England or India. But still there remain people among us who desire to stick to the servants' hall and take pride in the gold braid and livery of their service. . . . They call this Indianization. For them the problem is one of changing the color of the administration, or at most having a new administration. They never think in terms of a new State. . . .

The Congress attitude differs fundamentally from this because it seeks a new State and not just a different administration. What that new State is going to be may not be quite clear to the average Congressman, and opinions may differ about it. But it is common ground in the Congress (except perhaps for a moderate fringe) that present conditions and methods cannot and must not continue, and basic changes are essential. Herein lies the difference between Dominion status and independence. The former envisages the same old structure, with many bonds visible and invisible tying us to the British economic system; the latter gives us, or ought to give us, freedom to erect a new structure to suit our circumstances. . . .

Personally, I owe too much to England in my mental make-up ever to feel wholly alien to her. And, do what I will, I cannot get rid of the habits of mind, and the standards and ways of judging other countries as well as life generally, which I acquired at school and college in England. My predilections (apart from the political ones) are in favor of England and the English people, and, if I have become what is called an uncompromising opponent of British rule in India, it is almost in spite of these.

It is their rule, their domination, to which we object, and with which we cannot compromise willingly—not the English people. Let us by all means have the closest contacts with the English and other foreign peoples. We want fresh air in India, fresh and vital ideas, healthy co-operation; we have grown too musty with age. But, if the English come in the role of a tiger they can expect no friendship or co-operation. To the tiger of imperialism there will be only the fiercest opposition, and today our country has to deal with that ferocious animal. It may be possible to tame the wild tiger of the forest and to charm away his native ferocity, but there is no such possibility of tam-ing capitalism and imperialism when they combine and swoop down on an unhappy land. . . .

What has been the record of British rule in India? I doubt if it is possible for any Indian or Englishman to take an objective and dispassionate view of this long record. And, even if this were possible, it would be still more diffi-cult to weigh and measure the psychological and other immaterial factors. We are told that British rule "has given to India that which throughout the centuries she never possessed, a government whose authority is unquestioned in any part of the subcontinent;" it has established the rule of law and a just and efficient administration; it has brought to India Western conceptions of parliamentary government and personal liberties; and "by transforming British India into a single unitary state it has engendered amongst Indians a sense of political unity" and thus fostered the first beginnings of nationalism. That is the British case, and there is much truth in it, though the rule of law and personal liberties have not been evident for many years.

The Indian survey of this period lays stress on many other factors, and points out the injury, material and spiritual, that foreign rule has brought us. The viewpoint is so different that sometimes the very thing that is com-mended by British is condemned by Indians. . . .

Are we needlessly cantankerous and perverse if we suggest that some such technical progress would have come to us anyhow in this industrial age, and even without British rule? And, indeed, if we compare our lot with many other countries, may we not hazard a guess that such progress might have been greater if we had not had to contend against a stifling of that progress by the British themselves? Railways, telegraphs, telephones, wireless, and the like are hardly tests of the goodness or beneficence of British rule. They were welcome and necessary, and, because the British happened to be the agents who brought them first, we should be grateful to them. But even these her-alds of industrialism came to us primarily for the strengthening of British rule. They were the veins and arteries through which the nation's blood should have coursed, increasing its trade, carrying its produce, and bringing new life and wealth to its millions. It is true that in the long run some such result was likely, but they were designed and worked for another purpose—to strengthen the imperial hold and to capture markets for British goods—which they succeeded in achieving. I am all in favor of industrialization and the latest methods of transport, but sometimes, as I rushed across the Indian plains, the railway, that life-giver, has almost seemed to me like iron bands confining and imprisoning India.

The outstanding feature of British rule was their concentration on every-thing that went to strengthen their political and economic hold on the coun-try. Everything else was incidental. If they built up a powerful central government and an efficient police force, that was an achievement for which they can take credit, but the Indian people can hardly congratulate them-selves on it. Unity is a good thing, but unity in subjection is hardly a thing to be proud of. The very strength of a despotic government may become a greater burden for a people; and a police force, no doubt useful in many ways, can be, and has been often enough, turned against the very people it is supposed to protect.

Britain's supremacy in India brought us peace, and India was certainly in need of peace after the troubles and misfortunes that followed the breakup of the Moghal empire. Peace is a precious commodity, necessary for any progress, and it was welcome to us when it came. But even peace can be purchased at too great a price, and we can have the perfect peace of the grave, and the absolute safety of a cage or of prison. Or peace may be the sodden despair of men unable to better themselves. The peace which is imposed by an alien conqueror has hardly the restful and soothing qualities of the real article. . . .

They gave us political unity, and that was a desirable thing; but whether we had this unity or not, Indian nationalism would have grown and demanded that unity.

The political unity of India was achieved incidentally as a side product of the Empire's advance. In later years, when that unity allied itself to nationalism and challenged alien rule, we witnessed the deliberate promotion of disunity and sectarianism, formidable obstacles to our future progress. . . .

To the British we must be grateful for one splendid gift of which they were the bearers, the gift of science and its rich offspring. It is difficult, however, to forget or view with equanimity the efforts of the British Government in India to encourage the disruptive obscurantist, reactionary, sectarian, and opportunist elements in the country. Perhaps that too is a needed test and challenge for us, and, before India is reborn, it will have to go through again and again the fire that cleanses and tempers and bums up the weak, the impure, and the corrupt.

The Call for Pakistan (1940)

MUHAMMAD ALI JINNAH

The struggle for Indian independence from Great Britain soon became charged with issues of national identity. India's large Muslim minority feared its values would be lost in a united and overwhelmingly Hindu state. Although Muhammad Ali Jinnah (1876–1948) loyally supported joint Hindu-Muslim efforts to oust the British, he also argued that Hinduism and Islam demanded two nations, a point clearly made in this presidential address to the Muslim League (1940). In 1947, the British gave up their colony, partitioning it into the two separate states of India and Pakistan as they left.

The British government and Parliament, and more so the British nation, have been for many decades past brought up and nurtured with settled notions about India's future, based on developments in their own country which has built up the British constitution, functioning now through the Houses of Parliament and the system of cabinet. Their concept of party government functioning on political planes has become the ideal with them as the best form of government for every country, and the one-sided and powerful propaganda, which naturally appeals to the British, has led them into a serious blunder, in producing the constitution envisaged in the Government of India Act of 1935. We find that the most leading statesmen of Great Britain, saturated with these notions, have in their pronouncements seriously asserted and expressed a hope that the passage of time will harmonize the inconsistent elements of India.

A leading journal like the London Times, commenting on the Government of India Act of 1935, wrote: "Undoubtedly the differences between the Hindus and Muslims are not of religion in the strict sense of the word but also of law and culture, that they may be said, indeed, to represent two entirely distinct and separate civilizations. However, in the course of time, the superstition will die out and India will be molded into a single nation." So, according to the *London Times*, the only difficulties are superstitions. These fundamental and deep-rooted differences, spiritual, economic, cultural, social, and political, have been euphemized as mere "superstitions." But surely it is a flagrant disregard of the past history of the subcontinent of India as well as the fundamental Islamic conception of society vis-à-vis that of Hinduism to characterize them as mere "superstitions." Notwithstanding a thousand years of close contact, nationalities, which are as divergent today as ever, cannot at any time be expected to transform themselves into one nation merely by means of subjecting them to a democratic constitution and holding them forcibly together by unnatural and artificial methods of British parliamentary statute. What the unitary government of India for one hundred fifty years had failed to achieve cannot be realized by the imposition of a central federal government. It is inconceivable that the fiat or the writ of a government so constituted can ever command a willing and loyal obedience throughout the subcontinent by various nationalities except by means of armed force behind it.

The problem in India is not of an intercommunal character but manifestly of an international one, and it must be treated as such. So long as this basic and fundamental truth is not realized, any constitution that maybe built will result in disaster and will prove destructive and harmful not only to the Mussalmans but to the British and Hindus also. If the British government are really in earnest and sincere to secure [the] peace and happiness of the people of this subcontinent, the only course open to us all is to allow the major nations separate homelands by dividing India into "autonomous national states." There is no reason why these states should be antagonistic to each other. On the other hand, the rivalry and the natural desire and efforts on the part of one to dominate the social order and establish political supremacy over the other in the government of the country will disappear. It will lead more towards natural good will by international pacts between them, and they can live in complete harmony with their neighbors. This will lead further to a friendly settlement all the more easily with regard to minorities by reciprocal arrangements and adjustments between Muslim India and Hindu India, which will far more adequately and effectively safeguard the rights and interests of Muslims and various other minorities.

It is extremely difficult to appreciate why our Hindu friends fail to understand the real nature of Islam and Hinduism. They are not religions in the strict sense of the word, but are, in fact, different and distinct social orders, and it is a dream that the Hindus and Muslims can ever evolve a common nationality, and this misconception of one Indian nation has gone far beyond the limits and is the cause of most of your troubles and will lead India to destruction if we fail to revise our notions in time. The Hindus and Muslims belong to two different religious philosophies, social customs, literatures. They neither intermarry nor interdine together and, indeed, they belong to two different civilizations which are based mainly on conflicting ideas and conceptions. Their aspects on life and of life are different. It is quite clear that Hindus and Mussalmans derive their inspiration from different sources of history. They have different epics, different heroes, and different episodes. Very often the hero of one is a foe of the other and, likewise, their victories and defeats overlap. To yoke together two such nations under a single state, one as a numerical minority and the other as a majority, must lead to growing discontent and final destruction of any fabric that may be so built up for the government of such a state.

Muslim India cannot accept any constitution which must necessarily result in a Hindu majority government. Hindus and Muslims brought together under a democratic system forced upon the minorities can only mean Hindu rāj [rule]. Democracy of the kind with which the Congress High Command is enamored would mean the complete destruction of what is most precious in Islam. . . .

. . . Mussalmans are a nation according to any definition of a nation, and they must have their homelands, their territory, and their state. We wish to live in peace and harmony with our neighbors as a free and independent people. We wish our people to develop to the fullest our spiritual, cultural, economic, social, and political life in a way that we think best and in consonance with our own ideals and according to the genius of our people. Honesty demands and the vital interests of millions of our people impose a sacred duty upon us to find an honorable and peaceful solution, which would be just and fair to all. But at the same time we cannot be moved or diverted from our purpose and objective by threats or intimidations. We must be prepared to face all difficulties and consequences, make all the sacrifices that may be required of us to achieve the goal we have set in front of us.

Bandung Declaration (1955)

As Europe's mandates and colonies gained political independence, they found their economic independence was in jeopardy in a world squeezed by two giant politico-economic blocks: the Capitalist West and the Communist East. In April 1955, 29 African and Asian states met for a "third world conclave" in Bandung, a mountain town on the island of Java. The newly created nations represented a wide range of economic and political systems, but, as this Declaration indicates, all were united in their opposition to colonialism and in a mutual desire for cultural and economic cooperation.

Human Rights and Self Determination

1. The Asian-African Conference declared its full support of the fundamental principles of Human Rights as set forth in the Charter of the United Nations and took note of the universal declaration of Human Rights as a common standard of achievement for all peoples and all nations.

    The Conference declared its full support of the principle of self-determination of peoples and nations as set forth in the Charter of the United Nations and took note of the United Nations resolutions on the rights of peoples and nations to self-determination, which is a prerequisite of the full enjoyment of all fundamental Human Rights.

2. The Asian-African Conference deplored the policies and practices of racial segregation and discrimination which form the basis of government and human relations in large regions of Africa and in other parts of the world. Such conduct is not only a gross violation of human rights, but also a denial of the fundamental values of civilisation and the dignity of man.

    The Conference extended its warm sympathy and support for the courageous stand taken by the victims of racial discrimination, especially by the peoples of African and Indian and Pakistani origin in South Africa; applauded all those who sustain their cause; reaffirmed the determination of Asian-African peoples to eradicate every trace of racialism that might exist in their own countries; and pledged to use its full moral influence to guard against the danger of falling victims to the same evil in their struggle to eradicate it.

Problems of Dependent Peoples

1. The Asian-African Conference discussed the problems of dependent peoples and colonialism and the evils arising from the subjection of peoples to alien subjugation, domination and exploitation.

   The Conference is agreed:

   a. in declaring that colonialism in all its manifestations is an evil which should speedily be brought to an end;

   b. in affirming that the subjection of peoples to alien subjugation, domination and exploitation constitutes a denial of fundamental human rights, is contrary to the Charter of the United Nations and is an impediment to the promotion of world peace and cooperation;

   c. in declaring its support of the cause of freedom and independence for all such peoples; and

   d. in calling upon the powers concerned to grant freedom and independence to such peoples.

2. In view of the unsettled situation of North Africa and of the persisting denial to the peoples of North Africa of their right to self-determination, the Asian-African Conference declared its support of the rights of the people of Algeria, Morocco and Tunisia to self-determination and independence and urged the French Government to bring about a peaceful settlement of the issue without delay.

Ten Principles

Free from mistrust and fear, and with confidence and goodwill towards each other, nations should practice tolerance and live together in peace with one another as good neighbors and develop friendly cooperation on the basis of the following principles:

1. Respect for fundamental human rights and for the purposes and principles of the Charter of the United Nations.

2. Respect for the sovereignty and territorial integrity of all nations.

3. Recognition of the equality of all races and of the equality of all nations large and small.

4. Abstention from intervention or interference in the internal affairs of another country.

5. Respect for the right of each nation to defend itself singly or collectively, in conformity with the Charter of the United Nations.

6. a. Abstention from the use of arrangements of collective defence to serve the particular interests of any of the big powers.

   b. Abstention by any country from exerting pressures on other countries.

7. Refraining from acts or threats of aggression or the use of force against the territorial integrity or political independence of any country.

8. Settlement of all international disputes by peaceful means, such as negotiation, conciliation, arbitration or judicial settlement as well as other peaceful means of the parties' own choice, in conformity with the Charter of the United Nations.

9. Promotion of mutual interests and cooperation.

10. Respect for justice and international obligations.

The Asian and African Conference declares its conviction that friendly cooperation in accordance with these principles would effectively contribute to the maintenance and promotion of international peace and security, while cooperation in the economic, social and cultural fields would help bring about the common prosperity and well-being of all.

The 28th Anniversary of the Chinese Communist Party (1949)

MAO ZEDONG

In this speech to the Chinese Communist Party, delivered shortly before their final victory over the Nationalists, Mao Zedong (1893–1976) demonstrated his commitment to Marxist thought and his confidence in China's destiny. In Mao's understanding of nationalism, individuals holding politically opposing views were no longer part of the nation and so were not entitled to the state's protection.

"You are dictatorial." My dear sirs, you are right, that is just what we are. All the experience the Chinese people have accumulated through several decades teaches us to enforce the people's democratic dictatorship, that is, to deprive the reactionaries of the right to speak and let the people alone have that right.

Who are the people? At the present stage in China, they are the working class, the peasantry, the urban petty bourgeoisie and the national bourgeoisie. These classes, led by the working class and the Communist Party, unite to form their own state and elect their own government; they enforce their dictatorship over the running dogs of imperialism—the landlord class and bureaucrat-bourgeoisie, as well as the representative of those classes, the Kuomintang reactionaries and their accomplices—suppress them, allow them only to behave themselves and not to be unruly in word or deed. If they speak or act in an unruly way, they will be promptly stopped and punished. Democracy is practised within the ranks of the people, who enjoy the rights of freedom of speech, assembly, association and so on. The right to vote belongs only to the people, not to the reactionaries. The combination of these two aspects, democracy for the people and dictatorship over the reactionaries, is the people's democratic dictatorship. . . .

"Don't you want to abolish state power?" Yes, we do, but not right now; we cannot do it yet. Why? Because imperialism still exists, because domestic reaction still exists, because classes still exist in our country. Our present task is to strengthen the people's state apparatus—mainly the people's army, the people's police and the people's courts—in order to consolidate national defence and protect the people's interests. Given this condition, China can develop steadily, under the leadership of the working class and the Communist Party, from an agricultural into an industrial country and from a new-democratic into a socialist and communist society, can abolish classes and realize the Great Harmony. The state apparatus, including the army, the police and the courts, is the instrument by which one class oppresses another. It is an instrument for the oppression of antagonistic classes; it is violence and not benevolence.

"You are not benevolent." Quite so. We definitely do not apply a policy of benevolence to the reactionaries and towards the reactionary activities of the reactionary classes. Our policy of benevolence is applied only within the ranks of the people, not beyond them to the reactionaries or to the reactionary activities of the reactionary classes.

The people's state protects the people. Only when the people have such a state can they educate and remould themselves on a country-wide scale by democratic methods and . . . advance towards a socialist and communist society. Here, the method we employ is democratic, the method of persuasion, not of compulsion. When any one among the people breaks the law, he too should be punished, imprisoned or even sentenced to death; but this is a matter of few individual cases, and it differs in principle from the dictatorship exercised over the reactionaries as a class.

As for the members of the reactionary classes and individual reactionaries, so long as they do not rebel, sabotage or create trouble after their political power is overthrown, land and work will be given to them as well in order to allow them to live and remould themselves through labour into a new people. If they are not willing to work, the people's state will compel them to work. . . .

When it (remoulding of the reactionaries) is well-done, China's major exploiting classes, the landlord class and the bureaucrat-bourgeoisie (the monopoly-capitalist class) will be eliminated for good. There remain the national bourgeoisie; at the present stage, we can already do a good deal of suitable educational work with many of them. When the time comes to realize socialism, that is, to nationalize private enterprise, we shall carry the work of educating and remoulding them a step further. The people have a powerful state apparatus in their hands—there is no need to fear rebellion by the national bourgeoisie.

The serious problem is the education of the peasantry. The peasant economy is scattered, and the socialization of agriculture, judging by the Soviet Union's experience, will require a long time and painstaking work. Without socialization of agriculture, there can be no complete, consolidated socialism. The steps to socialize agriculture must be coordinated with the development of a powerful industry having state enterprise as its backbone. The state of the people's democratic dictatorship must systematically solve the problems of industrialization. . . .

To sum up our experience and concentrate it into one point, it is: the people's democratic dictatorship under the leadership of the working class (through the Communist Party) and based upon the alliance of workers and peasants. This dictatorship must unite as one with the international revolutionary forces. This is our formula, our principal experience, our main programme.

China Under Deng Xiaoping

As determined as Chairman Mao was to maintain the Communist Party's control of China, Deng Xiaoping (1904–1997) was more willing to experiment with economic reform and diplomatic compromise to increase China's prosperity and power. His 1978 speech at the National Science Conference argued for "four modernizations"—agriculture, industry, defense, and science/technology—at a time when he was still struggling to oust the "Gang of Four" determined to continue Mao's Cultural Revolution. Deng's 1984 "One Country, Two Systems" speech linked China's plans for the return of Hong Kong in 1997 to the introduction of capitalist "special economic zones" on the mainland and to China's desire to reincorporate Nationalist Taiwan.

Speech at the Opening Ceremony of the National Conference on Science (1978)

Our people are undertaking the historic mission of modernizing our agriculture, industry, national defence and science and technology within the present century, in order to transform China into a modern and powerful socialist state. We have waged a bitter struggle against the Gang of Four over the question of whether the four modernizations are needed or not. The Gang made the senseless statement that "the day the four modernizations programme is realized will mark the day of capitalist restoration". Their sabotage brought China's economy to the brink of collapse and led to a constant widening of the gap between us and the countries with the most advanced science and technology. Did the Gang really want to build socialism and oppose the restoration of capitalism? Not in the least. On the contrary, socialism sustained grave damage wherever their influence was strongest. Their misdeeds, serving as a negative example, make us realize all the more clearly that even though we have a dictatorship of the proletariat, unless we modernize our country, raise our scientific and technological level, develop our productive forces and thus strengthen our country and improve the material and cultural life of our people—unless we do all this, our socialist political and economic system cannot be fully consolidated, and there can be no sure guarantee for the country's security. The more our agriculture, industry, national defense and science and technology are modernized, the stronger we will be in the struggle against forces which sabotage socialism. Only if we make our country a modern, powerful socialist state can we more effectively consolidate the socialist system and cope with foreign aggression and subversion; only then can we be reasonably certain of gradually creating the material conditions for the advance to our great goal of communism.

The key to the four modernizations is the modernization of science and technology. Without modern science and technology, it is impossible to build modern agriculture, modern industry or modern national defense. . . .

. . . The Gang of Four raised a hue and cry over this, confounding right and wrong and sowing much confusion in people's minds. Marxism has consistently treated science and technology as part of the productive forces. . . .

The Gang of Four made the absurd claim that the more a person knew, the more reactionary he would become. . . .

Comrade Mao Zedong urged intellectuals to become both "red and expert."

❀

One Country, Two Systems (1984)

The Chinese Government is firm in its position, principles and policies on Hong Kong. We have stated that after China resumes the exercise of its sovereignty over Hong Kong in 1997, Hong Kong's current social and economic systems will remain unchanged, its legal system will remain basically unchanged, its way of life and its status as a free port and an international trade and monetary centre will remain unchanged and it can continue to maintain and develop economic relations with other countries and regions. We have also stated repeatedly that apart from stationing troops there, Beijing will not assign officials to the government of the Hong Kong special administrative region. This policy too will remain unchanged. We shall station troops there to safeguard our national security, not to interfere in Hong Kong's internal affairs. Our policies with regard to Hong Kong will remain unchanged for 50 years, and we mean this.

We are pursuing a policy of "one country, two systems". More specifically, this means that within the People's Republic of China, the mainland with its one billion people will practise socialism, while Hong Kong and Taiwan may practise capitalism. . . .

Our policy towards Hong Kong will remain unchanged for a long time to come, but this will not affect socialism on the mainland. The main system in China must be socialism. The socialist system is practised by the one billion people on the mainland, but a capitalist system will be allowed to exist in certain regions, such as Hong Kong and Taiwan. Opening a number of cities on the mainland and letting in some measure of capitalism will supplement the development of the socialist economy and benefit the growth of the socialist productive forces. For example, when foreign capital is invested in Shanghai, it does not mean that the entire city has gone capitalist. The same is true of Shenzhen (a special economic zone), where socialism still prevails. In China, socialism is the dominant system.

The concept of "one country, two systems" has been formulated to suit China's realities, and it has attracted international attention. China has not only the Hong Kong problem to tackle but the Taiwan problem. What is the solution to the Taiwan problem? Is it for socialism to swallow up Taiwan, or for the "Three People's Principles" preached by Taiwan to swallow up the mainland? The answer is neither. If the problem cannot be solved by peaceful means, then it must be solved by force. Neither side would benefit from that. Reunification of the motherland is the aspiration of the whole nation. If it cannot be accomplished in 100 years, it will be in 1000 years. . . .

Some requirements or qualifications should be established with regard to the administration of Hong Kong affairs by the people of Hong Kong. It must be required that patriots form the main body of administrators, that is, of the future government of Hong Kong. Of course it should include other people, too, as well as foreigners invited to serve as advisers. Who are patriots? The qualifications for a patriot are respect for the Chinese nation, sincere support for the motherland's resumption of sovereignty over Hong Kong and a desire not to impair Hong Kong's prosperity and stability. Those who meet these requirements are patriots, whether they believe in capitalism or feudalism or even slavery. We don't demand that they be in favour of China's socialist system; we only ask them to love the motherland and Hong Kong.

The Vietnamese Declaration of Independence (1945)

During the second half of the Nineteenth Century, as European states "scrambled" to obtain colonies, France seized control of Indo-China (modern day Vietnam, Laos, and Cambodia). Two world wars later, France still retained its title to Vietnam but it faced a vigorous independence movement led by Ho Chi Minh (1890–1969), founder of the Indochinese Communist Party in 1929. During World War II, Ho's nationalists fought Japanese occupation, taking possession of Hanoi as the fighting ended. On September 2, 1945, Ho proclaimed the independence of the Democratic Republic of Vietnam. Cold War policy dictated the splitting of Vietnam into two countries, however: a Communist state in the north and a pro-American state in the south. It would be another thirty years before all foreign troops were expelled from Vietnam's borders and the country reunited.

"All men are created equal. They are endowed by their Creator with certain inalienable Rights; among these are Life, Liberty and the pursuit of Happiness."

This immortal statement was made in the Declaration of Independence of the United States of America in 1776. In a broader sense, this means: All the peoples on the earth are equal from birth, all the peoples have a right to live and to be happy and free.

The Declaration, made in 1789 at the time of the French Revolution, on the Rights of Man and the Citizen, also states: "All men are born free and with equal rights, and must always remain free and have equal rights."

Those are undeniable truths.

Nevertheless, for more than eighty years, the French imperialists, abusing the standard of Liberty, Equality and Fraternity, have violated our Fatherland and oppressed our fellow-citizens. They have acted contrary to the ideals of humanity and justice.

In the field of politics, they have deprived our people of every democratic liberty.

They have enforced inhuman laws; they have set up three distinct political regimes in the North, the Center and the South of Viet Nam in order to wreck our national unity and prevent our people from being united.

They have built more prisons than schools. They have mercilessly slain our patriots; they have drowned our uprisings in rivers of blood. They have fettered public opinion; they have practiced obscurantism against our people. To weaken our race they have forced us to use opium and alcohol.

In the field of economics, they have fleeced us to the bone, impoverished our people and devastated our land.

They have robbed us of our ricefields, our mines, our forests, our raw materials. They have monopolized the issue of banknotes and the export trade.

They have invented numerous unjustifiable taxes, and reduced our people, especially our peasantry, to a state of extreme poverty.

They have hampered our national bourgeoisie from prospering; they have mercilessly exploited our workers.

In the autumn of 1940, when the Japanese fascists violated Indochina's territory to establish new bases against the Allies, the French imperialists went down on their bended knees and handed over our country to them.

Thus, from that date, our people were subjected to the double yoke of the French and the Japanese. Their sufferings and miseries increased. The result was that from the end of last year to the beginning of this year, from Quang Tri province to the North of Viet Nam, more than two million of our fellow-citizens died from starvation. On the 9th of March, French troops were disarmed by the Japanese. The French colonialists either fled or surrendered, showing that not only were they incapable of "protecting" us, but that, in the span of five years, they had twice sold our country to the Japanese.

On several occasions before the 9th of March, the Viet Minh league had urged the French to join forces with it against the Japanese. Instead of agreeing to this proposal, the French colonialists so intensified their terrorist activities against the Viet Minh members that before fleeing they massacred a great number of political prisoners detained at Yen Bay and Cao Bang.

Notwithstanding all this, our fellow-citizens have always manifested a tolerant and humane attitude towards the French. Even after the Japanese coup de force of March 1943, the Viet Minh League helped many Frenchmen to cross the frontier, rescued some of them from Japanese jails and protected French lives and property.

From the autumn of 1940, our country had in fact ceased to be a French colony and had become a Japanese possession.

After the Japanese had surrendered to the Allies, our whole people rose up to regain our national sovereignty and to found the Democratic Republic of Viet Nam.

The truth is that we have wrested our independence from the Japanese and not from the French.

The French have fled, the Japanese have capitulated. Emperor Bao Da has abdicated. Our people have broken the chains which for nearly a century have fettered us and have won independence for the Fatherland. Our people at the same time have overthrown the monarchic regime that has reigned supreme for tens of centuries. In its place has been established the present Democratic Republic.

For these reasons, we, members of the Provisional Government, representing the whole Vietnamese people, declare that from now on we break off all relations of a colonial character with France; we repeal all the international obligations that France has so far subscribed to on behalf of Viet Nam and we abolish all the special rights the French have unlawfully acquired in our Fatherland.

The whole Vietnamese people, animated by a common purpose, are determined to fight to the bitter end against any attempt by the French colonialists to reconquer our country.

We are convinced that the Allied nations, which at Teheran and San Francisco have acknowledged the principles of self-determination and equality of nations, will not refuse to recognize the independence of Viet Nam.

A people that has courageously opposed French domination for more than eighty years, a people that has fought side by side with the Allies against the fascists during these last years, such a people must be free and independent.

For those reasons, we, members of the Provisional Government of the Democratic Republic of Viet Nam, solemnly declare to the world that Viet Nam has the right to be free and independent, and in fact it is so already. The entire Vietnamese people are determined to mobilize all their physical and mental strength, to sacrifice their lives and property in order to safeguard their freedom and independence.

Camp David Agreement (1978)

The war between Israel and Arab states that broke out in 1948 is still without a complete peace. The 1948 cease fire has been punctuated by three full scale wars (1956, 1967, 1973) and numerous other conflicts. However, in 1978, thanks to the efforts of Egyptian President Anwar Sadat (1918–1981), Israeli Prime Minister Menachem Begin (1913–1992), and United States President Jimmy Carter (b. 1924), Israel was able to make peace with one Arab state when Sadat and Begin signed the Camp David Agreement. Egypt was immediately ostracized by the Arab League and Sadat was later assassinated for signing the agreement.

During the past 30 years, Israel and Egypt have waged war. But for the past 16 months, these same two great nations have waged peace.

Today we celebrate a victory, not of a bloody military campaign, but of an inspiring peace campaign. Two leaders who loom large in the history of nations, President Anwar Sadat and Prime Minister Menachem Begin, have conducted this campaign with all the courage, tenacity, brilliance and inspiration of any generals who have ever led men and machines onto the field of battle.

At the end of this campaign, the soil of the two lands is not drenched with young blood. The countrysides of both lands are free from the litter and the carnage of a wasteful war.

Mothers in Egypt and Israel are not weeping today for their children fallen in senseless battle. The dedication and determination of these two world statesmen have borne fruit. Peace has come to Israel and to Egypt.

I honor these two leaders and their Government officials who have hammered out this peace treaty which we have just signed. But most of all, I honor the people of these two lands whose yearning for peace kept alive the negotiations which today culminate in this glorious event.

First Step of Peace

We have won, at last, the first step of peace. A first step on a long and difficult road. We must not minimize the obstacles which still lie ahead. Differences still separate the signatories to this treaty from one another. And also from some of their neighbors who fear what they have just done.

To overcome these differences, to dispel these fears, we must rededicate ourselves to the goal of a broader peace with justice for all who have lived in a state of conflict in the Middle East.

We have no illusions. We have hopes, dreams and prayers, yes. But no illusions. There now remains the rest of the Arab world whose support and whose cooperation in the peace process is needed and honestly sought.

I am convinced that other Arab people need and want peace. But some of their leaders are not yet willing to honor these needs and desires for peace. We must now demonstrate the advantages of peace and expand its benefits to encompass all those who have suffered so much in the Middle East.

The Next Step

Obviously, time and understanding will be necessary for people, hitherto enemies, to become neighbors in the best sense of the word. Just because a paper is signed, all the problems will not automatically go away. Future days will require the best from us to give reality to these lofty aspirations.

Let those who would shatter peace, who would callously spill more blood, be aware that we three and all others who may join us will vigorously wage peace. So let history record that deep and ancient antagonisms can be settled without bloodshed and without staggering waste of precious lives, without rapacious destruction of the land.

It has been said, and I quote:

"Peace has one thing in common with its enemy, with the fiend it battles, with war: Peace is active, not passive; peace is doing, not waiting; peace is aggressive, attacking; peace plans its strategy and encircles the enemy; peace marshals its forces and storms the gates; peace gathers its weapons and pierces the defense. Peace, like war, is waged."

It is true that we cannot enforce trust and cooperation between nations, but we can use all our strength to see that nations do not again go to war. Our religious doctrines—all our religious doctrines give us hope.

Quoting the Prophet

In the Koran, we read: "But if the enemy inclines toward peace, do thou also incline towards peace. And trust in God, for He is the One that heareth and knoweth all things."

And the Prophet Isaiah said: "Nations shall beat their swords into plowshares, and their spears into pruning hooks. Nation shall not lift up sword against nation. Neither shall they learn war any more."

So let us now lay aside war; let us now reward all the children of Abraham who hunger for a comprehensive peace in the Middle East. Let us now enjoy the adventure of becoming fully human, fully neighbors, even brothers and sisters.

We pray God, we pray God together, that these dreams will come true. I believe they will.

Topic XII

Liberation and Dependency in Africa and Latin America

110

The Freedom Charter of the African National Congress (1955)

Founded in 1912 to combat Boer domination of South Africa, the African National Congress (ANC) pursued a course of Gandhi-inspired non-violent protest. The imposition of apartheid (strict racial separation) after the victory of the Afrikaner dominated Nationalist Party in 1948, gave the ANC a new impetus. This 1955 Freedom Charter reaffirmed the ANC's inclusive, multi-racial vision of South Africa.

Preamble

We, the people of South Africa, declare for all our country and the world to know:

That South Africa belongs to all who live in it, black and white, and that no government can justly claim authority unless it is based on the will of the people;

That our People have been robbed of their birthright to land, liberty and peace by a form of government founded on injustice and inequality;

That our country will never be prosperous or free until all our people live in brotherhood, enjoying equal rights and opportunities;

That only a democratic state, based on the will of all the people, can secure to all their birthright without distinction of color, race, sex or belief;

And therefore, we, the people of South Africa, black and white, together—equals, countrymen and brothers—adopt this FREEDOM CHARTER. And we pledge ourselves to strive together, sparing nothing of our strength and courage, until the democratic changes here set out have been won.

The People Shall Govern!

Every man and woman shall have the right to vote for and stand as a candidate for all bodies which make laws.

341

All the people shall be entitled to take part in the administration of the country.

The rights of people shall be the same regardless of race, color or sex.

All bodies of minority rule, advisory boards, councils and authorities shall be replaced by democratic organs of self-government.

All National Groups Shall Have Equal Rights!

There shall be equal status in the bodies of state, in the courts, and in the schools for all national groups and races;

All people shall have equal rights to use their own languages and to develop their own folk culture and customs;

All national groups shall be protected by law against insults to their race and national pride;

The preaching and practice of national, race or color discrimination and contempt shall be a punishable crime;

All apartheid laws and practices shall be set aside.

The People Shall Share in the Country's Wealth!

The national wealth of our country, the heritage of all South Africans, shall be restored to the people;

The mineral wealth beneath the soil, the banks and monopoly industry shall be transferred to the ownership of the people as a whole;

All other industries and trade shall be controlled to assist the well-being of the people;

All people shall have equal rights to trade where they choose, to manufacture and to enter all trades, crafts and professions.

The Land Shall Be Shared Among Those Who Work It!

Restriction of land ownership on a racial basis shall be ended, and all the land re-divided amongst those who work it, to banish famine and land hunger;

The state shall help the peasants with implements, seed, tractors and dams to save the soil and assist the tillers;

Freedom of movement shall be guaranteed to all who work on the land;

All shall have the right to occupy land wherever they choose;

People shall not be robbed of their cattle, and forced labor and farm prisons shall be abolished.

All Shall Be Equal Before the Law!

No one shall be imprisoned, deported or restricted without a fair trial;

No one shall be condemned by the order of any Government official;

The courts shall be representative of all the people;

Imprisonment shall be only for serious crimes against the people, and shall aim at re-education, not vengeance;

The police force and army shall be open to all on an equal basis and shall be the helpers and protectors of the people;

All laws which discriminate on grounds of race, color or belief shall be repealed.

All Shall Enjoy Equal Human Rights!

The law shall guarantee to all their right to speak, to organize, to meet together, to publish, to preach, to worship and to educate their children;

The privacy of the house from police raids shall be protected by law;

All shall be free to travel without restriction from countryside to town, from province to province, and from South Africa abroad;

Pass laws, permits and all other laws restricting these freedoms shall be abolished.

There Shall Be Work and Security!

All who work shall be free to form trade unions, to elect their officers and to make wage agreements with their employers;

The state shall recognize the right and duty of all to work; and to draw full unemployment benefits;

Men and women of all races shall receive equal pay for equal work;

There shall be a forty-hour working week, a national minimum wage, paid annual leave, and sick leave for all workers, and maternity leave on full pay for all working mothers;

Miners, domestic workers, farm workers and civil servants shall have the same rights as all others who work;

Child labor, compound labor, the tot system and contract labor shall be abolished.

The Doors of Learning and of Culture Shall Be Opened!

The government shall discover, develop and encourage national talent for the enhancement of our cultural life;

All the cultural treasures of mankind shall be open to all, by free exchange of books, ideas and contact with other lands;

The aim of education shall be to teach the youth to love their people and their culture, to honor human brotherhood, liberty and peace;

Education shall be free, compulsory, universal and equal for all children;

Higher education and technical training shall be opened to all by means of state allowances and scholarships awarded on the basis of merit;

Adult illiteracy shall be ended by a mass state education plan;

Teachers shall have all the rights of other citizens;

The color bar in cultural life, in sport and in education shall be abolished.

There Shall Be Houses, Security and Comfort!

All people shall have the right to live where they choose, to be decently housed, and to bring up their families in comfort and security;

Unused housing space to be made available to the people;

Rent and prices shall be lowered, food plentiful and no one shall go hungry;

A preventive health scheme shall be run by the state;

Free medical care and hospitalization shall be provided for all, with special care for mothers and young children;

Slums shall be a demolished, and new suburbs built where all have transport, roads, lighting, playing fields, crèches and social centers;

The aged, the orphans, the disabled and the sick shall be cared for by the state;

Rest, leisure and recreation shall be the right of all;

Fenced locations and ghettos shall be abolished, and laws which break up families shall be repealed.

There Shall Be Peace and Friendship!

South Africa shall be a fully independent state, which respects the rights and sovereignty of all nations;

South Africa shall strive to maintain world peace and the settlement of all international disputes by negotiation—not war;

Peace and friendship amongst all our people shall be secured by upholding the equal rights, opportunities and status of all;

The people of the protectorates—Basutoland, Bechuanaland and Swaziland—shall be free to decide for themselves their own future;

The right of all the peoples of Africa to independence and self-government shall be recognized, and shall be the basis of close co-operation.

Let all who love their people and their country now say, as we say here:

'THESE FREEDOMS WE WILL FIGHT FOR, SIDE BY SIDE, THROUGHOUT OUR LIVES, UNTIL WE HAVE WON OUR LIBERTY.'

South African Women's Charter (1954)

One year before the African National Congress proclaimed its Freedom Charter, *the multi-racial Federation of South African Women (which had evolved out of the ANC's Women's League) launched its own proclamation in the ongoing struggle for equality in South Africa. The FSAW successfully campaigned to have many (but not all) of its demands specific to the problems women faced included in that more well-known manifesto. Suppressed by the government in 1960, the Women's League was re-launched on August 9, 1990, to mark the anniversary of the Women's 1956 anti-pass law march in Pretoria—and to continue the struggle for women's rights in the new South Africa.*

Preamble: We, the women of South Africa, wives and mothers, working women and housewives, African, Indians, European and Colored, hereby declare our aim of striving for the removal of all laws, regulations, conventions and customs that discriminate against us as women, and that deprive us in any way of our inherent right to the advantages, responsibilities and opportunities that society offers to any one section of the population.

A Single Society: We women do not form a society separate from the men. There is only one society, and it is made up of both women and men. As women we share the problems and anxieties of our men, and join hands with them to remove social evils and obstacles to progress.

Test of Civilization: The level of civilization which any society has reached can be measured by the degree of freedom that its members enjoy. The status of women is a test of civilization. Measured by that standard, South Africa must be considered low in the scale of civilized nations.

Women's Lot: We women share with our menfolk the cares and anxieties imposed by poverty and its evils. As wives and mothers, it falls upon us to make small wages stretch a long way. It is we who feel the cries of our children when they are hungry and sick. It is our lot to keep and care for the homes that are too small, broken and dirty to be kept clean. We know the burden of looking after children and land when our husbands are away in the mines, on the farms, and in the towns earning our daily bread. We know what it is to keep family life going in pondokkies and shanties, or in over-crowded one-room apartments. We know the bitterness of children taken to lawless ways, of daughters becoming unmarried mothers whilst still at school, of boys and girls growing up without education, training or jobs at a living wage. Poor and Rich: These are evils that need not exist. They exist because the society in which we live is divided into poor and rich, into non-European and European. They exist because there are privileges for the few, discrimination and harsh treatment for the many. We women have stood and will stand shoulder to shoulder with our menfolk in a common struggle against poverty, race and class discrimination, and the evils of the color bar.

National Liberation: As members of the National Liberatory movements and Trade Unions, in and through our various organizations, we march forward with our men in the struggle for liberation and the defense of the working people. We pledge ourselves to keep high the banner of equality, fraternity and liberty. As women there rests upon us also the burden of removing from our society all the social differences developed in past times between men and women, which have the effect of keeping our sex in a position of inferiority and subordination.

Equality for Women: We resolve to struggle for the removal of laws and customs that deny African women the right to own, inherit or alienate property. We resolve to work for a change in the laws of marriage such as are found amongst our African, Malay and Indian people, which have the effect of placing wives in the position of legal subjection to husbands, and giving husbands the power to dispose of wives' property and earnings, and dictate to them in all matters affecting them and their children. We recognize that the women are treated as minors by these marriage and property laws because of ancient and revered traditions and customs which had their origin in the antiquity of the people and no doubt served purposes of great value in bygone times. There was a time in the African society when every woman reaching marriageable stage was assured of a husband, home, land and security. Then husbands and wives with their children belonged to families and clans that supplied most of their own material needs and were largely self-sufficient. Men and women were partners in a compact and closely integrated family unit.

Women who Labor: Those conditions have gone. The tribal and kinship society to which they belonged has been destroyed as a result of the loss of tribal land, migration of men away from the tribal home, the growth of towns and industries, and the rise of a great body of wage-earners on the farms and in the urban areas, who depend wholly or mainly on wages for a livelihood. Thousands of African women, like Indians, Colored and European women, are employed today in factories, homes, offices, shops, on farms, in professions as nurses, teachers and the like. As unmarried women, widows or divorcees they have to fend for themselves, often without the assistance of a male relative. Many of them are responsible not only for their own livelihood but also that of their children. Large numbers of women today are in fact the sole breadwinners and heads of their families.

Forever Minors: Nevertheless, the laws and practices derived from an earlier and different state of society are still applied to them. They are responsible for their own person and their children. Yet the law seeks to enforce upon them the status of a minor. Not only are African, Colored and Indian women denied political rights, but they are also in many parts of the Union denied the same status as men in such matters as the right to enter into contracts, to own and dispose of property, and to exercise guardianship over their children.

Obstacle to Progress: The law has lagged behind the development of society; it no longer corresponds to the actual social and economic position of women. The law has become an obstacle to progress of the women, and therefore a brake on the whole of society. This intolerable condition would not be allowed to continue were it not for the refusal of a large section of our menfolk to concede to us women the rights and privileges which they demand for themselves. We shall teach the men that they cannot hope to liberate themselves from the evils of discrimination and prejudice as long as they fail to extend to women complete and unqualified equality in law and in practice.

Need for Education: We also recognize that large numbers of our womenfolk continue to be bound by traditional practices and conventions, and fail to realize that these have become obsolete and a brake on progress. It is our duty and privilege to enlist all women in our struggle for emancipation and to bring to them all realization of the intimate relationship that exists between their status of inferiority as women and the inferior status to which their people are subjected by discriminatory laws and color prejudices. It is our intention to carry out a nation-wide program of education that will bring home to the men and women of all national groups the realization that freedom cannot be won for any one section or for the people as a whole as long as we women are kept in bondage.

An Appeal: We women appeal to all progressive organizations, to members of the great National Liberatory movements, to the trade unions and working class organizations, to the churches, educational and welfare organizations, to all progressive men and women who have the interests of the people at heart, to join with us in this great and noble endeavor.

Our Aims

We declare the following aims:

1. This organization is formed for the purpose of uniting women in common action for the removal of all political, legal, economic and social disabilities. We shall strive for women to obtain:

- The right to vote and to be elected to all State bodies, without restriction or discrimination.
- The right to full opportunities for employment with equal pay and possibilities of promotion in all spheres of work.
- Equal rights with men in relation to property, marriage and children, and for the removal of all laws and customs that deny women such equal rights.

2. For the development of every child through free compulsory education for all; for the protection of mother and child through maternity homes, welfare clinics, creches and nursery schools, in countryside and towns; through proper homes for all, and through the provision of water, light, transport, sanitation, and other amenities of modern civilization.

3. For the removal of all laws that restrict free movement, that prevent or hinder the right of free association and activity in democratic organizations, and the right to participate in the work of these organizations.

4. To build and strengthen women's sections in the National Liberatory movements, the organization of women in trade unions, and through the peoples' varied organization.

5. To cooperate with all other organizations that have similar aims in South Africa as well as throughout the world.

6. To strive for permanent peace throughout the world.

"The Widows of the Reserves" (1960)

PHYLLIS NTANTALA

Under apartheid, blacks were not considered citizens of South Africa, but of native "reserves"called Bantustans. These "reserves" were deliberately designed to be too small to support their inhabitants. Black South Africans were forced to seek underpaid work inside a South Africa in which they could only travel with official permission (nicknamed a "Pass"—short for passport). Phyllis Ntantala (b. 1920) was born into the small black African social elite of South Africa. A journalist and teacher, she emigrated to the United States with her family in the 1960s. In this article she explored the life of the women left behind in the "reserves."

Widowhood—a life of void and loneliness; a period of tension, unbalance, and strenuous adjustment. And what can it be to those thousands of African women—those adolescent girls married before they reach womanhood, thrown into a life of responsibility before they have completely passed from childhood to adulthood; those young women in the prime of early womanhood left to face life alone, burdened with the task of building a home and rearing a family; those young women doomed to nurse alone their sick babies, weep alone over their dead babies, dress and bury alone their corpses? What can it mean to those young brides whose purpose has been snatched away, overnight, leaving them bewildered and lost, leaving them with a thirst and hunger that cannot be stilled?

And yet this is the daily lot of tens of thousands of African women whose husbands are torn away from them to go and work in the cities, mines, and farms—husbands who because of the migratory labor system cannot take their wives with them and, because of the starvation wages they receive, are forced to remain in the work centers for long periods—strangers in a strange land—but equally strangers at home to their wives and children.

These women remain alone in the Reserves to build the homes, till the land, rear the stock, bring up the children. They watch alone the ravages of drought, when the scraggy cows cease to provide the milk, when the few stock drop one by one because there is no grass on the veld, and all the streams have been lapped dry by the scorching sun. They watch alone the crops in the fields wither in the scorching sun, their labor of months blighted in a few days. They witness alone the hailstorm sweep clean their mealie lands, alone they witness the wind lift bodily their huts as if they were pieces of paper, rendering them and their children homeless. Alone they bury their babies one by one and lastly their unknown lovers—their husbands, whose corpses alone are sent back to the Reserves. For the world of grinding machines has no use for men whose lungs are riddled with TB and miner's phthisis.

For miles around throughout the country, one sees nobody but these women—young and yet sternfaced with lines of care on their faces. This one climbing the slope with a bucket of water on her head and, if lucky, a baby on her back; that one going up the hill with a heavy bundle of wood on her head; another following behind with a span of six oxen drawing a sledge with plowing implements and a youngster of ten or twelve years as her help; and yet another driving home a scraggy herd of cattle or a flock of sheep numbering twenty at the very most, with yet another small boy by her side.

In the plowing season they are to be seen behind the span of oxen, holding the plow, leading the team of plowing oxen. In the cold winter months, alone with young girls and boys, they reap the fields, load the wagons, and bring in the harvest. A poor harvest! What else could it be? "Bad farming methods of the native," is the official attitude of South Africa. But how could it be otherwise when the farming is left to women and children, when the whole task of homebuilding is on their shoulders?

At home in the morning these lonely women see to it that their children get ready for school—those underfed and scantily dressed children whose breakfast is a piece of dry bread, mealie-pap without any milk, and for many just cold mush and beans. Their desire to see their children educated is so great that the women themselves go out with the stock in order to keep their children at school—to give them the education that will free them from poverty, the education that has given the other races so much knowledge and power.

At the close of day they light their fires to prepare the evening meal. The fortunate ones milk and shut in the stock, but for most there is no stock to shut in, and their children do not know the milk from the family cow. For some there is a letter of good news from the father and husband far away in the work center—the long-awaited letter with money has come—part of the debt at the trader's will be paid off. There will be bread, sugar, tea, and a few extras to eat for at least a few weeks. For others it is bad news. The loved one far away is ill, has met with an accident, has been thrown into jail because he failed to produce his papers when demanded by some government official. Not that he did not have them, but just that by mistake he forgot them in the pocket of his other jacket. A black man in South Africa cannot forget! It is a sad day for this one. Her children look up anxiously in her face. They fear to ask her any questions, and she does not know how much to tell them. "Tata sends his greetings," she manages to say at last, "but says we will have to be patient about the money we asked for; he has had some trouble and has used up all the money." The rest of the evening is spent in silence. And when they kneel down to pray, this lonely woman sends to heaven a prayer without an "Amen." Small wonder most of them are old women at the age of thirty, emaciated, tired, and worn-out. . . .

Tired of their hard life in the Reserves and in despair, they resort to all sorts of ways whereby they can get to the work centers in order to join their husbands. But the pass system which is used to control the movements of the whole African population throughout the country makes it well nigh impossible for them to do so. Under the influx control regulations, all the railway stations have been instructed not to sell tickets to Africans proceeding to any of the major cities in the Union, unless such Africans produce exit and entry permits from some government official. If the permit is for the purpose of consulting a specialist in the major cities—the only places where such specialists are to be found—a doctor's certificate to that effect has to be produced. But sometimes even with doctor's certificate, the official may refuse to grant such right of entry, if he is convinced in his own mind that the woman does not need specialist treatment. If the permit is for the purpose of tracing a lost husband, brother, or son, or rushing to the sickbed of a husband in the city, all relevant information—no matter how private and intimate—has to be given, and again it is the official who has to decide whether the matter is urgent. . . .

Those of them who are lucky to get jobs on arrival in the city are tied down to their employers under unbearable service conditions. The pass laws, the influx control regulations and the contract system which give their employers the right to cancel their permits and have them endorsed out of the area, give their employers also the power to bully and blackmail, to offer them low wages and the worst of service conditions.

Even many of those who have slipped through are hounded out and sent back to the Reserves, leaving their husbands behind. And those of them who are in service are required to "sleep in," while their children are sent back to the country whether or not there is someone to look after them after they get there.

In this way many African homes are broken up, families are split up. No wonder the people term the Women's Registration Office in Langa the "Divorce Court." And yet the Superintendent at Langa can say that he and his men will carry out this breaking-up of families as "humanely" as possible. But how can the splitting-up of families, the separation of wife, children and husband, be carried out "humanely"? How can anybody speak of acting "humanely " when the breaking-up involves so many thousands of women in Cape Town alone? Would these men consider it "humane," no matter how sweet and gentle the officials in charge, if it was their own wives and children who were being torn away from them? It is only in South Africa and when

351

dealing with the blacks that anybody can speak of carrying out such a break-ing-up "humanely"—an action that has brought suffering and misery to so many people, young and old. Back to the Reserves all these must go; back they must be sent to join those hundreds of others to whom each day is like another—one monotonous song of droning flies, sick babies, dying stock, hunger, starvation, and death.

"Our March to Freedom Is Irreversible" (1990)

NELSON ROLIHLAHLA MANDELA

Political protest was outlawed in South Africa following violent government suppression of a demonstration against the Pass Laws in 1960. As its leaders went into hiding or fled abroad, the ANC abandoned its nonviolent tactics for a policy of Umkhonto we Sizwe (Spear of the Nation). Protests within South Africa and international economic sanctions eventually forced the National Party to dismantle apartheid. But before the healing could begin, President F.W. deKlerk (b. 1936) had to enlist the aid of Nelson Mandela (b. 1918), a long imprisoned leader of the ANC and international symbol of African defiance. Mandela's release from prison paved the way for the all-party negotiations leading to South Africa's first free elections in 1994 and Mandela's presidency. This speech, made upon Mandela's release from prison, acknowledged the discrimination and sacrifices of the past while looking forward to a better future.

Friends, Comrades and fellow South Africans. I greet you all in the name of peace, democracy and freedom for all. I stand here before you not as a prophet but as a humble servant of you, the people. Your tireless and heroic sacrifices have made it possible for me to be here today. I therefore place the remaining years of my life in your hands. . . .

Today the majority of South Africans, black and white, recognize that apartheid has no future. It has to be ended by our own decisive mass action in order to build peace and security. The mass campaign of defiance and other actions of our organization and people can only culminate in the establishment of democracy.

The apartheid destruction on our subcontinent is incalculable. The fabric of family life of millions of my people has been shattered. Millions are homeless and unemployed. Our economy lies in ruins and our people are embroiled in political strife.

Our resort to the armed struggle in 1960 with the formation of the military wing of the ANC, *Umkhonto we Sizwe (Spear of the Nation)*, was a purely defensive action against the violence of apartheid. The factor which necessitated the armed struggle still exists today. We have no option but to continue. . . .

Negotiations on the dismantling of apartheid will have to address the overwhelming demand of our people for a democratic, non-racial and unitary South Africa.

There must be an end to white monopoly on political power, and a fundamental restructuring of our political and economic systems to ensure that the inequalities of apartheid are addressed and our society thoroughly democratized.

It must be added that Mr. deKlerk himself is a man of integrity, who is acutely aware of the dangers of a public figure not honouring his undertakings. But as an organization, we base our policy and strategy on the harsh reality we are faced with. And this reality is that we are still suffering under the policies of the Nationalist government.

Our struggle has reached a decisive moment. We call on our people to seize this moment, so that the process towards democracy is rapid and uninterrupted.

We have waited too long for our freedom! We can no longer wait. Now is the time to intensify the struggle on all fronts. To relax our efforts now would be a mistake which generations to come will not be able to forgive. The sight of freedom looming on the horizon should encourage us to redouble our efforts. It is only through disciplined mass action that our victory can be assured.

We call on our white compatriots to join us in the shaping of a new South Africa. The freedom movement is a political home for you, too. We call on the international community to continue the campaign to isolate the apartheid regime. To lift sanctions now would be to run the risk of aborting the process towards the complete eradication of apartheid.

Our march to freedom is irreversible. We must not allow fear to stand in our way. Universal suffrage on a common voters' roll in a united, democratic and non-racial South Africa is the only way to peace and racial harmony.

In conclusion I wish to go to my own words during my trial in 1964. They are as true today as they were then. I quote:

> I have fought against white domination and I have fought against black domination. I have cherished the ideal of a democratic and free society in which all persons live together in harmony and with equal opportunity. It is an ideal which I hope to live for and to achieve. But if needs be, it is an ideal for which I am prepared to die. *Amandla (power)!*

Four Years of Independence (1962)

AHMED SÉKOU TOURÉ

*In 1958 Ahmed Sékou Touré (1922–1984) became the first president of
an independent Guinea. Touré, a former trade unionist who despised
both France and tribal parochialism, nationalized Guinea's industry,
agriculture and banking, but later permitted a return to western Capitalism in the face of economic decline. In 1962 he published this assessment of affairs in Guinea after* Four Years of Independence *in which
he examined the continuing economic dependence of African states on
their former colonial masters. He believed Africa could only solve its
problems by relying on its authentic culture instead of Western or Eastern ideological imports.*

The vastness of the movement of national liberation which has abruptly
caused an entire continent to be reborn, making it turn towards an international life, is sufficient evidence of the strength of the current and of the
degree of force of collective conscience of our peoples. It is not by planting
in their concessions bamboo stakes bearing severed Angolese heads that the
Portuguese colonists, and colonialism in general, will arrest this impulse or
dam up this force of conscience. In order to accomplish this, too many heads
would have to roll. The truth is that an important evolution in History is taking place at present and its incidences, its direct or indirect consequences will
influence more and more the transformations of universal society. In fact the
liberation movement of the peoples will change international structures more
profoundly than did the two terrible world conflicts of 1914–1918 and
1939–1945. . . .

To believe that all has been attained, and that the efforts are to stop on
independence (which still remains to be consolidated for the majority of the
African peoples) is to close one's eyes to the human evidence, to deny historical evolution and to ignore the real existence of the needy countries
which, after having become aware of the injustices suffered, burn to exploit
judiciously all the potentials with which they are endowed, thus affirming the
historic rights which are theirs and which are returning to them in the struggle for progress and the safeguarding of the balance of the world, which is

conceived not as a balancing of opposing forces, but as an attainment of the necessary harmonization of levels of development among the peoples of the world.

For us, the need to satisfy our wants prevails over gratuitous philosophical reasoning or pure ideology, since it is those human wants which, bound up with man's consciousness of them and therefore of their reality, constitute the principal motive power of History, a power whose intensity is measured and exercised in proportion to the forces which thwart or oppose it.

It is in vain to hope that Africa will evolve according to this or that form that one might wish to impose on her from outside or which might be alien to her understanding of things. Africa will evolve within the bounds of her authenticity, according to her peculiarities and her personality as a function of the profound social aspirations of her peoples, until the moment when her economic conditions lose their peculiarly acute distinctions, that is to say until they become normal ones. This transformation is inscribed in the historical evolution of societies. It is a determinant in the establishment of a just international equilibrium without which the new universal society, on which depends as a last resort the destiny of all Humanity, would be unable to build itself and take shape.

It is in vain to seek to put Africa under tutelage, to give her alms which appease the conscience of some or momentarily retard or enfeeble the awakening of others and perpetuate unequal relationships between peoples by favoring the maintenance of barriers which create differences in their material conditions of existence.

It is equally vain to try to impose on Africa this or that course. Starting from the requirements of our destiny and the exigencies demanded by the advent of the Universal Society, fraternal, solid and conforming with the aspirations of man, it is more a question of allowing Africa the right to make her own way, bearing in mind her will, her resources, her intrinsic genius, her aptitudes and her original values.

It is a question of affirming our African-ness, that is to say our personality, without endeavoring to clothe it in a Western or Eastern manner, and therefore of favoring the harmonious construction, the rapid development, the complete expansion of an authentically African Africa.

Africa has her needs, her conceptions, her customs which are her very own. She does not want at all, still less does she search, to deck herself up in someone else's raiments which have not been tailored to her size. . . .

Considered on the international plane, Africa is a continent which, in relation to other continents, suffers a serious backwardness; but this backwardness, in what sphere is one to locate it? Is it under the index of a natural inequality between the black man and the white man? To this latter question it is easy to answer "No" because there are certain men of black race who, by their culture, have an intrinsic worth superior to that of others who are white men. Therefore, on the plane of intellectual capacity compared with the level of the individual personality, there exists no inequality between men whatever their color or race. Inequality dwells solely in conditions of life, in historical contingencies, that is to say in the political, economic and social situations which have governed and still do govern the development of different parts of the world: the political situations when the fact politic has, within the framework of the nations, hindered development, as is the case for certain European countries (Spain, Portugal, Greece); and the economic and social situations when foreign intervention has installed a policy of economic exploitation and social oppression, as is the case for all countries politically subjected, directly or indirectly, to a foreign authority.

But is this inequality located in the sphere of intelligence? We reply categorically "No"! Is this disparity found, for example, in the spheres of morals or of human thought in the two societies here compared? We again reply "No"! The African is not backward in the moral and spiritual spheres. In fact, the African possesses an acute awareness of the notions of good and evil, of justice, liberty, solidarity, the virtues of work and human charity, as well as of universal peace; he has the same sense of his responsibility as an inhabitant of Europe, America, Asia or Oceania. He has, to within a degree, the same scale of values, and on account of this fact one cannot consider him, even momentarily, as being even slightly backward in the moral and spiritual spheres. Consequently, inequality only exists in economic conditions. This inequality, far from being an absolute defect, is the consequence of the low level of scientific, technological and economic development of our countries. Although in the technical, scientific and economic spheres Africa may be backward by comparison with other continents, on the other hand she must not under-estimate her human personality, her economic, cultural and moral values, her spiritual force, nor the contribution that she is capable of making to world civilization. . . .

The unanimous aspiration of the African peoples for unity will not realize itself through one man, nor through one country, but through a concrete program, however minimal this may be. The rules of this union must favor and reinforce precise concepts of acquired citizenship: equality of nations great or small, brotherly solidarity in relationships, pooling of certain resources, respect of the personality and of the institutions of each State. None of them must seek to interfere in the internal affairs of another State, but must account it a duty to help resolve its problems. If we do not quickly attain this essential solidarity permitting a peaceful and rapid evolution of our countries, we run the risk of seeing the cold war soon arrive at our doors, that is to say, divide into opposing forces and hostile blocks the African States whose common future could not but be thereby further compromised.

The peaceful and harmonious evolution of our nations demands a loyal and broad mutual co-operation between our States. We have always believed that Africa must consider itself as a human body, from which once a finger is cut off, the whole body must suffer therefrom. The awareness of similarity of condition of the States and of the future of our peoples can only rationally direct our efforts towards the development of this mutual co-operation, towards the strengthening of this active solidarity, towards the concrete and conscious participation of Africa in universal progress.

When we talk then of rehabilitating the Man of Africa, we are not showing proof of racialism but are obeying rather an historic and moral imperative. We have suffered enough from the ignominy of the wickedness and scorn of others. We must cause them to respect us from now on and do that by our respecting first ourselves in the honest and competent exercise of our human responsibilities. It is indeed a problem of dignity and conscience!

Perón Expounds His Doctrine (1948)

JUAN DOMINGO PERÓN

Colonel Juan Domingo Perón (1895–1974) seized power in Argentina in 1946 and attempted to modernize a still feudal society. Perón and his wife Evita (1919–1952) enjoyed enormous support among the working class and Argentina's poorest citizens. Exiled in 1955, Perón later returned in 1973 and established a second dictatorship which he bequeathed to his second wife Isabelita (b. 1931). In 1948 Perón published a book of his speeches laying out his plans for industrialization and nationalization of Argentina's resources.

An attempt has been made to lead the public to believe that the oligarchy, that untoward lodge of demagogues, represented the ruling class in the country, its elite, and as such was made up of wise, rich and good people. We must observe that "the wise are seldom rich, and the rich seldom good." Nor must we forget that neither the wise nor the good found a place among Argentine politicians . . . .

From today onwards we shall industrialize the country so that our work may be done by Argentine workers and so that they may earn what foreign workers earned before. This is what industrialization means to us. To accomplish this cycle we shall complete and intensify the economic cycle of production and consumption, we shall produce more, and value that production in view of our own industrialization and commerce, avoiding exploitation and increasing the consumption. When this cycle is closed, we shall be able to provide our country with 80 or 90 per cent of our production and we shall only export 10 or 20 per cent, because it is necessary to convince ourselves that the money of a man from Catamarca or Santiago del Estero is worth as much as that of the English, Americans or Japanese. All this problem is in itself simple if one tries to solve it, but it gets complicated when one cannot or does not want to solve it. We have our orientation clearly defined and a plan of action that will take us directly to the achievement of the objectives we are looking for. . . .

Foundations have already been laid for the national tin-plate factory—an article of trade which is taking too long in getting to our country—in which the containers we need to export our production in will be manufactured. Due to the lack of a factory of tin-plate containers, the Republic has lost many thousands of millions of pesos; and we have not had any tin-plate factory before because certain foreigners that negotiated with our food production, objected to it. But in the future we shall have the containers that our production requires, the ships necessary to transport it, and those who in previous times commanded here as if they were in their own land, will have to submit and receive our products canned by Argentine hands, transported by Argentine railways and taken to Europe by Argentine ships. . . .

When I entered the government, there were persons in my country who were paid 20 centavos a day and peons who got as little as 10 or 15 pesos per month. Workers were killed barbarously in the sugar mills and fields because of criminal working conditions. In a country which had 45 million cows the inhabitants died for lack of food. Argentina was a country of fat bulls and undernourished peons.

Social security was practically unknown, though insignificant pensions were paid to a few public employees and army officers. We established retirement pay for all workers, including the employers. We created pensions for the aged and the sick, thus banishing from the country the sad spectacle of misery in the midst of abundance.

We legalized the existence of syndical organizations previously declared illegal by Argentine law, and we fostered the organization of the General Confederation of Labor which now has six million paid members.

We made possible absolutely free education for all who wanted to study, without distinction of class, creed, or religion, and in only eight years we built 8,000 schools of all kinds.

Great dams with their power plants increased the size of Argentine farmlands and more than 35,000 public works were the result of the first governmental five-year plan alone, among them the gas pipeline 1,800 kilometers long, the Pistarini Airport, the Eva Peron oil refinery (which the rebels wished to bombard in spite of its costing 400 million dollars and ten years of labor), the coal exploitation of Rio Turbo and its railroad, more than twenty great electric plants, etc., etc.

When I entered the government not even pins were made in Argentina. When I left buses, tractors, automobiles, locomotives, etc., were being manufactured. I left the railroads recovered for the nation, as well as telephones and gas. I left a merchant marine, an air fleet, etc. But why continue? All Argentines know this better than I do.

Now I hope that the People will be able to defend what has been achieved against the greed of their false liberators.

History Will Absolve Me (1953)

FIDEL CASTRO

On July 26, 1953, a Havana lawyer named Fidel Castro (b. 1926) attempted to overthrow Cuba's dictatorial regime. Castro's bid failed miserably, but his speech before the sentencing court has become a venerated text of Latin liberty. After serving two years in prison, Castro was exiled and later returned to lead another, more successful, revolt. Castro has been Cuba's communist dictator since 1959.

Honorable judges: If there is in your hearts a vestige of love for your country, love for humanity, love for justice, listen carefully. I know that I will be silenced for many years; I know that the regime will try to suppress the truth by all possible means; I know that there will be a conspiracy to bury me in oblivion. But my voice will not be stilled—it will rise from my breast even when I feel most alone, and my heart will give it all the fire that callous cowards deny it. . . .

From a shack in the mountains on Monday, July the 27th, I listened to the dictator's voice on the air while there were still eighteen of our men in arms against the government. Those who have never experienced similar moments will never know that kind of bitterness and indignation. While the long cherished hopes of freeing our people lay in ruins about us we heard those crushed hopes gloated over by a tyrant more vicious, more arrogant than ever. The endless stream of lies and slanders, poured forth in his crude, odious, repulsive language, may only be compared to the endless stream of clean young blood which had flowed since the previous night—with his knowledge, consent, complicity and approval—being spilled by the most inhuman gang of assassins it is possible to imagine.

To have believed him for a single moment would have sufficed to fill a man of conscience with remorse and shame for the rest of his life. At that time I could not even hope to brand his miserable forehead with the mark of truth which condemns him for the rest of his days and for all time to come. Already a circle of more than a thousand men, armed with weapons more powerful than ours and with peremptory orders to bring in our bodies, was closing in around us. Now that the truth is coming out, now that speaking before you I am carrying out the mission I set for myself, I may die peacefully and content. So I shall not mince any words about those savage murderers. . . .

Moncada Barracks were turned into a workshop of torture and death. Some shameful individuals turned their uniforms into butchers' aprons. The walls were splattered with blood. The bullets imbedded in the walls were encrusted with singed bits of skin, brains and human hair, the grisly reminders of rifle shots fired full in the face. The grass around the barracks was dark and sticky with human blood. The criminal hands that are guiding the destiny of Cuba had written for the prisoners at the entrance of that den of death the very inscription of Hell: "Forsake all hope."

They did not even attempt to cover appearances. They did not bother in the least to conceal what they were doing. They thought they had deceived the people with their lies and they ended up deceiving themselves. They felt themselves lords and masters of the universe, with power over life and death. So the fear they had experienced upon our attack at daybreak was dissipated in a feast of corpses, in a drunken orgy of blood . . . .

. . . At their hands the best and noblest Cubans perished: the most valiant, the most honest, the most idealistic. The tyrant called them mercenaries. There they were dying as heroes at the hands of men who collect a salary from the Republic and who, with the arms the Republic gave them to defend her, serve the interests of a clique and murder her best citizens.

Throughout their torturing of our comrades, the Army offered them the chance to save their lives by betraying their ideology and falsely declaring that Prío had given them money. When they indignantly rejected that proposition, the Army continued with its horrible tortures. They crushed their testicles and they tore out their eyes. But no one yielded. No complaint was heard nor a favour asked. Even when they had been deprived of their virile organs, our men were still a thousand times more men than all their tormentors together. Photographs, which do not lie, show the bodies torn to pieces. Other methods were used. Frustrated by the valour of the men, they tried to break the spirit of our women. With a bleeding human eye in their hands, a sergeant and several other men went to the cell where our comrades Melba Hernández and Haydée Santamaría were held. Addressing the latter, and showing her the eye, they said: "This eye belonged to your brother. If you will not tell us what he refused to say, we will tear out the other." She, who loved her valiant brother above all things, replied full of dignity: "If you tore out an eye and he did not speak, much less will I." Later they came back and burned their arms with lit cigarettes until at last, filled with spite, they told the young Haydée Santamaría: "You no longer have a fiancé because we have killed him too." But, still imperturbable, she answered: "He is not dead, because to die for one's country is to live forever." Never had the heroism and the dignity of Cuban womanhood reached such heights. . . .

We are Cubans and to be Cuban implies a duty; not to fulfil that duty is a crime, is treason. We are proud of the history of our country; we learned it in school and have grown up hearing of freedom, justice and human rights. We were taught to venerate the glorious example of our heroes and martyrs. Céspedes, Agramonte, Maceo, Gómez, and Martí were the first names engraved in our minds. . . . We were taught to cherish and defend the beloved flag of the lone star, and to sing every afternoon the verses of our National Anthem: "To live in chains is to live in disgrace and in opprobrium" and "To die for one's homeland is to live forever!" All this we learned and will never forget, even though today in our land there is murder and prison for the men who practise the ideas taught to them since the cradle. We were born in a free country that our parents bequeathed to us and the Island will sink into the sea before we consent to be slaves of anyone. . . .

I come to the close of my defence plea but I will not end it as lawyers usually do, asking that the accused be freed. I cannot ask freedom for myself while my comrades are already suffering in the ignominious prison of the Isle of Pines. Send me there to join them and to share their fate. It is understandable that honest men should be dead or in prison in a Republic where the President is a criminal and a thief. . . . I do not fear prison, as I do not fear the fury of the miserable tyrant who took the lives of seventy of my comrades. Condemn me. It does not matter. History will absolve me.

"The Death of Victor Jara" (1973)

The Chilean military establishment was outraged when, in a democratic election, the people chose the socialist candidate for president, Salvador Allende (1908–1973). Allende undertook major economic reforms, but was soon overthrown. With support from the United States, the Chilean military initiated a reign of terror that killed thousands of Chilean citizens. Victor Jara (1932–1973), a prominent singer, composer, and theatrical director, was an ardent supporter of Allende's reforms. Immediately following Allende's death, Jara was attacked at his job at the State Technical University, rounded up by the military, and taken to Chile Stadium together with thousands of other political prisoners. What happened next is described in the eye-witness account below.

Victor Jara was brought to the Chile Stadium, together with the employees and students of the Technical University after the assault on that institution, on Wednesday, September 12. There an officer of the *carabineros* (national police) discovered him: "You're Victor Jara, you son-of-a-bitch." And so began the calvary of the distinguished composer, folk singer, and stage director. The officer threw himself furiously on Victor and struck him with the butt of his rifle on his stomach, head, everywhere. Victor fell down and another soldier joined in his punishment. They kicked him and hurled insults at him. One kicked him in the face, and an eye filled with blood. They yelled an beat him savagely. Victor curled up, but made no sound.

The head of the "prisoner camp" arrived and said: "Let's cut off the hands of this son-of-a-bitch." He hit Victor with a stick. "Sing now, you bastard; get up!" he ordered. Then they bent him over, with his hands on a sawhorse, and began to beat his hands and wrists until they became a bloody mass. All this took place in a passage of the stadium. There were five thousand prisoners in the stadium and many were able to see the torture. Impotent tears streamed down the faces of all the witnesses. They had also received or were receiving their dose of punishment. Now Victor was down on the ground. They left him for a few minutes and then returned. They showed him off to the fascists who arrived as if he were a trophy of war. Three air force officers arrived and stopped in front of him, insulting and taking turns in kicking him. "Do you want a smoke, bastard?" they asked in a mocking tone. Victor did not respond. They put out a cigarette on one of his hands, a mass of wounds. The torture continued until very late in the afternoon of the twelfth. They left him unconscious all that night and the next day, the thirteenth, of course without food or water.

Then they seemed to forget him. They had other entertainments. Someone ordered that he should be taken away with the other prisoners. Signs of solidarity with Victor came from every corner of the stadium: pieces of bread, a biscuit, a jacket to keep him warm. Victor gradually came to himself. Now he was happy, though he suffered atrocious pain. He spoke of the future, of his wife and children. Meanwhile the stadium resounded with the groans of the victims of fascism. They killed and tortured in the presence of five thousand men. Some prisoners went mad and threw themselves down from the top of the stadium. Others cried and ran, and the lieutenants beat them till they died. From the underground rooms moans and cries rose day and night. Foreigners, "agents of international communism," suffered special agonies. Victor continued to recover, though his body was one large hematoma, his wounded eye continued to bleed, and his face showed the wounds he had received.

Saturday, the thirteenth, they announced a transfer of prisoners to the national stadium, and all thought that Victor would leave with the rest. It seemed they had finally forgotten him. That morning he began to dictate the verses that he entitled "Chile Stadium." He would never finish them. They took him, together with a group described as "Marxist specialists in explosives" out of the corridors. They took him into one of the rooms converted into torture chambers and the rain of blows began again. They stretched him out on the ground, spread his legs apart, and kicked him in the testicles. They attacked him with savage fury. They would leave and then return to the attack. A student who managed to come out of that inferno alive tells that at the end blood poured from his mouth, nostrils, ears, eyes. Thus died Victor Jara, who had sung of love, tenderness, and hope in the language of the humble. There he died, beaten to death by the irrational hatred of fascism. Afterwards, by way of an example to others, they left him lying in the foyer of the stadium.

Chiapas: The Southeast in Two Winds, A Storm and a Prophecy (1992)

SUBCOMANDANTE MARCOS

Neither the nineteenth century Reforma nor the 1917 Constitution restored control of their ancestral lands to Mexico's Indian population. In 1992, deep within the Lacondora jungle of Chiapas Province, a masked revolutionary calling himself Subcomandante Marcos began a movement that the Mexican government has been unable to suppress. This manifesto from the Zapatista Rebels (named to honor the nineteenth-century mestizo reformer, Emiliano Zapata) promises that the winds of change will unite to sweep Mexico into a new era of equality.

The First Wind: The One From Above

...Chiapas loses blood through many veins: Through oil and gas ducts, electric lines, railways, through bank accounts, trucks, vans, boats and planes, through clandestine paths, gaps, and forest trails. This land continues to pay tribute to the imperialists: petroleum, electricity, cattle, money, coffee, banana, honey, com, cacao, tobacco, sugar, soy, melon, sorghum, mamey, mango, tamarind, avocado, and Chiapaneco blood flows as a result of the thousand teeth sunk into the throat of the Mexican Southeast. These raw materials, thousands of millions of tons of them, flow to Mexican ports and railroads, air and truck transportation centers. From there they are sent to different parts of the world: The United States, Canada, Holland, Germany, Italy, Japan, but with the same fate—to feed imperialism. The fee that capitalism imposes on the Southeastern part of this country oozes, as it has since from the beginning, blood and mud. . . .

In Chiapas, Pemex [the national oil company] has 86 teeth clenched in the townships of Estacio'n Jua'rez, Reforma, Ostuaca'n, Pichucalco, and Ocosingo. Every day they suck out 92,000 barrels of petroleum and 517,000,000,000 cubic feet of gas. They take away the petroleum and gas, and in exchange leave behind the mark of capitalism: ecological destruction, agricultural plunder, hyperinflation, alcoholism, prostitution, and poverty. . . . The trees fall and dynamite explodes on land where campesinos are not allowed to cut down trees to cultivate. . . .

Chiapas also bleeds coffee. Thirty-five percent of the coffee produced in Mexico comes from this area. The industry employs 87,000 people. Forty-seven percent of the coffee is for national consumption and 53% is exported abroad, mainly to the United States and Europe. More than 100,000 tons of coffee are taken from this state to fatten the beast's bank accounts: in 1988 a kilo of pergamino coffee was sold abroad for 8,000 pesos. The Chiapaneco producers were paid 2,500 pesos or less.

The second most important plunder, after coffee, is beef. Three million head of cattle wait for middle-men and a small group of businessmen to take them away to fill refrigerators in Arriaga, Villahermosa, and Mexico City. The cattle are sold for 400 pesos per kilo by the poor farmers and resold by the middle-men and businessmen for up to ten times the price they paid for them.

The tribute that capitalism demands from Chiapas has no historical parallel. Fifty-five percent of national hydroelectric energy comes from this state, along with 20% of Mexico's total electricity. However, only a third of the homes in Chiapas have electricity. Where do the 12,907 kilowatts produced annually by hydroelectric plants in Chiapas go? . . .

What does the beast leave behind in exchange for all it takes away? . . .

Education? The worst in the country. At the elementary school level, 72 out of every 100 children don't finish the first grade. More than half of the schools only offer up to a third grade education and half of the schools only have one teacher for all the courses offered. There are statistics, although they are kept secret of course, that show that many Indigenous children are forced to drop out of school due to their families' need to incorporate them into the system of exploitation. In any Indigenous community it is common to see children carrying corn and wood, cooking, or washing clothes during school hours. Of the 16,058 classrooms in 1989, only 96 were in Indigenous zones. . . .

The health conditions of the people of Chiapas are a clear example of the capitalist imprint: One-and-a-half million people have no medical services at their disposal. There are 0.2 clinics for every 1,000 inhabitants, one-fifth of the national average. There are 0.3 hospital beds for every 1,000 Chiapanecos, one third the amount in the rest of Mexico. There is one operating room per 100,000 inhabitants, one half of the amount in the rest of Mexico. There are 0.5 doctors and 0.4 nurses per 1,000 people, one-half of the national average.

Health and nutrition go hand in hand in poverty. Fifty-four percent of the population of Chiapas suffer from malnutrition, and in the highlands and forest this percentage increases to 80%. A campesino's average diet consists of coffee, corn, tortillas, and beans.

This is what capitalism leaves as payment for everything that it takes away. . . .

367

The Second Wind: The Wind from Below

Collective work, democratic thinking, and subjection to the decisions of the majority are more than just traditions in Indigenous zones. They have been the only means of survival, resistance, dignity, and defiance. These "evil ideas," as they are seen by landholders and businessmen, go against the capitalist precept of "a lot in the hands of a few."

It has mistakenly been said that the Chiapas rebellion has no counterpart, that it is outside the national experience. This is a lie. The exploited Chiapaneco's specialty is the same as that of exploited people from Durango, Veracruz, or the plateau of northern Mexico: to fight and to lose. If the voices of those who write history speak excessively, it is because the voice of the oppressed does not speak—yet. There is no historic, national, or regional calendar that has documented each and every rebellion against this system that is imposed and maintained with blood and fire throughout the national territory. In Chiapas, this rebel voice is only heard when it shakes the world of the landowners and businesspeople. . . .

And this wind from below, that of rebellion and dignity, is not just an answer to the wind from above. It is not just an angry response or the destruction of an unjust and arbitrary system. Rather it carries with it a new proposal, a hope of converting rebellion and dignity into freedom and dignity.

How will this new voice make itself heard in these lands and across the country? How will this hidden wind blow, this wind which now blows only in the mountains and canyons without yet descending to the valleys where money rules and lies govern? This wind will come from the mountains. It is already being born under the trees and is conspiring for a new world, so new that it is barely an intuition in the collective heart that inspires it. . . .

In the town of Betania, in the outskirts of San Cristo'bal de las Casas, Indigenous people are regularly detained and harassed by judicial agents for cutting firewood for their homes. The judicial agents say that they are only doing this to protect the environment. The Indigenous people decide to stop being silent and kidnap three judicial officials. They take the Panamerican highway and cut off communications to the east of San Cristo'bal. At the intersection between Ocosingo and Comita'n, campesinos are holding the judiciaries and they demand to speak to the viceroy before they will agree to unblock the road. Business comes to a halt, tourism collapses. Negotiating commissions come and go. The conflict appears to resolve itself but the causes persist. . . .

In the municipal seat of Ocosingo, 4,000 Indigenous campesinos from the organization ANCIEZ march from different points of the city. Three marches converge in front of the Municipal building. The municipal president doesn't know what it's all about and flees. On the floor of his office is a calendar indicating the date: April 10, 1992. Outside Indigenous campesinos from Ocosingo, Oxchuc, Huixta'n, Chilo'n, Yajalon, Sabanilla, Salto de

Agua, Palenque, Altamirano, Margaritas, San Cristo'bal, San Andre's and Cancuc dance in front of a giant image of Zapata painted by one of them, recite poetry, sing, and speak. Only they are listening. The landowners, businessmen, and judicial officials are closed up in their homes and shops, the federal garrison appears deserted. The campesinos shout that Zapata lives and the struggle continues. . . .

The storm is here. From the clash of these two winds the storm will be born, its time has arrived. Now the wind from above rules, but the wind from below is coming.

The prophecy is here. When the storm calms, when rain and fire again leave the country in peace, the world will no longer be the world but something better.

Topic XIII

The Contemporary World

Civilization and Its Discontents (1930)

SIGMUND FREUD

*The theories of Sigmund Freud (1856–1939) have been so completely
absorbed by contemporary society that it is nearly impossible to recap-
ture their original revolutionary impact. Specializing in the treatment
of nervous disorders, Freud believed that instinctual drives, buried deep
beneath our conscious minds, were the causes of adult hysteria, depression, and neurosis. His new method of treatment, psychoanalysis, used
free association and dream analysis to probe the unconscious mind and
free patients from their emotional pain. In Civilization and its Discontents (1930), Freud expanded his analysis from the individual to a
society-wide scale. He felt there was a conflict between individual
aggressive instinct and the rules of society that no ideology (religious,
nationalist, capitalist, or socialist) could ever permanently resolve.*

Homo homini lupus. [Man is wolf to man.] Who, in the face of all his
experience of life and of history, will have the courage to dispute this assertion? As a rule this cruel aggressiveness waits for some provocation or puts
itself at the service of some other purpose, whose goal might also have been
reached by milder measures. In circumstances that are favourable to it, when
the mental counterforces which ordinarily inhibit it are out of action, it also
manifests itself spontaneously and reveals man as a savage beast to whom
consideration towards his own kind is something alien. Anyone who calls to
mind the atrocities committed during the racial migrations or the invasions
of the Huns, or by the people known as Mongols under Jenghiz Khan and
Tamerlane, or at the capture of Jerusalem by the pious Crusaders, or even,
indeed, the horrors of the recent World War—anyone who calls these things
to mind will have to bow humbly before the truth of this.

The existence of this inclination to aggression, which we can detect in
ourselves and justly assume to be present in others, is the factor which dis-
turbs our relations with our neighbour and which forces civilization into such
a high expenditure [of energy]. In consequence of this primary mutual hostility of human beings, civilized society is perpetually threatened with disintegration. The interest of work in common would not hold it together;

instinctual passions are stronger than reasonable interests. Civilization has to use its utmost efforts in order to set limits to man's aggressive instincts and to hold the manifestations of them in check by psychical reaction-formations. Hence, therefore, the use of methods intended to incite people into identifications and aim-inhibited relationships of love, hence the restriction upon sexual life, and hence too the ideal's commandment to love one's neighbour as oneself—a commandment which is really justified by the fact that nothing else runs so strongly counter to the original nature of man. In spite of every effort, these endeavours of civilization have not so far achieved very much. It hopes to prevent the crudest excesses of brutal violence by itself assuming the right to use violence against criminals, but the law is not able to lay hold of the more cautious and refined manifestations of human aggressiveness. The time comes when each one of us has to give up as illusions the expectations which, in his youth, he pinned upon his fellow men, and when he may learn how much difficulty and pain has been added to his life by their ill-will. At the same time, it would be unfair to reproach civilization with trying to eliminate strife and competition from human activity. These things are undoubtedly indispensable. But opposition is not necessarily enmity; it is merely misused and made an *occasion* for enmity.

The communists believe that they have found the path to deliverance from our evils. According to them, man is wholly good and is well-disposed to his neighbour; but the institution of private property has corrupted his nature. The ownership of private wealth gives the individual power, and with it the temptation to ill-treat his neighbour; while the man who is excluded from possession is bound to rebel in hostility against his oppressor. If private property were abolished, all wealth held in common, and everyone allowed to share in the enjoyment of it, ill-will and hostility would disappear among men. Since everyone's needs would be satisfied, no one would have any reason to regard another as his enemy; all would willingly undertake the work that was necessary. I have no concern with any economic criticisms of the communist system; I cannot enquire into whether the abolition of private property is expedient or advantageous. But I am able to recognize that the psychological premises on which the system is based are an untenable illusion. In abolishing private property we deprive the human love of aggression of one of its instruments, certainly a strong one, though certainly not the strongest; but we have in no way altered the differences in power and influence which are misused by aggressiveness, nor have we altered anything in its nature. Aggressiveness was not created by property. It reigned almost without limit in primitive times, when property was still very scanty, and it already shows itself in the nursery almost before property has given up its primal, anal form; it forms the basis of every relation of affection and love among people (with the single exception, perhaps, of the mother's relation to her male child). If we do away with personal rights over material wealth, there still remains prerogative in the field of sexual relationships, which is bound to become the source of the strongest dislike and the most violent hostility among men who in other respects are on an equal footing. If we were to remove this factor, too, by allowing complete freedom of sexual life and thus abolishing the family, the germ-cell of civilization, we cannot, it is true, easily foresee what new paths the development of civilization could take; but one thing we can expect, and that is that this indestructible feature of human nature will follow it there.

It is clearly not easy for men to give up the satisfaction of this inclination to aggression. They do not feel comfortable without it. The advantages which a comparatively small cultural group offers of allowing this instinct an outlet in the form of hostility against intruders is not to be despised. It is always possible to bind together a considerable number of people in love, as long as there are other people left over to receive the manifestations of their aggressions.

The Universal Declaration of Human Rights (1948)

The Universal Declaration of Human Rights was adopted by the United Nations General Assembly on December 10, 1948. Shepherded through adoption by Eleanor Roosevelt (1884–1962), the Declaration is both an affirmation and an expansion of Enlightenment ideals. The United Nations intended the Declaration to inspire a new era of justice and shared values, but the incorporation of the Declaration into many national constitutions has not brought universal adherence to its provisions.

Preamble.

Whereas recognition of the inherent dignity and of the equal and inalienable rights of all members of the human family is the foundation of freedom, justice and peace in the world,

Whereas disregard and contempt for human rights have resulted in barbarous acts which have outraged the conscience of mankind, and the advent of a world in which human beings shall enjoy freedom of speech and belief and freedom from fear and want has been proclaimed as the highest aspiration of the common people,

Whereas it is essential, if man is not compelled to have recourse, as a last resort, to rebellion against tyranny and oppression, that human rights should be protected by the rule of law,

Whereas it is essential to promote the development of friendly relations between nations,

Whereas the people of the United Nations have in the Charter reaffirmed their faith in fundamental human rights, in the dignity and worth of the human person and in the equal rights of men and women and have determined to promote social progress and better standards of life in larger freedom,

Whereas Member States have pledged themselves to achieve, in cooperation with the United Nations, the promotion of universal respect for and observance of human rights and fundamental freedoms,

Whereas a common understanding of these rights and freedoms is of the greatest importance for the full realization of this pledge,

Now, therefore,

The General Assembly

Proclaims this Universal Declaration of Human Rights, as a common standard of achievement for all peoples and all nations, to the end that every individual and every organ of society, keeping this Declaration constantly in mind, shall strive by teaching and education to promote respect for these rights and freedoms and by progressive measures, national and international, to secure their universal and effective recognition and observance, both among the peoples of Member States themselves and among the peoples of territories under their jurisdiction.

Article 1. All human beings are born free and equal in dignity and rights. They are endowed with reason and conscience and should act towards one another in a spirit of brotherhood.

Article 2. Everyone is entitled to all the rights and freedoms set forth in this Declaration, without distinction of any kind, such as race, colour, sex, language, religion, political or other opinion, national or social origin, property, birth or other status. Furthermore, no distinction shall be made on the basis of the political, jurisdictional or international status of the country or territory to which a person belongs, whether it be independent, trust, non-self-governing or under any other limitation of sovereignty.

Article 3. Everyone has the right to life, liberty, and the security of person.

Article 4. No one shall be held in slavery or servitude; slavery and the slave trade shall be prohibited in all their forms.

Article 5. No one shall be subjected to torture or to cruel, inhuman or degrading treatment or punishment.

Article 6. Everyone has the right to recognition everywhere as a person before the law.

Article 7. All are equal before the law and are entitled without any discrimination to equal protection of the law. All are entitled to equal protection against any discrimination in violation of this Declaration and against any incitement to such discrimination.

Article 8. Everyone has the right to an effective remedy by the competent national tribunals for acts violating the fundamental rights granted him by the constitution or law.

Article 9. No one shall be subjected to arbitrary arrest, detention or exile.

Article 10. Everyone is entitled in full equality to a fair and public hearing by an independent and impartial tribunal, in the determination of his rights and obligations and of any criminal charge against him.

Article 11. (1) Everyone charged with a penal offense has the right to be presumed innocent until proved guilty according to law in a public trial at which he has had all the guarantees necessary for his defence. (2) No one shall be held guilty of any penal offense on account of any act or omission which did not constitute a penal offense, under national or international law, at the time when it was committed. Nor shall a heavier penalty be imposed than the one that was applicable at the time the penal offense was committed.

Article 12. No one shall be subjected to arbitrary interference with his privacy, family, home or correspondence, nor to attacks upon his honour and reputation. Everyone has the right to the protection of the law against such interference or attacks.

Article 13. (1) Everyone has the right to freedom of movement and residence within the borders of each State. (2) Everyone has the right to leave any country including his own, and to return to his country.

Article 14. (1) Everyone has the right to seek and to enjoy in other countries asylum from persecution. (2) This right may not be invoked in the case of prosecutions genuinely arising from non-political crimes or from acts contrary to the purposes and principles of the United Nations.

Article 15. (1) Everyone has the right to a nationality. (2) No one shall be arbitrarily deprived of his nationality nor denied the right to change his nationality.

Article 16. (1) Men and women of full age, without any limitation due to race, nationality or religion, have the right to marry and to found a family. They are entitled to equal rights as to marriage, during marriage and at its dissolution. (2) Marriage shall be entered into only with the free and full consent of the intending spouses. (3) The family is the natural and fundamental group unit of society and is entitled to protection by society and the State.

Article 17. (1) Everyone has the right to own property alone as well as in association with others. (2) No one shall be arbitrarily deprived of his property.

Article 18. Everyone has the right to freedom of thought, conscience and religion; this right includes freedom to change his religion or belief, and freedom, either alone or in community with others and in public or private, to manifest his religion or belief in teaching, practice, worship and observance.

Article 19. Everyone had the right to freedom of opinion and expression; this right includes freedom to hold opinions without interference and to seek, receive and import information and ideas through any media and regardless of frontiers.

Article 20. (1) Everyone has the right to freedom of peaceful assembly and association. (2) No one many be compelled to belong to an association.

Article 21. (1) Everyone has the right to take part in the government of his country, directly or through freely chosen representatives. (2) Everyone has the right to equal access to public service in his country. (3) The will of the people shall be the basis of the authority of government; this shall be expressed in periodic and genuine elections which shall be by universal and equal suffrage and shall be held by secret vote or by equivalent free voting procedures.

Article 22. Everyone is a member of society, has the right to social security and is entitled to realization, through national effort and international cooperation and in accordance with the organization and resources of each State, of the economic, social and cultural rights indispensable for his dignity and the free development of his personality.

Article 23. (1) Everyone has the right to work, to free choice of employment, to just and favourable conditions of work and to protection against unemployment. (2) Everyone, without any discrimination, has the right to equal pay for equal work. (3) Everyone who works has the right to just and favourable remuneration ensuring for himself and his family an existence worthy of human dignity, and supplemented, if necessary, by other means of social protection.

Article 24. Everyone has the right to rest and leisure, including reasonable limitation of working hours and periodic holidays with pay.

Article 25. (1) Everyone has the right to a standard of living adequate for the health and well-being of himself and of his family, including food, clothing, housing and medical care and necessary social services, and the right to security in the event of unemployment, sickness, disability, widowhood, old age or other lack of livelihood in circumstances beyond his control. (2) Motherhood and childhood are entitled to special care and assistance. All children, whether born in or out of wedlock, shall enjoy the same social protection.

Article 26. (1) Everyone has the right to education. Education shall be free, at least in the elementary and fundamental stages. Elementary education shall be compulsory. Technical and professional education shall be made generally available and higher education shall be equally accessible to all on the basis of merit. (2) Education shall be directed to the full development of the human personality and to the strengthening of respect for human rights and fundamental freedoms. It shall promote understanding, tolerance and friendship among all nations, racial or religious groups, and shall further the activities of the United Nations for the maintenance of peace. (3) Parents have a prior right to choose the kind of education that shall be given to their children.

Article 27. (1) Everyone has the right freely to participate in the cultural life of the community, to enjoy the arts and to share in scientific advancement and its benefits. (2) Everyone has the right to the protection of the moral and material interests resulting from any scientific, literary or artistic production of which he is the author.

Article 28. Everyone is entitled to a social and international order in which the rights and freedoms set forth in this Declaration can be fully realized.

Article 29. (1) Everyone has duties to the community in which alone the free and full development of his personality is possible. (2) In the exercise of his rights and freedoms, everyone shall be subject only to such limitations as are determined by law solely for the purpose of securing due recognition and respect for the rights and freedoms of others and of meeting the just requirements of morality, public order and the general welfare in a democratic society. (3) These rights and freedoms may in no case be exercised contrary to the purposes and principles of the United Nations.

Article 30. Nothing in this Declaration may be interpreted as implying for any State, group or person any right to engage in any activity or to perform any act aimed at the destruction of any of the rights and freedoms set forth herein.

Brown v. Board of Education (1954)

In 1896 (in Plessy v. Ferguson) the United States Supreme Court held that "separate but equal" facilities fulfilled the nation's obligation to its black citizens. That position was not reversed until 1954, when (in Brown v. Board of Education of Topeka, Kansas), the Supreme Court reversed itself and declared "separate but equal" education to be inherently unequal and, therefore, unconstitutional. Both the 1896 and 1954 Supreme Court decisions rested on the power given the Federal government by the Fourteenth Amendment to overturn state laws that violated provisions of the Bill of Rights.

These cases come to us from the States of Kansas, South Carolina, Virginia, and Delaware. They are premised on different facts and different local conditions, but a common legal question justified their consideration together in this consolidated opinion.

In each of the cases, minors of the Negro race, through their legal representatives, seek the aid of the courts in obtaining admission to the public schools of their community on a nonsegregated basis. In each instance, they had been denied admission to schools attended by white children under laws requiring or permitting segregation according to race. This segregation was alleged to deprive the plaintiffs of the equal protection of the laws under the Fourteenth Amendment. In each of the cases other than the Delaware case, a three-judge federal district court denied relief to the plaintiffs on the so-called "separate but equal" doctrine announced by this Court in *Plessy v. Ferguson*, 163 U.S. 537. Under that doctrine, equality of treatment is accorded when the races are provided substantially equal facilities, even though these facilities be separate. In the Delaware case, the Supreme Court of Delaware adhered to that doctrine, but ordered that the plaintiffs be admitted to the white schools because of their superiority to the Negro schools.

The plaintiffs contend that segregated public schools are not "equal" and cannot be made "equal," and that hence they are deprived of the equal protection of the laws. . . .

Reargument was largely devoted to the circumstances surrounding the adoption of the Fourteenth Amendment in 1868. It covered exhaustively consideration of the Amendment in Congress, ratification by the states, then existing practices in racial segregation, and the views of proponents and opponents of the Amendment. This discussion and our own investigation convince us that, although these sources cast some light, it is not enough to resolve the problem with which we are faced. At best, they are inconclusive. The most avid proponents of the post-War Amendments undoubtedly intended them to remove all legal distinctions among "all persons born or naturalized in the United States." Their opponents, just as certainly, were antagonistic to both the letter and the spirit of the Amendments and wished them to have the most limited effect. What others in Congress and the state legislatures had in mind cannot be determined with any degree of certainty.

An additional reason for the inconclusive nature of the Amendment's history, with respect to segregated schools, is the status of public education at that time. In the South, the movement toward free common schools, supported by general taxation, had not yet taken hold. Education of white children was largely in the hands of private groups. Education of Negroes was almost nonexistent, and practically all of the race were illiterate. In fact, any education of Negroes was forbidden by law in some states. Today, in contrast, many Negroes have achieved outstanding success in the arts and sciences as well as in the business and professional world. It is true that public school education at the time of the Amendment had advanced further in the North, but the effect of the Amendment on Northern States was generally ignored in the congressional debates. Even in the North, the conditions of public education did not approximate those existing today. The curriculum was usually rudimentary; ungraded schools were common in rural areas; the school term was but three months a year in many states; and compulsory school attendance was virtually unknown. As a consequence, it is not surprising that there should be so little in the history of the Fourteenth Amendment relating to its intended effect on public education. . . .

In approaching this problem, we cannot turn the clock back to 1868 when the Amendment was adopted, or even to 1896 when *Plessy v. Ferguson* was written. We must consider public education in the light of its full development and its present place in American life throughout the Nation. Only in this way can it be determined if segregation in public schools deprives these plaintiffs of the equal protection of the laws.

Today, education is perhaps the most important function of state and local governments. Compulsory school attendance laws and the great expenditures for education both demonstrate our recognition of the importance of education to our democratic society. It is required in the performance of our most basic armed forces. It is the very foundation of good citizenship. Today it is a principal instrument in awakening the child to cultural values, in preparing him for later professional training, and in helping him to adjust normally to his environment. In these days, it is doubtful that any child may reasonably be expected to succeed in life if he is denied the opportunity of an education.

Such an opportunity, where the state has undertaken to provide it, is a right which must be made available to all on equal terms.

We come then to the question presented: Does segregation of children in public schools solely on the basis of race, even though the physical facilities and other "tangible" factors may be equal, deprive the children of the minority group of equal educational opportunities? We believe that it does. . . .

The effect of this separation on their educational opportunities was well stated by a finding in the Kansas case by a court which nevertheless felt compelled to rule against the Negro plaintiffs:

> "Segregation of white and colored children in public schools has a detrimental effect upon the colored children. The impact is greater when it has the sanction of the law; for the policy of separating the races is usually interpreted as denoting the inferiority of the negro group. A sense of inferiority affects the motivation of a child to learn. Segregation with the sanction of law, therefore, has a tendency to [retard] the educational and mental development of negro children and to deprive them of some of the benefits they would receive in a racial[ly] integrated school system."

Whatever may have been the extent of psychological knowledge at the time of *Plessy v. Ferguson*, this finding is amply supported by modern authority. Any language in *Plessy v. Ferguson* contrary to this finding is rejected.

We conclude that in the field of public education the doctrine of "separate but equal" has no place. Separate educational facilities are inherently unequal. Therefore, we hold that the plaintiffs and others similarly situated for whom the actions have been brought are, by reason of the segregation complained of, deprived of the equal protection of the laws guaranteed by the Fourteenth Amendment. This disposition makes unnecessary any discussion whether such segregation also violates the Due Process Clause of the Fourteenth Amendment.

"I Have a Dream" (1963)

MARTIN LUTHER KING, JR.

In the wake of the Supreme Court's decision in Brown v. the Board of Education to desegregate public schools, a movement demanding full equality for all American citizens swept the nation. Martin Luther King Jr. (1929–1968) was a minister who took on the cause of Civil Rights. He organized the Montgomery Bus Boycott, led the march to Selma Bridge, protested American involvement in Vietnam, and backed the wage demands of sanitation workers. In all his campaigns he demanded that Americans be true to their national ideals. His most famous speech was delivered in August 1963 before some 250,000 Americans of every race, color and creed. Those demonstrations led to the passage of the Civil Rights (1964), Voting Rights (1965), and Fair Housing (1968) Acts that finally ended official racial discrimination in the United States.

I am happy to join with you today in what will go down in history as the greatest demonstration for freedom in the history of the Nation.

Five score years ago, a great American, in whose symbolic shadow we stand today, signed the Emancipation Proclamation. This momentous decree came as a great beacon of light and hope to millions of Negro slaves who had been seared in the flames of withering injustice. It came as the joyous daybreak to end the long night of captivity.

But one hundred years later, the Negro still is not free. One hundred years later, the life of the Negro is still sadly crippled by the manacle of segregation and the chain of discrimination. One hundred years later, the Negro lives on a lonely island of poverty in the midst of a vast ocean of material prosperity. One hundred years later, the Negro is still languishing in the comer of American society and finds himself an exile in his own land. So we have come here today to dramatize a shameful condition.

In a sense we have come to the capital to cash a check. When the architects of our republic wrote the magnificent words of the Constitution and the Declaration of Independence, they were signing a promissory note to which every American was to fall heir. This note was a promise that all men—black men as well as white men—would be guaranteed the unalienable rights of life, liberty, and the pursuit of happiness.

But it is obvious today that America has defaulted on this promissory note insofar as her citizens of color are concerned. Instead of honoring this sacred obligation, America has given the Negro people a bad check—a check that has come back marked "insufficient funds." But we refuse to believe that the bank of justice is bankrupt. We refuse to believe that there are insufficient funds in the great vaults of opportunity in this Nation.

So we have come to cash this check. A check that will give us the riches of freedom and the security of justice.

We have also come to this hallowed spot to remind America that the fierce urgency is now. This is no time to engage in the luxury of cooling off or to take the tranquilizing drug of gradualism. Now is the time to make real the promise of democracy. Now is the time to rise from the dark and desolate valley of segregation to the sunlit path of racial justice. Now is the time to lift our Nation from the quicksands of racial injustice to the solid rock of brotherhood. Now is the time to make justice a reality for all of God's children.

It would be fatal for the Nation to overlook the urgency of the moment. This sweltering summer of the Negro's legitimate discontent will not pass until there is an invigorating autumn of freedom and equality. 1963 is not an end, but a beginning.

Those who hope that the Negro needed to blow off steam and will be content will have a rude awakening if the Nation returns to business as usual. There will be neither rest nor tranquillity in America until the Negro is granted his citizenship rights. The whirlwind of revolt will continue to shake the foundation of our Nation until the bright day of Justice emerges.

But there is something that I must say to my people who stand on the warm threshold which leads into the palace of justice. In the process of gaining our rightful place, we must not be guilty of wrongful deeds. Let us not seek to satisfy our thirst for freedom by drinking from the cup of bitterness and hatred.

We must forever continue our struggle on the high plane of dignity and discipline. We must not allow our creative protest to degenerate into physical violence. Again and again we must rise to the majestic heights of meeting physical force with soul force.

The marvelous new militancy which has engulfed the Negro community must not lead us to a distrust of all white people—for many of our white brothers, as evidenced by their presence here today, have come to realize that their destiny is inextricably tied up with our destiny. They have come to realize that their freedom is inextricably bound to our freedom.

We cannot walk alone, and as we walk, we must make the pledge that we shall always march ahead. We cannot turn back. There are those who are asking the devotees of civil rights: "When will you be satisfied?" We can never be satisfied as long as the Negro is the victim of unspeakable horrors of police brutality. We can never be satisfied as long as our bodies, heavy with the fatigue of travel, cannot gain lodging in the motels of the highways and the hotels of the cities. We can never be satisfied as long as the Negro's basic mobility is from a smaller ghetto to a larger one. We can never be satisfied as long as our children are stripped of their selfhood and robbed of their dignity by signs stating "For Whites Only."

We cannot be satisfied so long as the Negro in Mississippi cannot vote and the Negro in New York believes he has nothing for which to vote. No, no, we will not be satisfied until justice rolls down like water and righteousness like a mighty stream.

I am not unmindful that some of you have come here out of great trials and tribulations. Some of you have come from narrow jail cells. Some of you have come from areas where your quest for freedom left you battered by the storms of persecution and staggered by the winds of police brutality. You have been the veterans of creative suffering. Continue to work with the faith that unearned suffering is redemptive.

Go back to Mississippi. Go back to Alabama; go back to South Carolina; go back to Georgia; go back to Louisiana; go back to the slums and ghettoes of our northern cities knowing that somehow this situation can and will be changed. Let us not wallow in the valley of despair.

I say to you today, my friends, even though we face the difficulties of today and tomorrow, I still have a dream. It is a dream deeply rooted in the American dream. I have a dream that one day this Nation will rise up and live out the true meaning of its creeds—"we hold these truths to be self-evident that all men are created equal."

I have a dream that one day on the red hills of Georgia the sons of slaves and the sons of former slaveowners will be able to sit down together at the table of brotherhood. I have a dream that one day even the state of Mississippi, sweltering with the heat of injustice, sweltering with the heat of oppression, will be transformed into an oasis of freedom and justice.

I have a dream that my four little children will one day live in a Nation where they will not be judged by the color of their skins, but by the content of their character.

I have a dream that one day in Alabama, with this vicious racist, its Governor, having his lips dripping the words of interposition and nullification—one day right there in Alabama, little black boys and black girls will be able to join hands with little white boys and little white girls as brothers and sisters.

I have a dream that one day every valley shall be exalted: every hill and mountain shall be made low, the rough places will be made plane, the crooked places will be made straight and the glory of the Lord shall be revealed and all flesh shall see it together.

This is our hope. This is the faith that I go back to the South with. With this faith, we will be able to hew out of the mountains of despair a stone of hope. With this faith, we will be able to transform the jangling discord of our Nation into a beautiful symphony of brotherhood. With this faith, we will be able to work together; to play together; to struggle together; to go to jail together; to stand up for freedom together knowing that we will be free one day. . . .

"The Great Society" (1964)

LYNDON BAINES JOHNSON

After the assassination of John Fitzgerald Kennedy, Lyndon Baines Johnson (1908–1973) entered the White House determined to fulfill the programs of his predecessor. In his five years in office, Johnson pushed major government initiatives in civil rights, health care, and education through Congress. He summed up his vision of "The Great Society" in this May 1964 speech at the University of Michigan. Unfortunately, American involvement in the Vietnam War derailed his presidency, and he could not achieve his dream of using the nation's wealth to benefit all members of society regardless of ethnicity, color, sex, or social position.

I have come today from the turmoil of your Capital to the tranquility of your campus to speak about the future of your country.

The purpose of protecting the life of our Nation and preserving the liberty of our citizens is to pursue the happiness of our people. Our success in that pursuit is the test of our success as a Nation.

For a century we labored to settle and to subdue a continent. For half a century we called upon unbounded invention and untiring industry to create an order of plenty for all of our people.

The challenge of the next half century is whether we have the wisdom to use that wealth to enrich and elevate our national life, and to advance the quality of our American civilization.

Your imagination, your initiative, and your indignation will determine whether we build a society where progress is the servant of our needs, or a society where old values and new visions are buried under unbridled growth. For in your time we have the opportunity to move not only toward the rich society and the powerful society, but upward to the Great Society.

The Great Society rests on abundance and liberty for all. It demands an end to poverty and racial injustice, to which we are totally committed in our time. But that is just the beginning.

The Great Society is a place where every child can find knowledge to enrich his mind and to enlarge his talents. It is a place where leisure is a welcome chance to build and reflect, not a feared cause of boredom and restlessness. It is a place where the city of man serves not only the needs of the body and the demands of commerce but the desire for beauty and the hunger for community.

It is a place where man can renew contact with nature. It is a place which honors creation for its own sake and for what it adds to the understanding of the race. It is a place where men are more concerned with the quality of their goals than the quantity of their goods.

But most of all, the Great Society is not a safe harbor, a resting place, a final objective, a finished work. It is a challenge constantly renewed, beckoning us toward a destiny where the meaning of our lives matches the marvelous products of our labor.

So I want to talk to you today about three places where we begin to build the Great Society—in our cities, in our countryside, and in our classrooms.

Many of you will live to see the day, perhaps 50 years from now, when there will be 400 million Americans—four-fifths of them in urban areas. In the remainder of this century urban population will double, city land will double, and we will have to build homes, highways, and facilities equal to all those built since this country was first settled. So in the next 40 years we must rebuild the entire urban United States.

Aristotle said: "Men come together in cities in order to live, but they remain together in order to live the good life." It is harder and harder to live the good life in American cities today.

The catalog of ills is long: there is the decay of the centers and the despoiling of the suburbs. There is not enough housing for our people or transportation for our traffic. Open land is vanishing and old landmarks are violated.

Worst of all expansion is eroding the precious and time honored values of community with neighbors and communion with nature. The loss of these values breeds loneliness and boredom and indifference.

Our society will never be great until our cities are great. Today the frontier of imagination and innovation is inside those cities and not beyond their borders. . . .

A second place where we begin to build the Great Society is in our countryside. We have always prided ourselves on being not only America the strong and America the free, but America the beautiful. Today that beauty is in danger. The water we drink, the food we eat, the very air that we breathe, are threatened with pollution. Our parks are overcrowded, our seashores overburdened. Green fields and dense forests are disappearing. . . .

A third place to build the Great Society is in the classrooms of America. There your children's lives will be shaped. Our society will not be great until every young mind is set free to scan the farthest reaches of thought and imagination. We are still far from that goal. . . .

In many places, classrooms are overcrowded and curricula are outdated. Most of our qualified teachers are underpaid, and many of our paid teachers are unqualified. So we must give every child a place to sit and a teacher to learn from. Poverty must not be a bar to learning, and learning must offer an escape from poverty. . . .

These are three of the central issues of the Great Society. While our Government has many programs directed at those issues, I do not pretend that we have the full answer to those problems.

But I do promise this: We are going to assemble the best thought and the broadest knowledge from all over the world to find those answers for America. I intend to establish working groups to prepare a series of White House conferences and meetings—on the cities, on natural beauty, on the quality of education, and on other emerging challenges. And from these meetings and from this inspiration and from these studies we will begin to set our course toward the Great Society.

The solution to these problems does not rest on a massive program in Washington, nor can it rely solely on the strained resources of local authority. They require us to create new concepts of cooperation, a creative federalism, between the National Capital and the leaders of local communities. . . .

For better or for worse, your generation has been appointed by history to deal with those problems and to lead America toward a new age. You have the chance never before afforded to any people in any age. You can help build a society where the demands of morality, and the needs of the spirit, can be realized in the life of the Nation.

So, will you join in the battle to give every citizen the full equality which God enjoins and the law requires, whatever his belief, or race, or the color of his skin?

Will you join in the battle to give every citizen an escape from the crushing weight of poverty?

Will you join in the battle to make it possible for all nations to live in enduring peace—as neighbors and not as mortal enemies?

Will you join in the battle to build the Great Society, to prove that our material progress is only the foundation on which we will build a richer life of mind and spirit?

There are those timid souls who say this battle cannot be won; that we are condemned to a soulless wealth. I do not agree. We have the power to shape the civilization that we want. But we need your will, your labor, your hearts, if we are to build that kind of society.

Those who came to this land sought to build more than just a new country. They sought a new world. So I have come here today to your campus to say that you can make their vision our reality. So let us from this moment begin our work so that in the future men will look back and say: It was then, after a long and weary way, that man turned the exploits of his genius to the full enrichment of his life.

The Feminine Mystique (1963)

BETTY FRIEDAN

With so many American men away at the front during World War II, American women were encouraged to take their place at America's assembly lines. After the war, those same women were expected to devote their lives to home and family in America's new suburbs. Women who expressed dissatisfaction with the lack of intellectual or professional challenge in their lives were dismissed as neurotic. In The Feminine Mystique *(1963), the groundbreaking feminist Betty Friedan (1921–2006) explored the problem "that had no name" and challenged the preconception that women wanted limited lives. Her book helped usher in a new women's right's movement.*

The problem lay buried, unspoken, for many years in the minds of American women. It was a strange stirring, a sense of dissatisfaction, a yearning that women suffered in the middle of the twentieth century in the United States. Each suburban wife struggled with it alone. As she made the beds, shopped for groceries, matched slipcover material, ate peanut butter sandwiches with her children, chauffeured Cub Scouts and Brownies, lay beside her husband at night—she was afraid to ask even of herself the silent question—"Is this all?"

For over fifteen years there was no word of this yearning in the millions of words written about women, for women, in all the columns, books and articles by experts telling women their role was to seek fulfillment as wives and mothers. Over and over women heard in voices of tradition and of Freudian sophistication that they could desire no greater destiny than to glory in their own femininity. Experts told them how to catch a man and keep him, how to breastfeed children and handle their toilet training, how to cope with sibling rivalry and adolescent rebellion; how to buy a dishwasher, bake bread, cook gourmet snails, and build a swimming pool with their own hands; how to dress, look, and act more feminine and make marriage more exciting; how to keep their husbands from dying young and their sons from growing into delinquents. They were taught to pity the neurotic, unfeminine, unhappy women who wanted to be poets or physicists or presidents. They learned that truly feminine women do not want careers, higher education, political rights-the independence and the opportunities that the old-fashioned feminists fought for. Some women, in their forties and fifties, still remembered painfully giving up those dreams, but most of the younger women no longer even thought about them. . . . Fewer and fewer women were entering professional work. The shortages in the nursing, social work, and teaching professions caused crises in almost every American city. Concerned over the Soviet Union's lead in the space race, scientists noted that America's greatest source of unused brain-power was women. But girls would not study physics: it was "unfeminine." A girl refused a science fellowship at Johns Hopkins to take a job in a real-estate office. All she wanted, she said, was what every other American girl wanted—to get married, have four children and live in a nice house in a nice suburb.

The suburban housewife—she was the dream image of the young American women and the envy, it was said, of women all over the world. The American housewife—freed by science and labor-saving appliances from the drudgery, the dangers of childbirth and the illnesses of her grandmother. She was healthy, beautiful, educated, concerned only about her husband, her children, her home. She had found true feminine fulfillment. As a housewife and mother, she was respected as a full and equal partner to man in his world. She was free to choose automobiles, clothes, appliances, supermarkets; she had everything that women ever dreamed of. . . .

If a woman had a problem in the 1950's and 1960's, she knew that something must be wrong with her marriage, or with herself. Other women were satisfied with their lives, she thought. What kind of a woman was she if she did not feel this mysterious fulfillment waxing the kitchen floor? She was so ashamed to admit her dissatisfaction that she never knew how many other women shared it. If she tried to tell her husband, he didn't understand what she was talking about. She did not really understand it herself. For over fifteen years women in America found it harder to talk about this problem than about sex. Even the psychoanalysts had no name for it. When a woman went to a psychiatrist for help, as many women did, she would say, "I'm so ashamed," or "I must be hopelessly neurotic." "I don't know what's wrong with women today," a suburban psychiatrist said uneasily. "I only know something is wrong because most of my patients happen to be women. And their problem isn't sexual." Most women with this problem did not go to see a psychoanalyst, however. "There's nothing wrong really," they kept telling themselves. "There isn't any problem."

But on an April morning in 1959, I heard a mother of four, having coffee with four other mothers in a suburban development fifteen miles from New York, say in a tone of quiet desperation, "the problem." And the others knew, without words, that she was not talking about a problem with her husband, or her children, or her home. Suddenly they realized they all shared the same problem, the problem that has no name. They began, hesitantly, to talk about it. Later, after they had picked up their children at nursery school and taken them home to nap, two of the women cried, in sheer relief, just to know they were not alone.

Gradually I came to realize that the problem that has no name was shared by countless women in America. As a magazine writer I often interviewed women about problems with their children, or their marriages, or their houses, or their communities. But after a while I began to recognize the telltale signs of this other problem. I saw the same signs in suburban ranch houses and split-levels on Long Island and in New Jersey and Westchester County; in colonial houses in a small Massachusetts town; on patios in Memphis; in suburban and city apartments; in living rooms in the Midwest. Sometimes I sensed the problem, not as a reporter, but as a suburban house-wife, for during this time I was also bringing up my own three children in Rockland County, New York. I heard echoes of the problem in college dormitories and semi-private maternity wards, at PTA meetings and luncheons of the League of Women Voters, at suburban cocktail parties, in station wagons waiting for trains, and in snatches of conversation overheard at Schrafft's. The groping words I heard from other women, on quiet afternoons when children were at school or on quiet evenings when husbands worked late, I think I understood first as a woman long before I understood their larger social and psychological implications.

Just what was this problem that has no name? What were the words women used when they tried to express it? Sometimes a woman would say "I feel empty somehow . . . incomplete." Or she would say, "I feel as if I don't exist." Sometimes she blotted out the feeling with a tranquilizer. Sometimes she thought the problem was with her husband, or her children, or that what she really needed was to redecorate her house, or move to a better neighborhood, or have an affair, or another baby. Sometimes, she went to a doctor with symptoms she could hardly describe: "A tired feeling . . . I get so angry with the children it scares me . . . I feel like crying without any reason." (A Cleveland doctor called it "the housewife's syndrome.") A number of women told me about great bleeding blisters that break out on their hands and arms. "I call it the housewife's blight," said a family doctor in Pennsylvania. "I see it so often lately in these young women with four, five and six children who bury themselves in their dishpans. But it isn't caused by detergent and it isn't cured by cortisone."

. . . I began to see new dimensions to old problems that have long been taken for granted among women: menstrual difficulties, sexual frigidity, promiscuity, pregnancy fears, childbirth depression, the high incidence of emotional breakdown and suicide among women in their twenties and thirties, the menopause crises, the so-called passivity and immaturity of American men, the discrepancy between women's tested intellectual abilities in childhood and their adult achievement, the changing incidence of adult sexual orgasm in American women, and persistent problems in psychotherapy and in women's education.

If I am right, the problem that has no name stirring in the minds of so many American women today is not a matter of loss of femininity or too much education, or the demands of domesticity. It is far more important than anyone recognizes. It is the key to these other new and old problems which have been torturing women and their husbands and children, and puzzling their doctors and educators for years. It may well be the key to our future as a nation and a culture. We can no longer ignore that voice within women that says: "I want something more than my husband and my children and my home."

Roe v. Wade (1973)

In January 1973 the Supreme Court admitted that women had the right to control what went on inside their own bodies. The case involved the right of an unmarried woman to end an unwanted pregnancy in Texas, where abortion was a criminal offense. Deciding that a "right of personal privacy" existed under several clauses of the Constitution, a 7–2 majority of the Court approved a woman's right to terminate her pregnancy. Though much denounced by "right to life" critics, the Court has upheld and expanded the Roe decision to cover second trimester abortions.

[Texas statutes] make it a crime to "procure an abortion," as therein defined, or to attempt one, except with respect to "an abortion procured or attempted by medical advice for the purpose of saving the life of the mother." Similar statutes are in existence in a majority of the States. . . .

The principal thrust of the appellant's attack on the Texas statutes is that they improperly invade a right, said to be possessed by the pregnant woman, to choose to terminate her pregnancy. Appellant would discover this right in the concept of personal "liberty" embodied in the Fourteenth Amendment's Due Process Clause; or in personal, marital, familial, and sexual privacy said to be protected by the Bill of Rights or its penumbras. . . .

The Constitution does not explicitly mention any right of privacy. In a line of decisions, however, going back perhaps as far as *Union Pacific R. Co. v. Botsford* (1891), the Court has recognized that a right of personal privacy, or a guarantee of certain areas or zones of privacy, does exist under the Constitution. In varying contexts the Court or individual justices have indeed found at least the roots of that right in the First Amendment . . . in the Fourth and Fifth Amendments . . . in the penumbras of the Bill of Rights . . . in the Ninth Amendment . . . or in the concept of liberty guaranteed by the first section of the Fourteenth Amendment. . . . These decisions make it clear that only personal rights that can be deemed "fundamental" or "implicit in the concept of ordered liberty" . . . are included in this guarantee of personal privacy. They also make it clear that the right has some extension to activities relating to marriage . . . procreation, contraception, family relationships, and child rearing and education.

This right of privacy, whether it be founded in the Fourteenth Amendment's concept of personal liberty and restrictions upon state action, as we feel it is, or, as the District Court determined, in the Ninth Amendment's reservation of rights to the people, is broad enough to encompass a woman's decision whether or not to terminate her pregnancy. The detriment that the State would impose upon the pregnant woman by denying this choice altogether is apparent. Specific and direct harm medically diagnosable even in early pregnancy may be involved. Maternity, or additional offspring, may force upon the woman a distressful life and future. Psychological harm may be imminent. Mental and physical health may be taxed by child care. There is also the distress, for all concerned, associated with the unwanted child, and there is the problem of bringing a child into a family already unable, psychologically and otherwise, to care for it. In other cases, as in this one, the additional difficulties and continuing stigma of unwed motherhood may be involved. All these are factors the woman and her responsible physician necessarily will consider in consultation. . . .

We therefore conclude that the right of personal privacy includes the abortion decision, but that this right is not unqualified and must be considered against important state interests in regulation. . . .

[The State of Texas argues] that the fetus is a "person" within the language and meaning of the Fourteenth Amendment. . . .

The Constitution does not define "person" in so many words. Section I of the Fourteenth Amendment contains three references to "person." The first, in defining "citizens," speaks of "persons born or naturalized in the United States." The word also appears both in the Due Process Clause and in the Equal Protection Clause. "Person" is used in other places in the Constitution. . . . But in nearly all these instances, the use of the word is such that it has application only postnatally. None indicates, with any assurance, that it has any possible prenatal application. . . .

Texas urges that, apart from the Fourteenth Amendment, life begins at conception and is present throughout pregnancy, and that, therefore, the State has a compelling interest in protecting that life from and after conception. We need not resolve the difficult question of when life begins. When those trained in the respective disciplines of medicine, philosophy, and theology are unable to arrive at any consensus, the judiciary, at this point in the development of man's knowledge, is not in a position to speculate as to the answer. . . .

We do not agree that, by adopting one theory of life, Texas may override the rights of the pregnant woman that are at stake. We repeat, however, that the State does have an important and legitimate interest in preserving and protecting the health of the pregnant woman, whether she be a resident of the State or a nonresident who seeks medical consultation and treatment there, and that it has still *another* important and legitimate interest in protecting the potentiality of human life. These interests are separate and distinct. Each grows in substantiality as the woman approaches term and, at a point during pregnancy, each becomes "compelling."

With respect to the State's important and legitimate interest in the health of the mother, the "compelling" point, in the light of present medical knowledge, is at approximately the end of the first trimester. This is so because of the now established medical fact . . . that until the end of the first trimester mortality in abortion is less than mortality in normal childbirth. It follows that, from and after this point, a State may regulate the abortion procedure to the extent that the regulation reasonably relates to the preservation and protection of maternal health. Examples of permissible state regulation in this area are requirements as to the qualifications of the person who is to perform the abortion; as to the licensure of that person; as to the facility in which the procedure is to be performed, that is, whether it must be a hospital or may be a clinic or some other place of less-than-hospital status; as to the licensing of the facility; and the like.

This means, on the other hand, that, for the period of pregnancy prior to this "compelling" point, the attending physician, in consultation with his patient, is free to determine, without regulation by the State, that in his medical judgment the patient's pregnancy should be terminated. If that decision is reached, the judgment may be effectuated by an abortion free of interference by the State. . . .

With respect to the State's important and legitimate interest in potential life, the "compelling" point is at viability. This is so because the fetus then presumably has the capability of meaningful life outside the mother's womb. State regulation protective of fetal life after viability thus has both logical and biological justifications. If the State is interested in protecting fetal life after viability, it may go so far as to proscribe abortion during that period except when it is necessary to preserve the life or health of the mother.

Measured against these standards Texas, in restricting legal abortion to those "procured or attempted by medical advice for the purpose of saving the life of the mother," sweeps too broadly. The statute makes no distinction between abortions performed early in pregnancy and those performed later, and it limits to a single reason, "saving" the mother's life, the legal justification for the procedure. The statute, therefore, cannot survive the constitutional attack made upon it here. . . .

A Lakota at Boarding School

LUTHER STANDING BEAR

Luther Standing Bear (1868–1939), born Ota Kte, was an Oglala Lakota writer and actor. His traditional life came to an end when his father sent him to Carlisle Industrial School in Pennsylvania. Carlisle was one of a chain of schools set up under the supervision of the United States Bureau of Indian Affairs to assimilate Native Americans into the dominant national culture and train them for jobs in the industrial economy. In this selection from his memoirs, Land of the Spotted Eagle *(1933), this education included changes of name, dress, language and culture. After graduation, Luther Standing Bear worked for a while as a storekeeper at the Pine Ridge Reservation in South Dakota, but went on to become an actor in Buffalo Bill's Wild West Show and several early western movies.*

I grew up leading the traditional life of my people, learning the crafts of hunter, scout, and warrior from father, kindness to the old and feeble from mother, respect for wisdom and council from our wise men, and was trained by grandfather and older boys in the devotional rites to the Great Mystery. This was the scheme of existence as followed by my forefathers for many centuries, and more centuries might have come and gone in much the same way had it not been for a strange people who came from a far land to change and reshape our world.

At the age of eleven years, ancestral life for me and my people was most abruptly ended without regard for our wishes, comforts, or rights in the matter. At once I was thrust into an alien world, into an environment as different from the one into which I had been born as it is possible to imagine, to remake myself, if I could, into the likeness of the invader. By 1879, my people were no longer free, but were subjects confined on reservations under the rule of agents. One day there came to the agency a party of white people from the East. Their presence aroused considerable excitement when it became known that these people were school teachers who wanted some Indian boys and girls to take away with them to train as were white boys and girls.

Now, father was a "blanket Indian [a traditionalist]," but he was wise. He listened to the white strangers, their offers and promises that if they took his son they would care well for him, teach him how to read and write, and how to wear white man's clothes. But to father all this was just "sweet talk," and I know that it was with great misgivings that he left the decision to me and asked if I cared to go with these people. I, of course, shared with the rest of my tribe a distrust of the white people, so I know that for all my dear father's anxiety he was proud to hear me say "Yes." That meant that I was brave.

I could think of no reason why white people wanted Indian boys and girls except to kill them, and not having the remotest idea of what a school was, I thought we were going East to die. But so well had courage and bravery been trained into us that it became a part of our unconscious thinking and acting, and personal life was nothing when it came time to do something for the tribe. . . . Thus, in giving myself up to go East I was proving to my father that he was honored with a brave son. . . . On our way to school we saw many white people, more than we ever dreamed existed, and the manner in which they acted when they saw us quite indicated their opinion of us. It was only about three years after the Custer battle, and the general opinion was that the Plains people merely infested the earth as nuisances. . . . At one place we were taken off the train and marched a distance down the street to a restaurant. We walked down the street between two rows of uniformed men whom we called soldiers, though I suppose they were policemen. This must have been done to protect us, for it was surely known that we boys and girls could do no harm. Back of the rows of uniformed men stood the white people craning their necks, talking, laughing, and making a great noise. They yelled and tried to mimic us by giving what they thought were war-whoops. We did not like this, and some of the children were naturally very much frightened. . . .

At last at Carlisle the transforming, the "civilizing" process began. It began with clothes. Never, no matter what our philosophy or spiritual quality, could we be civilized while wearing the moccasin and blanket. The task before us was not only that of accepting new ideas and adopting new manners, but actual physical changes and discomfort has to be borne uncomplainingly until the body adjusted itself to new tastes and habits. Our accustomed dress was taken and replaced with clothing that felt cumbersome and awkward. Against trousers and handkerchiefs we had a distinct feeling—they were unsanitary and the trousers kept us from breathing well. High collars, stiff-bosomed shirts, and suspenders fully three inches in width were uncomfortable, while leather boots caused actual suffering. We longed to go barefoot, but were told that the dew on the grass would give us colds. . . . red flannel undergarments were given us for winter wear, and for me, at least, discomfort grew into actual torture. I used to endure it as long as possible, then run upstairs and quickly take off the flannel gannents and hide them. . . . I still remember those horrid, sticky garments which we had to wear next to the skin, and I still squirm and itch when I think of them. Of course, our hair was cut, and then there was much disapproval. But that was part of the transformation process and in some mysterious way long hair stood in the path of our development. For all the grumbling among the bigger boys, we soon had our heads shaven. How strange I felt! Involuntarily, time and time again, my hands went to my head, and that night it was a long time before I went to sleep. . . .

Almost immediately our names were changed to those in common use in the English language. Instead of translating our names into English and calling Zinkcaziwin, Yellow Bird, and Wanbli K'leska, Spotted Eagle, which in itself would have been educational, we were just John, Henry, or Maggie, as the case might be. I was told to take a pointer and select a name for myself from the list written on the blackboard. I did, and since one was just as good as another, and as I could not distinguish any difference in them, I placed the pointer on the name Luther. I then learned to call myself by that name and got used to hearing others call me by it, too. By that time we had been forbidden to speak our mother tongue, which is the rule in all boarding-schools. This rule is uncalled for, and today is not only robbing the Indian, but America of a rich heritage. The language of a people is part of their history. . . .

Of all the changes we were forced to make, that of diet was doubtless the most injurious, for it was immediate and drastic. White bread we had for the first meal and thereafter, as well as coffee and sugar. Had we been allowed our own simple diet of meat, either boiled with soup or dried, and fruit, with perhaps a few vegetables, we should have thrived. But the change in clothing, housing, food, and confinement combined with lonesomeness was too much, and in three years nearly one half of the children from the Plains were dead and through with all earthly schools. In the graveyard at Carlisle most of the graves are those of little ones. . . .

When I had been in school a year, father made his first trip to see me. After I had received permission to speak to him, he told me that on his journey he had seen that the land was full of "Long Knives." "They greatly outnumber us and are here to stay," he said, and advised me, "Son, learn all you can of the white man's ways and try to be like him." . . . He did not say that he thought the white man's ways better than our own; neither did he say that I could be like a white man. He said, "Son, try to be like a white man." So, in two more years I had been "made over." I was Luther Standing Bear wearing the blue uniform of the school, shorn of my hair, and trying hard to walk naturally and easily in stiff-soled cowhide boots. I was now "civilized" enough to go to work in John Wanamaker's fine store in Philadelphia.

I returned from the East at about the age of sixteen, after five years' contact with the white people, to resume life upon the reservation. But I returned, to spend some thirty years before again leaving, just as I had gone—a Lakota. Outwardly I lived the life of the white man, yet all the while I kept in direct contact with tribal life. While I had learned all that I could of the white man's culture, I never forgot that of my people. I kept the language, tribal manners and usages, sang the songs and danced the dances. I still listened to and respected the advice of the older people of the tribe. I did not come home so "progressive" that I could not speak the language of my father and mother. I did not learn the vices of chewing tobacco, smoking, drinking, and swearing, and for all this I am grateful. I have never, in fact, "progressed" that far.

But I soon began to see the sad sight, so common today, of returned students who could not speak their native tongue, or, worse yet, some who pretended they could no longer converse in the mother tongue. They had become ashamed and this led them into deception and trickery. . . . . We went to school to copy, to imitate; not to exchange languages and ideas, and not to develop the best traits that had come out of uncountable experiences of hundreds and thousands of years living upon this continent. Our annals, all happenings of human import, were stored in our song and dance rituals. our history differing in that it was not stored in books, but in the living memory. So, while the white people had much to teach us, we had much to teach them, and what a school could have been established upon that idea! However, this was not the attitude of the day, though the teachers were sympathetic and kind, and some came to be my lifelong friends. But in the main, Indian qualities were undivined and Indian virtues not conceded. And I can well remember when Indians in those days were stoned upon the streets as were the dogs that roamed them. We were "savages," and all who had not come under the influence of the missionary were "heathen," and Wakan Tanka [the Great Mystery], who had since the beginning watched over the Lakota and his land, was denied by these men of God. Should we not have been justified in thinking them heathen? And so the "civilizing" process went on, killing us as it went.

The Quranic School

ASSIA DJEBAR

Assia Djebar (b. 1936) is an Algerian novelist, film-maker, and histo-
rian. L'Amour, La Fantasia *(1985), from which this selection is taken,*
is the first of four volumes in which she tells the story of women's lives
in Algeria under French rule (1827–1962) through a mixture of his-
torical recreation, her own personal memoirs, and the oral histories of
women involved in the struggle for independence. Here, she depicts the
mixture of difficulties and opportunities that come from growing up
under two contrasting (and sometimes conflicting) cultures, a type of
experience shared by inhabitants of colonies everywhere. For the 23
years before this novel appeared Djebar gave up writing in French (in
which she had already published four other novels) in order to concen-
trate on exploring the history of her own country in its own language.

At the age when I should be veiled already, I can still move about I freely
thanks to the French school: Every Monday the village bus takes me to the
boarding school in the nearby town, and brings me back on Saturday to my
parents' home.

I have a friend who is half Italian and who goes home every weekend to a
fishing port on the coast; we go together to catch our respective buses and
are tempted by all sorts of escapades. . . . With beating hearts we make our
way into the center of the town; to enter a smart cake-shop, wander along
the edge of the park, stroll along the boulevard, which only runs alongside
common barracks, seems the acme of freedom, after a week of boarding
school! Excited by the proximity of forbidden pleasures, we eventually each
catch our bus; the thrill lay in the risk of missing it!

As a young teenager I enjoy the exhilarating hours spent every Thursday
in training on the sports field. I only have one worry: fear that my father
might come to visit me! How can I tell him that it's compulsory for me to
wear shorts, in other words, I have to show my legs? I keep this fear a secret,
unable to confide in any of my school friends; unlike me, they haven't got
cousins who do not show their ankles or their arms, who do not even expose
their faces. My panic is also compounded by an Arab woman's "shame." The

French girls whirl around me; they do not suspect that my body is caught in invisible snares.

"Doesn't your daughter wear a veil yet?" asks one or other of the matrons, gazing questioningly at my mother with suspicious kohl-rimmed eyes, on the occasion of one of the summer weddings. I must be thirteen, or possibly fourteen.

"She reads!" my mother replies stiffly.

Everyone is swallowed up in the embarrassed silence that ensues. And in my own silence.

"She reads," that is to say in Arabic, "she studies." I think now that this command "to read" was not just casually included in the Quranic revelation made by the Angel Gabriel in the cave. . . "She reads" is tantamount to saying that writing to be read, including that of the unbelievers, is always a source of revelation: in my case of the morality of my body, and so of my future freedom.

When I am growing up—shortly before my native land throws off the colonial yoke—while the man still has the right to four legitimate wives, we girls, big and little, have at our command four languages to express desire before all that is left for us is sighs and moans: French or secret missives; Arabic for our stifled aspirations towards God-the-Father, the God of the religions of the Book; Lybico-Berber which takes us back to the pagan idols—mother-gods—of pre-Islamic Mecca. The fourth language, for all females, young or old, cloistered or half-emancipated, remains that of the body: the body which male neighbors' and cousins' eyes require to be deaf and blind, since they cannot completely incarcerate it; the body which, in trances, dances or vociferations, in fits of hope or despair, rebels, and unable to read or write, seeks some unknown shore as destination for its message of love.

In our towns, the first woman-reality is the voice, a dart which flies off into space, an arrow which slowly falls to earth; next comes writing with the scratching pointed quill forming amorous snares with its liana letters. By way of compensation, the need is felt to blot out women's bodies and they must be muffled up, tightly swathed, swaddled like infants or shrouded like corpses. Exposed, a woman's body would offend every eye, be an assault on the dimmest of desires, emphasize every separation. The voice, on the other hand, acts like a perfume, a draft of water for the dry throat; and when it is savored, it can be enjoyed by several simultaneously; a secret, polygamous pleasure. . .

When the hand writes, slow positioning of the arm, carefully bending forward or leaning to one side, crouching, swaying to and fro, as in an act of love. When reading, the eyes take their time, delight in caressing the curves, while the calligraphy suggests the rhythm of the scansion: as if the writing marked the beginning and the end of possession.

Writing: Everywhere, a wealth of burnished gold and in its vicinity there is no place for other imagery from either animal or vegetable kingdom; it looks in the mirror of its scrolls and curlicues and sees itself as woman, not the reflection of a voice. It emphasizes by its presence alone where to begin and where to retreat; it suggests, by the song that smoulders in its heart, the dance floor for rejoicing and hair-shirt for the ascetic; I speak of the Arabic script; to be separated from it is to be separated from a great love. This script, which I mastered only to write the sacred words, I see now spread out before me cloaked in innocence and whispering arabesques,—and ever since, all other scripts (French, English, Greek) seem only to babble, are never cathartic; they may contain truth, indeed, but a blemished truth.

Just as the pentathlon runner of old needed the starter, so, as soon as I learned the foreign script, my body began to move as if by instinct.

As if the French language suddenly had eyes, and lent them me to see into liberty; as if the French language blinded the peeping-toms of my clan and, at this price, I could move freely, run headlong down every street, annex the outdoors for my cloistered companions, for the matriarchs of my family who endured a living death. As if. . . Its script is a public unveiling in front of sniggering onlookers. . .

In my earliest childhood—from the age of five to ten—I attended the French school in the village, and every day after lessons there I went on to the Quranic school.

Classes were held in a back room lent by a grocer, one of the village notables. I can recall the place, and its dim light: Was it because the time for the lessons was just before dark, or because the lighting of the room was so parsimonious? . . .

The master's image has remained singularly clear: delicate features, pale complexion, a scholar's sunken cheeks; about forty families supported him. I was struck by the elegance of his bearing and his traditional attire: A spotless light muslin was wrapped around his headdress and floated behind his neck; his serge tunic was dazzling white. I never saw this man except sitting.

In comparison, the horde of misbehaving little urchins squatting on straw mats—sons of *fellaheen* [peasants] for the most part—seemed crude riffraff, from whom I kept my distance.

We were only four or five little girls. I suppose that our sex kept us apart, rather than my supercilious amazement at their behavior. In his aristocratic bearing, the *taleb* [teacher] did not hesitate to lift his cane and bring it down on the fingers of a recalcitrant or slow-witted lad. (I can still hear it whistle through the air.) We girls were spared this regular punishment.

I can remember the little impromptu parties my mother devised in our flat when I brought home (as later my brother was to do) the walnut table decorated with arabesques. This was the master's reward when we had learnt a long *sura* by heart. My mother and our village nanny, who was a second mother to us, then let out that semi-barbaric "you-you." That prolonged, irregular, spasmodic cooing, which in our reserved for teachers' families—all European except for ours—must have appeared incongruous, a truly primitive cry. My mother considered the circumstances (the study of the Quran undertaken by her children) sufficiently important for her to let out this ancestral cry of jubilation in the middle of the village where she nevertheless felt herself an exile.

At every prize-giving ceremony at the French school, every prize I obtained strengthened my solidarity with my own family; but I felt there was more glory in this ostentatious clamour. The Quranic school, that dim cavern in which the haughty figure of the Sheikh was enthroned above the poor village children, this school became, thanks to the joy my mother demonstrated in this way, an island of bliss—Paradise regained.

Back in my native city, I learned that another Arab school was being opened, also funded by private contributions. One of my cousins attended it; she took me there. I was disappointed. The buildings, the timetable, the modern appearance of the masters, made it no different from a common-or-garden French school. . .

I understood later that in the village I had participated in the last of popular, secular teaching. In the city, thanks to the Nationalist movement of "Modernist Muslims," a new generation of Arab culture was being forged.

Since then these *medrasas* have sprung up everywhere. If I had attended one of them (if I'd grown up in the town where I was born) I would have found it quite natural to swathe my head in a turban, to hide my hair, to cover my arms and calves, in a word to move about doors like a Muslim nun!

After the age of ten or eleven, shortly before puberty, I was no longer allowed to attend the Quranic school. At this age, boys are suddenly excluded from the women's Turkish bath—that emollient world of naked bodies stifling in a whirl of scalding steam. . . The same thing happened to my companions, the little village girls, one of whom I would like to describe here.

The daughter of the Kabyle baker must, like me, have attended the French school simultaneously with the Quranic school. But I can only recall her presence squatting at my side in front of the Sheikh: side by side, half smiling to each other, both already finding it uncomfortable to sit cross-legged! . . . My legs must have been too long, because of my height: It wasn't easy for me to hide them under my skirt.

For this reason alone I think that I would in any case have been weaned from Quranic instruction at this age: There is no doubt that it's easier to sit cross-legged when wearing a *seroual;* a young girl's body that is beginning to develop more easily conceals its form under the ample folds of the traditional costume. But my skirts, justified by my attendance at the French school, were ill adapted to such a posture.

When I was eleven I started secondary school and became a boarder. What happened to the baker's daughter? Certainly veiled, withdrawn overnight from school: betrayed by her figure. Her swelling breasts, her slender legs, in a word, the emergence of her woman's personality transformed her into an incarcerated body!

I remember how much this Quranic learning, as it is progressively acquired, is linked to the body.

The portion of the sacred verse, inscribed on both sides of the walnut tablet, had to be wiped off at least once a week, after We had shown that We could recite it off by heart. We scrubbed the piece of wood thoroughly, just like other people wash their clothes: The time it took to dry seemed to ensure the interval that the memory needed to digest What it had swallowed. . .

The learning was absorbed by the fingers, the arms, through the physical effort. The act of cleaning the tablet seemed like ingesting a portion of the Quranic text. The writing—itself a copy of writing which is considered immutable—could only continue to unfold before us if it relied, clause by clause, on this osmosis. . .

As the hand traces the liana-script, the mouth opens to repeat the word, obedient to their rhythm. . . The shrill voices of the drowsy children rise up in a monotonous, sing-song chorus.

Stumbling on, swaying from side to side, care taken to observe the tonic accents, to differentiate between long and short vowels, attentive to the rhythm of the chant; muscles of the larynx as well as the torso in harmony. Controlling the breath to allow the correct emission of the voice, and letting the understanding advance precariously along its tight-rope. Respecting the grammar by speaking it aloud, it part of the chant.

This language which I learn demands the correct posture for the body, on which the memory rests for its support. The childish hand, spurred on—as in training for some sport—by willpower worthy of an adult, begins to write. "Read!" The fingers laboring on the tablet send back the signs to the body, which is simultaneously reader and servant. The lips having finished their muttering, the hand will once more do the washing, proceeding to wipe out what is written on the tablet: This is the moment of absolution, like touching the hem of death's garment. Again, it is the turn of writing, and the circle is completed.

And when I sit curled up like this to study my native language it is as though my body reproduces the architecture of my native city: the *medinas* with their tortuous alleyways closed off to the outside world, their secret life. When I write and read the foreign language, my body travels far in subversive space, in spite of the neighbors and suspicious matrons; it would not need much for it to take wing and fly away!

As I approach a marriageable age, these two different apprenticeships, undertaken simultaneously, land me in a dichotomy of location. My father's preference will decide for me: light rather than darkness. I do not realize that an irrevocable choice is being made: the outdoors and the risk, instead of the prison of my peers. This stroke of luck brings me to the verge of breakdown.

I write and speak French outside: The words I use convey no flesh-and-blood reality. I learn the names of birds I've never seen, trees I shall take ten years or more to identify, lists of flowers and plants that ever smell until I travel north of the Mediterranean. In this respect, all vocabulary expresses what is missing in my life, exoticism without mystery, causing a kind of visual humiliation that it is not seemly to admit to . . . Settings and episodes in children's books are but theoretical concepts; in the French family the mother comes to fetch her daughter or son from school; in the French street, the parents walk quite naturally side by side. . . So, the world of the school is expunged from the daily life of my native city, as it is from the life of my family. The latter is refused any referential role.

My conscious mind is here, huddled against my mothers knees, in darkest corners of the flat which she never leaves. The ambit of the school is elsewhere: My search, my eyes are fixed on other regions. I do realize, no-one around me realizes, that, in the conflict between these two worlds, lies an incipient vertigo.

The Hidden Face of Eve

NAWAL EL SAADAWI

*The definition of "universal" human rights expressed by the United
Nations 1948 Declaration sidestepped the problem of cultural values.
Nawal El Saadawi (b. 1931), an Egyptian doctor and woman's rights
activist, is the child of educated parents who loved her deeply. Yet at the
age of six, she was subjected by her parents to clitoral circumcision, a rit-
ual demanded by customs that pre-date the spread of Islam throughout
the Middle East and Northern Africa. The Egyptian government
imprisoned Saadawi (1981–1982) because of her campaigns on behalf
of women's rights and banned her books. In 1997, an Egyptian court
overturned the government's own year-old ban on female circumcision.
Here, Saadawi recounts her own experience with the custom.*

I was six years old that night when I lay in my bed, warm and peaceful in
that pleasurable state which lies half way between wakefulness and sleep,
with the rosy dreams of childhood flitting by, like gentle fairies in quick succession. I felt something move under the blankets, something like a huge
hand, cold and rough, fumbling over my body, as though looking for something. Almost simultaneously another hand, as cold and as rough and as big
as the first one, was clapped over my mouth, to prevent me from screaming.

They carried me to the bathroom. I do not know how many of them there
were, nor do I remember their faces, or whether they were men or women. The
world to me seemed enveloped in a dark fog which prevented me from seeing,
Or perhaps they put some kind of a cover over my eyes. All I remember is that
I was frightened and that there were many of them, and that something like an
iron grasp caught hold of my hand and my arms and my thighs, so that I
became unable to resist or even to move. I also remember the icy touch of the
bathroom tiles under my naked body, and unknown voices and humming
sounds interrupted now and again by a rasping metallic sound which reminded
me of the butcher when he used to sharpen his knife before slaughtering a
sheep for the *Eid* [the Festival at the end of the Holy Month of *Ramadan*].

My blood was frozen in my veins. It looked to me as though some thieves
had broken into my room and kidnapped me from my bed. They were get-

ting ready to cut my throat which was always what happened with disobedient girls like myself in the stories that my old rural grandmother was so fond of telling me.

I strained my ears trying to catch the rasp of the metallic sound. The moment it ceased, it was as though my heart stopped beating with it. I was unable to see, and somehow my breathing seemed also to have stopped. Yet I imagined the thing that was making the rasping sound coming closer and closer to me. Somehow it was not approaching my neck as I had expected but another part of my body. Somewhere below my belly, as though seeking something buried between my thighs. At that very moment I realized that my thighs had been pulled wide apart, and that each of my lower limbs was being held as far away from the other as possible, gripped by steel fingers that never relinquished their pressure. I felt that the rasping knife or blade was heading straight down towards my throat. Then suddenly the sharp metallic edge seemed to drop between my thighs and there cut off a piece of flesh from my body.

I screamed with pain despite the tight hand held over my mouth, for the pain was not just a pain, it was like a searing flame that went through my whole body. After a few moments, I saw a red pool of blood around my hips.

I did not know what they had cut off from my body, and I did not try to find out. I just wept, and called out to my mother for help. But the worst shock of all was when I looked around and found her standing by my side. Yes, it was her, I could not be mistaken, in flesh and blood, right in the midst of these strangers, talking to them and smiling at them, as though they had not participated in slaughtering her daughter just a few moments ago. . . .

My family was not an uneducated Egyptian family. On the contrary, both my parents had been fortunate enough to have a very good education, by the standards of those days. My father was a university graduate and that year (1937) had been appointed General Controller of Education for the Province of Menoufia in the Delta region to the North of Cairo. My mother had been taught in French schools by her father who was Director-General of Army Recruitment. Nevertheless, the custom of circumcising girls was very prevalent at the time, and no girl could escape having her clitoris amputated, irrespective of whether her family lived in a rural or an urban area. When I returned to school after having recovered from the operation, I asked my classmates and friends about what had happened to me, only to discover that all of them without exception, had been through the same experience, no matter what social class they came from (upper class, middle or lower-middle class). . . .

The memory of circumcision continued to track me down like a nightmare. I had a feeling of insecurity, of the unknown waiting for me at every step I took into the future. I did not even know if there were new surprises being stored up for me by my mother and father, or my grandmother, or the people around me. Society had made me feel, since that day that I opened my eyes on life, that I was a girl, and that the word *Bint* (girl) when pronounced by anyone is almost always accompanied by a frown. . . .

'Message' to UNCED (1992)

FIDEL CASTRO

Problems of ecological devastation and global warming have raised a new debate between the industrialized states of the "First World" and the still-industrializing states of the "Third." In 1992, 178 countries attended the United Nations Conference on Environment and Development (UNCED) in Brazil. In this speech, Cuban Premier Fidel Castro (b. 1926) summarized the perspectives of both groups but argued that continuing Third World development could not be sacrificed to pay for the past blunders of the First World.

Messrs. Heads of State or Government

Each of us attending this UNCED is aware of the significance of this meeting and the urgency of reaching decisions that will allow effective measures to defend the very survival of mankind.

The accelerated and spiralling deterioration of the environment is today possible the most serious long-term threat to mankind as a whole, and most especially to what is still called the Third World. . . .

Never in the history of mankind has such a generalized and destructive aggression taken place against all of the world's vital systems. In the underdeveloped world, underdevelopment and poverty itself are the main factors that today have a multiplying effect on the pressure exerted on the environment. The over exploitation of arable or grazing land, improper agricultural practices, and the lack of financial and technical resources add to the harmful effect of adverse climates. In addition, the eagerness to obtain the greatest profit margin of natural resources and industrial capacities—in the case of capitalist exploitation, national or multinational, in or outside the Third World—adds its serious destructive quota and adds additional ways of contamination and degradation to the environment.

In the developed world, there are lifestyles that encourage irrational consumption and encourage waste and destruction of nonrenewable resources. These lifestyles multiply the tensions and effects to local and world physical environments as unprecedented and previously unimaginable levels. . . .

If you examine the deterioration of the environment from a historical view-point you will see, generally speaking, that the greatest damage to the global ecosystem has been caused by the development patterns followed by the most industrialized countries. Meanwhile, the conditions of poverty in which the immense majority of the world's population lives also severely affects the environment. . . . [but] it is absurd to demand the same degree of responsibility for the deterioration of the environment from a citizen with relatively high income, used to a consumer-oriented, developed country with wasteful ways, as from the poor inhabitant of any one of the more backward countries of the underdeveloped world. The poor man's daily concern is to find—with increasing difficulty—ways of preventing his children from starving. . . .

In the Third World what is in danger first is not the quality of life, but life itself and the right to life. In environmental issues, the main concern in these countries has to be the availability of water, the lack of firewood, and the exhaustion of agricultural land. . . .

To act in favor of the conservation and improvement of the environment, then, unavoidably means to act against the causes that foster the degrading poverty displayed by the Third world as it approaches the 21st century. Without a doubt, this will require a series of social and economic changes, both on a national and international level. Such changes could begin with a just and lasting solution to the issue of foreign debt in the underdeveloped nations and with the redirection of available financial and monetary resources to these development plans. . . . From that perspective, the starting point of any negociation on the environment and development must be the recognition of the ecological debt the industrialized nations have contracted. . . .

The member countries of the OECD represent barely 16 percent of the world population and 24 percent of the total world surface. Their economies contribute 72 percent of the global GNP and generate approximately 76 percent of the total world commerce, including 73 percent of exports of chemical products and almost the same percentage of imports of timber products. The OECD countries are also responsible for 45 percent of the world's emission of carbon dioxide, 40 percent of the sulfur dioxide emissions, and 50 percent of the nitrogen oxide emissions. They produce 60 percent of the world's industrial waste and generate 90 percent of the toxic waste. In 1984, the United States, the EEC, and Japan produced 86 percent of the world's chlorofluorocarbons, whereas the Third world countries produced only 4.4 percent. . . .

From an historical standpoint, the developed countries have been the chief promoters and beneficiaries of deforestation in the [under]developed countries. It was due to the colonial regime, and later to the economic expansion of the major capitalist powers and the neocolonial exploitation of the natural resources of the Third World, that the indiscriminate felling of forests in vast areas of the world and the exploitation of timber took place. It turned these forest areas into agricultural land destined to be used for the production of food and raw materials to be exported to those industrialized countries.

If the phenomenon is analyzed from a broader perspective, the inevitable conclusion is that the ultimate responsibility for the accumulated deterioration of the environment in the Third World as a whole falls on the developed capitalist world. . . .

According to preliminary estimates, all underdeveloped countries would require no less than $40 billion extra per year to invest in programs aimed at achieving environment sustainability, based on 1990 level[s] of economic activity. This amount represents 25 percent of the total payments made by these countries to service their foreign debt during that year. . . . Nobody is denying the need for underdeveloped countries to work in designing their own strategies for socioeconomic development to ensure the sustained expansion of their productive capacity, cope with serious social problems, correct environmental problems of the past, and avoid a subsequent deterioration of the environment based on the available resources. It is evident, however, that foreign financing plays a major role. This is the first way to pay the ecological debt of the developed world.

Foreign financing for sustainable development cannot be the result of a redistribution of the already scarce financial resources that reach the underdeveloped countries, but a flow of new capital. Otherwise, the topic of the environment would only constitute a new condition imposed on the foreign aid. . . .

In the past 20 years, the world has wasted over $13 billion on military expenses. Even in 1991, having overcome the Cold War and the threat of confrontation between the great powers, military spending reached almost $1 billion. There are the resources to finance these programs.

The success of this conference will be measured by the actions that result from it. We represent humanity, and that moral duty, that political obligation, that exceptional and historical responsibility, demands decisions, specific measures, and a commitment that can no longer be delayed.